Albert Camus and the
Philosophy of the Ordinary

Also Available from Bloomsbury

Sartre's Existential Psychoanalysis: Knowing Others,
Mary Edwards
The Parallel Philosophies of Sartre and Nietzsche: Ethics, Ontology and the Self,
Nik Farrell Fox
Kierkegaard and Philosophical Eros: Between Ironic Reflection and Aesthetic Meaning,
Ulrika Carlsson

Albert Camus and the Philosophy of the Ordinary

Raymond D. Boisvert

BLOOMSBURY ACADEMIC
LONDON • NEW YORK • OXFORD • NEW DELHI • SYDNEY

BLOOMSBURY ACADEMIC
Bloomsbury Publishing Plc
50 Bedford Square, London, WC1B 3DP, UK
1385 Broadway, New York, NY 10018, USA
29 Earlsfort Terrace, Dublin 2, Ireland

BLOOMSBURY, BLOOMSBURY ACADEMIC and the Diana logo are trademarks of
Bloomsbury Publishing Plc

First published in Great Britain 2023
This paperback published in 2024

Copyright © Raymond D. Boisvert, 2023

Raymond D. Boisvert has asserted his right under the Copyright, Designs and Patents Act,
1988, to be identified as Author of this work.

For legal purposes the Acknowledgements on p. viii constitute an extension of this
copyright page.

Cover design by Charlotte Daniels
Cover image: Albert Camus, French-Algerian author, philosopher and journalist
(© Pictorial Press Ltd / Alamy Stock Photo)

All rights reserved. No part of this publication may be reproduced or transmitted
in any form or by any means, electronic or mechanical, including photocopying, recording,
or any information storage or retrieval system, without prior permission in writing
from the publishers.

Bloomsbury Publishing Plc does not have any control over, or responsibility for, any
third-party websites referred to or in this book. All internet addresses given in this
book were correct at the time of going to press. The author and publisher regret any
inconvenience caused if addresses have changed or sites have ceased to exist, but can
accept no responsibility for any such changes.

A catalogue record for this book is available from the British Library.

A catalog record for this book is available from the Library of Congress.

ISBN: HB: 978-1-3503-4791-5
PB: 978-1-3503-4795-3
ePDF: 978-1-3503-4792-2
eBook: 978-1-3503-4793-9

Typeset by Deanta Global Publishing Services, Chennai, India

To find out more about our authors and books visit www.bloomsbury.com and sign up for
our newsletters.

Contents

Acknowledgments		viii
Abbreviations: Works by Camus		ix
1	Introduction	1
	Camus: Unending Searcher	1
	Beyond Absurdism	4
	Philosophy as a Drawback	6
2	Defiant Humanism: Reflections on Camus's *The Myth of Sisyphus*, I	9
	Inflated Expectations, Disappointed Realizations, I	9
	Nihilism: Facing Life without Religious or Scientific Faith	11
	Buridan's Ass	12
	Defiant Humanism	14
	The Great Bifurcation	15
	Absurd, or Just "Surd"	18
	Sisyphus as a Guiding Image	19
3	Defiant Humanism in Question: Reflections on Camus's *The Myth of Sisyphus*, II	23
	Inflated Expectations, Disappointed Realizations, II	23
	Irony, Not Absurdity	25
	Resisting Tidy-Mindedness	29
	Imagining Sisyphus Happy?	31
4	*The Stranger*	35
	The Stranger as a *Reductio ad Absurdum*	35
	Statues and Outsiders	38
	L'Étranger: Meursault as a Statue-Self	41
	Meursault and the Preconditions for Evil	43
	Authenticity and Society at Odds	48
5	*The Plague*	51
	Indifference Is Always an Option	51
	When Indifference Is Difficult to Assume	55

	The Problem of Good	56
	Saying Yes to the Ordinary	60
	Seeking a Third Way	63
6	Reflections on *The Rebel*, I	69
	Beyond Boo-hurrah Ethics	69
	Indignant Man versus Absurd Man	72
	The Ascendancy of Nihilism	75
	Rehabilitating Human Nature, I	77
7	Reflections on *The Rebel*, II	81
	Sade as a Test Case	81
	Rehabilitating Human Nature, II	83
	Worries about an Overdone Plot	89
8	*The Fall*	95
	The Plate Glass of Indifference	95
	Moral Fallibilism Is Real	97
	Recapitulation: Building up to *The Fall*	99
	The Fall: Something Is Amiss	102
	Manipulanda, Indifference, Call and Response	103
	Judge-Penitent: Living in a Pan-prosecutorial World	105
	Hints for a Paradigm Shift	108
9	*Exile and the Kingdom*, I: The Backward-Looking Stories	113
	"Better Sometimes to Remain Confused"	113
	Changing the Paradigm	116
	The Backward-Looking Stories: 1	120
	The Backward-Looking Stories: 2	123
	Saying "No" to Ordinary Life	126
10	*Exile and the Kingdom*, II: The Transitional Stories	129
	Liquidity and Minerality	129
	The Quotidian Almost Rehabilitated: 1	131
	The Quotidian Almost Rehabilitated: 2	136
11	*Exile and the Kingdom*, III: The Forward-Looking Stories	143
	Xenia and *Agape*	143
	Accepting the Responsibilities of Xenia	145
	Guest/Host Reciprocity	149
	Rehabilitating the Ordinary	154

12	*The First Man I*, What Is "First"?	157
	A Work in Progress	157
	The "First," or the Father-of-Oneself Fantasy	158
	Being from Nothingness	162
	Relato, not Isolato	163
	Countering Nietzsche's "Last Man"	165
	From Nihilism to Pan-Semioticism	167
13	*The First Man II*, What Is Love?	173
	The *Aporia* of Love	173
	Love as Debt	175
	I am the Sum of My Affections	181
	Eros as Problematic	183
	What It All Means	186
14	Conclusion	189
	Literature Is Not the Handmaiden of Philosophy	189
	Philosophy without the Great Bifurcation	191
	Three (Potentially) Paradigm-Shifting Essays	198
	"The Enigma"	198
	"Helen's Exile"	200
	"The Almond Trees"	203
	Evaluating Camus	204
Notes		207
Bibliography		219
Index		229

Acknowledgments

Anyone who writes on Camus is indebted to the commentators who have come before. I make no pretense to having read all or even most of the secondary literature on Camus. I will readily admit, however, having benefited from the reading I have done. For those seeking guidance, I would suggest books by Robert Zaretsky and Robert Meagher. Both write engaging prose and both know Camus well. The entries in this book's Bibliography offer other suggestions.

In 2013, I was fortunate to take part in a session commemorating the centennial of Camus's birth. The session took place at the meeting of the American Philosophical Association's Eastern Division in Baltimore. It was an enriching session, and I am grateful to the other participants, John Burkey, Ron Srigley, and Sophie Bastien.

This book was a long time in the making. After hearing me complain one too many times about how the process seemed interminable, my wife, Jayne, suggested that I set other projects aside and concentrate on the text with a fixed timetable, advice that did the trick.

As is often the case, I benefited from comments made by referees for the press. This is especially true as regards the most recent referee, one with a good grasp of philosophy and an eye for weaknesses in the manuscript.

For helpful practical advice, two friends, John Stuhr and Tim Madigan, provided much-appreciated guidance.

At Bloomsbury publishing, Liza Thompson's encouraging attitude served as a wonderful motivator.

Abbreviations: Works by Camus

C1	*Carnets, Janvier 1942–Mars 1951*
C3	*Carnets III, Mars 1951–Décembre 1959*
Ch	*La Chute*
EE	*L'envers et l'endroit*
EK	*Exile and the Kingdom*
ER	*L'Exil et le Royaume*
ESS	*Essais*. Bibliothèque de la Pléiade
ETR	*L'Étranger*
F	*The Fall*
FM	*The First Man*
HR	*L'Homme Révolté*
LaP	*La Peste*
LRB	*Lettre d'Albert Camus à Roland Barthes sur "La Peste"*
LCE	*Lyrical and Critical Essays*
MS	*The Myth of Sisyphus and Other Essays*
N	*Noces suivi de L'été*
OC	*Oeuvres Complètes, vol. III*
Pl	*The Plague*
PH	*Le Premier Homme*
PS	Preface to *The Stranger*

1

Introduction

Camus: Unending Searcher

The book you are about to read, a study of Albert Camus, aims at being appreciative but not hagiographic. It is appreciative because there is much to admire in Camus. It is not hagiographic because, as is the case with everyone, Camus was a product of his time and lived out some of its limitations. On the appreciative side, Camus has much going for him. He was a wonderful artist, writing beautifully in various forms: philosophical essays, lyrical essays, works of fiction. A consistent friend of freedom and justice, he joined the French Resistance and, in the years following the Second World War, expended lots of energy supporting the oppressed and the persecuted. For him, the commonly uttered freedom-and-responsibility linkage was more than a matter of snappy phraseology. In the 1950s, when many intellectuals remained fellow travelers, he railed against the horrors of Stalinist communism. Undeserved suffering and narrow-minded vengefulness, along with absence of justice, were his enemies, whether in Franco's Spain, the Russian Gulag, terrorism's indiscriminate violence, or the death penalty.

He was also someone engaged in constant searching. As I will indicate, one common, yet understandable, misconception is to identify Camus with his earliest and most famous works, *The Myth of Sisyphus* and *The Stranger*. Camus, the constant searcher, specifically and openly envisioned a trajectory that would move beyond both *The Myth of Sisyphus* and *The Stranger*. He envisioned a three-cycle plan for his works. Each cycle was to be associated with a figure in Greek mythology. *Sisyphus* and *Prometheus* were to symbolize the first two cycles. The third, less well known because incomplete, was to be developed under the patronage of *Nemesis*, goddess of measure and limits.

Modern European thought, as Camus tells us in his essay "Helen's Exile," had ignored limits. Historically, it is important here to recognize that "Modern" identifies a particular period in European history, the period opened by Descartes (1596–1650) and closed by Nietzsche (1844–1900). As indicating a particular epoch in Western history, the term is to be distinguished from the adjective "modern" meaning "now." Camus's complaint can thus be read as the critique of a position which had become dominant at a particular time. Highlighting *Nemesis* was his way of restoring an ancient sensibility that had been lost: despite a wide degree of flexibility and a wide spectrum of variability, there remain limits that humans should not transgress.

Without limits, responsibility loses most of its substantive force. So long as *Nemesis* is present, acting responsibly means remaining within the (capacious but not unlimited) boundaries patrolled by her. Making *Nemesis* a real presence is a way of emphasizing how the pairing of freedom and responsibility is a real pairing. Selecting among options (freedom) should be preceded by an attempt to discern how the options fare as regards better and worse. Better and worse, in turn, are not completely arbitrary. *Nemesis*, goddess of limits and measure ("measure" was another ancient Greek conception welcomed by Camus), symbolizes a dimension of reality that is operative but enigmatic. Error in attempting to discern better and worse is always possible. That is the whole point of emphasizing limits. The boundaries may not be obvious. Sedimented ones can be overly narrow. Still, totalizing comments that deny their existence altogether, ones that dismiss *Nemesis* entirely, have to be recognized as exaggerated overreactions.

Camus, as we shall see, set himself in opposition to what epitomized such overreactions, the position known as "nihilism."[1] This label emerged to describe a situation in which there were no operative limits, nothing (*nihil*) in the fabric of things to separate better from worse. All standards and norms were merely cultural inventions. Religion, as Nietzsche surprisingly but insightfully suggested, had paved the way. For religion, all limits, all rules came from divine commands. There was no moral syntax operative in the conditions of lived experience. The religious perspective, as Nietzsche saw it, was that of nihilism-plus-divine-commands. The combination was always a tenuous, artificial one. It also set the stage for establishing a generalized nihilism. Once the divine commander was removed, nothing, *nihil*, was left to warrant judgments about differential worthiness.

This kind of sharp separation seemed problematic to Camus. It erected a divide which completely ignored *Nemesis*: on one side, the natural world as neutral and value-free; on the other, a divinity and, after the death of God, humans, legislating value and meaning. Thus Camus's wish to undo what he called "Helen's exile" and his willingness to adopt *Nemesis* as a representative figure. For Camus, the combination of freedom and responsibility had to be taken seriously. Being taken seriously meant that freedom could be misused. Choices are elections among options. They are not proclamations. They can be mistaken. This is where the ancient Greeks, as Camus saw it, were closer to the mark. If there were some operative moral syntax, responsibility (selecting among options after careful deliberation) would be a serious matter. It would be a serious matter because the option selected could, since its value was not dependent on either a divine or human proclamation, turn out to be mistaken.

In a world of nihilism, one of general meaninglessness, the comfortable slogan (freedom and responsibility) could continue to be uttered. Substantively, though, the weight of responsibility was diminished. After all, if there is no moral template, if all evaluations of better and worse are just conventional, the word "responsibility" may remain, but it is no longer burdensome. Nothing like *Nemesis* is involved. Perhaps a conventional rule will be broken, but, what's the big deal, it's only an arbitrary, culturally specific regulation. Aldous Huxley tells us that, for him, a general philosophy of meaninglessness meant license to engage in whatever self-serving activities he desired (in Klein, 96). When Jean-Paul Sartre was asked for advice by a student unsure of what choice to make, Sartre did not suggest a detailed analysis, did not counsel thoughtful thinking-through of ramifications, but rather urged the student to "choose." To "choose," within the Sartrean philosophical landscape, was not to elect among options for good reasons. It meant, rather, proclaim, or "invent" (Sartre 1996, 33). After all, the absence of a moral syntax meant that there were no operative patterns which humans should seek to understand. At the same time, the absence of a moral syntax changed the meaning of "responsibility." Where *Nemesis* is a part of the moral atmosphere, better and worse mean something. Responsibility, in a substantive sense, assumes that "elect among options" is not the same as "invent." In the strongest sense of the term, "invent" actually weakens the force of responsibility. Why? Because the criteria for better and worse are no longer considered to be dependent on the entire situation. They have been "invented" by the fact of choosing. This makes it difficult to have been wrong. It puts *Nemesis* out of business.

One of Camus's most straightforward claims of his position came in a war-related text entitled *Letters to a German Friend*. The relevant passage is worth quoting at length:

> You never believed in the meaning of this world, and you therefore deduced the idea that everything was equivalent and that good and evil could be defined according to one's wishes. You supposed that in the absence of any human or divine code the only values were those of the animal world—in other words, violence and cunning. Hence you concluded that man was negligible and that his soul could be killed, that in the maddest of histories the only pursuit for the individual was the adventure of power and his own morality, the realism of conquest. (Camus, RRD, 27)

Keeping *Nemesis* in business was central to Camus's mature project. Doing so in a consistent manner proved, however, to be a challenge. Although Camus wished to move beyond the cycles devoted to *Sisyhpus* and to *Prometheus*, that is, the cycles associated with absurdity and revolt, this third stage was one he could not quite bring to a culmination. Here we arrive at the limitations that dogged Camus. We also arrive at the central axis around which my reading turns: Camus just never had the philosophical tools to match his humanist and artistic aspirations. To be quite specific, Camus, although resisting the full ramifications of his philosophical inheritance, remained too much in the grip of that inheritance. As a result he could do little more than sound an alarm.

Ron Srigley has directly articulated the problem. Camus's project was "unworkable," Srigley asserts. Why? Because his project "rested on the assumption that one could find a way beyond modernity's conclusions while remaining faithful to its premises" (Srigley, 8). My book in a sense is an elaboration on this claim. The main point of divergence with Srigley has to do with the centrality of Camus's short story collection *Exile and the Kingdom*. For Srigley, *The Rebel* is Camus's pivotal text. "After its publication," Srigley asserts, Camus's works began to "dry up" (Srigley, 8).[2] What I will suggest is that a pivotal place should be granted to the single major work published after *The Rebel*, a work mostly dismissed by commentators, the short stories gathered in *Exile and the Kingdom*. Those stories indicate a real struggle with central issues and actually, this is what I will defend, point in the direction of rethinking assumptions. Srigley is right to assert that Camus never really made a paradigm shift. When the short stories are taken seriously, readers get a good sense of the growth in Camus's general orientation, a growth that was moving toward a paradigm shift, even if, here Srigley is right, Camus never did make the needed shift.

Because it was not within his intellectual ambit to rethink assumptions in ways that would allow him to weave a new intellectual fabric, Camus could only serve as a kind of prophet longing for an altered future condition. All he could offer was (1) rebellion against what the prevailing philosophical paradigm seemed to demand and (2) some tentative, preliminary moves toward a much-needed new paradigm. The moves, as tentative and preliminary, were not comprehensive enough to revise the entire intellectual climate. Such a reframing would have impacted key terms like "absurd," "revolt," "fall," and "exile." The serious paradigm shift that philosophers like Whitehead, William James, and Heidegger were undertaking would (1) result in a major shifting of the context within which such terms held specific meanings, and, as a result, (2) the terms themselves would become more peripheral than central. Twentieth-century philosophical movements would do much to remap the intellectual territory. But these movements had little impact on Camus.

Beyond Absurdism

My reading takes seriously Camus's own claim that labels like "absurd" were not meant to be his final word. The particular focus on absurdity resulted, he tells us, from attempts to explore a theme dominant at his time. Instead of treating Camus as the artist of "the absurd," the present book aims to read him as he was: someone changing, seeking, growing as a thinker; someone whose quest for meaning did not remain fixed and stagnant. He was an artist sensitive to how ideas played themselves out in life experience. Although his most famous works had involved an attempt to develop an understanding of, and an orientation toward, the "absurd," his more enduring project had to do with resisting nihilism and reestablishing the centrality of Greek notions like "beauty" and "limit" (embodied as Helen and Nemesis). When readers come to his work via the lens of absurdity, they, except for his two most famous works, distort this underlying and ongoing concern. Or, at the very least, they prioritize a youthful phase over one that dominated his more mature years.

If my efforts meet with some success, the name "Camus" will no longer automatically and inevitably be associated with "absurdity." The label "absurdist philosopher" will no longer fall so easily from the lips of commentators. Phrasing the same point in terms of his works, my efforts will have succeeded if *The Stranger* and *The Myth of Sisyphus* are no longer thought to represent *the* essential Camus.

Instead I will suggest ways in which his entire trajectory, centered on challenging nihilism, needs to be taken into account. Positively, this will involve his move toward rehabilitating the notion of "human nature." This rehabilitation will encompass several dimensions associated with his projected *Nemesis* cycle. These dimensions and their implications remain mostly out of intellectual fashion. The Camusian position of accepting the operative significance of a moral syntax, of limits and of measure, points in a direction of affirming the existence of some pre-wiring in humans, pre-wiring which encourages some attunement to limits and measures as more worthy than others. Such an awareness, at the very least, indicates the general drift of Camus's searching.

Besides exploring this dimension, I will also be suggesting that he could not bring his searching and seeking to a satisfactory conclusion. He could, as he did in *The Plague*, describe different characters: a doctor tirelessly struggling against the epidemic; a black marketeer profiting personally from the infectious scourge that has descended on the city. When confronted with such characters, it's hard to avoid labels like "better" and "worse." This unavoidability of judgment then raises a follow-up problem. If we accept nihilism in its full ramifications, value judgments have no standing apart from being subjective pronouncements (what has been called the "boo-hurrah" theory of ethics, explored in Chapter 5). Camus's main worry is identified here. He is concerned that without some real ballast, value judgments don't mean much. His take: bring in *Nemesis* to suggest that, although it may be hard to formulate, something more complicated is at work. The received either/or, *either* all objective *or* all subjective, offers too simplified and too un-Greek an analysis. "Better" and "worse" have some substantive force.

My take thus explicitly understands Camus to be a divided self: (1) someone who had a sense of unease with the nihilism he found around him; (2) at the same time, he retained an unstinting commitment to what I call the "Great Bifurcation," the Cartesian framework which separated humans from their natural setting and provided the foundation for nihilism. But (1) and (2) do not fit well together; it is hard to critique nihilism while accepting one of the key presuppositions underpinning it. One result: his position was much like that of a prophet crying in the wilderness. His "here I stand" would, as a result, have to remain mostly oppositional, an insistence that something in the dominant climate of opinion was awry. As such, he remained a transitional figure. He was aware of, and indignant about, where inherited ideas led. He could not, however, set out a new groundmap, one that would (1) capture more adequately the complexities and interrelationships of lived experience and (2) alter the very ways in which issues and problems were articulated.

Such alternative groundmaps would emerge in twentieth-century philosophy. They would be associated with names like Alfred North Whitehead, William James, Martin Heidegger, and, later, Ludwig Wittgenstein. Despite their differences, the movements associated with these individuals would redescribe the conditions within which humans find themselves. Such redescriptions would be variously formulated. They would, though, (1) identify a central foil, Descartes, and (2) emphasize interdependence in a field. They would also resonate around a central theme: emphasizing how human beings were humans, not just minds set off against an external world. They would, in other words, displace what I call the Great Bifurcation, the separation of humans, as minds, from the world, understood as mostly matter. Humans would be taken seriously as living beings in a living world. That world would make sense as a proper home for humans.

So long as the Great Bifurcation remained in place, a very different take on the human condition would prevail. Within that framework, it would seem only natural to envision "man" as an outsider, a stranger, an alien. Such a move, since it brought with it the removal of all value from the "objective" realm of the world and localized it in the "subjective" humans, provided the generative context which would lead, ultimately, to nihilism.

Philosophy as a Drawback

My diagnosis of Camus as a divided self is accompanied by an important evaluative judgment: philosophy is what holds Camus back. His philosophical inheritance (the Great Bifurcation) is the one which, by imposing an artificial grid onto lived experience, keeps Camus from engaging more fully in what is needed to challenge nihilism: the rehabilitation of the ordinary. Such a rehabilitation, one which thinks of the ordinary, not as a "fallen" realm (religious version) or as "mere" matter (scientism version) but as a cluster of possibilities, including those which, in line with appropriate human responses, could bring positive, justice, and freedom-enhancing culminations.

This is where the side of Camus as a literary artist becomes helpful. Literature's explorations of lived experience can help bring out the limitations and artificiality of an overly abstract philosophical grid. The literary effort, as I understand it, is freer to explore the complexities of lived experience, and of complexities that do not always fit within an entrenched philosophical framework. My claim as a student of philosophy is straightforward: Camus's endeavor was shackled by the philosophical framework he inherited. This stands out most clearly when considering the literary works written in conjunction with a philosophical treatise. In those works, Camus is not so much a literary artist seeking to explore, and thus learn, from life experience. Rather the aim is to exemplify, in story form, an already adopted philosophical position. Given such an evaluative context, a work like *The Stranger*, great and influential as it may have been, represents what is the weakest side of Camus, the one deriving from an overly dualistic, abstract, and eliminationist philosophy. Rather than open up modes of lived experience, the story actually imposes a rather rigid interpretive grid on that experience.

In terms of his literary artistry, my commentary will come to a culmination that is atypical in Camus scholarship: a high point of Camus's literary works is not just his famous novels. It is also his often marginalized collection of short stories, *Exile and the Kingdom*. These stories, I will suggest, reveal Camus moving away from the limiting philosophical assumptions that are dominant in his other literary works. Importantly, the stories no longer read like philosophical fables, providing images and characters whose role is to express predetermined ideas. The stories open, in tentative and piecemeal ways, a prophetic dimension, one that reveals rather than conceals the rich possibilities within lived experience. They undertake a move toward rehabilitating the ordinary.

Keeping such a background in mind, what I hope to show is that although Camus had a side strongly sympathetic to the rehabilitation of the ordinary, his other side remained firmly within the grip of the Great Bifurcation. So long as this remained a major part of his orientation, his sympathy for lived experience would not culminate in a paradigm shift. Because his orientation would always preserve the belief that human life is alien to, and estranged from, the world, all he could do was to engage in criticism and rebellion.

My book is explicitly and consciously a philosophy book. It centers around a general orientation accepted as primordial, and a cluster of ideas which, in the words of Susanne Langer, are generative. The poet Rilke, in "Presaging," compared himself to a flag feeling the oncoming winds. By the time Camus began writing, the issue which weighed upon him, the loss of meaning, was already in the intellectual air. Mathew Arnold had given it poetic articulation in "Dover Beach." In that poem he described a situation in which humans could no longer find guidance in Faith. The result: a world which "Hath really neither joy, nor love, nor light, Nor certitude, nor peace, nor help for pain." From the scientific side, Thomas Henry Huxley was, as we shall see in the conclusion, forced to admit that ethics and knowledge had to be opposed. Science revealed a world devoid of meaning; ethics demanded it. From the philosophical side, someone who had a great influence on Camus, Friedrich Nietzsche, worried about the "nihilism" which would result after the death of God. Camus, because of his great talent, captured the public imagination with his own take on the loss of meaning. More specifically, as I hope my book will show, Camus spent his life working out various permutations associated with this inherited issue.

In developing this novel path for Camus's interpretation, I will make use of recurring trail markers. Among them are

- a hungry donkey unable to decide between two identical haystacks;
- the Greek word *oikos* ("home") from which comes the prefix *eco* as in "ecology";
- a Spanish philosopher who kept philosophy down to earth with a specific understanding of "irony" and an emphasis on *razón vital*;
- an English philosopher who, like Camus, worked to reestablish the legitimacy of "human nature," but her wider orientation rejected the understanding of humans as strangers, insisting instead that this world was our *oikos*, our proper home;
- Herman Melville via his neologism "isolato";
- ordinary examples like breathing and eating which break down the bifurcation between humans and the world they inhabit;
- giving birth and children, to counterbalance the narrow philosophical fetishization of a single individual and his "being-unto-death";
- entering Camus into conversation with various thinkers who work outside the framework of the Great Bifurcation.

Camus, as we shall see, was in possession of many pieces which could have led to a major reconstruction of the philosophical paradigm he inherited. That such work was accomplished not by him but by people like James, Heidegger, Whitehead, and Wittgenstein is not to diminish his importance. It is simply to say that he lived when he did and where he did. What does diminish his importance is a general interpretive tradition which freezes him in time and thinks of him only as a philosopher of absurdism.

2

Defiant Humanism

Reflections on Camus's *The Myth of Sisyphus*, I

Inflated Expectations, Disappointed Realizations, I

Philosophy means, literally, the "love of wisdom." "Wisdom" connotes intelligence used to guide living. Philosophers, it could be said, seek to cultivate an understanding that will guide humans toward living meaningful lives in an intelligible world.[1] I say "could" because by the middle of the twentieth century such a formulation had been put into question. The key assumptions, "meaningful" life and "intelligible" world, no longer reinforced each other. By the time Camus published *The Myth of Sisyphus* (1942), intelligence and meaning had actually become foes. The conflict was phrased most pithily in the late 1970s by the Nobel Prize–winning physicist Steven Weinberg: "the more the universe seems comprehensible, the more it seems pointless" (Weinberg, 154).[2] Intelligence, when applied via science, discovered not a meaningful world but a pointless one.

The position articulated by Weinberg was already philosophical boilerplate in the early 1940s. This meant that philosophy, the search for wisdom, had to adapt to the new intellectual landscape. Humans continued to crave meaning and value. Intelligence continued to point out their objective absence. Somehow the disconnect would have to be addressed.

To make this challenge more complicated, humans had grown comfortable within an older, more self-serving orientation. The eighteenth century, an era of optimism, had reworked the image of God. The multiple gods of the ancients had long ago been set aside. Now the Biblical God, contradictory, puzzling, and often disappointing, was given an important makeover. He (the masculine dominated) metamorphosed into a Grand Designer. The universe too had been metamorphosed. It was understood, via Newtonian mechanics, as a well-structured machine. Just as any machine required a designer, so the universe now needed one too.

This Designer God, it was believed, had crafted the well-oiled machine that science had revealed. In doing so, taking a page from the Adam and Eve story, the Designer had thoughtfully made the universe a very friendly place for His favorite creature. As a successful designer, all products were made to serve specific purposes. Since humans were at the center of it all, the purposes of lesser creatures often catered to specifically human ends. Bertrand Russell (1872–1970) parodied this view, pointing out that one of its consequences was to be thankful for the white rabbit tails. Why? That made them so much easier to shoot (Russell).

The intellectual situation inherited by Camus emerged from just such a context. There were, on one hand, the optimistic, self-serving expectations of Designer teleology; on the other, there was the brute materialism of scientific description. The results were not pretty. Humans, after all, had come to expect that the world was designed for them. Value and meaning should be everywhere, even in the rabbit's white tail. Though comforting, this older attitude could no longer be uncritically accepted. Rabbits, deer, and other animals, it turned out, went their own way and lived quite full lives without ending up on anyone's plate. More generally, what was true for edible animals was even more true for the universe understood as a machine whirring away on its own. Humans, once benefactors of intelligent design, now found themselves in a world indifferent to their concerns, needs, and desires. Viruses, bacteria, earthquakes, hurricanes, and tornadoes, not to mention the difficulties associated with community life, offered dramatic indications.

The inflated assumptions associated with a Designer God, together with a comforting, self-centered picturing of their situation, set up humans for a great disappointment. At some stage they would relearn the sobering lesson that was boilerplate in the past. It was a lesson recognized in ancient Greek tragedy and admitted in the book of Job: the world is not designed to make life easy for us. Humans are, it is true, unique participants. They have considerable intellectual capabilities. They can survive in almost any ecosystem. At the same time, humans are physiological entities, component parts of a world that is their habitat. An important and nuanced realization ensues. Although the world offers plenty of possibilities of which humans can make use, the entities and events that make it up are not designed to subserve human ends. A creator God, as opposed to a Designer God, would not have so narrow a focus.

Having forgotten the lessons of Greek and Hebrew antiquity, Modern thinkers embraced the newer, self-congratulatory depictions of post-Renaissance thought. By doing so, they inflated expectations to such a degree that, when the more realistic, deflated outcomes emerged; they were received as nothing short of calamitous. The initial Designer setup had already, though this went unrecognized, paved the way. All meaning and value were situated in the mind of the Great Designer. The lifeworld was described as "fallen." Meaning and value derived from the Designer's plan. That plan was accompanied by a set of divine commands. It was an "all eggs in one basket" kind of situation. It was also exceptionally fragile: remove the Grand Designer, the promulgator of moral directives, and down would fall the entire valuational house of cards.

When Bertrand Russell gave the address in which he used the rabbit example, he explicitly identified the resulting philosophical challenge. His essay was called "Why I am not a Christian." After laying out the givens of intelligence, essentially a materialist scenario which culminates in the heat death of our universe, he raised a concern that Camus was also to confront: "I am told that that sort of view is depressing, and people will sometimes tell you that if they believed that they would not be able to go on living." With good old-fashioned, don't-worry-about-what-you-have-no-contr ol-over, optimism, Russell simply rejected that position. "Do not believe it; it is all nonsense. Nobody really worries much about what is going to happen millions of years hence. Even if they think they are worrying much about that, they are really deceiving themselves" (Russell).

By the end of the essay, Russell had actually gotten quite buoyant. Intelligence and meaning could still be reconciled. Welcoming what we know about the universe need not lead to pessimism and suicide. Taking up the mantle of technological, as opposed to religious, salvation, he promoted looking at facts squarely in the face, rolling up our sleeves, and getting to work. We can shape our destinies. Domination and control are within our power.

> Conquer the world by intelligence, and not merely by being slavishly subdued by the terror that comes from it. . . . A good world needs knowledge, kindliness, and courage; it does not need a regretful hankering after the past, or a fettering of the free intelligence by the words uttered long ago by ignorant men. It needs a fearless outlook and a free intelligence. It needs hope for the future, not looking back all the time towards a past that is dead, which we trust will be far surpassed by the future that our intelligence can create. (Russell)

Thus, Russell, hopeful and optimistic, promoted a kind of triumphalism. Humans with their intelligence can make things better, more meaningful. Let's go ahead and do so.

What about the inconsistency between working as if our activities were meaningful and the ultimate meaninglessness of things? Russell anticipated this problem by conflating meaninglessness with the heat death of the universe. That's a long way off. There is plenty of time in the interim. We can make good use of that time by harnessing our know-how to make the present better. What about the people, acknowledged by Russell, who say that in the face of a meaningless universe "they would not be able to go on living"? Dismiss the thought! Welcome the promise of technology. Do the best you can. The two components of philosophical wisdom, seeking to live intelligible lives in a meaningful world, need not be held together. Intelligible lives simply did not require a meaningful world. This was Great Britain in 1927. Faith in religion might have become a thing of the past. Faith in science, technology, and progress remained strong. The spirit of Prometheus held sway.

Nihilism: Facing Life without Religious or Scientific Faith

When, some ten years later, Camus engaged in a similar reflection, he started with analogous, but not identical, assumptions. One philosopher, barely on Russell's radar, loomed large for Camus. This was Friedrich Nietzsche (1844–1900). In his address upon receiving the Nobel Prize, Camus specifically highlighted a major theme from Nietzsche: "nihilism."[3] "Nihilism" is a wide-ranging term. Philosophically, its core meaning reflects the word at its root, *nihil*, "nothing." Adding the suffix "ism" transforms the straightforward term into a sweeping diagnosis: there is nothing that warrants or sanctions or underwrites value determinations. Friends of the Great Designer begged to differ. Such underwriting was guaranteed by divine command morality. For Nietzsche, this only served as an admission that the here and now, without the divine lawgiver, was a space of nihilism. Once that designer was removed, as with Nietzsche's famous pronouncement that God is dead, the full force of the latent nihilism would be felt.

One might think that this opened the door for Bertrand Russell-style Prometheanism. That judgment would be too hasty. Nietzsche was, if anything, a wide-ranging iconoclast. Religion offered a clear target, a false idol proclaiming certitudes in the face of which humans had to bow. For Nietzsche, though, science also offered a similar idol. Both science and religion shared in the "ascetic ideal," the desire to rise above the complicated, changing, realm of the here and now. Both aspired to the life-denying ideal of final, inflexible, perfect, absolute pronouncements. Supernatural escapism and techno-philic utopianism were both to be resisted.

Ordinary humans, living in a world of change and probabilities, should accept the circumstances in which living took place. Theirs was a realm of approximations, not certitudes, a fallible realm demanding constant vigilance and revision. The ascetic class (in clerical garb or lab coats) with its "will to truth," its certainties, its self-proclaimed power to command submission might come in both religious and scientific flavors. Still, the driving motivation, that of once and for all arriving at a point of fixity, "that unconditional will to truth, is *faith in the ascetic ideal itself*" (Nietzsche 1887/1994, 112).[4]

What this double iconoclasm meant for Camus was that Russell-style optimism was closed off. Science had simply become a new God. After Nietzsche, all gods were dead. The nihilistic fallout: no fixed, absolute grounds remained for selecting among options, that is, making reasoned and reasonable value decisions. Neither the commands of a divinity nor the absolute certitudes of the sciences could be latched onto as definitive sanctions for particular evaluative discriminations. After the death of all gods, nothing, *nihil*, could provide such warrantability. Nihilism ruled.

Buridan's Ass

One more philosophical detour, I ask the reader's indulgence, and the context for situating and properly understanding Camus will have been set. I've already mentioned a nineteenth-century figure, Nietzsche, and a twentieth-century one, Russell. A third figure takes us back to the fourteenth century, when the older Medieval ways were sliding into Modern ones. It's someone who had his finger on the pulse of what was to come. It's also someone who came up with a memorable thought experiment. The figure is Jean Buridan, a fourteenth-century logician. His experiment goes by the name "Buridan's ass." It represents an important foreshadowing. With it, Buridan envisioned, well before the label "nihilism" could be invented, the plight of someone for whom there was no evidence to guide intelligence. The "ass" in question is not the human backside but a donkey, specifically a hungry donkey.

The tale comes in various versions. The central elements are as follows. Imagine an ass who is (1) hungry and (2) set between two absolutely identical bales of hay. Because the options are identical in every way, there are no differential data; there is no evidence justifying the superiority of one choice over the other. Nothing in the nature of things (here's the foreshadowing of *nihi*lism) determines how the donkey should opt. Therefore the rational donkey, with nothing to guide his reason, starves. Starves, that is, unless some other factor comes into play. Starvation is an awful fate. It can be avoided. How? Admitting the futility of ratiocination, the donkey exercises a sheer act of will. He just goes to one haystack and begins happily munching.

If there are no factors providing guidance for intelligence (i.e., the situation is akin to what will come to be described as "nihilism"), all is not lost. When "mind" finds nothing to direct it, another faculty, "will," can pick up the slack. In such a scenario, one in which "mind" and "will" present themselves as two isolated functions, the very word "choice" alters its meaning. Its original signification indicated "electing among options on the basis of good reasons." Now, fully consistent with Buridan's ass and the nihilism it foreshadows, "choice" alters its meaning. It comes to signify "thus I will it." Without the possibility for a logical, evidence-based sanctioning, there remains only a sheer act of will, "choice" in its new meaning as "thus I will it."

What does this mean for Camus? The Russell option of rejecting nihilism by embracing science is, following Nietzsche, closed. A religious "leap of faith," recognizing this world as nihilistic but projecting another, transcendent, non-nihilistic domain, is specifically dismissed in *The Myth of Sisyphus* as a cowardly act of evasion. What options remain? There is one in line with Buridan's ass. It involves several components: (a) accept that in life, as with Buridan's hungry donkey, value determinations have to be made; (b) accept also that those value determinations, electing among options, will result from a "choice" in its new meaning of "thus I will it." Expressed differently the combination could be phrased in this way: (1) value selections are inevitable; (2) the world investigated by intelligence yields dry as dust, non-guiding, value-neutral facts. Simultaneously embracing (1) and (2) demands, in a positive sense, honesty and courage. In a more realistic sense, it indicates the central role of will, and freedom now defined as an act of will liberated from any external strictures. The *Myth of Sisyphus*'s dramatic opening line forces a reckoning: "Judging whether life is or is not worth living amounts to answering the fundamental question of philosophy" (MS, 3). The "fundamental question" requires a response. The Russellian path (science and technology) and the one fostered by Søren Kierkegaard (a leap of religious faith) represent modes of evasion rather than answers. Though the specifics are different, the evasion works similarly in both cases. Each invents an imaginary, beneficent, future realm. Each denies the full force of nihilism.

Camus's response? Well, humans, like Buridan's donkey, have to eat. We could pretend that religion or technology, in a future realm, will provide food. Those might be happy depictions, but hunger is gnawing at us here and now. Fortunately, like the donkey, we can undertake a free act. For Camus, freedom to chart our own path is primordial. We can activate freedom in a way that recognizes nihilism and circumvents escapism. Better to use one's freedom and embrace life, in spite of the fact that there is no secure foundation for its meaning. The other options represent liberticidal servility. Accepting suicide in a nihilist context amounts to abdicating one's freedom. It involves subservience to the indifference and pointlessness of the world. Taking the leap of faith whether in religion or science also involves an abdication of freedom. In both cases the free individual is constrained by some idealized realm.

Camus's greatness as a thinker results from his attempt to hold together seemingly incompatible positions: accept the death of all gods, yet refuse to accept life-denying consequences associated with the nihilism that follows. He turned away from the seemingly inexorable implications of nihilism because, as a champion of liberty, he would not prostrate himself to any inexorability. Axiological agnosticism, embodied in Buridan's ass, simply did not, he felt, encompass the entire story. Specifically, such axiological agnosticism (1) minimized freedom and (2) did not square with his love of life, a love well expressed in his lyrical essays.

Defiant Humanism

The Myth of Sisyphus's opening focuses on the issue in a dazzling way. If rationality tells us that all is meaningless, then why not end one's life? There are, after all, no reasons not to, and, given general meaninglessness, it may in fact stand as the more consistent path. So sayeth cold rationality. Still, the young man who loved sun and sea almost could not help himself, on a more purely gut level, from embracing life. Camus's challenge in *The Myth of Sisyphus* is thus set. Like Buridan's ass we *must* opt one way or another. Camus' *amor vitae* leans in the direction of continued living. Yet, given his philosophical inheritance, there can be no definitive *ratio decidendi*, no clear-cut mandate justifying such a decision.

What, then, is a philosophically inclined fellow, living in the first half of the twentieth century to do? Camus's answer: embrace contradiction. Say "yes" to what intelligence discovers about the meaninglessness of life. Then, remembering one's status as a free being, say "no" to what such meaninglessness would logically entail metaphysical nihilism might be inevitable. Ethical nihilism, though, remains a matter of personal decision.

Lucidity, realism, and courage guide Camus's adventure. The result is an openly embraced paradox. It all revolves around the term on which Camus focused: "absurd." Our condition, envisioned with pure objective lucidity, can best be described as "absurd." Humans seek clarity, meaning, certitude. The universe, in exactly those respects, is opaque, "silent" as Camus puts it (MS, 28). This contrast, between what humans need and what the universe provides, defines the absurdity of our condition. As rational beings, we are compelled to accept this reality. As free agents we need not submit to its pessimistic implications. We can say "no."[5] We can work to foster meaning in a meaningless world.

Metaphysical meaninglessness and ethical nihilism might be inseparable in a world devoid of freedom. They can be pried apart in a world where liberty is operative. Camus separates them by choosing the path of self-determination. He embraces a position which balances the loss of logical purity with the gain of personal freedom. The position thus ends up being a sort of heroic one. It resists the easier paths of escapism: escaping the absurd via suicide; escaping the absurd by positing a transcendent realm. It embraces contradiction and welcomes the trials and efforts that will result.

Although Camus eventually grew tired of being considered primarily as an "absurdist" thinker,[6] his reflections continue to have resonance, even today. That resonance, to a great degree, is due to the ways in which we remain inheritors of the intellectual climate of opinion that shaped Camus. In other ways, ways that have moved beyond that climate of opinion, Camus's analysis is just not as compelling as it once was.

The Great Bifurcation

Criticism of Camus can take a generous form as with the literary critic Susan Sontag. Her praise for Camus includes this recognition of illogic: "Starting from the premises of a popular nihilism, he moves the reader—solely by the power of his own tranquil voice and tone—to humanist and humanitarian conclusions *in no way entailed* by his premises" (Sontag, italics added). A more brutal critique, one which highlights a basic flaw, one central to my analysis, comes from the philosopher Mary Midgley. After quoting Camus asserting that "man feels like an alien, a stranger," Midgley adds, caustically, "This is nothing but the fantasy of a child who, because he is disappointed in his actual parents, decides to view himself as a kidnapped and disinherited prince" (Midgley 1978, 198–9). Though the image is harsh, the point is well taken: the key error is that of envisioning oneself as a kind of alien in this world.

That depiction revolves around a theme I touched upon earlier: false expectations. These result from a flawed initial move: placing ourselves at the center of things and thinking that our surroundings should have been designed for us. It's like being hungry and believing that our surroundings should be, as in popular American imagery, a "Big Rock Candy Mountain." The flaw derives from hubristic anthropocentrism. The alternatives then come to be oversimplified in terms of a narrow either/or. Either the world is like a Big Rock Candy Mountain or we starve. Shorn of the hobo-inspired imagery, the position could be formulated this way: *either* the world responds perfectly to our need for meaning, *or* our situation is absurd. The diagnosis of absurdity thus starts from a doubly flawed self-understanding: (1) imagining that the world should be made for us, and, when disappointed, (2) thinking of ourselves as aliens, strangers, or outsiders. We are not, Midgley explains, aliens in this world. We are home. Being in our home does not mean that we live in a world where rabbit tails have been specifically designed to serve as easy targets. Being at home does not mean "having an environment that has been especially designed for you. It means having one where you belong" (Midgley 1978, 195).

Being "where you belong," in turn, means *not* being an outsider or a stranger. It suggests, rather, recognizing some continuity with the living world of which we are a part. The stranger/outsider attitude overexaggerates our specificity. Unique though we may be, we continue to have kinship with other living things (Midgley 1978, 196). Forgetting this, giving in to *hubris*, tempts us to adopt a "childish and megalomaniac notion," demanding that "this universe—all of it—should be made *for us*" (Midgley 1978, 195).

We are here brought back to the situation of inflated expectations and disappointed realizations. Once we assume that the world should be made for us, disappointments are inevitable. One reaction to such disappointments: proclaim that our situation is absurd. Such an overreaction is exactly what we get from Camus. In a sense, the overreaction is understandable. After all, given the presupposition that the world should be made for us, our actual situation will seem nonsensical and calamitous. Midgley's judgment: Camus has things backward. "What we need, in order to feel at home in the world, is certainly *not* a belief that it was made for us. We are at home in this world *because we were made for it*" (Midgley 1978, 195).

What is important in listening to Midgley, but also Sontag, is how reading Camus from a later time allows for a more critical perspective. A 2019 review of Camus's *The Fall*, again in kinder, more Sontag-spirited terms, indicates this directly. The reviewer begins by expressing satisfaction that he first encountered the novel in adolescence. Looking back now, from the vantage point of the twenty-first century, the "fixation on cosmic indifference, seems like the troubled adolescence of humankind: it was a phase we were going through" (Doyle).

Sontag and Doyle admire Camus's eloquence but resist going full bore with him. Midgley, the philosopher, helps explain why. For all his talent, Camus remained within a worldview that too sharply segregated humans from their surroundings. That worldview was dominant when Camus was undergoing his philosophical education. It offered a story with a guiding theme, what I call the "Great Bifurcation." So long as the Great Bifurcation dominated the climate of opinion, *The Myth of Sisyphus* represented the best one could do. Moving beyond its illogic (Sontag) and its "childish and megalomaniac" notions (Midgley) would require de-emphasizing or rethinking entirely the framework provided by the Great Bifurcation. These represented moves that Camus would never make.

It is important to take account of the Great Bifurcation because without this background it is hard to envision why someone would think of humans as outsiders, strangers, alien-like entities, finding themselves in a world not just challenging and obstacle-laden but that is *totally* foreign and recalcitrant to their aspirations. The diagnosis of absurdity, Camus insists, derives from just such a status. The entire issue of absurdity would not arise if he were "a tree among trees, a cat among animals." In those cases "I should *belong to this world*" (MS, 51, italics added). That he possesses "consciousness" and "reason" disqualifies him (read: not a nuanced, partial disqualification, but a full-and-complete one) from such belonging. As someone endowed with consciousness, he is alien-like. Instead of pointing out how human intelligence is in some ways continuous with, while in others frustratingly divorced from, ways of dealing with surroundings, there is rather a totalizing claim. Mind "is what sets me in opposition to all creation" (MS, 51). Why? Rationality will not settle for less than absolute certitude. The world, however, maintains an "unreasonable silence" (MS, 28). Such a demand for total certitude is (a) overblown. In addition, (b) the "silence" of the world is not qualified, not partial, not contextualized. It also is characterized as total. The confrontation between a mind that demands certitude and a world wholly intransigent defines the absurd condition.

Midgley, writing some three decades later, inhabits a quite different intellectual landscape. It is one that had, from the nineteenth century, absorbed important ramifications from Darwinism and, from the twentieth, had learned much from the ecological sciences. Within this altered context there is room for both uniqueness and continuity. No longer is there a felt need to treat continuity with our embodied, physiological sides, as a "weakness," as a dethroning of humans from their perch above nature (Midgley 1978, 288).[7]

There is a lengthy intellectual history leading to the emphasis on separation and opposition instead of continuity. It begins in post-Aristotelian, Hellenistic philosophy, with an articulation that the spiritual and the bodily exist in opposition, gets taken up by influential figures in Christianity, suffers a bit of a setback when Aristotelian philosophy dominates in the thirteenth century, but returns in full force in the early seventeenth century with René Descartes (1596–1650). He, more than any other philosopher, helped crystallize, demarcate, and institutionalize the Great Bifurcation.

The Great Bifurcation insisted that humans were not really of this world. Endowed with minds, humans were more like spectators looking out onto an "external" world. The "we are strangers, outsiders" dimension manifests itself in Descartes' *Second Meditation*. There, in a move that repudiates how humans live in, by, with, and on account of the world, he actually wishes it away. "I suppose, accordingly, that all the things which I see are false (fictitious); I believe that none of those objects which my fallacious memory represents ever existed; I suppose that I possess no senses; I believe that body, figure, extension, motion, and place are merely fictions of my mind" (Descartes Meditation 2, par 2). The natural, embodied aspects of our lives are shameful weaknesses. The possibilities associated with natural life do not provide opportunities for culminations which blend material and spiritual. We would do better if we could rise completely above our material dimensions. Then, continuing this rupture from surroundings, Descartes famously concludes that he is, really and essentially, not a living being in a living world but a "thinking thing" (Descartes, Meditation 2, par. 8). Such a move, the specific sundering of humans from their milieux, is what I call the "Great Bifurcation."

Once the bifurcation had become the default mode of thinking, the way was paved for nihilism. The world, no longer the home or habitat by which, in which, with which, on account of which humans make their way, gets transformed. It now becomes "external," an entity populated with "objects." The interest of those "objects" to the "subject" now moves from practical to epistemological. Practical concerns revolved around issues such as how the intersection of humans and their natural surroundings could be brought to their proper, optimal, culminations. Epistemological concerns tended to sidestep the ethical dimension altogether. The world now more "external" than "lived" came to be the realm most properly examined by those studies (the sciences) which leave aside value considerations. It is then but a small step to identify the objective realm as the locus of mere "facts" separated from "values." Better and worse simply do not apply, in any objective way, to this realm. There is, within it, *nihil*, nothing, that guides intelligence when it comes to evaluations. Evaluations derive strictly from the other side of the bifurcation, the subjective one.

We thus return to the setting described by Buridan. Objective criteria do not offer differential indicators. The donkey is stymied if it seeks to be guided by evidence. Still, it must eat. So, in order to survive, its only option is the voluntaristic one: "thus I will it, this is the hay bale I choose." There are no factual differences that make a difference. Axiological agnosticism rules. Nothing about what we know (*gnosis*) guides reflection when it comes to judging matters of worth (*axia*). Decisions, though, still have to be made. "Choice," as we have seen, shifts its meaning. It moves from "elect among options for good reasons" to "thus I will it."[8]

The Great Bifurcation thus sets up the opposition that defines the absurd condition and enables nihilism. One result: the situation confronted by Camus, a muddle from which there is no escape. No escape, that is, so long as the Great Bifurcation, along with the totalizing pronouncements it encourages, continues to be taken for granted. Qualifications, matters of degree, phrases like "in a way" tend to be considered soft and unworthy of the elevated status of mind. Exaggerations are encouraged. Camus, with his penchant for dramatic, attention-grabbing pronouncements, was well suited to such a setting. Well suited to a particular philosophical framework, however, does not mean sensitive to the subtleties and complexities of lived experience.

Absurd, or Just "Surd"

Are all human longings satisfied fully and perfectly? No. Does this mean that the world is completely "silent" as regards those longings? No as well. Hunger, as with Buridan's ass, serves as a good example. If the world were made just to satisfy hungry humans, it would be like a Big Rock Candy Mountain. It is not. Does this mean that the world is "silent," completely indifferent to the nutritional needs of humans? Well, no. It is true that the needs of nutrition are not met easily and automatically. It is also true that humans, like other world-inhabiting creatures, can find ways for maximizing the possibilities offered by nature. Camus's rhetoric, in the shadow of the Great Bifurcation, favors sharp either/or formulations. There is lots of room between a dream-world (childish and monomaniacal) embodied by Big Rock Candy Mountain and complete deprivation The diagnosis of absurdity depends on denying the reality of this in-between. Stated more negatively, it uncritically takes for granted assumptions that embrace the anthropocentric, hubristic belief that the world should perfectly match our aspirations.

Shifting terms a bit, we could say that, in many ways, our interchanges with the world leave plenty of room for misunderstanding. It is as if both we and the world suffered from partial deafness. "Deaf," in French is *sourd*, a word derived from the Latin *surdus*. An ab-surd world is one that is absolutely deaf to our pleas. "This world itself is not reasonable, that is all that can be said. But what is absurd is the confrontation of this irrational and the wild longing for clarity whose call echoes in the human heart" (MS, 21). The presence of a Big Rock Candy Mountain, by contrast, would instantiate a world free of absurdity. It would be one which responded, immediately and thoroughly, to human solicitations.

Is there an in-between, a world that is, in many ways, frustrating, painful, aggravating while at the same time offering opportunities for harmonious and happy consummations? Could it be that the world has a "surdish" dimension without being fully absurd? Within the confines of the Great Bifurcation and its demand that all issues be framed as either/or dilemmas, the answer has to be "no." Outside its confines, in an intellectual climate where degrees of difference, approximations, spectra, and complexities are recognized, the answer becomes "yes."

A "surdish" world is one in which perfect formulations are rare, one in which even today's best science can be altered tomorrow. Today's ethical certainties turn out to be temporally and culturally conditioned. Our best-intentioned and best-designed projects are never perfectly successful. Resolutions of antecedent problems can generate novel ones. Utopian dreams turn into nightmares. Even if a particular life is successful, mortality will bring it, along with unfinished projects, to a frustrating end. All of this can be acknowledged without the single-minded exaggeration that proclaims universal, ontological absurdity.

Sisyphus as a Guiding Image

Such a transformation, however, is encouraged by the Great Bifurcation. The only way out would be to challenge the assumption that dismisses continua and degrees of difference. So long as formulations of our situation and its conditions are channeled into absolutist pronouncements, accompanied by inflexible either/or formulations, the Camusian take is as good as can be expected. He encouraged humans to accept the opportunity and burden of freedom. It is because of freedom that a spirit need not be broken by external circumstances. The suggested stance, one of ethical heroism has nothing to do with, in fact, specifically stands apart from both the *deus* of traditional religion and the *Prometheus* of Russell-style faith in science and technology. Rather, as Camus's title indicates, the prototypical figure is *Sisyphus*. Sisyphus serves as a model because he neither evades truths nor gives in to them. He remains undaunted and steadfast. Unlike those who are more timid and self-deluded, this valiant champion of lucidity takes satisfaction in his own determination not to be sidetracked by illusion or wishful thinking. If we can envision such a figure, Camus concludes, then we "must imagine Sisyphus happy" (MS, 123).

Sisyphus exercises liberty by resisting, rebelling, refusing to give in. He embraces the paradoxical human condition, saying "yes" to the Absurd *and* "yes" to life. The main issue turns around living with a conjunction that could easily be discarded. On one hand, rationality must be given its due. "I want to know whether I can live with what I know and with that alone" (MS, 40). On the other hand, for free individuals, the question whether the absurd dictates death remains an open one (MS, 7–8). Two traditional paths for dealing with this question have been prominent in the tradition: either accept that absurdity entails suicide and submit to the dictates of logic or accept that the absurd pushes us toward a leap of faith and submit to the dictates of religion.

Camus has a sense that there is more to the story, but he does not have the philosophical tools to reconstruct the semantic landscape he has inherited. All he can do is what Sontag recognizes he has done: offer a celebratory championing of a position which he wishes to defend. This position is taken, even though, as Sontag put it, its "humanist and humanitarian conclusions" are "in no way entailed by his premises." Camus's own phrasing is that he opts to avoid the easy paths open to him, preferring to remain on the "dizzying crest" (MS, 50). Humans need not submit. They are free to struggle against the conditions within which they find themselves. Defiant humanism suggests that they avail themselves to this option.

Accepted claims bring with them some expectable follow-ups. The subsequent responses, though, are multiple. One asks: are the claims true? Another asks: can we live in accordance with them? For Camus, in more technical terms, the issue is whether metaphysical nihilism (true as far as he is concerned) should be accompanied by ethical nihilism (suspect for him). Staying on the "dizzying crest" for Camus means accepting the former while resisting the latter. If this entails embracing contradiction, so much the worse for logic. The whole point is to be rigorously honest and courageous. This means recognizing the reality of the absurd, "keeping it alive" by "contemplating it" while not giving in to it (MS, 54). The response which combines freedom and courage has a name. Camus says that the "coherent" philosophical position "is thus revolt" (MS, 54). "Revolt" here involves embracing both intelligence and freedom. Intelligence declares our situation to be absurd. Freedom allows us to elect options at variance with what such an acknowledgment would logically entail.

Pure logic seeks final, perfect resolutions. Such resolutions, however, are only possible in an imaginary realm. "But I know that in order to keep alive, the absurd cannot be settled" (MS, 54). Embracing our absurd condition means that we accept how existence always eludes perfect resolution. The dream of a neat resolution is the illusion fostered by the friends of faith, the friends of utopian fantasies, and the friends of perfect rationality. The absurd, by contrast, means that there are no neat resolutions. Humans embrace this realization when they exercise their freedom and choose continuing existence.

Engaging his penchant for striking formulations, Camus suggests that the original form of the question had gotten things backward. Traditionally, the belief is that life is worth living only if it has meaning. "It now becomes clear, on the contrary, that it will be lived all the better if it has no meaning" (MS, 53). The formulation is both striking and puzzling. Still, it's possible to make sense of it. To begin with, there is the issue of freedom. After all, there is a major difference between being condemned to death (mostly out of our control) and suicide (a choice we can make). The former describes a situation of minimal freedom. The latter depicts a situation in which freedom is manifest. Responsibility is absent in the former case but enhanced in the latter. Second, if our lives have no prearranged scripts, no "meaning" mandated for us, we are gifted with an opening and can craft our lives in any of a variety of ways. Each of these, though, requires an initial step, revolt. We must say no to the siren call of suicide.

The mythological character who best exemplifies the revolt-and-freedom combination is Sisyphus. In Camus's telling, Sisyphus, though condemned to a mind-and-body-breaking punishment, can, by an internal effort of scorn and revolt, emerge "superior to his fate" (MS, 121). The punishment is disheartening and frustrating: pushing a rock up a hill only to have it roll down again, with the process repeated over and over. The situation is made worse by awareness that it is unending. There is no hope of reprieve, pardon, or escape.

Still, even in such a predicament, Camus insists that Sisyphus can engage his consciousness in revolt. He can refuse to be broken. "The lucidity that was to constitute his torture at the same time crowns his victory. There is no fate that cannot be surmounted by scorn" (MS, 121). The Great Bifurcation here plays itself out in the separation between inner and outer. No matter how bad are external conditions, there is always the possibility of a free internal judgment about those conditions. For Camus, this possibility is realized by Sisyphus as he descends to begin the uphill trek anew. "If the descent is thus sometimes performed in sorrow, it can also take place in joy" (MS, 121). External conditions may be terrible and cruel, but, internally, Sisyphus is not broken. "All Sisyphus' silent joy is contained therein. His fate belongs to him" (MS, 123). His (external) fate may be dire, but his (internal) "fate belongs to him." In the end this refusal to acquiesce, this revolt, this scorn, this "struggle itself toward the heights is enough to fill a man's heart." As a result, in the essay's final words, "One must imagine Sisyphus happy" (MS, 123).

3

Defiant Humanism in Question

Reflections on Camus's *The Myth of Sisyphus*, II

Inflated Expectations, Disappointed Realizations, II

"One must imagine Sisyphus happy." It's a great closing line. It's also all wrong. The situation of Sisyphus, a punishment invented by the gods, is rather dire. The task is physically painful and, with the rock always rolling back, frustrating. There is, in addition, no chance of escape nor hope for a reprieve. Sisyphus toils in full awareness of his fate. Despite all of this, Camus still suggests that we *must* imagine Sisyphus *happy*. The recommendation is both dogmatic and slippery. "Must" (*il faut*) is dogmatic; "imagine" is slippery. We can always "imagine" counterintuitively. It is, in a narrow sense, *possible* to imagine prisoners happy, slaves happy, people in difficult circumstances happy. But that possibility has little to do with likelihood. It is a fanciful projection that, most of the time, would be mistaken.[1] Thus the necessity of adding *must*, a directive which Camus wishes to impose on his readers.

For Camus's exhortation to make sense, a series of conditionals has to be accepted: *if* the Great Bifurcation holds, *if* outer events can be totally disconnected from inner evaluations, *if* happiness is just a matter of deciding what one's inner attitude will be. These conditionals may have once seemed boilerplate. Today, they seem hyperbolic. They isolate, simplify, and misconstrue lived experience. They radically segregate *inner* attitude from *external* conditions. They suggest that all human predicaments, like the one of Camus's Sisyphus, can be neatly sorted into external conditions that have nothing to do with inner attitude. As a result, and quite in opposition to reformist tendencies, such a neat segregation supports, as a default position, not change of conditions but a shift in inner attitude. Problematic as is the perspective, Camus needs to preserve it. It provides the prerequisites for both the diagnosis of absurdity and the judgment that we must imagine Sisyphus happy. Without it, the diagnosis and the judgment have little support.

"Little" identifies an important qualification. The position of Camus is built around partial truths that get metastasized before ending up as grandiose, overexaggerated, absolutist falsehoods. There are many aspects of lived experience which, in ordinary language, can be described as "absurd." This does not support the blanket claim that, in its fundamental structure, the human condition is absurd. Before this claim can be asserted, a general philosophical assumption, what I've called the Great Bifurcation, has to be accepted. Ontological absurdity would then emerge as a spillover of the bifurcation: the contrast between, on one side, human aspirations and, on the other, a silent, indifferent world.

The claim of ontological absurdity is flawed, but only flawed because it is made without qualifications. The absence of qualifications depends, we also saw this in the first chapter, on a particular expectation: that reality should match perfectly the mental grids humans have concocted. The "real," as a neo-Hegelian slogan had it, is imagined straightforwardly and completely to be "rational." Maybe the real is not rational in this neat sense. Maybe, at the same time, it is not irrational. Maybe it is intellig*ible*, understand*able*, pregnant with indications inviting human inquiries. Maybe the world, though presenting intellectual challenges, is neither totally, completely forthcoming nor totally, completely "silent."

Camus, to his credit, recognizes the presence of "irrationals" (MS, 27). So far so good. The real, after all, is superabundant, that is, *not* a simple rational grid. The human setting, as Camus sees it, is thus inherently frustrating. On one side, there is a longing for perfect rationality; on the other, an awareness that such rationality is nowhere to be found. This is a tension that must be preserved. Some philosophers, Husserl is the example given by Camus, have had the temerity to assert that "reason eventually has no limits" (MS, 49). A religious philosopher like Kierkegaard follows a different path to avoid the tension. The specifics of his strategy differentiate him from Husserl. Kierkegaard, friend of religious faith, gives up one aspect inherent to the tension. Husserl dreams of a world where rationality is like a perfect eyeball. Kierkegaard gives up the desire for total, perfect rational clarity (MS, 49). The absurd man of Camus, by contrast, insists on living in this world. He rejects the escape via rationalism *and* the escape via fideism.

This too is good. But, here's the rub, why exaggerate the impact of reality having a surdish dimension? Why set up the issue in a way assuming, of course, that humans should expect *perfect, total* clarity. Why create the artificial desire in the first place? This move, creating an artificial desire, is the lynchpin that leads to the diagnosis of absurdity. It creates expectations which, within this philosophical atmosphere, seem obvious and self-evident. They are also expectations bound to be frustrated. The divorce between expectations and realizations then underwrites the claim of absurdity. "That evidence is the absurd. It is that divorce between the mind that desires and the world that disappoints, my nostalgia for unity, this fragmented universe, and the contradiction that binds them together" (MS, 50).

Two points are important as we parse this passage. First, the French word *évidence* has the connotation of self-evident, obvious, incontrovertible. Such a starting point, in other words, is foundational; it cannot be gainsaid. Second, there is the issue with which this chapter opened: what presuppositions must be assumed before the conclusion makes sense? What if the world "disappoints" *somewhat*? What if *total* disappointment depends on the faulty expectation of perfect mind/reality mirroring? What if the lure of perfect clarity, along with the "nostalgia for unity," is part and parcel of an inherited philosophical tradition and not neutral, obvious (self-evident) expectations? What happens, in other words, if we added qualifications like "somewhat," "to some degree," or "in some ways" to the claim that the world "disappoints." Then "absurdity" would seem a diagnosis without a foundation or a diagnosis occasioned by presuppositions that have little to do with ordinary, quotidian human life. The presuppositions create exaggerated expectations. Those expectations, when not met, occasion the overblown reaction of applying the label "absurd."

Irony, Not Absurdity

A philosophical detour (yes I know, this book has many of them) helps appraise the diagnosis of absurdity. This time the philosopher in question is not a twentieth-century science/technology optimist like Russell, nor a nineteenth-century prophet like Nietzsche, nor a medieval logician like Buridan. He's the important twentieth-century philosopher José Ortega y Gasset (1883–1955). Gasset's significance derives from formulations that move philosophy into an orbit other than that of the Great Bifurcation. Once philosophy's planetary system is shifted, it becomes possible to welcome another take on the human condition, one not built around the axiom "we are like aliens." It becomes possible to embrace the complexities of life without imposing the narrow, binary grid that separates "mind" and "world." Once that grid is set aside, the door is opened for thinking of human intelligence, not as the cold rationality practiced by a mind detached from the world but rather as *razón vital*, living reason.[2] After all, in a post-Bifurcation era, we can once again think of ourselves as living beings in a living world. The intellectual capacities of such beings can best be characterized not as a rationality that seeks to rise above life but as *razón vital*, reasoning in life.

In place of the Great Bifurcation, Ortega emphasized lived experience. He summarized that experience in the slogan "I am I and my circumstance" (Ortega 1963, 13). The formulation emphasizes conjunction rather than bifurcation. The inherited framework had insisted on separation: humans as minds over here; the world over there. In its place, Ortega proposes a more ordinary situatedness with all the conjunctions that accompany a social, affective, normative, inquisitive creature. Humans no longer need to be understood primarily as outsiders or detached spectators. Their condition can be appreciated as that of living participants in ongoing processes.

Ortega's shift in philosophical paradigm provides a way of situating Camus. Camus mostly remained within the older (we are like aliens, so life seems absurd) landscape. The Camusian starting point: the gap between human aspirations and what the world can provide. As we have seen, he states it specifically in terms of total rupture. It's the "divorce between the mind that desires and the world that disappoints" (MS, 50). This represents the Camusian bedrock, the assumption that is so obvious (*évidence*) that it serves as the foundation on which future reflection is based. Because he understands it as an *évidence*, he cannot, as other early twentieth-century philosophers were doing, think of it as one way of attempting an adequate attunement with how things are. Instead of regarding it as a schema articulated at a particular time and place in response to particular circumstances, he gives it an atemporal, self-evident status.

The formulation in terms of a "divorce" offers an indication of Camusian hyperbole. It is built on a partial truth: humans are unique in important ways. But, as the saying goes, "a half-truth is a whole lie." This is especially so when the partial truth is not recognized as partial. Humans, besides being unique, are also, in important ways, continuous with other organisms. The uniqueness *and* the continuities both need to be recognized. If, instead, the two are divorced, humans can be thought of as strangers, aliens, or outsiders to the lifeworld. A more humble, more concrete depiction would admit, Ortega-style, the interpenetration of "I" and its "circumstances." After all, the "I" survives as an entity in, with, and on account of the milieu of which it forms a part.

Ortega, recognizing such interdependence, offers a more suitable starting point. "I find that there is one primary and fundamental fact which carries its own assurance. This fact is the joint existence of a self, a subjectivity, and of its world. . . . Therefore the basic and undeniable fact is not my existence, but my coexistence with the world" (Ortega 1964, 200).

Isolated units as insulated blocks are abstractions. Humans, organisms who breathe, eat, come from the union of sperm and egg, have gestated in a female, need lengthy care as children, are already, always, within a context. Experienced concretely, the lifeworld manifests "coexistence," that is, interrelationships, not bifurcation. Such coexistence, Ortega cautions, should be thought of as genuinely interactive, not as indicating merely that "one thing stands besides another." Our "circumstances" implicate us and other participants in networks marked by mutuality. We are not like a pile of shot stuffed into a gun shell. The live creature "sees the world, thinks about it, touches it, loves it or detests it, is enthusiastic about it or irritated at it, transforms it, exhausts it, suffers it--this is what has always been called 'living'" (Ortega 1964, 210).

Such living and the loves, enthusiasms, irritations, attempts at transformation that characterize it provide occasions for reflection. They give *razón vital* something to do. *Razón vital* in turn has no need of inventing a neutral ground zero. Living reason, this is significant, is quite different from Cartesian rationality. Cartesian rationality thinks of mind as a kind of combination container-mirror. In that container are "ideas." Those ideas, in turn, are supposed to mirror perfectly the objects outside the container. It's a unidimensional, "snapshot-isolating-a-moment-in-time" kind of depiction. It's also one that begins by a division between mind and world, a division which separates valuation from fact. *Razón vital*, by contrast, is operative both temporally and in the midst of things. The "circumstances" to which it is attentive are not just neutral objects. They are matters of concern.

The epistemic ideal shifts away from just perfect mirroring of neutral (or neutered) objects. "Accuracy" can now regain its etymological sense as "done with care." Done with care, or done with the best care of which we, in this time and place, are capable, does not encourage closure, does not suggest the kind of finality fostered by the mind-as-container/mirror imagery. The resulting shift (accuracy understood as proceeding with great care *versus* accuracy as perfect mirroring) is a major one. It also carries implications for understanding Camus since it can be summarized as the contrast between irony and absurdity.

Camus, as is widely known, defends, in *The Myth of Sisyphus*, the position of absurdity. Ortega's emphasis on irony offers a contrast which can encompass much of what Camus says without engaging in Camusian hyperbole. To understand how this is so, it is important to get a sense of what Ortegan "irony" is all about.

Irony, as most commonly understood, is a literary or rhetorical device. Central to irony is double meaning. There is often an obvious meaning which is then doubled up by another. Early in the movie *Titanic*, Jack Dawson wins a poker game. The prize: a ticket across the Atlantic. It's a "lucky" hand, and, upon boarding, Jack exclaims, "We're the luckiest sons of bitches in the world." The "luck," for a viewer aware of the ship's upcoming iceberg encounter, is ironic. Jack's utterance involves oppositional simultaneity. His claim connotes, at the same time, a typical meaning (what good fortune to win a ticket on the *Titanic*) and its opposite (what bad luck to be a passenger on this particular ship).

Philosophically the most famous use is in the phrase "Socratic irony." Here the meaning is that Socrates, while claiming lack of awareness, is actually in control of the conversation. He may proclaim lack of insight or understanding, but this is a ruse. Socrates proclaims ignorance while being very much in possession of knowledge.

Ortega, whose writing style was praised by Camus,[3] tweaked this notion in an important way. Philosophers who could blithely proclaim (proclaim without qualifications) that the real is rational and the rational is real had lost a fundamental sense of irony. Ortega, no longer captivated by the depiction of ideas as little mirrors in the container called mind, rejects the notion of perfect, final, never-revisable mind-object mirroring. Instead, truer to the workings of *razón vital*, he points out that every philosophical formulation is inherently and irrevocably "ironic." Why? Because inquiries, no matter how much care is put into them (i.e., no matter how much being "accurate" is a goal), can never provide formulations that will fully, perfectly, once and for all articulate the thick complexity of existence. As a result, even successful articulations (1) always leave a residuum and (2) are open to revision in some ways. They are thus "ironic." On one hand, they grasp something of importance. On the other hand, they leave something out. Ortega's explanation employs the metaphor of a diamond ring:

> Every concept, the simplest and most technical, is framed in its own irony as the geometrically cut diamond is held in its setting of gold. The concept tells us quite seriously: "This thing is A, that thing is B." But the seriousness is that of the man who is playing a joke on you, the unstable seriousness of one who is swallowing a laugh, which will burst out if he does not keep his lips tight-closed. It knows very well that this thing is not just merely A, or that thing just merely B. What the concept really thinks is a little bit different from what it says, and herein the irony lies. What it really thinks is this: I know that, strictly speaking, this thing is not A, nor that thing B; but by taking them as A and B, I come to an understanding with myself for the purposes of my practical attitude towards both of these things. (Ortega 1932, 130–1)

As part of philosophy's move away from the primacy of ideas over life, Ortega recognizes how the lifeworld will always be richer, fuller, have more density than will any conceptual scheme attempting to map it. Philosophical irony then becomes something quite ordinary and humble: the awareness that no matter how helpful conceptual frameworks are, they will always fall short in some ways. They will always be in need of further elaboration, tinkering, or reform. The dream of a final resting place, what philosophers call a "final vocabulary," one that would bring thinking and commentary to a close, is misguided. The presence of "irony" in Ortega's sense is precisely what keeps philosophers from succumbing to the temptation of coming up with *the, single, final* formulation.[4] Truths are obtain*able*, the world is intellig*ible*, but a final direct, pure, unmediated, flawless, mirroring of reality by mind is not only illusory but also a dangerous precursor of totalitarian tendencies.

Absurdity encourages rebellion against the typical circumstances within which we find ourselves. Irony is more welcoming. But, consistent with its admonishing side, the welcoming does not mean that all is perfect. The difficulties identified by Camus need not be swept under any rug. Nor need they lead to a hasty conclusion about absurdity. As live creatures who think, touch, love, esteem and abominate, humans will come up against obstacles, feel some frustration. After all, as Mary Midgley reminded us in the last chapter, the world is not made for us, we are made for it.

This is the point at which Camusian overreaction becomes significant. Disappointment, resulting from faulty expectations, leads to an exaggerated overreaction, the hyperbolic, qualification-free, claim about how the world "disappoints" or how it is "unintelligible" (MS, 50, 21). Half-truths are whole lies. Even though there may not be absolutely final rational clarity, there is not complete unintelligibility. Irony allows degrees of accuracy. It discourages thinking in absolute *Either/Or* terms.

In emphasizing a particular understanding of irony, Ortega encouraged a major shift in outlook. Instead of assuming that we are on the brink of a final, incontrovertible, complete rational formulation, there are now altered expectations. Fallibility is recognized as unavoidable. The continuous need for revision is taken for granted. The "ironic turn," as we might call it, may have been radical in the first half of the twentieth century. Today it has become widely accepted. It has even made an impact in the sciences. One contemporary physicist has phrased it in wonderfully clear terms.

> All the laws of nature discovered by scientists are considered provisional. They are considered to be approximations of deeper laws. The laws are constantly being revised as new experimental evidence is found or new, and testable, ideas are proposed. In fact, what we call "laws of nature" should really be called "approximate laws of nature." But that expression is a mouthful. (Lightman, 93–4)[5]

Recognizing approximation and revisability as integral to their profession, physicists do not throw up their arms and proclaim "It's all absurd." Better would be the Ortegan-inspired formulation: irony is just part and parcel of *razón vital*. To proclaim "it's all absurd" is possible. It can actually make some sense, but only within a particular philosophical landscape, one which gives rise to over-elevated expectations that have little to do with the situation and setting of humans.

Resisting Tidy-Mindedness

Camus's position, at least as evidenced by *The Myth of Sisyphus*, remains one caught in the trajectory of inflated expectations, disappointments, and the hyperbolic claims that ensue. His take on things assumes that if irony (as Ortega understands it) is inevitable, if perfect clarity is unachievable, these are indications that our situation is absurd. Consciousness sets humans in opposition to the world. *Razón vital* is an oxymoron.

There are "two certainties," according to Camus, and they cannot logically be held together. "And these two certainties—my appetite for the absolute and for unity and the impossibility of reducing this world to a rational and reasonable principle—I also know that I cannot reconcile them" (MS, 51). Several familiar themes are present here. The most important is an insistence on purity and thoroughness. No approximations allowed. A contemporary physicist like Alan Lightman, as we have seen, can accept that "laws of nature" really means "approximate laws of nature." In the early 1940s, Camus's philosophical inheritance blocked him from making a similar admission. Purity, perfection, totality were the received marching orders. "The appetite for the absolute and for unity" is taken as fixed and infallible. And indeed it is a fixed and infallible demand for disembodied minds but not for flesh-and-blood humans.

Living, multidimensional creatures, participating in living environments, will have much more appreciation for the ordinary, for approximations, for fallibility. They will resist fanciful dreams, like that of escaping into the realm of pure, clean, disconnected consciousness. Such live creatures in living environments, however, are not at all what Camus envisions humans to be. A key passage, cited partially in the previous chapter, is worth quoting at length:

> If I were a tree among trees, a cat among animals, this life would have a meaning, or rather this problem would not arise, for I should belong to this world. I should *be* this world to which I am now opposed by my whole consciousness and my whole insistence upon familiarity. (MS, 51)

The either/or in this passage is blunt. On one hand, *either* complete immersion in the physico-material world, be a "tree among trees, a cat among animals." Such a status would leave humans without consciousness. It would, by this very fact, convey an advantage: mind-deprived beings do not long for "the absolute and for unity." Theirs is a world free of absurdity. This represents the *either*.

Its complement, the *or*, makes clear how, for Camus, there is no in-between. If we are not just animals among animals, that is because we are endowed with consciousness. Such consciousness marks a *total* separation from the realm of being another animal among animals. Consciousness (1) sets humans (or, staying close to Camusian terminology, "man") in opposition to the world; (2) it creates a demand to which man must submit: "the appetite for the absolute and for unity"; (3) what results is an irresolvable situation which leads to the verdict of absurdity. The range of in-between options, ones that would seek to formulate the whole truth, that humans are *both* physiological and psychological, is ruled out. Not just ruled out, but the two components are set in unalterable opposition. To think in terms requiring qualifications, distinctions; to utilize expressions like "in some ways," "to some degree," such procedures are anathema. They represent a mixed and muddled picture, one that might be suitable for *razón vital* but which violates the narrow strictures of pure rationality.

Pure thought might be good in some contexts, say Euclidean geometry, a model field for much of Modern philosophy. In the ordinary context of living, "vital reason" (or "vital reasonableness") offers a more suitable competency. What Mary Midgley calls "tidy-minded" types (those who favor pure rationality over vital reason) simply do not like the effort associated with being human. They want shortcuts and simplifications. They thus rebel against the everyday, actual conditions within which genuine inquiries take place. They prefer the purified, abstract, artificial, realm represented by mind disconnected from body.[6] From such a restricted, purified take, it may be possible, as Ludwig Wittgenstein remarked, to say things about "abstruse questions of logic." Such an ability, though, has little to do with philosophy's search for wisdom. What good, Wittgenstein continues, is the study of philosophy "if it does not improve your thinking about important questions of everyday life?" (in Midgley 1989, 239).

Such improvement will not come about when we begin by promoting, as does Camus, faulty ideals constructed on the mistaken belief that the highest human attainment is reaching absolute once-and-for-all certitude. So long as this demand remains the guiding ideal, *razón vital* will seem an impoverished, unsatisfactory substitute. It will never provide the perfect, irrefutable, absolutely certain conclusions associated with deductive logic. All it can do is work within the context of "accuracy," that is, proceed with care. Such care can be manifested by marshaling evidence, making a strong case, striving for a warranted and reasonable account. All of this is done within the context of "irony." Conclusions reached will always leave some loose ends, some questions still to be resolved. Who could favor such a deficient, muddled, defective (as opposed to pure rational certitude) approach? Well, us: humans as living beings in a living world. Why begin with the assumption that we should be disembodied minds? The kind of reasonableness associated with *razón vital* may not be suited for a disembodied mind, but it's a good fit for humans. Attentive, accuracy-conditioned reasonableness is a good fit because of who we are. Mary Midgley articulates it well. We are "social, integrated, affectionate, language-using beings." The reasonableness suited for such beings, she goes on, is not an arbitrary imposition. "It is continuous with the rest of life" (Midgley 1991, 26).

"Continuous with the rest of life." That is an admission which philosophers, sadly, have too often resisted. Camus, dissatisfied with the escapisms he found around him, would appear to be someone who would embrace quotidian experience and an understanding of intelligence as continuous with the rest of life. As his quest developed, he, later, would make tentative moves in this direction. His earliest publications, though, continue to be shaped by the Great Bifurcation. "I want everything to be explained to me or nothing" (MS, 27). Such a rigid, exclusionary demand vitiates, from the beginning, the Wittgensteinian call for philosophy to improve (note "improve," not settle once and for all) our "thinking about important questions of everyday life." The "everything explained to me or nothing" attitude cannot be "continuous with the rest of life." It has backed itself into a corner, one in which "consciousness" (not everyday intelligence) *must* envision itself as opposed to the ordinary lifeworld.

Imagining Sisyphus Happy?

Such an antithesis, following upon the inner/outer compartmentalization, allows Camus to end his essay with the famous pronouncement *il faut imaginer Sisyphe heureux*. Despite the severe, unending punishment that has been visited upon Sisyphus, despite the total absence of hope, "one must imagine Sisyphus happy" (MS, 123). This *must* is difficult to accept. The gods have designed an especially frustrating, demeaning chastisement. Sisyhpus is compelled, with great toil, to roll a rock uphill, only to have it roll down again, forcing him, over and over, to repeat the bitter task. This punishment will be unending. There is no hope of reprieve. How, then, can Camus conclude that his readers must *judge* Sisyphus *happy?* True, he says "imagine," but the semantic range of that word allows Camus to play a little game. He can mandate a specific position while preserving some plausible deniability. After all, "imagination" allows for lots of possibilities.

Defending the judgment of happiness requires commitment to a familiar orientation, that of the Great Bifurcation. A rigid barrier has to be erected ("fabricated" would be more accurate) between inner and outer, between objective facts and subjective evaluations. Camus accepts the existence of such a bulwark. This is not a disjunction which he invents. He absorbs it from his academic schooling. (Yes, reader, another philosophical detour is coming.) The disjunction with which Camus is working represents a long-existing and long-lasting strand in European philosophy.

Some of its most prominent formulations date from post-Aristotelian "Hellenistic" philosophy. The clearest statements can be found in schools sometimes set in opposition to one another: Stoicism and Epicureanism. On the issue of inner/outer segregation, there is plenty of overlap. The overlap: isolate completely human (internal) subjectivity from the objectivity (external) of surrounding conditions. In a famous letter, Epicurus (341–270 BCE) went so far as to urge a follower, Menoeceus, to consider independence from outward things "as a great good" (Epicurus). From the Stoic side, a paradigmatic utterance comes from the Roman Emperor Marcus Aurelius (121–180 CE). In place of a mutuality, a living interplay between individuals and the circumstances in which they find themselves, the Roman emperor suggests a rigid separation:

> External things are not the problem. It's your assessment of them. Which you can erase right now. (Aurelius, 110)

Sisyphus, as Camus describes him, lives out the compartmentalization described by Aurelius: the autonomy of "assessment," its disconnection from surrounding events. The proclamation is one that does not emphasize awareness of, and appropriate response to, circumstances. The proclamation suggests rather that a total disconnection of the two is a high human ideal. The pivotal moment is associated with partial truth: there are many ways to react to a situation. It is possible and often important not to let a situation completely crush one's spirit. The grain of truth is exemplified in Camus's description of Sisyphus's descent. The rock has rolled, once again, downhill. Sisyphus is condemned to restart his unending task. In that pause, however, Sisyphus can insist on a self-determining judgment. This is the moment during which Marcus Aurelius' subjectivity of "assessment" takes on significance. Consciousness allows Sisyphus to maintain some detachment. Regardless of external circumstances, he can, inwardly, celebrate what got him there: "scorn of the gods," "hatred for death," and "passion for life" (MS, 120). "There is no fate," Camus concludes, "that cannot be surmounted by scorn." As a result, the descent of Sisyphus, with his consciousness intact, can "take place in joy," and the word "joy," Camus emphasizes, "is not too much" (MS, 121).

Some of us, I for one, may beg to differ. What Camus has given us, sorry if this is getting too repetitive, is hyperbole. It is a flight of fancy deriving from an exaggerated either/or cleavage. Qualifications, distinctions, matters of degree, contextualization of claims—these find no place in the totalizing directive to judge Sisyphus happy. Camus moves, without justification, from partial truth to a grandiose claim. The grandiose claim, in its absence of qualifications, transforms partial truth into a misleading exaggeration. Keep in mind that Camus is not just asserting how Sisyphus can experience moments of happiness, or can, internally/mentally, preserve commitments which are dear to him, or can decide to make the best of a horrible situation. He is not just saying that Sisyphus always possesses a kind of freedom: one to adopt a particular attitude toward his situation. The claim that "we must imagine Sisyphus happy" goes beyond such a realization. Viktor Frankl's reflections on life in concentration camps, camps already in operation when *The Myth of Sisyphus* was published, provide testimony to the dangers of overstatement. The partial truth remains. One can assert, as Frankl does, that "life holds a potential meaning under any conditions" (Frankl, 16). It would be quite another for outside observers to assert that Frankl must be considered to have been "happy" while a prisoner.

In order to make his claim about Sisyphus, Camus has drawn on the Hellenistic partition between inner and outer. Marcus Aurelius, picturing himself as a detached spectator, could pronounce that such disconnection was possible. Epicurus could proclaim that the disconnection was a good thing. Camus's continuation of this tradition, along with his talent for dramatic pronouncement, led to his powerful, gripping, but dangerous overstatement. Using our own imaginative powers, we can caricature the depiction of Sisyphus envisioned by Camus. "Let me see," we can imagine Sisyphus saying. "Should I choose to feel happy or not? The situation I find myself in is irrelevant. Therefore, since happiness is more pleasing, I choose, ignoring entirely my situation, to feel, in an unqualified way, happy."

Marcus Aurelius might approve of this scenario. After all, for him "assessment" was a matter of free choice allied to self-control and detached from lived conditions. We can always, if we follow the neo-Stoic dispensation, choose, completely choose, how we are to feel. *If we follow the neo-Stoic dispensation*—that's a big "if." When humans conceive of themselves as engaged participants, when they embrace Ortega's "I am I and my circumstance," the foundation for the "I can just choose how to feel'" position begins to crumble. With that foundation less secure, they are more likely to emphasize the proper reading of a situation, a reading that does not disallow hopefulness and resilience. They are also less likely to engage in Camusian hyperbole. That hyperbole, after all, dismisses *entirely* the impact of external conditions on internal feeling. A more moderate position is available. External conditions may not mandate completely what our judgments and feelings will be. At the same time, those judgments and feelings do not just represent capricious, fully subjective impositions indifferent to the milieu in which we find ourselves. Grief, a major theme at the opening of *The Stranger*, need not be understood as a weakness or pure choice. We grieve because we love. We are not like aliens disconnected from our surroundings.

If my forward-looking reference to *The Stranger* was not persuasive, perhaps an actual historical anecdote will be more successful. For compelling testimony we can draw on another famous Roman, one born some 200 years before Marcus Aurelius. He's the famous statesman, orator, and philosopher Cicero. In his early fifties Cicero was shaken by an event in "outward things." His adult daughter Tullia died from complications in childbirth. Cicero became a grieving father.[7] This grief was not arbitrary. It was not as if he staged a mental discussion: "Tullia has died. Should I grieve or not?" Rather, attached to his offspring, he could not disconnect himself, could not "erase" his "assessment" of this event. No matter that the event took place in the realm which Epicurus and Marcus Aurelius would identify as that of "external" things. From their perspective Cicero's grieving would have been a sign of weakness, a sign that his "internal" assessment was what philosophers call "heteronomous," not fully within his control.

The case of Cicero is instructive as we think about Camus. We can *imagine* some cases in which a father would not grieve the death of his daughter. Such an imaginative projection, though possible, would probably not match the reactions of most fathers to the loss of a child. Nor would equanimity, lack of feeling, be a *desirable* response. The freedom from outward things that Epicurus considers "a great good" comes at a great cost: excision of the affective, emotive, caring dimensions that characterize an engaged, involved, committed, and concerned life.

Grieving, yes, upsets the ideal of equanimity. Yes, it appears to be a feeling which we cannot dominate or control. It, thus, represents a limitation on autonomy. But, we grieve because we love, and we love because we are involved participants, not cold, detached spectators. Such involvement makes room for the full panoply of human responses, including feelings and emotions. The latter are not, as the bi-level ideal would have it, intrusive distractions, just body-and-matter induced weaknesses which the mind, representing the best in us, should be able to rise above.

Camus envisions Sisyphus as someone who can rise above such weaknesses. Sisyphus is so much in control that we can judge him, although in awful straits, to be "happy." No matter what the external conditions, he can always resist, can always opt for defiance over submission. This is the strength of Camus's assessment. The ability to keep alive the struggle, the struggle itself, can be assessed as offering great satisfaction. It can provide some solace even in the direst of circumstances. Whether it is enough, in an unqualified sense, to "fill a man's heart" (MS, 123) is questionable.

Sisyphus, true to neo-Stoic ideals, is out-of-the-ordinary in significant ways: someone whose internal life is completely insulated from external events, someone immune to typical disappointments and frustrations. He can, as a result, choose to be "happy." Whether such an individual can be multiplied and, more importantly, whether such an individual *should* be multiplied are questions not as readily answered as the young Camus would have us answer them.

The use of Sisyphus as an exemplary, archetypal figure helps highlight some central characteristics of a prototypical Camusian individual. Such an individual would, first, be depicted as rising above affective and emotional dispositions. Second, it would mean developing a character for whom no one and no thing would be held dear. Attachments of all sorts would have to be sundered. Detachment, disconnection, "objectivity" (in the sense of all-purpose neutrality) would have to be cultivated. Once cultivated, such a detached individual could easily consider himself to be an alien, an outsider, a stranger. How would life play out for such an individual? Articulating an answer to this question is just what Camus does in his most famous novel.

4

The Stranger

The Stranger as a *Reductio ad Absurdum*

Reading Camus's most famous novel in the twenty-first century is not like reading it when it was first published. The standard modes of interpretation were set by Jean-Paul Sartre and by Camus himself. Sartre drew a direct parallel between *The Stranger* and *The Myth of Sisyphus*. The latter offered a detailed *philosophical* exploration of the "absurd." The former, published first, had presented a *literary* treatment. "In *the Myth of Sisyphus*, which appeared a few months later, Camus provided us with a precise commentary upon his work." Sartre pointed out that *The Stranger*'s main character was "neither good nor bad, neither moral nor immoral." He can be classified as a member of "a very particular species for which the author reserves the word 'absurd'" (Sartre 1947/1962, 108).

Camus reinforced this approach in several self-interpretations. The first is found in Camus's review of Sartre's *Nausea*. Camus, in his mid-twenties, opened the review with a dramatic pronouncement: "A novel is never anything but a philosophy expressed in images" (LCE, 199). He goes on to explain that this can be done well or clumsily, but the initial claim remains: first comes a philosophy and then a story that embodies it. In addition to such comments touching on literature in general, Camus has left us other comments on *The Stranger*. One remark asserts that his story was an "exercise in objectivity and detachment" (OC, 416). Another can be found in the preface to a classroom edition of *The Stranger*. Camus there claims that he had tried to shape Meursault as a sacrificial victim, as "the only Christ we deserve." The main character was "condemned because he did not want to play the game demanded by society" (PS).

What are we, readers in the twenty-first century, to make of such comments? From the perspective of the history of ideas, they are certainly situated in a time-specific intellectual landscape. The Great Bifurcation sets the context. That bifurcation takes many subordinate forms: nature/culture; art/nature; man/world; faith/reason; mind/matter are among the most prominent. In his review of Sartre, Camus reveals another: ideas/being. This segregation has implications for literature in general, not just *The Stranger*. What Camus insists on is the primacy of ideas over being (as philosophers would put it). Literature is not understood as a first-order exploration of the thickness and density of the lifeworld. Rather, it is understood as an ancillary to philosophy. Literature serves a specific, secondary function: translating an antecedently accepted philosophical perspective into story form.

In terms specific to *The Stranger*, the bifurcation emerges in Camus's explicit comment that he was undertaking an "exercise in objectivity and detachment." This makes the main character essentially an epistemological subject, a spectator-mind set off against a world which is "external." Literature, rooted in language, might be expected to emphasize dialogue, a suitable metaphor for the back and forth, the give and take marking the existence of an engaged participant in a particular milieu. *The Stranger* steers clear of such a setting. Instead, a particular take on philosophy, one centered on the metaphor of spectatorship, takes center stage. One result: the main character understands himself primarily as a spectator, a recipient of neutral, indifferent data. He rises above the dialogical hubbub of ordinary life. He takes on the stance of data-recipient. Such data, coming from the "external" world, becomes separable from any "assessment" of them.

Such separation is easy for outside spectators, not so much for engaged conversants ("converse," etymologically, signals "living or dwelling with"). For conversants, individuals as engaged participants in the hubbub of quotidian life, such a life is a realm, not of neutrality, but of concern and mattering. By contrast, for the spectator/epistemological subject, the lifeworld becomes (1) an external stage, and (2) its components are reduced to neutral data. It is not "mattering" but "matter" that predominates. Conversants, already woven into a milieu, tend, Socrates-style, to seek wisdom via dialogue. Theirs is a call-and-response kind of world. Their concerns center around a question like "what makes for a flourishing, fulfilling life." Meursault, the epistemological subject, seeks rather for what can be labeled "authenticity." Given the separation of inner and outer, the older Greek emphasis on virtues cannot be supported. Defining a good life as a virtuous one makes sense only if the social condition of that life is recognized. Trustworthiness, courage, justice, and gratitude imply an irrevocable social element. They identify traits of optimality when it comes to being a good member of a community.

This latter dimension falls to the wayside with the Great Bifurcation. The notion of a "good" life changes accordingly. For an ancient like Aristotle, a life could be described as better or worse in terms of how well the cluster of virtues was manifested in the light of wisdom. All of this took place within a context recognized as interactive and communal. Once the Great Bifurcation separates individuals from their social milieu, a revised understanding of optimality is called for. The highest good can no longer be formulated in terms of the proper cluster of virtues manifested within social interaction. The optimal good is now transformed. The kind of transformation is one that makes it strictly internal. It is phrased in terms like "being true to oneself." The social circuitry having been set aside, what now counts is an isometry between one's feelings and expression. The focus for such isometry is the encapsulated self. In philosophy, this falls under the label of "authenticity." Meursault fits the pattern well. His highest ideal is a refusal to lie, where lying means pretending to have feelings, emotions, sensitivities which one does not have. Such authenticity, in turn, is supposed to be admired by readers. After all, in the realm of bifurcation, the authentic individual and the artifice known as "society" are inherently opposed. The authentic individual receives data that is neutral. Valuation is an artificial superimposition. Any expression indicating some attitude other than basal neutrality is immediately classified as simulated or manufactured.

Such preliminary considerations help identify three pillars which support the standard reading of *The Stranger*: (a) literature as the handmaiden of philosophy; (b) humans as epistemological subjects; (c) authenticity as a major human aspiration. Each, I hope to show, is less secure today than it was in the middle of the twentieth century. In terms of *The Stranger*, what I will suggest is that the significance and relevance of the novel now lie elsewhere, that is not where Sartre and Camus placed them. My reading accepts Camus's claim that the work is an "exercise in objectivity and detachment." Such an opening, though, does not automatically lead to the conclusions formulated by Sartre and Camus. It is time to break with the readings of *The Stranger*, which (1) assert that the protagonist is "neither good nor bad, neither moral nor immoral," and (2) want us to see Meursault as "the only Christ we deserve." Instead, Camus's depiction of Meursault can be read as a *reductio ad absurdum*. It stands as a powerful illustration and thus a forceful indictment of the philosophical perspective which, prizing spectatorship over dialogue, portrays humans essentially as detached observers. Meursault is indeed what such a character would be like. Perhaps Camus wished him to be viewed as a model. Today we can see him as a foil.

Later, as his ways of thinking developed, Camus actually voiced a perspective close to one which would treat *The Stranger* as a *reductio*. In the introduction to *The Rebel*, he acknowledged that the perspective of "absurdity" offered only a starting point, an attempt to clear the ground. By itself it does little but leave us "in a blind alley," literally "at an impasse" (R, 10, HR, 21). An "impasse" was not a good place in which to remain. New pathways would have to be tried out. The first claim, "this is not a good place in which to remain," was as far as Camus could get. He could identify the problems associated with inherited ideas. But because he continued to be situated within the framework committed to the Great Bifurcation, he could offer no groundmap which would chart a serious alternative. Although he never was able to make the needed paradigm shift, Camus provided a powerful voice indicating the need for such a shift. *The Stranger*, read in the twenty-first century, provides just such an indication.

Other commentators, taking for granted the perspectives of the spectator subject and authenticity, suffer from a major blind spot. Meursault, we should not have to remind ourselves, is a murderer, and a rather cold-blooded one at that. Too many interpretations reveal an unusual *insensitivity* to the murder victim.[1] That we are dealing with a murderer should mean, at the very least, that Sartre was wrong in his blithe assertion that Meursault was "neither good nor bad, neither moral nor immoral."

What Sartre should have said is that *The Stranger*, rather than taking us beyond good and evil, allows us a glimpse into some concrete preconditions for evil. Specifically, it offers a complementary analysis to what Hannah Arendt called the "banality of evil." We can say that Meursault was neither good nor bad only if our sole focus is whether he had good or bad intentions. These, it is true, are missing. Indeed, there is much missing in his character. Such absences offer an important lesson from reading *The Stranger* today: the link between absence and evil. The conditions for the possibility of evil are present when there is a major absence, mostly a deficit in affectivity. The novel gives us a setting in which we can paradoxically assert "he is not a bad guy" (not especially malignant, ill-tempered, or vile in his intentions) while at the same time asserting "he is a bad guy" (not only a cold and indifferent accomplice to an unjustified beating but also a murderer). His life is both banal and evil. Meursault may not be the Christ for our time that Camus envisioned, but he is a figure for our time, one offering us a frightening morality tale.

Statues and Outsiders

To arrive at this reading, it is helpful to begin with statues. Yes, here, though disguised, is yet another philosophical detour. Philosophers in Modernity (roughly from the Renaissance to the end of the First World War) were uncomfortable with regular flesh-and-blood individuals, persons who combined sentiment, emotion, reason, attachments—individuals embedded within physiological, cultural, and temporally conditioned settings. Instead, they bought into the streamlined variant what I call the Great Bifurcation. Within it, humans were not only de-biologized, they were generally understood via divorce and rupture. Mind versus body offered a prominent example. Gilbert Ryle (1900–76) parodied such dualism by saying that Cartesianism amounted to thinking of mind and body along the model of a "ghost in the machine" (Ryle, 5). Studying texts from the sixteenth to the eighteenth centuries, we might tweak the terminology a bit and speak of the statue that cogitates. Descartes's *res cogitans*, the "thinking thing," becomes the *statua cogitans*, the statue that cogitates. It's a lot like the ghost in the machine, but mind-in-a-statue is more consistent with typical examples used by key figures in developing Modern thought.

Galileo (1564–1642) led the statues-are-us way. Let's imagine, he suggested, an inanimate representation of a human being, that is, a statue. Now, let's imagine that we run our fingers along certain key areas, the back of the knees, the soles of the feet, under the arms. There is motion, but there is no such thing as "tickling." The statue remains impassive (Drake, 274). Inner and outer, as Epicurus and Marcus Aurelius had long before claimed, stand decisively apart. There is physical movement in the outer world. There is also a separate inner world. "Tickling" is strictly an internally invented phenomenon. The activity in the outer world can only be described objectively as what it is: matter-in-motion. Interaction and interplay are minimized. In their place Galileo offers disjunction: the divorce between qualities as internal and matter-in-motion as external. Qualities, Galileo insisted, "have no real existence save in us" (Drake, 276–7).[2]

Jean-Jacques Rousseau (1712–78) took the example in a different direction. He opened his *Discourse on the Origin of Inequality* by referring to the statue of a Greek sea-god, Glaucus. Having been disfigured by time, water, and natural elements, the statue bore little resemblance to its original. Just so, society, a corrupting influence, transformed humans from their original, natural condition. A lesser-known contemporary of Rousseau, Étienne Bonnot de Condillac (1715–80), also followed the trend. Condillac was what we would today call a "reductionist." The statue example fits right in with his notions of reducing complex humanity to basic components. Like the others who favored statue similes, he resists accepting what ordinary experience would have taught, that humans are human. For friends-of-statue supporters, much of what is distinctively human has been sheared off.

The resulting statue-like creatures have one advantage: they are really not that complicated. There is now a shortcut to understanding: break them down to simpler components. Condillac makes this clear:

> I wish the reader to notice particularly that it is most important for him to put himself in imagination exactly in the place of the statue we are going to observe. He must enter into its life, begin where it begins, have but one single sense when it has only one, acquire only the ideas which it acquires, contract only the habits which it contracts: in a word he must fancy himself to become just what the statue is.

He ends with a magisterial understatement: "I believe that the readers who put themselves exactly in its place, will have no difficulty in understanding this work; those who do not will meet with enormous difficulties" (Condillac, xxxvii). In other words, if humans will just imagine themselves as nonhuman statues, Condillac's whole exposition, full of simplifications and shortcuts, will make perfect sense.

It was all a purely fantasized and, as a result, faulty point of departure. Don't start, it suggested, with flesh-and-blood human beings. Assume instead some artificially construed, simplified, starting point. Such a starting point will make things easier. Such ease, we can now say, comes at a considerable cost. It requires plenty of bracketing and sequestering. The biological realm of fleshy interactions, reciprocities, cares, and concerns—set that aside. Transform it all into a realm much more suitable for disembodied minds: a geometric grid populated by entities best studied by (a) ignoring the interdependent contexts within which they live and (b) breaking them up into component parts.

Such a "bracket and eliminate" strategy depended on a major excision: the complete de-socialization of human life. The older Aristotelian understanding that humans, by nature, were social animals, and that flourishing lives could best be achieved in properly constituted cultures emphasizing the right combination of virtues, was sidelined. The newer story, consistent with the reductionist pattern of bracket and eliminate, insisted that humans were primordially and essentially autonomous units. The resulting depiction invented an initial status for humans that did away with (1) the social context within which humans actually find themselves and even (2) minimized dependence on ancestors, especially mothers. Purging the social and biological dimensions, it came up with something called the "state of nature."

This state of nature had little to do with ordinary life. Interdependence was downplayed, autonomy romanticized. Such an autonomous state would be populated by humans, "men," as independent units, completely outside of community. The bracket-and-eliminate mode could then add another dimension. Since interdependence and interrelationships were minimized, feelings like affection and love were considered to be not part of one's natural dispositions but, like the distortions of Glaucus, later accretions. They showed up when the initial autonomous existence was abandoned for community life. In general, the bracket-and-eliminate mode could pretend that humans were not really suited for social life. This occasioned a new addition to the Great Bifurcation. Not only were individuals thought of as set apart from nature. Now a new opposition was added: that between individual and society. The statue-self came to be a doubly insulated one, a stranger both to nature and to society.

The statue-like data-reception unit, self-sufficient in its autonomy, defined essentially as an epistemological subject, is, let's face it, odd. Much better, much closer to concrete reality, would be to describe humans as living beings in a living and complicated world. As mentioned in the previous chapter, José Ortega y Gasset helped redress the balance. He offered his own alternative to the data-receiving unit, an alternative which reverses the statue paradigm. His scenario goes like this: imagine the room of a dying man, someone well known and well regarded; his wife sits beside him; a doctor is in attendance; the patient's fame has occasioned the presence of a reporter.

The participants are differentially related to the situation. They thus attend to varying aspects of what is going on. The event is oversaturated with meanings. Given such a setting, an eliminationist, abstraction-friendly, intellectual could go the shortcut/simplification route and say "there's only one 'really real' story here and the way to get at it is via objective detachment." Otherwise, all we have is the merely subjective perspectives of various attendees. Ortega tends toward a more concrete, thick rendition. He situates participants within a context of interactions, not one of subjects set over against objects. The participants, it is true, are differentially attentive. This is because they are not statues.

There is a difference in "the emotional distance between each person and the event they all witness." The wife, emotionally involved, stands closest to the dense thickness of the situation. Her loving relationship means that she grasps dimensions of what is going on to which other onlookers are blind. She does not simply "behold" the scene; she "lives" it (Ortega 1925/1968, 15). She is, in other words, as little statue-like as possible. This is not, for her, a *scene* merely to be *observed*. The physician is attentive in a different way. He pays attention to changes in the patient that might escape the wife's notice. He is not a statue. He is concerned, but in a different way from the wife. The reporter, by contrast, goes a long way in the statue direction. His profession mandates a neutral impartiality. "To him the event is a mere scene, a pure spectacle." He does not "live" the event. He observes a tableau. He is "emotionally free, an outsider" (Ortega 1925/1968, 16). He comes closest to representing a statue-containing-a-mind.

Reversing Modern assumptions, Ortega prioritizes "'lived' over the 'outsider' take of 'observed' reality" (Ortega 1925/1968, 17). The fullest sense of what is real, the more primordial one, the encompassing complexity "from which all the others derive and which they all presuppose" is the participatory one, the one immersed in ordinary, involved, lived experience. There is a kind of "practical" and "normative" primacy at work here (Ortega 1925/1968, 15). This kind of primacy seems sensible enough. Sensible enough, at least, if we keep to who we are, resisting the temptation to envision ourselves as statues or ghosts in machines.

Once thinkers make the statue-containing-a-mind move, the default, primordial position becomes that of a disinterested observer. For the detached spectator, practical and normative primacy recede. A new ethic comes into being. Disengaged, uninvolved ratiocination becomes the highest good, the most direct mode of dealing with impressions coming from the external world. Fecund, lived, reality is forgotten.

Sanitized, cogitated reality takes its place. The standpoint that comes to be assumed as primordial is that of an outsider. In French the outsider is an *étranger*.

L'Étranger: Meursault as a Statue-Self

Camus's book has been translated as both *The Stranger* and *The Outsider*. Both are apt.[3] Camus did not compose his text in a vacuum. His intellectual inheritance, mostly unnoticed and unacknowledged, included tendencies (1) to work within the framework of the statue-self and (2) to embrace authenticity. Given such guiding assumptions, it makes sense to proclaim, as does Sartre, that Meursault is "neither good nor bad, neither moral nor immoral." Once we move beyond the guiding assumptions, such a proclamation loses much of its conviction.

The same can be said for Camus's own proclamation about the "only Christ we deserve." Camus did not just state this position. He elaborated on it. How does Meursault avoid playing society's games? "He refuses to lie." Camus then specifies what this means.

> To lie is not only to say what isn't true. It is also and above all, to say more than is true, and, as far as the human heart is concerned, to express more than one feels. This is what we all do, every day, to simplify life. He [Meursault] says what he is, he refuses to hide his feelings, and immediately society feels threatened. (PS)

Meursault is a straightforward individual. He goes about his affairs free of aggressivity, ambition, or duplicity. Several themes converge here. Meursault can be contrasted to the statue of Glaucus. Unlike the actual statue, Meursault is immune to the tarnishing and corruptions occasioned by the duplicities of social game-playing. The regimentation and role-playing that society seeks to impose simply do not stick. He is free of pretense. He does not adjust his utterances, as others do, "to simplify life."[4] He remains true to himself.

His pronouncements live out a particular ideal: *adaequatio mentis secum*. Honesty and truth mean, above all, saying what is inside one's mind and only that—that is, not pretending that some feeling is present when it is not. Such an isometry, however, depends on some preliminary formatting. Neutrality, not concerns of various sorts, is projected as ground zero. The older, medieval notion characterized truth as *adaequatio mentis ad rem*. Within this older, interactionist, model the quest for truth overlapped with the attempt to provide formulations that adequately revealed dimensions of the lived world. After the inward turn of Modernity a new model was put in place. The only adequacy that now counted was that which matched external utterances with inner feelings—all of this within a context presupposing that the most basal level was one of neutrality. The result: an ideal in which (a) the mind would agree with itself—*adaequatio mentis secum*, and (b) such an agreement had to admit a basal neutrality. The Great Bifurcation, by sundering self from world, altered what counts as truth. The external world and one's responses were now redefined as facts separated from values. Truth now came to mean both that the contents of the mind are straightforwardly articulated with no dissimulation and that this absence of dissimulation had to mean a primordial neutrality. So long as one (within this new context) agrees with oneself, truthfulness is guaranteed. One's life is authentic.[5]

Authenticity then becomes the yardstick for evaluation. An authentic individual embodies honest expression rather than hypocrisy. Honest expression, in turn, means avoiding the artificialities of cultural and ethical expectations. Authenticity and goodness then slide together. An authentic individual, by definition, is good. This, as we have seen by drawing on some comments from Camus, appears to have been one of his aims. Somewhere along the line, though, his artistry got in the way. The Meursault he created, when examined in a twenty-first-century context, undermines the very assumptions that the philosophy of absurdity took for granted. In a post-ecology era we are more sensitive to the imbedded-in-a-context-of-interactions setting which defines the human condition. Camus believed that adjusting our utterances to our audience was little more than a way to "simplify life." Here he has things backward. It is the assumptions of (1) initial neutrality and (2) the overriding demand of authenticity that simplify life.

These encourage a single, absolute command for any and every context. The difficulties and perplexities that come with responsibility are downplayed. There is no need to take account of a complex situation, one in which prized values might conflict. There is no need to worry about hurting the feelings of others, or of wondering whether in a particular case (to protect someone from a vengeful beating) it might be better to lie. Whereas responsibility involves *responding* properly, a perplexing, challenging, complicated endeavor, authenticity simply calls for submission to a single absolute. Within the framework of authenticity, responsibility is not all that complicated. The simplified life of the detached spectator, whose only concern is for the purity of his inner life, makes such a streamlined, that is, reduced, sense of responsibility not only possible but also attractive.

The Stranger, as an exercise in detachment and objectivity, centers on a statue-cogito. Meursault does behave as an outsider. His statue-self offers insulation from attachments. The responsibility for determining which differences make a difference, when and how, is set aside. The statue-self is thus liberated from the concerns, cares, and obligations that accompany attachments. Mary Midgley, as usual, states the matter bluntly. The protagonist of Camus's novel is indeed an outsider. "But he is so because he is an emotional cripple, someone apparently incapable of sharing human feelings" (Midgley 1978, 199). Camus may believe that he has created a character for whom a good life is fully and comprehensively defined as one in which pretense, dissimulation, and artifice are anathema. Midgley, though, judges him as the consummate counterfeit, someone who refuses to admit that he has "normal powers and feelings." "There is nothing stoical," she continues, "about *acting* lame" (Midgley 1978, 199, note 28, italics in original).

Meursault does not think of himself as an actor. Quite the opposite. He thinks of himself as the archetype of authenticity, someone free of artifice, someone who never dissembles. Midgley's comment prompts us to think of Meursault apart from his self-image. Seen in another light, he is someone who has so suppressed affection, concern, caring, "mattering" in general that his entire character can be understood as one great artifice. Attachments, along with the concerns and responsibilities they bring with them, might, in a particular philosophical context, seem to define unmanly weaknesses. A character might then wish to rise above such "entanglements." Such a character might be helped by a philosophical position which defines the entire realm of "mattering" to be strictly subjective. In that case, the character might come to believe that the more fundamental, more basal level of human existence would be one of sheer neutral data reception. This, for Midgley, has nothing to do with authenticity. It represents the height of self-deception.

The resulting life-orientation is not just one self-dissimulation, it is also pernicious. Its malignant side emerges because the axiologically neutered character suffers from a crucial absence. Meursault is someone who, from his perch as spectator, has a real void, an emptiness where characteristic human sensibilities typically reside. Camus chafed at a critic who referred to Meursault as a "sorry excuse for a human being" (*cette piètre humanité*) (Pingaud, 161). The critic, writing in *Le Figaro*, had complained about how, with Meursault, Camus had given his readers "a man mutilated of all that makes for the worth of humans" (*Il nous propose un homme mutilé de tout ce qui fait la valeur de l'homme*) (Pingaud, 161).[6] Midgley says Meurseault is "lame." The *Figaro* reviewer described the main character as "mutilated." Both are correct. Both point in the direction of revealing fully what it means to do what Camus said he was doing, undertaking an exercise in detachment and objectivity.

Meursault and the Preconditions for Evil

To grasp how this is so, we have to recall how Meursault, as a statue-cogito, simply lives a life characterized by absences. Using older English we might speak of "wants." "Want" can mean both something missing and something that ought to be present and is thus desired. For Meursault, important constitutive ingredients are "wanting." Because he is unaware, they are not felt as absences or deficiencies. They are "wanting" but not "wanted." His assumption is that the authentic, free-of-artifice human is one who is disengaged from the affective, emotive, caring dimensions of existence. These are considered to form part of a subjective realm, invented, abetted, and reinforced by social conventions.

He aims, as we have seen, to be a consummate truth-teller. Truth-telling, in his sense, means stating only what is basic (i.e., not adulterated, sentimental, socially mandated). Meursault, inhabiting a realm above such lower-level vulnerabilities, carries out his project authentically. He does not express grief at the death of his mother. He resists the word "love," telling Marie (the woman he has agreed to marry) that the term is meaningless. He says "yes" to his shady neighbor's request to write a note ensuring that a female will be unjustly beaten. Later, after becoming a murderer, he blames it on the sun.

In each case, Meursault does not represent the standard exemplar of evil. He would not be immediately described as a "bad" or "depraved" person. One can even envision Meursault saying "I'm a nice, easy-going individual." He is not a crude self-interested manipulator. He neither has a violent temper nor a cruel, nasty heart. Here, I suggest, is just the point at which the story can speak to us today. It opens an awareness of evil that goes beyond the easy Gnostic/Manichean identification of evil: as having a bad will, as giving in to the bodily inclinations, as having a dark, evil character. Meursault falls into none of these categories. *The Stranger* explores ruthlessly and carefully what happens when evil results from absence: absence of sentiment, absence of emotional connection, absence of well-justified differential response to surroundings.

We continue to live in a world marked by lingering elements of Modernity: inner/outer segregation, the "subjectivity" of emotional/moral reactions, the prizing of authenticity. Because of this *The Stranger* continues to be important. Why? Because Camus, in spite of his overt comments, has shown us how easy it is for evil to be both present and disguised. *The Plague* as we shall see is the novel typically thought to deal with the problem of evil. As regards the theological problem of evil, this is true. *The Stranger* deals with the anthropological problem of evil. It reveals what it is about humans that makes wickedness a possibility, even in someone who reveals no signs of vindictiveness, hatred, or meanness. When we only think of evil through the lens of the violent slaveholder, the cruel dictator, or the murderous drug lord, we overlook the conditions for the possibility of a more ordinary evil. Such conditions might even, because they minimize the burden of responsibility, seem attractive. They involve the marginalizing, if not total anesthetizing, of capacities, especially those associated with emotion and feeling. Hans Stark, head of admissions at Auschwitz, kept a sign above his desk. It read "compassion is weakness" (Langbein, 282). Evil and cold detachment are joined at the hip.

Responsibility, as differential response, moves in a different direction. Instead of the neutered perspective, it recognizes how differences make a difference. "Information," Gregory Bateson was fond of saying, "consists of differences that make a difference" (Bateson, 110). Even for a minimally sentient being like a larval tick sitting on a branch, it is not neutrality that reigns. The tick's milieu is anything but indifferent. It's a welter of informational differences. Differences that matter. When sweat is detected, the tick falls, hopefully dropping onto a mammal. The sensation of sweat is one difference that makes a difference, a difference to which the tick is selectively attentive. If, after a while, the tick smells no sweat, another difference that makes a difference, it drops "and goes to climb another tree" (Bateson, 51).

When information is taken seriously, the notion of indifference as primordial becomes less plausible. Intelligence, what Ortega y Gasset characterized as *razón vital*, means attentiveness to differences. Ethics, sorting out better from worse, is successful to the degree that we properly understand which differences make a difference, when, and how. The statue approach nullifies all of this. It has fancifully imagined itself into a state of insulated neutrality. We are here brought back to Buridan's ass and its two haystacks. When indifference, general equivalence, is thought to characterize external events, both attentiveness and intelligence are marginalized. After all, one of their roles is to establish which differences make a difference, how, and when. When intelligence, as the proper responsiveness to surrounding conditions, is minimized, an inward turn is maximized. Buridan's haystacks are then thought to exemplify the rule, not the exception. One ramification: the only moral maxim now defensible has to do with being true to oneself. This "oneself," though, has undergone alteration. It now separates itself from whatever might be "soft" or "tender hearted." Better to stay with the hard, nonsubjective perspective that rises above sensitivities to difference.

When the world is understood to be a realm of indifference, one in which differences do not make a difference, then a general leveling results. Moral equivalence becomes the default perspective. Write a letter that will lead to a young woman being beaten? Or, not write such a letter? It's all the same to the epistemological subject. There are no indications in one's surroundings, no differences that make a difference, nothing which would move intelligence in one direction rather than another. The statue-self, oblivious to difference, has a slogan. It is one repeated over and over by Meursault: *ça m'est égal*, it's all the same to me.

The *ça m'est égal* attitude emerges directly from ontological neutrality. Its practical upshot, however, is anything but neutral. *The Stranger* is relentless in depicting what life as a statue-self might mean. An attractive young woman with whom Meursault is having an affair suggests marriage. He acquiesces. She asks whether he loves her. She wonders, in effect, if she, this particular person, makes any difference to him. Would he, for example, say yes to a similar proposal from another woman? Indeed, he would and, committed to authenticity, has no problem responding "Sure" (S, 42). The French says *naturellement* (ETR, 68), and "naturally" provides a better translation than "sure." It indicates how Meursault is just going along with what he considers to be "natural," the general rule of indifference.

Marie or another woman: it's all the same to him. His mother's death or the death of another: it's all the same to him. Cicero felt sorrow and actually shed tears when his daughter died. What an odd reaction! Or, stated differently, what a strictly subjective choice. The data-receiving, absolutely objective statue neither feels grief nor feels obligated to pretend grief. Shedding tears is one among many options. It represents a social charade, an activity engaged in to please others.

The novel tells us that others weep. His mother, for instance, cried a lot when she first moved into the home for the aged. This is treated dismissively. Later on, having gotten used to the home, departing would have moved her to tears. It's all just a matter of getting used to things (S, 5). At the wake, one of the mother's friends is crying. This, for Meursault, not only makes no sense, it is actually annoying. Meursault wishes "he didn't have to listen to her anymore" (S, 10). Then there's the mother's *fiancé*. Camus's descriptions highlight a major contrast between the impassivity of the son and the tears shed by Thomas Pérez. In the retirement home, Pérez, more flesh-and-blood human than statue, had grown close to the dead woman. Other residents referred to her as his *fiancée*. Because of their relationship, he is taking her death "very hard" (S, 13).

It is Pérez who comes closest to the lived presence exemplified by the wife in Ortega's sickroom scene. Meursault, at his mother's wake, is more like the reporter.[7] As an outside spectator he pays little attention to the event-at-hand or even to the corpse in the coffin. Rather, his attentiveness is occupied by data collection: the chairs, the supports for the casket, even the screws on the coffin's lid (S, 6).[8] When his mother's friends leave, they shake his hand, a gesture he finds odd (S, 12). After all, no words have been exchanged. Nothing has happened to bring the friends and him closer together. In reality they were strangers to each other. Why pretend otherwise?

Meursault's behavior up to this point is atypical, a bit too aloof and detached, but not especially wicked or malevolent. He is, thus far, living out rather innocuously Camus's exercise in detachment and objectivity. Other events in Meursault's life make it harder to support Sartre's claim about Meursault being "neither good nor bad, neither moral nor immoral." At the very least, Meursault's behavior moves in the direction of worse rather than better. Take his relationship with Marie. Here is a woman who becomes his lover and whom he promises to marry. In this kind of situation, if anywhere, one would expect difference and deference to play major roles. The differences that characterize this particular woman would explain why Meursault would undertake a special deferential relationship with her. Such is not the case. Describing his attraction, Meursault avoids traits specific to this particular person. He praises her sandals, her dress, the curve of her breasts (S, 34). He only registers objective data, and generic data at that. The particular qualities of this particular person make no difference at all.

Once again, as with Meursault's mother, this behavior is bizarre and surprising, disagreeable and distasteful perhaps, but not malevolent. The next scenario, already referred to, crosses that line. It involves Meursault's neighbor Raymond Sintès. Not only does Sintès have a bad reputation, but one conversation with him should be enough to signal how self-serving and malicious is his focus. Meursault, neutral data-recording machine that he is, easily brackets such indicators. He finds the whole story Sintès relates simply "interesting" (S, 32). Sintès has hatched a plan. One aspect would involve Meursault. Sintès needs someone articulate. If Meursault would compose a letter, Sintès could draw his former mistress back to his apartment. It would be a trap. It's all a scheme to get violent revenge on the young woman.

Meursault, typically, is not revulsed by the proposal. When Sintès first broaches the favor, Meursault responds with his usual, "it's all the same to me," "*J'ai dit que ça m'était égal*" (ETR, 47). The English translation, rendering the phrase as "it was fine with me," misses the leveling effect of the answer, that is, one option or the other—they are equivalent (S, 29). Even after obtaining details of what he was getting into, Meursault acquiesces. After all, he "had no reason" not to please his neighbor (S, 32). Had he allowed his intelligence to register the complete ramifications of what was going on, red flags and reasons galore would have been discerned. Meursault, as is his statue-cogito wont, pays no attention to differences that make a difference. Write a letter inviting a friend to come visit *or* write a letter of entrapment—it's all the same. *Ça m'est égal* remains the outsider's slogan.

This is the point at which the Camus experiment in creating a character built around objectivity and detachment begins to reveal its iniquitous side. Meursault's *ça m'est égal* has led him to become an accomplice in setting a trap, one that will lead to a young woman being beaten. On the day when Sintès beats his former mistress, her cries can be heard throughout the building. A non-amputated accounting would include words like "appalling," "vengeful," "cruel," "vicious." Indeed, Marie describes the event as "terrible" (S, 36). Most of the neighbors see it this way. For Marie, the whole scene, the beating and screams, was too much. She loses her appetite. It would take a special effort of intentional detachment, a detachment that would distort the full dimensions of what was actually going on, to treat the sounds and sights as mere neutral data. But that is just how Meursault responds. Marie may have lost her appetite, but not Meursault. "I ate almost everything" (S, 37).

As these examples reveal, objectivity and detachment slide into iniquity without any need for initial evil intent. Failure to be moved by fairly clear signals in one's milieu offers opportunity enough. Meursault's level of malevolence, as the story progresses, rises beyond complicity in the beating of a young woman. He becomes a cold, indifferent murderer. Once again, a bad will, the specific aim of undertaking evil, plays no role. In some of the most powerful writing in the novel, a series of contingencies move Meursault toward the fateful moment. The entire scene develops in perfect accord with the mechanical working out of what Jacques Monod called "chance and necessity." There are a series of happenstance occurrences. There is also a clear sequence of causal antecedents. The whole event is just a neutral sequence of physical causes.

Meursault is spending a Sunday at the seashore. Several relatives and acquaintances of the woman Raymond has beaten are out for revenge. In one encounter, Raymond is cut. Meursault prevents him from using his revolver. The gun ends up in Meursault's possession. Later, alone, walking on the beach, Meursault comes across one of the Arabs. The sun is beating down. Camus turns everything, the power of the sun, even the sea, into fire and metal.[9] Meursault's eyes sting from salty sweat. The knife wielded by the Arab flashes in the sunlight and sends what seems to be a shard of blinding steel in Meursault's direction. "The light shot off the steel and it was like a long flashing blade cutting at my forehead. . . . The scorching blade slashed at my eyelashes and stabbed at my stinging eyes" (S, 59). He reaches for the pistol. The "trigger gave" (note the absence of agency). The Arab falls. Then, four more squeezes of the trigger and four more bullets into the cadaver (S, 59).[10]

Those four extra bullets have posed a special puzzle for interpreters. A single bullet would have sufficed to end the perceived threat. Why then have him fire four more times? This becomes less of a puzzle when we think of Camus as showing, in a detailed and consistent manner, the ramifications of being a statue-man. For the perfectly detached outsider there is no significant difference between putting a bullet into a live individual and putting a bullet into a fallen one.[11] The causal sequence, described in detached, data-neutral terms, remains the same: trigger gives, bullet moves, enters object.

Because Meursault is a study in statue-being, there are deficiency and absence where there should be a thick, multifaceted response. In terms of character, there is lack of feeling where there should be full humanity.[12] Instead of authenticity understood in terms of goodness and honesty, there is a deep deception at the heart of Meursault's character. Meursault's life, far from one of honesty, is one of acquiescence to deception, a failure to recognize how important aspects of being human have been expurgated.

Part one of the novel thus ends with a tracing out of what it would mean to be an outsider, someone untouched by the more typical sentiments and sensitivities of ordinary flesh-and-blood individuals. Such a person could seem harmless and innocent enough. Those appearances would deceive. Disinterest, along with detachment and abstract thinking, often praised, are here reevaluated. They become precursors to malevolence. The permanent outsider, the rational spectator who abstracts from differences, turning all events into mere data, ends up being not someone beyond good and evil but a paradigm of evil.

Authenticity and Society at Odds

Part one of the novel, read today, ends on a note at odds with the standard "it's all about absurdity" interpretation. Something similar can be said of part two. The novel's second half is rather heavy-handed in its treatment of authenticity's foil, "society." Camus here almost loses his artistic grace.[13] He gives ample room to his Rousseau side, his sense that bourgeois society is automatically, completely, and irrevocably corrupt, hypocritical, and inauthentic. As far as Meursault himself, despite a few exceptions, he remains within the statue-setting. Even though deeply implicated in the occasion, he is on trial for murder after all; he cannot help viewing it from the perspective an outsider. The entire event is not so much lived occurrence. It is, rather, observed spectacle.[14]

The Stranger's second half also introduces a new theme: a critique of religion. Meursault, typically dispassionate, detached, uninvolved, becomes passionate and enraged at the prison chaplain. The chaplain wants Meursault to betray what is his great ethical absolute. The chaplain wants him to pronounce a belief in God and a desire for forgiveness, that is, make public claims at odds with his inner disposition. In this way the priest, like the judge, the examining magistrate, even the defense attorney, represents the false, hypocritical realm of "society." The defense attorney may mean well, but he is caught up in society's game of pretense. The lawyer asks whether he can say that on the funeral day, Meursault had suppressed his "natural feelings." Meursault's predictable response: "No, because it's not true" (S, 65). The novel says little to describe the lawyer's reaction. Given the societal charade of which he is a part, it could easily be envisioned along these lines: "Good gracious, man, just a little equivocation and the jury will cut you some slack."

This, though, is just what Meursault will not do. A collision is inevitable: on one side, officials whose main concern is to play by society's rules; on the other, Meursault, committed to a basal neutrality and inflexible in his authenticity. For the officials, the canons imposed by civilized society must be respected. When a mother dies, sorrow must be manifested. Whether it's real or feigned is unimportant. Civilized society, in turn, is reinforced by religion, with its own demands of regimentation. There must be regret for sins. Forgiveness must be sought as a prerequisite for eternal life. The judge, the lawyers, and the priest may think of themselves as quite unique. For Meursault, they are similar. They serve as agents of domination, imposing a manufactured, artificial mold on all members of the community.

Meursault reserves special scorn for the priest. The latter thinks he holds a trump card: fear of death. But Meursault, even facing imminent death, is not about to betray his deepest commitment. The certainties accepted by the priest—desire for eternal life, admission of having sinned, salvation from eternal damnation—mean nothing to Meursault. He must, above all, remain true to himself. What he can avow honestly is a limited set of certitudes. "But I was sure about me, about everything, surer than he could ever be, sure of my life and sure of the death I had waiting for me" (S, 120). He also remained true to his detached, spectator status: "Nothing, nothing, mattered" (S, 121). Death has little to do with the priest's fantasies about an afterlife. Death is what guarantees general indifference and moral flattening of all valuation. No matter how important any life project or projects may seem, death negates them all. This absolute fact of mortality "leveled whatever was offered to me at the time, in years no more real than the ones I was living" (S, 121).

Death is not only final. It is also retroactive. It annuls whatever supposed valuations accompanied a life. What difference could anything make in light of the great certitude that one was fated for nothingness? Meursault's priest-occasioned outburst cuts to the *ça m´est égal* core of things: "What did other people's deaths or a mother's love matter to me; what did his God or the lives people choose or the fate they think they elect matter to me when we're all elected by the same fate" (S, 121). Self-deceptions about how differences were real, and thus could serve to warrant differential evaluations, are now exposed for what they are, delusions. "What did it matter that Raymond was as much my friend as Céleste, who was worth a lot more than him? What did it matter that Marie now offered her lips to a new Meursault" (S, 121–2). Individual mortality is a great solvent. If nothing else, it cleanses away illusions and leaves the most basic truth of all: indifference rules. Differences do not make a difference. Values are all flattened. The general equivalence highlighted in Buridan's thought experiment now becomes ontological bedrock. *Ça m´est égal* is the only honest attitude. In the end, nothing really matters. That, for Meursault, is ground zero, the baseline that guides his life.

Society, unable to admit this painful fact, offers various palliatives. But these simulations are false. We thus have a choice: live in the world of reality or escape into the realm of appearance and illusion. Meursault chooses what he envisions as the high road of authenticity. He remains true to himself and the cold, neutral facts of existence. Others like the judge, the priest, the prosecuting and defense attorneys opt for self-deception. For them, the real danger is authenticity. It undermines the contrived, manufactured realm in which they are comfortable. As a result, Meursault's unwillingness to betray his truth becomes, for them, the worst transgression. Meursault, like anyone who refuses to participate in the charade, must be sacrificed. His condemnation, as befits a world of pretense, does not result from the actual murder.

Meursault's last ruminations emphasize the generalized equivalence which provides his ontological orientation. He opens himself to the "gentle indifference of the world" (S, 122). He, recognizing the duplicities of society, opts to live in accordance with the truths of nature. He comes to realize how the natural world, envisioned as indifferent, was "so much like myself" (S, 122). That, ultimately, is the main point. Camus has worked out as well as anyone could the ramifications of a human existence paralleling a nature that is understood in a particular way. A life committed to truth will be one consistent with the objectively real realm of nature. Since the reality of the external world is characterized by generalized indifference, he who wishes to remain on the side of reality and not appearance will live his life accordingly. Such a character, as the last epiphany makes clear, matches the indifference of the world.

He and the world share something like a fraternal bond, "so like a brother, really" (S, 123). Meursault, statue-like in his encapsulated, insulated self, matches the supposed indifference of the world. This is how *The Stranger* serves as a *reductio ad absurdum*. The novel, read in the twenty-first century, teaches us about the human condition: something is amiss in the way of thinking that can create a Meursault. The novel thus encourages fundamental reassessments of assumptions concerning who we are and the kind of world that provides our habitat.

5

The Plague

Indifference Is Always an Option

One of the more striking images in *The Plague* is that of an elderly asthmatic. His wish: die a very old man. This is surprising. His life, by choice, is restrained. Once a dry-goods dealer, he decided, entering life's second half, to withdraw from social encounters. He spends his days moving peas from one container to another. Clocks are absent. Temporality is measured according to the frequency in which one container is emptied and the other filled. After fifteen transfers, he takes a food break. According to his wife, nothing has really ever interested him. Following a religious dictum that (1) descent characterizes life's second half and (2) death could come at any moment, he concluded it was best to do nothing (Pl, 116–18).

In creating this character, Camus is doing two things. He is setting up a contrast with the active, committed hero of the book, Dr. Rieux. He is also looking back to his earlier works examining absurdity. Those books had followed the model set out by Descartes: a radical clearing of the ground. Such a clearing, so Descartes insisted, was a necessary prerequisite to any rebuilding. *The Myth of Sisyphus* took the Cartesian clearing for granted. Such an amputation led to an immediate ramification: once humans had set themselves over against an amputated world, the issue of whether life was worthwhile came to be central. The issue of meaning arose because the Cartesian clearing had created a major incongruity between self and world. On one side, the self as mind longing for meaning and purpose. On the other, a world as matter, silent and indifferent (actually silent and indifferent because the Cartesian bulldozer had razed the interactive elements which made meaning possible).

The resulting diagnosis: life is absurd. This diagnosis, in turn, forced humans to ask: what am I to do? Camus dramatized this question by framing it in terms of suicide. His essay was a plea to avoid all forms of escapism, including the option of suicide. *The Myth of Sisyphus*'s message: embrace life while recognizing it for what it is. Resist acquiescence, welcome freedom. Embrace revolt and passion. Live fully, consciously. Living in revolt meant fully living while acknowledging the absurdity that marks the human situation.

The Plague explores further what this last advice might mean. Choosing to live is an important first step. Then comes the question of how to live. The transfer-of-peas man exemplifies one option: withdraw, pass time in a way that is both innocuous and sheltered from aggravations. That option is, given the framework of nihilism, as good as any other. Absence of clues and indicators renders all options ethically equivalent. Since differences do not make any deep, serious difference, one mode of living is morally equivalent to any other. So, why not sit at home, shut out the world's problems, and move peas from one container to the other?

As a general model for emulation, the position may not be that attractive. Still, the position, given a particular philosophical backdrop, is defensible. If life is absurd, the transfer-of-peas man has (1) chosen an option that is as good as any other, and (2) he is relatively harmless. He is definitely no Meursault, acquiescing in the entrapment and beating of a young woman, and guilty of murder.

Our friend who transfers peas might even, Sisyphus-style, proclaim himself to be "happy." People around him, however, might suggest (1) that he is working with a narrow understanding of happiness, and (2) his understanding of happiness has nothing to do with meaningfulness. His main aim: avoid anxiety, remain undisturbed. For him an anxiety-minimal life is a maximally happy one. It could be argued, though, that his understanding of happiness is an understanding that not only ignores the distinction between meaningfulness and happiness, it is one that disallows meaningfulness. His main aim is, as mentioned earlier, to avoid anxiety. For him happiness is identified with the neo-Stoic ideal of imperturbability. But his effort at achieving equanimity comes at a price. He has to insulate himself from the benefits, challenges, opportunities, and responsibilities associated with the give-and-take world of ordinary existence.

One of the best philosophical examinations of meaningfulness helps us understand why. The author is Susan Wolf. Her book is entitled *Meaning in Life and Why It Matters*. In that work, Wolf seeks to avoid two tempting oversimplifications: (1) meaning derives from rigorous rule-following; (2) meaning is whatever we make it. For Wolf, there's plenty of middle ground. She summarizes her conclusion in this formulation: "meaning arises when subjective attraction meets objective attractiveness" (Wolf, 62). There are, she suggests, wide ranges of activities that can count as meaningful. What they have in common: a worthiness that is not simply whatever is defined as worthy by the subject. A life is meaningful, as she puts it "insofar as it is actively and lovingly engaged in projects of worth" (Wolf, 35).

There exists a range of activities that can be characterized as "worthy." The notion of range, at the same time, suggests the presence of limits. As an example of someone outside the limits, Wolf speaks not of an individual counting peas but of someone counting bathroom tiles (Wolf, 43). Radical subjectivism's kernel of truth is to reject narrow absolutism. Its error is to overlook the notion of range and go to the other extreme: assert that that meaning is simply whatever people define it as.

Camus, with his projected third stage, exemplified by *Nemesis*, goddess of limits, was gesturing in exactly Wolf's direction. Unfortunately, as we shall see, the tug of a philosophy which assumed a self-world separation was just too strong. So long as the more ecological position (humans are made for this world which is their home; there are operative limits within the ecosphere) was not an available option, Camus could only identify a problem and not provide substantive moves beyond it.

The Plague offers a good example of how Camus identifies the problem. The story is written in such a way that readers are led to make a value judgment: the life trajectory and activities of Dr. Rieux are better than are the life trajectory and activities of the man-with-the-peas. Given how Camus has constructed his story, it would be hard for readers to proclaim that the life of the man-with-the-peas is as admirable as that of Dr. Rieux. Hard to proclaim, in practice at least. In theory, the "we are like aliens in an indifferent world" attitude associated with *The Myth of Sisyphus* has eliminated the possibility of experientially well-founded judgments of better and worse. Theoretically, the world is silent. Equivalence and indifference dominate. Therefore, all value judgments are leveled.

Practically, things are quite different. Humans make value judgments all the time. Such a theory/practice disconnect did not escape Camus. He explored the issue in some of his essays. A silent and indifferent world is, at the same time, morally neutral. Axiological equivalence, the leveling of all valuations, is one offshoot of the Great Bifurcation. In practice, though, people are always making value judgments. Camus phrases the rupture in a complicated but direct enough manner. "For the absurd is contradictory in existence. It, in fact, excludes judgments of value and there are judgments of value. There are such judgments because they are linked to the very fact of existence. We must thus displace the reasoning about the absurd and substitute its equivalent in existence, which is revolt" (ESS, 1696–7, my translation).[1]

Several important dimensions are highlighted in this passage.

1. There is a recognition of how significant is *praxis*. Humans are agents, active participants in their ambients. Such a *praxis*-centered awareness has to be held in tandem with, not in opposition to, theoretical reflection.
2. In line with an appreciation for *praxis*, Camus insists on something like a rehabilitation of the ordinary. Thinking of oneself as an engaged participant is quite different from thinking of oneself as an outsider or a stranger in a strange land. The outsider can more readily be assimilated to a spectator rather than a participant. Praxis, actual doings, undergoings, undertakings take place in the here and now. The here and now (realm of dealings which characterizes praxis for the participant) is pervaded by value judgments. In the here and now "there are such judgments because they are linked to the very fact of existence." For concrete living, radical subjectivism seems inadequate. Differences make a difference.
3. Once religion and its otherworldly escape scenarios are set aside, what remains is the need to live in the only realm that we have. Such living, as we have just seen, involves making evaluations, that is, judgments of better and worse. Such evaluations will encourage certain practices and discourage others. This is where "revolt," the theme of Camus's second cycle, comes into play. Those who accept divine command morality do not think in terms of revolt. For them "all the answers have already been given." For others, like Camus, such an evasion of responsibility is not possible. They are "forced to demand a human order where all responses will be human" (ESS, 1688, my translation).[2] Such a demand necessitates a reformist attitude, a changing of how things are, that is, acting in revolt against extant conditions.
4. Finally, a critical comment. Camus, as is often his wont, engages in overstatement. The term "revolt" is used without nuance, without distinctions,

without an awareness of semantic complexity. The implication: such an unqualified revolt is total. "Rieux believed himself to be on the right road—in fighting *against creation* as he found it" (Pl, 127, italics added). In formulating such a claim Rieux forgets that, as a physician, he both works with nature (he aims to restore health) and against it (he combats illness). In *The Rebel* Camus provides a more balanced position. He there criticizes "metaphysical rebellion" precisely because of its totalizing attitude. The ancient Greeks, a model culture for him, would have no part in such an unconditional rejection.

> In their most audacious flights they always remain faithful to the idea of moderation, a concept they deified. Their rebel does not range himself against all creation, but against Zeus, who is never anything more than one god among many and who himself was mortal. . . . It is a question of settling a particular account, of a dispute about what is good, and not a universal struggle between good and evil. (TR, 27)

The Plague, despite Dr. Rieux's overstatement about fighting *against* creation, mostly works within the realm of human-centered reform rather than metaphysical revolt. The novel emphasizes several themes.³ The widest context is set by the second cycle Camus envisioned for his work: a focus on revolt. The guiding figure here is Prometheus. Goodbye to the captive *Sisyphus* and his enforced frustrating, repetitive, that is, nonproductive, work. Hello to emancipated *Prometheus* whose gifts are fire (the arts, the abilities to transform) and freedom (liberation from the gods).

Emphasizing revolt, effort, and struggle, the novel makes the man-with-the-peas a foil. It is difficult to suspend judgment when comparing him to those who risk health and life to combat the plague. Despite the context of theoretical nihilism (normative leveling), *The Plague* strikes out in a different direction, one which highlights participation. It offers an alternative to the approach which identifies humans as aliens in a strange land, more outside spectators than engaged participants. In *The Plague* the category of participants is mostly forced on individuals. It remains possible to assume the attitude of "we are like aliens, more spectators than participants." Possible, but, given the plague, less likely.

In order to put the spectator attitude into question, Camus introduces a reporter. By profession Rambert should privilege spectatorship over engagement. Given his practical circumstances as someone trapped in a plague-infested city, he reverses the order: participatory engagement trumps spectatorship. The quarantine has forced Rambert to remain in the disease-threatened city. His love interest lives in Paris. This estrangement occasions a reflection about how detached spectatorship is not primordial. He wasn't, Rambert says, "brought into the world to write newspaper articles. But, it's quite likely I was brought into this world to live with a woman" (Pl, 85). He ends his complaint by saying "*Cela n'est-il pas dans l'ordre?*" (LaP, 82). The standard translation reads "That's reasonable enough isn't it?" (Pl, 85). What Rambert literally says situates him more squarely in the midst of lived experience and a lived experience characterized in a particular way: "Isn't that in the order of things." The *order* here is assumed to set a benchmark. Wherever there is a benchmark, there exist various possibilities: excess, deficiency, and hitting the mark or at least approximating it. An "order" of things challenges the position of general indifference and equivalence.

When Indifference Is Difficult to Assume

To emphasize that there is an order of things, a kind of existential fitness which provides a range within which value determinations can be warranted, Camus creates a crisis situation. It is always possible, *Étranger*-style, to deny that there is an order of things. In that case attunement to the order simply disappears as a desideratum. Mattering can be subjectivized. Radical relativism (subjectivism) can rule. Rationality, far from being an enemy, can actually reinforce such subjectivism. "Rational agents" can step back, can envision themselves as individuals whose main task is filing "objective" dispatches. Such self-imposed aloofness, although always possible, becomes harder to maintain once a plague has come to town. The danger of painful illness culminating in death is personal. Sequestration in a quarantined city is uncomfortable. The need for help in combating the disease is urgent. Incompetent, self-serving city officials are more a hindrance than a help. Black marketeering, smuggling, and the temptation of illegal escape are real.

Mattering, determinations of better and worse, no longer seems wholly, completely discretionary. Indifference, embodied by the man-with-the-peas, will, it is true, always remain a possibility. Given the context of nihilism and absurdity, that is, a context of axiological leveling, there is no theoretical reason for dismissing indifference. It, given a certain understanding of "objectivity," can even seem to be the default position—in theory at least. Within the world of praxis, especially when a puzzling ailment haunts the community, things are different. Mattering, in the realm of praxis, is hard to ignore. *Ça m'est égal* and moral leveling might be attractive for disembodied cogitators seeking above all else to avoid anxiety. They are hard, under usual conditions, to live out in practice. In the midst of a plague their appeal dwindles, if it does not wholly disappear. Various responses offer themselves. Praxis does not treat them as equivalent. Some are better than others. They are better, not just because of arbitrary choice. So long as the presence of *Nemesis* is recognized, good reasons can be given in their support. The inherited position which forces a language that opposes "objective" and "subjective" now seems overly narrow and constricted.

Such an eventual progression can be recognized even in the early stages of Camus's development, the one moving from *Sisyphus* to *Prometheus*. The latter is, for Camus, a special benefactor. He provides gifts which allow for greatness: (a) liberty and (b) the arts. Prometheus symbolizes both freedom to choose and the skills, the abilities to carry out projects. In plague-infested Oran that combination is best exemplified in the person of a physician. Dr. Rieux chooses freely to help the afflicted. His training provides the skills needed to be effective.

One gift not bequeathed by *Prometheus* is paradise. In paradise, neither freedom nor talent is important. There is no need to make choices regarding better and worse. Everything is always fine. Risk, sweat, and anxiety are unknown. There is no need for talent. Nothing requires repairing. Responsibility simply disappears as a consideration.

The gifts of Prometheus, though genuine, have nothing of the utopian about them. They are for humans living in the here and now.

In that setting, there is illness, there has always been illness, there will always be illness. Responsibility, rather than being superfluous, now becomes crucial. The gift of freedom is double-edged. Because *Nemesis* has not yet entered upon the scene, humans can always opt for indifference. They can always identify personal happiness as the highest goal, and identify happiness with absence of worry. That is the case for the man-with-the-peas. In the (heavily theoretical) world taken as basal in both *The Myth of Sisyphus* and *The Stranger*, indifference is fundamental and mattering is discretionary. *The Plague*, situated in a concrete context, reveals the weakness in such a generalized leveling of value judgments.

The Problem of Good

That, at least, is what *The Plague* suggests. It tilts in a clear direction: that of admiring Rieux. Camus, though, faces a special challenge: how to justify such admiration, which, after all, is a value judgment? If he were religious, this challenge would disappear. He could appeal to divine directives. At the same time, a new difficulty would arise, the problem of evil.[4] For Rieux and his partners, the problem is reversed. They face the problem of good. Adherents of religion must confront the task of reconciling undeserved suffering with belief in a benevolent, all-powerful divinity. Those who take, in the wake of Nietzsche, a nonreligious path, confront a different concern. It's an issue that piggybacks on that of theory/practice. One of *The Plague*'s main characters, Tarrou, broaches the issue explicitly. He asks about motivation. This adds a psychological dimension to the epistemological/ethical one. The epistemological/ethical question asks how, given the all-leveling context of nihilism, it is possible to provide reasonable grounds for validating the judgment that it is better to help others. The psychological question moves this issue one step closer to the sphere of action. Under what conditions will people actually be motivated to engage in benevolent projects? If nothing in the nature of things suggests that the Rieux option is better than the man-with-the-peas option, why undertake the more rigorous and more dangerous path? Why not just seek one's own self-interest? Why not admit how, in the grand scheme of things, indifference is just as valid a response as is heroic helpfulness.

Not yet having introduced *Nemesis*, Camus's answer is built around the theme of his second cycle "revolt." "Revolt" means not giving in to surrounding conditions. Minimally, it encourages resistance. Maximally it promotes concerted efforts to join with others in ameliorating existing conditions. Responsibility and revolt can reinforce each other. Post death of God individuals don't have to worry about reconciling a benevolent God and a far-from-benevolent creation. Already situated in a world marked by suffering, by multiple calls for help, their main concern is responsibility, that is, how to respond. When a plague has descended on a city, the alternatives are brought into focus: remove oneself from the fray; benefit personally from the crisis (the black marketeer "Cottard" follows this path); work to relieve suffering.

Such an emphasis on praxis does not eliminate reflection. It transfers theoretical concerns from one register to another. This new register forms the heart of *The Plague*. After the death of God, the problem is not so much that of evil as that of good. This is where the contrast between the man-with-the-peas and Dr. Rieux forces the issue. Nihilism proclaims that the world is silent. There are no indications or clues offering guidance for human intelligence. Rational data gathering results only in facts, not values. Buridan's ass is stymied; will always be stymied. Stymied intellectually, at least. There remains the sheer act of will. This is a will that is completely free. It is completely free because there is *nihil*, nothing in the external world that commands it to opt one way or another. The path of the man-with-the-peas or the path of Rieux, there is no absolute foundation for determining one as better than the other. Since all commitments are matters of free choice, a familiar conundrum emerges: why not opt for the path of least resistance, least effort, least vexation?

This is the point at which *The Plague* brings attention to weaknesses in the dominant philosophy. It highlights a key anomalous instance, the gap between theory and practice. Theoretically, there are no warrants for differential evaluations. Still, there is a need to make decisions. But, there can be no good reasons for judging some decisions as better than others. A Buridan-style gap has made itself felt. Only sheer willfulness, only radical subjectivity drives actions. The necessity of action is real, but an evaluative ranking of the options seems impossible. The alternatives have shrunk to two: (a) perfect infallible certitude or (b) subjective willfulness. Bringing attention to the gap between them is about as far as Camus can go. Remaining within the semantic landscape of the Great Bifurcation, he cannot rehabilitate ordinary experience. It remains a realm of mere fact isolated from value. Indifference is the basal ontological category. The Great Bifurcation, as is its wont, sets up the conditions of knowledge as a dilemma: either absolute certitude or mere opinion. Because ordinary life experience cannot provide absolute certitude, all decision-making is automatically considered to fall under the realm of mere opinion.

Such an either/or setting, while problematic in terms of fostering an all-or-nothing-approach, is actually attractive from the perspective of sidestepping responsibility and its attendant anxiety. For the absolutist, the answers are apodictic, infallible. Responsibility involves no risk. Why struggle with facts, evidence, norms, consequences? Like the aptly named Mr. Square in Henry Fielding's *Tom Jones*, it's all simply a matter of following the (already established, easily recognized) "rule of right" (Fielding, 94). Life is made a whole lot easier. Strangely enough, the same impulse away from responsibility and toward ease results from opponents of absolutism, those who embrace "it's all merely opinion." For them skepticism and subjectivity rule. Where skepticism and subjectivity rule, the onerous burden of figuring out how, properly, to respond, disappears. "It's up to the individual" becomes the guiding slogan. Burdensome responsibility wanes as simplified, risk-minimized, flexibility waxes.

The practical challenge for *The Plague* is thus set. Can responsibility mean anything in an intellectual setting dominated by nihilism? In practice, people elect a response to the pandemic. Dr. Rieux elects one response. The novel suggests that his response is noble. In doing so, the novel intimates that his response, when compared to others, is *better*. At the same time, readers, even if identifying with Rieux, are boxed in. Boxed in, at least, if they remain within the general framework of the Great Bifurcation. If there is nothing in the experiential realm that offers signs, clues, indicators which, taken together, could offer reasonable guidance for favoring one option over others, then all such favorings will derive from raw acts of will. Evaluations there have always been and always will be. Praise and blame, though, can within the Great Bifurcation only result from pronouncements which, when translated, mean "I personally proclaim that X is commendable/deplorable."

Camus was dissatisfied with such relativistic subjectivism. He realized that the nihilism underlying such subjectivism led to dead ends, contradictions, dangerous practical ramifications. In the scathing letter he addressed to Sartre, responding to a harshly negative review of *The Rebel* in the latter's journal *Les Temps Modernes*, Camus emphasized how "we can no longer do without positive values" (ESS, 751). He reinforced this point in his Nobel address, asserting that most people (*la plupart d'entre nous*) today "reject nihilism and have taken up the task of seeking a legitimacy" ("*ont refusé ce nihilisme et se sont mis à la recherche d'une légitimité*") (ESS, 1073).[5]

So far so good. But without a turn toward *Nemesis*, Camus remained under the influence of the Cartesian disembodied *cogito*. He made neither the move needed to recognize how (a) interactions, and not a Great Bifurcation, are primordial nor (b) the ecologically friendly move that would recognize limits (*Nemesis*) and not indifference as operative in how things are. As a result, he could only channel his hopefulness in the direction of "thought in revolt." He could not envision how *recherche d'une légitimité,* the attempt to legitimate valuation, can best be carried out after a paradigm change, specifically a move away from depicting humans as set off against the world.

The Cartesian *cogito* is not the only way of describing how humans relate to the world. *Razón vital,* for example, does not begin by self-sequestration from surroundings. It does not insist on a ground zero. It does not confuse truth with certitude. Its efforts begin from the assumption that (1) we are at home in the world and (2) there are, in our surroundings, *indicia,* clues, hints, signs that allow the formation of reasonable judgments. These will, it is true, be fallible. But fallibility, "this position might be wrong," suggests at the same time that it might be on the right track. Between absolutist claims of perfect certitude and subjectivist claims that "it's all relative" there is lots of room for fallible, evidence-based reasonableness.

One indication of how Rieux, given the assumptions Camus is working with, remains mostly within the "judgments are subjective" blueprint comes in an exchange with the journalist Rambert. Rambert is working with underworld figures to plot an illegal escape. He speaks openly about his plans. The good doctor, staying in the city, fighting the plague, in need of volunteers, could respond by attempting dissuasion. Rieux most likely thinks it would be *better* if individuals, having spent time in a plague-infested city, did not escape; would be *better* if Rambert signed on as a volunteer; would be *better* if Rambert used his journalistic skills to share what it is like to live in a quarantined city. Rieux, though, does no such thing. He refuses to stand in judgment. "You're right, Rambert, quite right, and for nothing in the world would I try to dissuade you from what you're going to do; it seems to me absolutely right and proper" (Pl, 163). Rieux here lives out both a sense of compassion and the leveling force of indifference.

He realizes how difficult it is for Rambert (and others) to be separated from loved ones. At the same time, he recognizes the challenges imposed by the plague, challenges that make difficult decisions necessary. He is caught in a situation in which evaluations about the relative significance of compassion and healing have to be made.

Deep down he has a sense of better and worse. But, given a particular philosophical background, there is nothing in the lifeworld that intelligence or reasonableness can latch onto which would justify such an evaluation. Buridan's ass rules. Judgments are just subjective. So, without any real support for better and worse, Rieux's reaction cannot go far beyond the attitude of "to each his own."

Disembodied cogitation, abstracting from the specifics of the situation, can proclaim its neutrality. It can relieve itself of responsibility and risk. It can proclaim the rigidly isolationist position that making evaluative judgments is, in the end, an arbitrary act. Sheer, autonomous choosing is all that can be expected. "Will" is not only opposed to "intellect." It now rules as imperial master. That Rieux remains within this framework is made evident in his proclamation that Rambert's plans are "absolutely right and proper." There are *reasons* why the quarantine has been imposed; there are *reasons* why, in this context, it is *better* to stay and help. There are also reasons why lovers should be in each other's company. Yet now, when a judgment is called for, the doctor cannot allow himself to weigh the different considerations on an axiological scale. Judgments of better and worse can only be envisioned as versions of "thus I will it." "You are absolutely right" translates into "each of us by our pronouncements and decisions, is the final arbiter of what is better and what is worse."

There is no in-between, no room for justified belief, for evaluations warranted by facts of the case, for evaluations of which differences make a difference, how, and when. When it comes to justifying his own commitment to stay and struggle, Rieux, dismissing reasonable justifications, can only say "it's a matter of common decency" (Pl, 163). The French word is *honnêteté*. It's a term rich in connotations, as the translator´s rendition of it as "common decency" reveals. The term's semantic range includes uprightness, integrity, sense of honor, probity, living out one's deepest commitments. The significance of this semantic scope is its overlap with the ideal of authenticity. Rieux could well be saying "I am being true to myself, as you, Rambert, are being true to yourself. That is why I can say with total authenticity, your chosen plan is 'absolutely right and proper.'"

Within such a setting, responsibility, as more than an honorific slogan, fades to the periphery. The effort required to determine and justify an appropriate, fitting, response is eliminated. Instead a shortcut is put in place: you choose your way, I choose mine. Don't try to figure things out. Distinctions of better and worse cannot be made on the basis of indications rooted in the lifeworld, lived experience, and history. You have to choose. But, since there is nothing in the nature of things that validates one choice over another, you are free, you can make your choice without the need to think things through, to gauge the relative importance of the situation's complex factors, to risk being mistaken, to arrive at a position warranted not by absolute certitude but by justified belief.

That's all so messy. Better to be simple and direct. Better if fallibility and risk could be avoided. Better to circumvent intelligence and the need for reasons. So long as the nihilistic landscape remains dominant, even someone like Rieux is limited in what he can say. He has no grounds for any assertion beyond "that is what you have chosen, so it is fine." You choose one way, I choose another. End of story.

Saying Yes to the Ordinary

The theory/praxis dilemma expressed in *The Plague* presents a context within which Camus comes close to rehabilitating the ordinary. All the ingredients are present for altering the dominant paradigm. That paradigm (humans as outsiders set over against a world that is "external") encourages a harsh "no" to the possibilities and opportunities already latent in ordinary life. Such a "no" is an inevitable byproduct of a philosophical landscape characterized by disembodied rationality, self-evidence, the demand for absolute certitude, and a world considered to be "external." One alternative, represented by *razón vital*, begins with live beings *and* the circumstances without which living would not be possible. Immersion and interaction are primordial. This world can be understood as our proper home.

Changing the terminology, we could say that "occupation" is primordial. This would be so in two senses: (1) being situated in a place and (2) engaging in pursuits. Even better would be to speak of humans as already "pre-occupied," that is, primordially situated, and in the midst of ongoing projects. For beings so pre-occupied, "mattering" is coordinate with being. Meaning and value are not imposed by an outside will. They are constitutive components of converse and intercourse. Ordinary life experience, far from a realm dominated by *nihil*, abounds with possibilities. Those possibilities act as "calls," calls to which *razón vital* responds. Such a realm, to be sure, is more complicated than that of the disembodied cogito confronting an external world of neutral data. It is also more complicated in the sense that it welcomes, rather than evades, risk and responsibility.

The eliminationist anesthetizer of disembodied cogitation can, of course, benumb dimensions like mattering, context, emotions, tradition, physiology. In fact, eliminative rationality, consistent with the Great Bifurcation and encouraged by the shortcut of minimizing responsibility, does just that. The highest ideal is that of complete rest, an anxiety-limiting closed loop which in cutting off interaction with circumstances can circumvent responsibility by two strategies which ignore middle ground. One says there are fixed rules and dictates which I am following. The other says, there are no rules, it's all up to the individual.

Such evasions, while attractive to aliens and detached spectators, are odd for active, living, engaged beings. Once again we are reminded that value judgments take place all the time. In a city besieged by a plague, such inevitability is made glaringly prominent. Responsibility, taking action in response to surrounding conditions, is unavoidable. The philosophical tradition inherited by Camus offered only two modes of acting. Both fall under the category I would call "thin" responsibility. Both offer shortcuts. For religious absolutists the shortcut becomes: submit to the divine will. For those within the orbit of nihilism, the formulation becomes: it's all relative. The alternatives boil down to "Thus God wills it" and "Thus I will it." What the two options leave out: "thick" responsibility. This position assumes a setting thick with possibilities. It welcomes risk and responsibility. It makes an effort, while admitting fallibility, to get things right.

When "thus I will it" stands as the last word after the death of God, the issue of motivation, the one raised by Tarrou, emerges more clearly. Having to opt among options is not the issue. Even Buridan's donkey has to choose. Why though, do so with enthusiasm and boundless energy? As is often the case, the religious have a ready response: because their deity commands such effort and determination. What about people like Rieux? As someone outside of religion, such an explanation does not apply. Tarrou forces the issue. He asks why Rieux is so passionate and devoted, "considering you don't believe in God?" Rieux's answer inverts the standard religious perspective. If he were a believer, Rieux would leave curing the sick to God (Pl, 127). Rieux adds that no one really believes in such a God, not even the prominent priest, Fr. Paneloux. The religious merely *claim* to revere this kind of God. Rieux, though not an aggressive atheist,[6] has no time for such religious polemics

The position Dr. Rieux formulates is at once post-Modern and pre-Modern. It is post-Modern in that it assumes, with Nietzsche, that the God of Christianity is dead. It is pre-Modern in that it revives what Camus calls the "tragic optimism" of ancient Greece (ESS, 1163). Tragic optimism is an attitude that (1) is attuned to the actual condition of humans, (2) recognizes the presence of evil and suffering in that condition, and (3) refuses escapisms and utopias. It's an attitude that is commonplace for physicians. Disease is always present (the tragic aspect). Health is not a subjective condition. It is real and can be restored (the optimistic dimension). The "tragic" sets the context; the "optimistic" provides the motivation. The motivation leads to responsible action. Responsible action, in turn, is (1) action by humans, with (2) a particular aim: repairing what is damaged. "Man in revolt," Camus asserts, "is man cast outside the sacred and makes demands for a human order where all the answers are human ones" (ESS, 1688,).

What other option is there? Absolutes, as divine commands, are illusory. Absolutes disguised as radical subjectivism are unsatisfactory. Both positions are of the absolutizing, anxiety-eliminating sort. One identifies the divine as the absolute; the other absolutizes the human subject. Their modes of actions and answers are not really "human ones." Humans inhabit a realm in between complete light and complete darkness. Camus signals this by situating Rieux "still in shadow" (Pl, 127), that is, without perfect knowledge or awareness.

The absence of either divine commands or radically subjectivist certitude only sharpens the question of Tarrou. What motivates Rieux? Is it just that he is an anti-Father Paneloux? The priest exemplifies the worst attitudes of believers. His two sermons devoted to the plague either blamed the populace (God is punishing us; repent) or preached acquiescence (God's ways are inscrutable; we must submit to his will). In either case the upshot is the same: do not, as a primary response, roll up your sleeves, get out there, and work to restore health. This is the kind of advice that bothers Rieux. It is why he believes it is better to situate oneself within a context of unbelief. "Since the order of the world is shaped by death, mightn't it be better for God if we refuse to believe in Him and struggle with all our might against death, without raising our eyes toward the heaven where He sits in silence?" (Pl, 128).

Rieux is here on such solid ground that even observant individuals have come around. The trappist monk Thomas Merton, who was a fan of Camus, is prominent among them. Merton specifically worries about how Fr. Paneloux describes a God who "acts like an arbitrary tyrant." "Grace" in this context is a kind of drug which provides "the power to submit to a will we do not understand and even to adore and love what appears horrible." "This is an idea," Merton continues, "that Camus finds revolting. And he is right. It is also an idea which Camus believes to be essential to Christianity, and he is wrong: the idea that God is essentially unjust, and to be loved as such!" (Merton, 213).[7]

Rieux, outside of religion, has little interest in such theological subtleties. He is a man of action. He listens to believers. He knows the kind of God they accept. Paying attention to how people act is what matters. Since creation is characterized by suffering and death, our first response must be to struggle against it (Pl, 127). Paneloux serves as a foil. No matter how intelligent and articulate, he, in the end, promotes inaction. His overall tone sends a single message: submit to the divine will. So much is this the case that such submission is called for even when, as in one of the novel's most moving scenes, what has to be accepted is the innocent suffering of a child. "True, the agony of a child was humiliating to the heart and to the mind. But that was why we had to come to terms with it. And that, too, was why—and here Paneloux assured those present that it was not easy to say what he was about to say—since it was God's will, we, too, should will it" (Pl, 225). Such a call to acquiescence is reinforced when Rieux overhears two other priests talking about Paneloux. He, Paneloux, is writing a text with a telling thesis: "That it's illogical for a priest to call in a doctor." And, indeed, when Fr. Paneloux becomes ill, he brushes aside requests that a physician be called in (Pl, 229–31).

Much better, Rieux thinks, to wager on Prometheus than on Yahweh. There is nothing Promethean in Fr. Paneloux's call to submission. Repugnance (at the sight of an innocent child suffering) is negated by the priest's call to acquiescence. Prometheus opens a different path, that of revolt. In this case the path is one from repugnance to revolt to effective action.

Prometheus is the force most allied to responsibility. Such responsibility is manifested as the movement from abhorrence to action. The most consistent participants in such a revolt are, for Camus, the nonbelievers. Neither Rieux nor his friend Jean Tarrou begins with a commitment to a creation that is good. Neither of them has much time for belief in God. The great need is to struggle, "to save the greatest possible number of persons from dying and being doomed to unending separation. And to do this there was only one resource: to fight the plague" (Pl, 133). The world will always manifest a dimension that is broken, will always be marked by illness, injustice, and other sorts of suffering. The everyday Promethean figure, the one who best combines commitment (freedom) and skill (art) is the healer, the physician. Tarrou, the most reflective character in the novel, says so explicitly, urging the need for "true healers" (Pl, 254). Such true healers are the real saints, whether they believe in God or, as the case with Tarrou and Rieux, do not (Pl, 255).

Seeking a Third Way

Father Paneloux represents a totalizing kind of affirmation. It's a blanket "yes" without nuance. It's an imperialistic yes, with no room for difference. The "yes" is embedded within an "all or nothing" landscape. Dr. Rieux, it would seem, is situated within a different landscape. Surprisingly, this is not so. What twenty-first-century readers can begin to appreciate is how Rieux represents a mirror image of Paneloux. For Paneloux, the bottom line is an ultimate, absolute "yes" to creation. For Rieux, the bottom line is an absolute, ultimate "no" to creation. He undertakes a fight "against creation." The "all or nothing" attitude is alive and well in both positions.

A different take, a less absolute and imperialistic one, would not fit well within the all-or-nothing paradigm. Why should the imperialistic assumption (creation is absolutely good or creation is absolutely bad) be taken for granted? Camus's much-admired Greeks wrote both tragedies and comedies. Humans inhabit a world which suggests the wisdom of such a move: the lived world is one of difference and multiplicity. Why automatically discredit a nuanced, mixed position, one that would assert "yes" *in some ways* and "no" in others. Such a mixed position could still accept a general "yea-saying" to the human situation. But it would be a yea-saying that acknowledged also how responsibility was part of the human situation. This, in turn, would necessitate an element of nay-saying: first identifying and subsequently rectifying what needed to be changed.

Tarrou bemoans the lack of such a third option. He utters a heartfelt disquisition which culminates in his claim that "it's up to us, so far as possible, not to join forces with the pestilences" (Pl, 253–4). Acting responsibly, he believes, means working against pestilences. But acting responsibly as an intelligent agent also means paying attention to consistency and motivation. Tarrou admits a strong dose of voluntarism in his position. Accepting responsibility was not brought about by reasoned discourse. His "yes" (a) results from a "thus I will it" style choice and (b) is absolute. Like Rieux and Paneloux, he inhabits an intellectual landscape dominated by an all-or-nothing attitude. As a result his notion of responsibility is absolutist. He has decided "to take, in every predicament, the victims' side" (Pl, 254). If all-or-nothing it must be, then at least opt for the path that favors the afflicted.

In the midst of his discourse, Tarrou longs for a more humane, more reasonable path. This is the point at which he introduces the phrase "true healers." He provides little elaboration about this alternative, but the phrase itself is telling. It suggests physicians as models of a "third way." Physicians can serve as a prototype because they do not fit neatly into the all-or-nothing scheme. They work both with and against creation, for and against the order of the world. The optimal condition, good health, manifests itself in the world. Dis-ease, the state of being un-well is also prevalent in life. The physician says both "yes" and "no." Yes to the optimal conditions which define health. "No" to the infirmities which impede the healthy state.

Rieux's formulation asserting that he is one-dimensionally fighting against creation is an overstatement. As a good physician, he works both with and against creation. Rieux is convinced that the real abomination is acting in ways that do *not* fix what needs to be fixed. The novel sides with him in this regard. We are here taken back to the unresolved contradiction between theory and practice. Camus creates a story in which making evaluative decisions is unavoidable. At the same time, the shadow of the Great Bifurcation looms large. Within its shadow, evaluations are *either* subjective or objective. Because the absolute certitude associated with the "objective" side is not realizable, all that remains is the subjectivity of evaluation. Third-way options, the ways of intelligent inquiry followed by commitments based on the best available evidence, are out of bounds. Out of bounds, at least, given the philosophical inheritance that is taken for granted.

Today's readers, having entered the twenty-first century, no longer need feel as committed to the inheritance taken for granted by Camus. Challenged from a variety of perspectives, the Great Bifurcation no longer holds complete sway. One result: space is opened up for novel formulations, for "third ways." No single, dominant third way has made an appearance, but the terrain is less restricted than it once was. This is certainly true for issues raised in *The Plague*, especially that which opposed Dr. Rieux to Fr. Paneloux. So long as the issue is framed, Great Bifurcation style, as an either/or, the trajectory is clear: Rieux or Paneloux, the secular or the religious. Such was indeed the dominant stance when Camus composed his novel.

How about today? Philosophical reflection, after all, does not stand still. An important shift in sentiment was announced by someone who was a giant in twentieth-century thought, Jürgen Habermas. As the twenty-first century opened, he announced that a new era was dawning, a "post-secular" one (Habermas). "Post-secular" is a bit strong. The prefix "post," if it is taken to indicate complete abandonment, is surely exaggerated. The formulation would then remain within the orbit of dilemma-driven, either/or thinking. It would suggest that secularism has been overcome. It would leave little room for the reformulation of basic questions, for new amalgams. In other words, "post," taken too literally, would dismiss "third" options.

The label, though, does get something right. Once the grip of the Great Bifurcation begins to fade, much of what flowed from it will move from center to periphery. When it does, the perfunctory mandate for framing all issues in terms of rigid dilemmas will no longer be felt as an imperative. The era announced by Habermas might not be *post*-secular in the sense of treating the secular era as a self-enclosed unit, now set aside. But it can mean that an era, which is no longer imperialistically secular, will allow for new amalgams, novel combinations, heretofore unimagined realignments.

The Plague, despite Tarrou's plea, makes no substantive moves in this direction. There is, though, one fertile point raised by Tarrou: motivation. As we have seen, the issue was quickly addressed by Dr. Rieux. The options are clear: the doctor on one side, the priest on the other. The position favored in the novel is that of Rieux. Motivation makes more sense, if one does *not* accept the existence of God.

In the middle of the twentieth century, the Fr. Paneloux versus Dr. Rieux opposition could be starkly posed. In the twenty-first century, things are more complicated. Those who challenge the *either* Rieux *or* Paneloux dilemma might over hastily be classified as "post-secular." The "post" would be hasty if it indicated a sense jettisoning the entire heritage associated with secularism, replacing it with a traditionalist understanding of religion. This would involve simply moving neatly defined, already established pieces, around. It would do little to explore third ways, ways of reweaving the intellectual fabric by a novel manner of intertwinings from various epochs.

Several philosophers have taken up the Tarrou challenge of focusing on motivation. One third-way explorer is Charles Taylor (1931–). Like the Trappist monk Merton, Taylor agrees with Camus in many ways. He prizes solidarity and what he calls "together goods."[8] Rieux, Grand, Tarrou, and Rambert exemplify "together goods" in practice. As a result, their lives can be described as revealing a certain "fullness." Taylor is also, like Camus, an admirer and champion of the advantages that secularization brought to the West. The world inhabited by Dr. Rieux is a world that welcomes scientific inquiry and champions political liberties, human rights, equality, and democratic republics. These gains would not have been realized had secularization, the separation of politics from religion, not taken place (Taylor 1999, 29). In this regard, even adherents of religion should be grateful for the emancipatory effects of secularization.

Thus far there is lots of Camus/Taylor overlap. It is Tarrou's prescient question, the one about motivation, that marks a dividing line. Tarrou's emphasis on motivation highlights the importance of praxis. Taylor phrases it this way: "but don't you see that it *also matters* whether people can actually bring themselves to *do* the right thing?" (Taylor 1999, 120). It is at this point that Taylor, friendly to religion, moves beyond the Rieux/Paneloux opposition. He strikes out in a direction undertaken by neither of those figures. Paneloux's only interest in motivation is related narrowly either to repentance or quiescence. For Rieux, that response identifies precisely the major drawback of religion: it eliminates the motivation for actually doing good. Taylor introduces a different tack. Discussing Camus specifically, he says the following:

> In the end, the question becomes a maximum one: how to have the greatest degree of philanthropic action with the minimum hope in mankind. A figure like Dr. Rieu [sic] in Camus' *La Peste* stands as a possible solution to this problem. But that is fiction. What is possible in real life? (Taylor 1999, 35)

In the world created by Camus, a Dr. Rieux, a Jean Tarrou, a Joseph Grand respond in unselfish ways to the challenges forced upon them. How deep, Taylor wonders, will the motivation be, how long will it last, without a sense of responding to some ultimate benevolence which is the source of all things?[9]

With sickness and suffering all around, in a context of unbelief, Tarrou had proposed a solution. Perhaps the presence and operative power of "sympathy" might be motivation enough (Pl, 254). Here, exactly, is where the Camus and the Taylor perspectives differ. To understand the difference, it is important to take into account some postcolonial and feminist criticisms of *The Plague*. In terms of the characters created by Camus, Louise Horowitz identifies the problem succinctly: "That Albert Camus systematically excluded-one is tempted to say eradicated-both women and the colonial Arab population of North Africa from his work is a literary fact" (Horowitz, 54).[10] The charge here is that Camus, thinking in strictly European terms, could write a novel set in Algeria but populate it almost entirely with European males.

The European/Algerian segregation takes on special significance when we think about sympathy as a motivator. Phrased critically, the issue is the following: how strong is the sympathy/similarity connection. Stated more descriptively, how likely is it that sympathy will be a strong motivator when the afflicted populace is of a different race, nationality, or ethnicity? *The Plague* sidesteps this issue by telling a story which, as Horowitz notes, has "eradicated" the majority indigenous population. Ethnic homogeneity, praxis, sympathy, and benevolence intersect in an important way. Studies have shown that humans tend to be more sympathetic, more willing to offer help, to show concern, to sacrifice, when the beneficiaries are people like them.[11] Tarrou, Grand, and Rieux, Europeans all, work tirelessly to help fellow Europeans who happen to be living in Oran. The question is simply not raised whether their sympathy would provide sufficient motivation for extending their tireless efforts to the indigenous population. Nor is the question raised about what their response would be if they, themselves, were not part of the victimized population. What if there was an illness that only impacted the Arab and Berber quarters?

The Taylor position, in its most dramatic formulation, asks about motivation in exactly those cases, that is, when those who need the help are "other," when the potential healers could retreat to an island of safety. Taylor's position: the motivating power of sympathy will simply not suffice. In a context dominated by otherness and difference, a context which requires ongoing effort and is often marked by frustration, sympathy will diminish *unless* there is some countervailing force. That countervailing force, here the post-secular dimension, is best articulated as in terms of an ultimate benevolence that is the ground of all being.

Taylor's comments are not unique in the post-secular intellectual landscape opened by the retreat of the Great Bifurcation. Another forceful articulation, this one concentrating on the question of otherness, has been articulated by John Cottingham. The details follow the pattern enunciated by Taylor. In *The Plague*, the call for help comes from within a homogeneous population (or, the focus is on a homogeneous population). What if the need for help would be located in a population different from that of the healers? Would the motivation to help be as strongly felt? Would a strong sense of responsibility seem as urgent? For Cottingham, the all-too-typical answer is no. A stronger motivational impetus is required, one associated with commitment to a transcendent reality that serves as a lure toward goodness. He begins his formulation with a pair of conditionals:

- if "the ultimate nature of reality contains no bias towards the good as opposed to the vicious,"
- if when we work for good, there is "no particular reason to think that our pursuit of the good is any more than a temporary fragile disposition possessed by a percentage (perhaps a minority) of a certain class of anthropoids."

These are followed by his conclusion. "Then at the very least it is hard to see how we can achieve the necessary confidence and resolution to follow the path of goodness; and at the worst the very idea that some lives can be more meaningful than others begins to seem a fantasy" (Cottingham, 72).

This final claim takes us back to the man-with-the-peas. By the end of *The Plague*, readers are disposed to think that Rieux's life was more meaningful than that of the secluded pea shuffler. It is safe to assume that Camus, critic of nihilism, wants readers to be so disposed. The Taylors and Cottinghams of the world agree. Where they part company with Camus is insisting on a next step. For them, that step would leave behind both the vindictive, dictatorial God of Paneloux and Rieux's understanding of religion as necessitating an interventionist God who discourages human effort. Motivation, the issue raised by Tarrou, is crucial. Real motivation, in practice, emerges in *The Plague,* from sympathy. Taylor and Cottingham counter by claiming that the most demanding motivation requires commitment to some ultimate benevolence which draws humans toward goodness. *The Plague* allows the issue to come to a head. Would Dr. Rieux's zeal for healing diminish, if it meant leaving the familiar side of town and going into non-European neighborhoods ravaged by the disease? Camus, by populating his novel with Europeans, does not face the question directly. Based on his generosity of spirit we can envision that he would want the answer to be "yes." When we place Camus in conversation with the later generation of people like Taylor and Cottingham, we find individuals who disagree.

Camus, who wished to move beyond nihilism, who had Tarrou raise the issue of a third way, could only offer the standard Paneloux-versus-Rieux dilemma. Religion offered little more than an escape, a way of shunning responsibility and risk. To his credit Camus encouraged readers to avoid this religious path. They must admit where they are, within this world. In this world "all responses will be human" (ESS, 1688). Given such a setting, the main question becomes: "can man, by himself and without the help of the eternal, create his proper values?" Not surprisingly, Camus answers yes, "it is possible to respond affirmatively" (ESS, 1696, 1695, my translation).[12]

Philosophers like Taylor and Cottingham, working within an altered paradigm, would, following Tarrou, reformulate the question. The issue is not just that of creating values. It is also that of being drawn by a powerful motivation to do good, not just in the face of frustrations and disappointments, but in contexts where the beneficiaries share neither one's ethnicity nor culture. To the question of whether humans can create values, Camus answers "yes." To the question whether humans without a divine lure can be motivated for devoted selfless acts of goodness, Taylor and Cottingham answer "no."

In reading *The Plague,* we should take Tarrou's aim of seeking a "third path" seriously. No third path is charted, but its necessity is recognized. The best Camus could do was point out the disparity between a *praxis* in which value determinations had to be made and a *theoria* which disallowed the reasonableness of those very judgments. Though he was only in an early stage of exploring the need for an alternative, he had already refused the perfunctory labels associated with the Great Bifurcation and its demand that all issues be framed in binary, either/or terms. Not being religious, he could be pigeonholed into the category of humanist. This was a label he resisted. Humanists were too optimistic. They placed too much belief in rationality, its certitudes, and its possibilities (ESS, 742, 1159).

Camus's position is best described in the label, already mentioned, that he used to characterize his friend René Char: "tragic optimism." Humanists are right to reject transcendence. Camus is with them on this score. At the same time, he shares with the religious a strong sense of evil and of how misplaced is the faith that rationality and its utopias will overcome it. It is up to us, *The Plague* is saying, to stand up, to right wrongs, to heal illness, to repair the world where it is broken. In the novel's final reflection,

Rieux says that, although we cannot be saints, we can be physicians. The French has a rhyme in it, *saints* rhymes with the last syllable in méde*cins*. This poetic turn makes the point more dramatically: "*tous les hommes qui, ne pouvant être des saints et refusant d'admettre des fléaux, s'efforcent cependant d'être des médecins*" (LaP, 279). There are many ways and many opportunities to heal. *The Plague*, avoiding utopian humanism and religious otherworldliness, dismisses the desire to become either a religious or a secular saint. Better to take on the more ordinary role of human healer, one who deals with the problem of evil and suffering by bringing some relief.

6

Reflections on *The Rebel*, I

Beyond Boo-hurrah Ethics

The Plague invites, even more encourages, differential valuation. Rieux, Grand, Tarrou are admirable. They are friends of life. Another character, Cottard, thrives via illegal activity. Significantly, when we first meet him, he is attempting suicide. He is a friend of death. He falls on the more despicable, detestable side of things. The man-with-the-peas, as we have seen, does not fare much better. Rieux and friends struggle against the disease. Cottard uses it to his advantage. The retired dry-goods dealer just withdraws, pursuing individual happiness via anxiety-minimized self-isolation.

Given the way Camus crafted the story, it is hard for readers to remain neutral. The novel plants seeds of doubt about what Camus considered to be the intellectual and practical scourge of his time: nihilism. Doubts about nihilism first emerge in the ways we deal with our circumstances. When we make value judgments, when we sort out better from worse, then, as a matter of practice at least, we move toward thinking that something in our situation provides clues, hints, suggestions. This, in turn, makes room for reasonable justifications. In the theoretical realm, nihilism is harder to challenge. The Great Bifurcation makes the fact/value disjunction seem axiomatic. The realm of facts, neutral in itself, is indifferent to evaluations. These latter can only be impositions from the realm of value, human subjectivity.

Besides flowing readily from the Great Bifurcation, nihilism, and the general indifference that accompanies it, can also be personally attractive. The self-serving aspect derives from two considerations. (1) The position is clean, neat, and easy. First, separate two purified realms. Then assert that valuations derive, neatly and solely, from one side in isolation. That side: the human who bestows meaning on a meaningless world. (2) Then, there is another, perhaps surprising, attractiveness. Nihilism, ignoring how differences make a difference, can do away with bothersome ethical considerations. The general diagnosis of meaninglessness removes limitations on unrestricted self-indulgence. Aldous Huxley articulated this dimension particularly well. "The philosopher who finds no meaning for this world is not concerned exclusively with the problem of pure metaphysics; he is also concerned to prove that there is no valid reason why he personally should not do as he wants to. . . . For myself . . . the philosophy of meaninglessness was essentially an instrument of liberation, sexual and political" (in Klein, 96). Nihilism's theoretical plausibility is thus reinforced by the self-serving dimensions of neatness and liberation. The position's allure increases directly in proportion to the way it maximizes ideological purity while minimizing moral constraints.

Within English-speaking philosophy, the neat, compartmentalized position came to be known as the "boo-hurrah" theory of ethics. Someone is embezzling funds? "Boo," "I condemn stealing as bad." So say some. "Hurrah, someone striking out against evil corporations," say others. Nothing in the realm of facts can prove that this embezzlement is bad or good. The facts are neutral (unnoticed is how philosophy has *invented* a neat fact/value separation which now just seems "natural"). Once "facts" are defined in a certain way, value judgments can only be subjective pronouncements imposed on objective data. An ecology-related claim like "carrying capacity" challenges the neat bifurcation, but this shift away from strict fact/value segregation had no impact on Camus. "Boo" and "hurrah" were (1) where the Great Bifurcation ultimately led, and (2) it is exactly here that Camus wishes to sound an alarm. If nothing apart from personal predilections underwrites determinations of better and worse, then, thinking of *The Plague*, judgments about worthiness do not have any significant purchase. It's all a matter of "boo" or "hurrah."

"It's all a matter of 'boo' or 'hurrah'" has worked its way, as philosophical positions tend to do, into everyday consciousness. The intellectual landscape of nihilism, if pushed to its logical conclusion, culminates in slogans like "it's up to the individual," "whatever floats your boat," "it's all subjective," "it's all a matter of opinion," "don't make value judgments." Even Shakespeare got in on the act, having Hamlet say "there is nothing either good or bad, but thinking makes it so." Such slogans contain a grain of truth. Each evaluation is made by some person or persons. Monolithic, universal agreement is nowhere to be found. However, as blanket claims without qualifications, without admission of the interactive setting in which humans find themselves, such slogans bring with them the corrosive influence that troubled Camus.

They impede thinking and encourage laziness. In ethical contexts, such expressions diminish the value of judgments. If "it's all a matter of opinion," then praise for Rieux does not mean all that much. In a wider philosophical context, such expressions abet a more general corrosive influence, one that is especially problematic for philosophy: they discourage thinking. How do they do this? They propose, as a starting assumption, that judgments are noncognitive, that they derive from nonrational preferences (feeling or emotion are often given as examples). Once that sharp separation (judgments segregated from the cognitive) is made, evaluative judgments are automatically placed in a bin entitled "non-cognitive: it's just boo and hurrah." If that is the case, intelligent effort to gather evidence, to make a strong case, is unnecessary. The nihilistic framework has to be understood, as Huxley understood it, as more than a metaphysical position. It brings with it some personal allure. It's clean and neat; it can encourage self-indulgence; it is comfortable with intellectual slothfulness.

Attractive, maybe, but as *The Plague* indicates, it is possible to shake up such comfortable complacency by creating conditions within which "it's all subjective" and "it's just a matter of opinion" seem inadequate. Once they provide the definitive, unqualified, final word, there is no way to countenance a judgment that the path of

Rieux is better than that of the pea-shifting man or of Cottard. Examined critically, a phrase like "it's up to the individual" can be understood as conflating two positions that need to be kept separate: (1) it *is* up to the individual to stake out a path; (2) it is *not* up to the individual whether the selected path is better or not. Claim (1) asserts the need to elect among options. This is unavoidable. In Camus's novel, a plague forces the issue. Rieux, Cottard, the man-with-peas, each stakes out a path. "It's up to the individual" is, in this sense, defensible. The claim is flawed when the force of position 2 is forgotten. Then, the act of selecting one option over others automatically validates the choice. The grain of truth: it is up to individuals to select among options. The problem with overgeneralization: it is *not* up to the individual whether the selected option is the worthier one. Take lunchtime. An individual selects what to ingest. It's up to the individual to make that selection. What's *not* up to the individual: whether the particular selection is nutritious or not.

This latter position is one which Camus sensed had to be somehow preserved. He sensed how its opposite position, the totalizing "it's all subjective" formulation, oversimplified the human condition. The unqualified "it's up to the individual" position does, it is true, make things easy. It does minimize the anxiety associated with reasonable deliberation. So if relief from anxiety is the highest aspiration, then this is the path to follow. What it misses is how some activities—for example, those of Dr. Rieux and his associates—are worthier than those of Cottard and the man-with-the-peas. The stakes are higher than "boo" and "hurrah."

In his second cycle, the one devoted to revolt, Camus builds on this intuition. He has a sense that the flattening or leveling that disallows substantive judgments about the moral superiority of Rieux flows directly from nihilism. What this means, for Camus, is that maybe it's time to take criticism to the source. Since nihilism depicts ordinary lived experience as a realm devoid of operative mattering, rethinking can start with the rehabilitation of the ordinary. Perhaps ordinary experience has been artificially neutered. Perhaps if we begin with "I-and-my-circumstances," perhaps if we move away from the point of departure which asserts "man set over against an *external* world," new pathways will become possible. Within the newly opened pathways, the "boo-hurrah" approach can be revealed as simplistic and, though containing a grain of truth, flawed.

The Plague, as a narrative, could only go so far in terms of overhauling nihilism's bowdlerizing of the ordinary. As a next step, it would be important to craft a formulation which offered an alternative orientation. Such was the task of Camus's lengthy book *L'Homme Révolté*, translated as *The Rebel*. The essay created quite a stir because it precipitated a famous break between Camus and the philosophical star of the day, Jean-Paul Sartre. That break is most often presented within the context of political differences. Camus was a harsh critic of communist countries. Sartre continued to think in terms favorable to communism's positive aspirations. What I would like to suggest is that the split was more serious. It involved a major difference in philosophical anthropology. *L´Homme Révolté*, as Robert Emmet Meagher has emphasized,[1] defended a position that was absolutely anathema to Sartre, the existence of something that could be called "human nature."

Indignant Man versus Absurd Man

In *The Rebel* Camus actually challenged plenty of sacred cows (sacred cows at least for the Parisian intelligentsia). Beyond attacking Soviet communism, Camus critiqued the excesses of the French Revolution, surrealism, romanticism, and freedom as a stand-alone value. All of it revolved around a central pivot, defending the reality of "human nature." This seemed to the *bien pensants* nothing more than a ridiculous anachronism. Sartre and his crowd had tossed the notion of human nature onto the rubbish heap of antiquated thought. It was the political criticism of Soviet totalitarianism that got the most publicity, but Camus's defense of human nature opened just as deep a philosophical breach.

As we look back on *L'Homme Révolté* today, two important points need to be noted. First, the English title should be something more like *Indignant Man*. Second, because of the press-friendly brouhaha which erupted after its publication, the book's more central thread, a critique of nihilism built around a theory of human nature, was marginalized. This marginalization occurred despite a straightforward articulation in the first pages of Camus's introduction.

> We see that the affirmation implicit in every act of rebellion (*tout acte de révolte*) is extended to something that transcends the individual in so far as it withdraws him from his supposed solitude and provides him with a reason to act. But it is already worth noting that this concept of values as it is pre-existant [sic] to any kind of action contradicts the purely historical philosophies, in which values are acquired (if they are ever acquired) after the action has been completed Analysis of rebellion leads at least to the suspicion that, contrary to the postulates of contemporary thought, a human nature does exist, as the Greeks believed. Why rebel if there is nothing permanent in oneself worth preserving? (R, 16)

Aristotle had, long before, included two chapters on friendship in his lectures on ethics. Why? Because being human is neither completely plastic nor flexible. Friendship is important. Humans are social animals, and having others to count on represents an important, nonarbitrary, good. Reviving an older notion like human nature was, however, a path littered with philosophical minefields. Several decades before the appearance of *L'Homme Révolté*, a German philosopher undertook the task of providing a serious analysis and defense of human nature. Recognizing the presence of the intellectual minefield, Martin Heidegger in his *Being and Time* (1927) explored human nature without using those words. Instead, he spoke of a special kind of being, which he called *Dasein*.

Camus seems not to have been impacted by Heidegger. One result: Camus held on to the traditional expression "human nature." He did so, however, while remaining within the framework of the Great Bifurcation. Many years later, Mary Midgley could, in defending "human nature," insist that "We are not, and do not need to be, disembodied intellects. We are creatures of a definite species on this planet, and this shapes our values'" (Midgley 1978, xxii). Camus, as my analysis seeks to make clear, despite his desiderata, could not make such a pronouncement. His commitment to the Great Bifurcation, a commitment strongly inclined to accept the understanding of humans as "disembodied intellects" blocked any attempts at continuity with other natural beings. Thus, the quandary: his philosophical inheritance encouraged a "we are disembodied intellects whose unlimited forays in self-creation need accept no limitations." At the same time, his experiential inclinations encouraged him to adopt a different position: "human nature" is an expression with some traction; some of our inclinations, when fulfilled, are, because they are more consistent with what is best in our nature, more worthwhile. Camus's recognition of how *Nemesis* would be crucial to his consummatory formulations suggests that this was not just an adventitious position for him.

By the time he was composing *The Rebel*, all Camus could do was articulate some dissatisfaction with the tension between inherited philosophy and felt inclinations. What he did was impressive enough to awaken the ire of Sartre and his followers. Camus's tentative steps begin with the claim that revolt emerges from somewhere. It stems from taking umbrage, feeling indignation in the face of transgression. The indignation, in turn, is not just a subjective attitude, not just a version of "boo, I feel this is bad." It results from a judgment that something is objectionable, not simply distasteful. There is, as Camus claims, "a reason to act." Thinking this through leads, ultimately, to a suspicion that the ancient Greek belief, "a human nature does exist," deserves a new look.

The Myth of Sisyphus had followed more closely the philosophical principles of the day, that is, generalized indifference resulting from the Great Bifurcation and its denial of human nature. The second word in the expression, "nature," was automatically suspect for humans defined in opposition to "nature."

The steps Camus took may have been tentative; they may not have been as dramatic as Heidegger's reformulations in terms of *Dasein*. They did, however, move in the direction of rehabilitation. There is, first of all, some clearing up of confusions. Accepting the notion of "human nature" did not mean being committed to narrow teleological claims like humans are by nature selfish. It did mean, though, moving away, tentatively, but substantively, from claims like "humans are strangers who find themselves in an indifferent world." Camus could not yet embrace a *Nemesis*-friendly formulation, one more consistent with the rise of ecology, that humans are at home in this world, one for which they are made. What accepting human nature could mean at this second stage is that indignation need not be understood as radically subjective. What it can do is justify a fitting response to an indignity. The indignity is really an indignity because it is a violation of something central to human flourishing. Because we are not calculating machines programmed for infallible certitude, all such claims can be contested. What is important is the recognition that such a claim would make little or no sense if humans were completely open-ended, completely malleable, with no central array of proper aspirations.

This shift brings ramifications with it. If there is a "human nature," as opposed to initially malleable, autonomous self-creation, then mattering has to do with what best suits the flourishing of those situated, social, physiological, affective creatures who are human. The "absurd," it is worth recalling, arises from the contrast between the human need "for reason" and "this unreasonable silence of the world" (MS, 28). That contrast, in turn, is built upon a notion of humans as (a) essentially minds (b) radically separate from the world. The world *becomes* silent if humans are not continuous with it, a continuity implicated in the notion of "human *nature*." The world as indifferent (because humans, as epistemological spectators, have been artificially segregated from it) provides no guidance for intelligence. It provides no such guidance if a particular understanding of the human condition is taken as basal: that humans are essentially minds wholly detached from natural conditions and thus having nothing of nature about them.

Camus, now in his second cycle, is seeking to articulate his own intuitions rather than echo the dominant ideas of his time. In this regard he worries about how the intellectual soil identified as crucial by Nietzsche, that of nihilism, does foster the germination of dangerous cultural flora. Nihilism suppresses hope and dismisses the notion (important for a Camus who lived the horrors of Nazi occupation) of "limit" (R, 282). If intelligence cannot really fathom differences that make a difference; if normative considerations do not make the attempt of sorting out which differences make a difference, how and when, then the consistent conclusion is clear and problematic: "it is a matter of indifference to kill when the victim is already condemned to death" (i.e., there is no difference between dying now by murder and dying later of old age) (R, 283). To these more intellectual formulations from Camus, I would add the comparison of characters in *The Plague*. If there are no factors in the lifeworld that provide clues for intelligence, then nothing beyond a subjective, emotive "hurrah" supports the judgment that Rieux's life activities were the worthier ones

In the all-or-nothing world abetted by the Great Bifurcation, the boo/hurrah attitude is the only game in town. This position is reinforced by recognition that a fundamental demand of the Great Bifurcation can never be met. No human or company of humans will ever arrive at a perfect mathematical-type proof that Rieux's life was the more worthwhile one. Such judgments will always remain contestable and contested. The assumption that intellectually justifiable means absolute certainty is both a philosophically inflected demand and a practical impossibility. In the all-or-nothing world, if absolute certitude is demanded for knowing, and that certitude is absent, then what remains is the "or, " that is, mere opinion, arbitrary, subjective preference. The wide swath in-between, the swath that includes making a strong, reasonable, thoughtful case, is simply dismissed outright. Abstract purity must rule. The messier, more nuanced, more muddled approaches of intelligence and reasonableness (*razón vital*) are summarily dismissed. The human has, via philosophical presuppositions, been sequestered from the natural realm. (There is no human *nature*). The not surprising result: the realm of experienced life becomes one of an *internal* cogito spectating an *external* world. The external world, in turn, is understood as totally neutral and indifferent. It becomes a realm of mere "facts," one in which this term acquires an innovative, segregated, de-contextualized meaning. "Facts" in the new semantic landscape are envisioned as "indifferent."

This notion of indifference is one way in which the second cycle envisioned by Camus, that highlighting "revolt," differed from the first, centered on the "absurd." With *The Plague*, and *L'Homme Révolté*, indifference moves from an unquestioned assumption to a problematic, question-encouraging one. The issue is not just a matter of labels.

Indifference and the kind of "revolt" Camus favors are, quite simply, incompatible. Or, at least incompatible if evaluations go beyond the "boo/hurrah" variety. Righteous indignation depends on *noting* differences that make a difference and then *responding in light of what has been heeded*. Such discernment leads to "revolt," that is, efforts that seek to repair what is broken. The trajectory moves according to a certain pattern: (1) taking umbrage in light of differences that make a difference; (2) following up with responsible action. This is the pattern of Tarrou's "true healers." It is also a pattern that cannot thrive in the landscape of nihilism.

This is so on a very basic level: differences do make a difference. It is important to make an effort at sorting out which differences make a difference, how, and when. Black market profiteering during a plague is not only different from the effort at healing; the difference comes with an evaluative valence: one activity is better than the other. In addition, this "better" does not mean much if it simply indicates an arbitrary emotion-laden predilection. When the whole setting is taken into account, when the world is not treated as "external," when the imposed solvent of nihilism is not applied, the milieu of which humans form a part can only with difficulty be thought of as neutral or indifferent. It is true that divine commands are missing, true also that perfect rational intuitions into the nature of the good are nowhere to be found. But, only within a philosophical rulebook mandating "either/or" does their absence entail subjective relativism. The presence of middle ground, once automatically rejected, has become more congenial to twenty-first-century individuals who are familiar with ecological assertions like "carrying capacity" and the physiological processes of homeostasis.

Camus's worry is that once the nihilistic solvent has been applied, difficulties, especially of the theory/practice sort, emerge. With the memory of the Nazi takeover still fresh, there is little, Camus worries, to safeguard against the human tendency of moving beyond limits, of breaching the optimal range, of death-dealing. "If our age admits, with equanimity, that murder has its justifications, it is because of this indifference to life which is the mark of nihilism" (R, 6).

The Ascendancy of Nihilism

Because "nihilism" is the main target in *L'Homme Révolté*, it is worth revisiting a few key themes. The first has to do with devaluing ordinary experience. To prepare the soil for nihilism, some major an*nihil*ation had to take place. Worth, value, optimal culminations, ideals are all purged from the interactive nexus of ordinary life. Indeed, interactivity itself is excised. The Great Bifurcation encourages a basic isolation: the human as mind set over against a world as matter. Such a bifurcation suggests that if values and ideals exist, they must be housed in some mind (either an absolute Mind or after the death of God, human minds). Such a rendition is why Nietzsche believed that religion, setting all values in a supernatural world and its divine command morality, was nihilistic. Since the everyday, interactive realm had been shorn of meaning and value, these could only come from another source. That source, traditionally, had been depicted as a divinity laying down rules the way a dictator would. For a long time the fragility of such an all-or-nothing scenario went unnoticed. Once the "all" was gone (with the death of God), humans were left with "nothing," or at least nothing but "boo" and "hurrah." Ordinary life experience had been eviscerated. No guidance could be expected for deliberations seeking to distinguish better from worse.

The second theme follows this absence of guidance. Responsibility becomes an empty honorific. The lifeworld (before it was discredited) stood as a realm in which responsibility (making commitments on the basis of solid but not infallible considerations) was hard to avoid. This meant that risk and anxiety were also unavoidable. Humans, though, are masters at developing strategies for avoidance. Divine commands offer one technique. Apodictic rational certainty provides another. Skepticism offers a third. In each of those cases, responsibility, which requires thinking to figure things out, is minimized. Two of them (divine commands and apodictic certainty) simply proclaim that the proper answers are already there, just waiting to be espied. The last one (skepticism) says there are no objective answers, so making one's own meaning is the only option. All three strategies highlight a highest ideal: eliminate anxiety.

Camus, sensitive to these modes of evasion, offers some preliminary moves toward Tarrou's "third way." What that third way would look like is not clear. Several criteria, though, stand out.

- It must be willing to welcome qualifications and lived tensions, saying both "yes" (in a way) and "no" (in a way).
- It must avoid seeking solutions that come from divine commands.
- It must avoid the illusion of attaining, via rationality, absolute certitude.
- It must avoid formulations that echo the dilemma-demanded option: *either* absolute, uncontestable certitude, *or* mere opinion.
- It must avoid the "boo-hurrah" simplification.
- It must locate the third way within the context of concrete human experience.

Camus, in exploring what a third way might entail, thinks he can get help by returning to the ancients. The Greeks did not consider the world to be indifferent. It was a mix of active forces. Humans were players within that mix. There were also gods, many of them. The whole system exhibited a sort of moral grammar or ontological cybernetics. The grammar or the cybernetic processes, though operative, were (somewhat) flexible, open to historical changes, not always clearly understood, and generous in allowing modifications. Nonetheless, the communication and feedback loops were operative. Because the loops were, to some degree, flexible, they would not best be made manifest in enunciated commands, whether of the philosophical or religious sort. They would be best manifested by exemplars, good and bad, in history/stories (the French word *histoire* combines both meanings).

Prophets, sages, and soothsayers spoke truths, but, unlike the sponsors of cold rationality, they spoke in enigmas. Their utterances were not like orders to be met by submission and obedience. They necessitated a human response, if only to figure out what the utterance meant. In other words, they initiated a story. Such stories involved flexibility, differences, contingencies. Still, they (think *Nemesis* here) would work within functioning boundaries. Such boundaries were real enough that egregious transgressions were met with negative consequences. When the boundaries had been transgressed in a major way, say a son killing his father and then marrying his mother, begetting children/siblings by her, the cosmos itself was affected. Then, as in *Oedipus Rex*, a plague might descend on the city, an indication of how, contrary to the dictates of the Great Bifurcation, the human, the natural, and the normative were inextricably interwoven.

The implication for the central concern of *The Rebel* is this: in such a world, nihilism makes little sense. The intellectual climate inherited by Camus had altered quite significantly from that of ancient Greece. By the early twentieth century, nihilism was not only possible. It, as Nietzsche had foreseen, provided the default inherited framework. The denigration of the ordinary had become so sedimented that a prophet like Nietzsche had to use all his rhetorical talent to highlight how problematic it was. One sign of how entrenched it was is how both friends of religion and friends of secularism took the denigration of the ordinary for granted. For the former it assumed the form of divine command morality; for the latter, "boo-hurrah" ethics. Different as the positions were, they shared a key assumption: the annihilation of mattering, an annihilation that turned the lifeworld into an external arena filled with neutral, value-free objects. A difficult challenge was thus set for Camus: seeking a third way. Nietzsche had helped by dismissing the God of divine command morality. The next step was to prove more challenging: getting contemporaries to give up their deeply held anti-essentialism and to accept something like the moral cybernetics of the ancient Greeks. Could such a step succeed?

Rehabilitating Human Nature, I

Camus's answer was "yes," a "yes" it took him almost 400 pages to explore, explain, and defend. His defense would turn, as we saw earlier, on the issue that had been famously sent to the rubble heap by Jean-Paul Sartre, the notion that there is such a thing as "human nature." Camus does not address Sartre's position directly, but the latter's popular talk *Existentialism Is a Humanism* offers a handy foil. In that talk, Sartre included what has become a well-known example. A son, living in occupied France, faces a difficult choice: whether to stay home and care for his mother or go off to join the Resistance. Sartre's advice: choose for yourself.

Sartre has constructed this particular problem to suit his polemical, anti-essentialist aims. Specifically, it is constructed to (a) diminish the importance of intelligence trying to figure things out and (b) emphasize how values are contrivances that accrue to decisions in the act of deciding. The story's overarching moral: to choose is *not* to select on the basis of intelligence, experience, cultural values, and differential valuation. This would be to forfeit freedom. Rather, to choose is to make a declaration on the order of "thus I will it." We create our values, "invent" them in the act of choosing. Sartre's advice is unequivocal: "You are free, so choose; in other words, invent. No general code of ethics can tell you what you ought to do; there are no signs in this world" (Sartre 1996, 33).

This is impressive as a test case. However, flaws emerge once we alter some details. Suppose the young man were interested in collaborating with the Nazis? Would Sartre, in that case, have given the same advice? Hopefully not. A better approach: ask the young man to think things through, that is, to pay attention (a) to the entire context, (b) to signs and indications, (c) to consequences, maybe even (d) consider some principles inherited from ethics, and (e) keep in mind that there are always borderline situations in which decisions are especially difficult. Such an alternative, emphasizing responsibility over autonomy, draws attention to a thick sense of interactive embeddedness, one that would avoid the shortcut of "invent."

Sartre's recommendation to "invent" combines two aspects that, as we saw earlier, need to be kept separate. First, there is the "subjective" or idio-centric dimension. This recognizes the individual's active role. It says "you are the one who needs to commit to a resolution." This dimension is properly emphasized. Then comes a stronger claim. "Invent" means "as you select among options, you are fashioning the very criteria that guide the selection." This dimension takes the individual out of the ancient Greek orbit Camus wished to reinstate. It makes humans little gods formulating their own divine command moralities. It sterilizes ordinary experience. It accepts "boo-hurrah" ethics. It reinforces nihilism.

For Sartre, any hint of "human nature" represented a limitation on freedom. It would mean having decisions determined by preexisting normative criteria. For Camus, the situation was not that simple. He specifically contrasted "revolt," which he favored, with "total freedom," which he criticized. The latter could easily slide over into license. Total freedom, without any qualifications or countervailing forces, offered a path for sidestepping responsibility. It could morph into a *carte blanche*. "Invent" brings with it no restrictions. It is thus different from *la révolte*. Rebellion is suspicious of the imperialistic reach of total freedom. It works within the more complex setting of republicanism. Values emerge from the condition of humans in the world. They are plural, and, Greek style, values have to be balanced off against one another. Rebellion puts total freedom "up for trial" (or "on trial," I would translate) (R, 284).

To this we could add the comments of Mary Midgley about how the isolation and metastasization of a single ideal, even an important one like freedom, poses a threat to other values: "It has spread itself to cover the isolation of the individual from all connection with others, therefore from most of what gives life meaning: tradition, influence, affection, personal and local ties, natural roots and sympathies, Hume's 'sentiment of humanity'" (Midgley 1978, 288). Camus, sensitive to Midgley-style concerns about disconnecting oneself from care, affection, and attachments of all sorts, worries that the notion of total freedom means removing oneself from the arena where normative benchmarks apply.

Midgley has, in addition, well articulated how the acceptance of human nature need not be understood automatically and wholly impinging on freedom. "The notion that we 'have nature,' far from threatening the concept of freedom, is absolutely essential to it. If we were genuinely plastic and indeterminate at birth, there is no reason why society should not stamp us into any shape that might suit it" (xviii). Camus put it more dramatically, paraphrasing his philosophy teacher Jean Grenier: "absolute freedom is the destruction of all value" (R, 288, note 2).

The dismissal of human nature and the sequestered apotheosizing of freedom not only allow the sidestepping of responsibility. They also, this repeats a theme from earlier in the chapter, represent an excuse for avoiding the difficult work of thinking. The guiding rule is straightforward: maximize freedom, invent values. "Invent," charts out a path that is a lot easier than "work things out in relation to context and evidence." The former claims to be allied with freedom and, for Sartre, with responsibility. Those would be good things. In reality, the "invent" position is linked (a) to the "absolute freedom" that accompanies the "destruction of all value" and (b) allows a detour around the serious thinking that would normally define intelligent responsibility.

7

Reflections on *The Rebel*, II

Sade as a Test Case

The considerations surrounding responsibility that ended the previous chapter offer an explanation for why Camus spends so much time (R, 37–47) discussing the Marquis de Sade (1740–1814). Sade is kind of a poster boy for the excesses of Modern thought. He worked within a particular semantic landscape. It revolved around two key pivots: (1) the priority of "I am" (as opposed to the more attentive-to-circumstances "we are") and (2) commitment to a single overriding value, absolute freedom. The first separates him from fellow beings. It makes it easier to treat them as "objects" to be manipulated and used. The second provides unrestricted leeway for such manipulation and use. What behavioral cluster emerges? A single desire considered (a) in isolation from the concerns of others (b) is judged to be good (the individual says "hoorah"), and (c) its free exercise is considered as unequivocally proper. A famous passage from Sade exemplifies this conjunction (the primacy of self, subjectivity of valuation, absolute freedom).

> A man who would like to enjoy whatever woman or girl will henceforth be able, if the laws you promulgate are just, to have her summoned at once to duty at one of the houses; and there, under the supervision of the matrons of that temple of Venus, she will be surrendered to him, to satisfy, humbly and with submission, all the fancies in which he will be pleased to indulge with her, however strange or irregular they may be, since there is no extravagance which is not in Nature, none which she does not acknowledge as her own. There remains but to fix the woman's age; now, I maintain it cannot be fixed without restricting the freedom of a man who desires a girl of any given age. (Sade, 130)

A passage like this raised alarm bells for Camus. Exaggerated as it may be, it marks out, in practice, the culmination of ideas that have become central. A level of disquiet about that culmination leads to a further consideration: maybe it is time to examine the context which gave rise to this particular cluster.

Camus, living at the time he does, still works within the primacy of "I am." Despite recognizing its limitations, he has not shifted to a paradigm which would move decisively in an ecologically sensitive direction, one that would move beyond "boo/hurrah" morality. The primacy of "I am" as untouchable leaves "absolute freedom" as a target. Sade's understanding of freedom is straightforward, simple, and without nuance: to be free is to act out, in an unimpeded way, whatever desire or inclination is felt. Ancient Greek polytheism with its concomitant pluralism of values had once provided an alternative to the isolation of freedom from other goods. Because there was a multiplicity of goods, optimality had to be discerned by working out the best mixture, the best balance. Such a balance would limit the absolutizing of any single good.

But balance, moderation, and limits were, though admired by the ancients, dismissed *en bloc* by the Moderns. Camus, going against the contemporary tide, finds inspiration in the ancients. Such inspiration should not be translated into simple importation of Greek notions. Camus is a denizen of the twentieth century. He has to undertake his own balancing act. With Nietzsche, he accepts that God is dead. In one sense, then, Camus and Sade share some common ground. Neither believes in a God who sends down absolute commands. Beyond this overlap there remain real differences. For Sade, fully immersed in Modernity, the self, newly liberated from divine commands and standing apart from natural patterns of goodness, is self-defining in its newfound emancipation. A direct, unencumbered path is blown open for the encumbrance-free realization of one's inclinations. In terms of abstract consistency, the new Modern package made a kind of sense: eliminate human nature; isolate freedom as the highest good; live a life that aims, above all, to maximize one's individual freedom.

The pattern manifested in Sade will form a template for the various positions criticized by Camus. Several themes run through his critique.

- The notion of maximizing a single good needs to be countered by a more ancient goal, that of seeking an optimal balance among multiple natural goods.
- Thinking in terms of an optimal balance suggests that, if "optimal" is not to be just an arbitrarily imposed term, something like a normative cybernetic system must be accepted.
- Nihilism, because it rejects any version of such a moral grammar, has to be overcome.
- The apotheosis of freedom is attractive because it provides shortcuts; it eliminates, from the beginning, the difficult, fallible work associated with acting responsibly, the work of deliberation, dialogue, and investigation.
- Absolute freedom, unburdened by the limits associated with the need to balance a cluster of values, translates into the cult of efficiency. "Thinking" loses its older meaning and comes to be understood as "instrumental rationality." The main task of mental activity becomes that of identifying the most efficient means to achieve whatever aim has been proclaimed.

Each of these identifies a component of Camus's challenge to nihilism. If we want to understand *L'Homme Révolté* as the important philosophical text that it was, Sade offers a good point of contrast. He helps highlight what is crucial to the Camusian position: replacing the imperialism of a single value by the republicanism of multiple values, values that have to be kept in proper balance. "Limit" becomes an important technical term. For the anti-essentialists, "limit" was automatically pejorative. It could only be understood as a restriction on absolute freedom. For Camus, "limit" is honorific. It delineates the proper human ideal: finding the right measure or balance among a cluster of values.

A setting which admits of an irreducible cluster of values need not dismiss freedom. What happens rather is that, as the generative philosophical landscape changes, so do the connotations of terms. When "freedom" means the capacity to select among options, intelligence becomes not a liberty-reducing factor but an important cooperating factor. The scenario of Buridan's ass is recognized as exception rather than rule. Intelligence, as examination of evidence, provides guidance as one deliberates on how to make the best selection among options. In the "all or nothing" context that gave support for absolute freedom, "guidance by intelligence" is understood as a form of freedom-constricting determinism. The will, on this view, cannot be absolutely free if it is susceptible to the influence of intelligence. It certainly cannot be totally autonomous if the deliberations of intelligence, deliberations which guide free choice, have to do with criteria, exemplary cases, historical precedents, consequences, benchmarks associated with human nature.

Supporters of the absolutely autonomous will can repeat over and over how freedom and responsibility are linked. In practice, an emphasis on the autonomous will has, effectively, disconnected the two. Here is where the pairing of autonomous will and responsibility faces a challenge. So long as there are no criteria operative apart from the act of choosing, there are no measures for determining whether one is acting responsibly or not. Responsibility becomes little more than an arbitrarily imposed honorific label. It's "responsibility" free from the anxiety of fallibility. All it demands is honesty on the order of "yes I admit having chosen this way," a version of *adaequatio mentis secum*.

Responsibility in a stronger, fuller sense can best become functional when the possibility of error is real. That condition comes into play when intelligent examination of evidence works in concert with the ability to select among options. In that case there is neither shortcut nor simplification, no advice just to "invent," no elimination of fallibilism and anxiety. Instead, the promoted path encourages thoughtfulness. Freedom, as an integral component of a flesh and-blood human (i.e., not of a disembodied mind), means taking on the responsibility of trying to discern how best to optimize the conditions for a fulfilling life. Such freedom, when allied to responsibility, necessarily brings risk with it. Getting the balance of values right is never the matter of a simple algorithm. Identifying boundaries and limits presents a challenge. In a world that takes balance, measure, and limits seriously, failure is always possible. All decisions are contestable. This is the setting within which responsibility, in the fullest sense, becomes a genuine concern. If we invented our own guidelines, the possibility of error, and the anxiety associated with responsibility, would vanish to nothing.[1]

Rehabilitating Human Nature, II

The anxiety/responsibility/risk interplay becomes important for the Camusian emphasis on revolt/indignation. There are many occasions when it is appropriate to challenge the status quo. Often, these involve a perceived injustice. A behavior is recognized as unjust when it, without proper justification, impedes factors fundamental to a fulfilled life. As counterintuitive as it may seem, emphasis on freedom can serve oppression, as the case of Sade attests. At least this is so if (1) absolute freedom is established as the single dominant ideal, and (2) a particular class believes it alone gets to exercise absolute freedom in light of a particular goal.

Without any limits or factors to counterbalance it, absolute freedom easily morphs into the power of rulers to do what they will, especially if they believe themselves to be new high priests in possession of absolute truth. Using the dominant example of his day, Camus says that Hitler and his minions were aided by such a faulty notion of freedom. They were not burdened by annoying ethical considerations. They had identified the proper structure of the state, and the only considerations that mattered were the instrumental ones relating to efficiency. They did not realize that "real freedom is an inner submission to a value which defies history and its successes" (R, 186). Although the general orientation of nihilism denies the reality of values, this denial works best, as we have seen, in the realm of theory. In practice what happens is quite different. Traditional values are backgrounded, and different ones move to the center. The newer values tend to be instrumental: expediency, power, quantitative measures of success.

When Camus speaks of "a value which defies history and its successes," he is using "history" in a sense made possible by the Great Bifurcation. "History" stands for the human realm, completely separated from "nature." "History" is the realm in which the "thus I will it" attitude dominates. Contours, boundaries, limits are thought to be mere conventions. When a ruling class believes itself to be in possession of an absolute truth about the direction of history, the results are catastrophic. That group then considers itself to be perfectly free to take whatever steps are necessary to bring about the utopia promised by the arrow of history.

To counter such a total instrumentalization of thought and valuation, along with the very real horrors they entailed, Camus proposed a more mundane approach, one he believed represented a revival of ancient Greek thought. Theoretically, it rejects radical voluntarism (the imperialistic absolutization of will and freedom). In practice, it promotes the path highlighted in *The Plague*: become "true healers." Camus's kingdom is always a kingdom of this world, of the here and now. True healers relieve suffering and make this world a better place. The absolutizing of freedom ("thus I will it") and the fantasy of utopia ("thus the absolute movement of history wills it") both ignore "nature" and the guidance it provides. Embracing "human nature" means, at the very least, putting a dent in nihilism.

Recognizing "human nature" is a move that encourages a kind of freedom allied to, not independent from, intelligence. It accepts how fallibility, anxiety, and approximations form part and parcel of the overall package of accepting responsibility. Freedom as the ability to elect among options is not diminished when it follows the guidance of reasonableness. A disembodied *cogito* can envision a self-enclosed, encapsulated abstraction called "freedom of the unguided will." That abstraction, as envisioned, is easily tarnished. Its purity can be contaminated, for example, if, in any way, it subjects itself to influences from the outside.

Appalled by what he experienced during the Nazi occupation, outraged by what he sees happening both in Stalin's Russia and Franco's Spain, Camus responds as the intellectual that he is. He aims to articulate a general orientation in which the defense of justice-freedom-fairness is more substantial than a declaration of "hoorah." Since dominant *theoria*, guided by nihilism, insists that there is no rational foundation for evaluation, he begins by stressing *praxis*. The rebel targets what is happening on the ground: mass killings, incarcerations, police state, secret police, informants, the hunt for "heretics," tight control over what can be published or taught. Righteous indignation is the first step. Beyond that, for beings endowed with intelligence, comes an important requirement: the need for a reasonable account justifying the indignation and the response it engenders.

Nihilism, at this point, raises a stop sign. But it's a stop sign with some allure. It says: stop thinking, take the easy path, be a slacker and a shirker. After all, you will never provide a perfect, absolute, infallible account. Evaluations are *just* subjective. In *The Myth of Sisyphus* Camus gave voice to such an all-or-nothing position. Now, in his new cycle, that of revolt, things get more complicated. He seeks out third ways. Maybe there is room for accounts that, while not apodictic, while contestable, are nonetheless reasonable, intelligible, defensible. What Camus insists on, and what sets him in opposition to Sartre and his followers, is that such reasonableness requires the rehabilitation of "human nature." "True healers" in the moral and political realm are analogous to those in the physiological realm. The aspirational end-state, health in one case, a good society in the other, are not just inventions of the imagination. Their contours have to be established by utilizing intelligence and experience. Neither is a pure human projection.

Rejecting the rigid *either/or* approach, Camus, early in *The Rebel*, acknowledges that with revolt, as with medicine, there exists both a nay-saying and a yea-saying dimension. The one seeking improvement, like the physician, begins with the awareness that something is amiss. This involves "a value judgment in the name of which the rebel refuses to approve the condition in which he finds himself." Camus goes on to explain that such a diagnosis depends on awareness of a standard. Without such a standard, without a "common value, recognized by all as existing in each one, then man is incomprehensible to man" (R, 23). As is often the case with Camus, this assertion includes an overstatement. In this passage it is the hyperbolic "recognized by all." This is not always the case. Only within the parameters of Modern philosophy and its Great Bifurcation was it a mandate. "Widely recognized," or "generally part of an inherited tradition," or "based on a reasonable assessment" would be more adequate.

Despite his exaggerated way of making the claim, Camus's point remains valid. Like his beloved ancient Greeks, like Plato, for example, certain moral Forms (norms we might say), though not perceptible to the senses, have to be admitted as having some kind of reality and as being operative. They are more than socially created prejudices. We might never be able to grasp perfectly, infallibly, what, say, justice, love, or friendship is, but their status as lures, occasioning thoughtfulness, is real and actual. Real and actual at least for that friend of the ancients, Camus. *The Rebel* wishes to emphasize the operative force of such values. Without them, as he witnessed with Fascism, and is witnessing with Soviet communism, even intelligent people can justify oppression. Even worse, murder on a massive scale can actually be condoned. Camus, in the opening pages of *The Rebel*, identified such justification as "logical crime." His essay, he announced, was to "examine meticulously the arguments by which it is justified" (R, 3).

Actually, its aim involved not just examination but criticism. It is in developing his criticism that Camus comes to realize how crucial is the controversial notion of "human nature." Without it, value judgments revert to the "boo-hurrah" category. He worries that within the inherited philosophical climate, a commitment to intellectual purity has overridden lived experience. "Ideology," he proclaims, has triumphed over "psychology" (R, 131).

To be fair, it's not just ideological purity which dismissed "human nature." Some defenders of the notion were also responsible for its poor reputation. This is where philosophical reflection, especially attentiveness to definitions and distinctions, becomes important. The issue turns on exactly what is, and what is not, meant by "human nature." The shortcut/simplification temptation does not just afflict anti-essentialists. It also afflicts supporters of human nature. In this latter case "human nature" becomes a polemical weapon for narrow social and political ends. One thinks here of rigid, old-guard types repeating "you can't change human nature." There are also those for whom "human nature" has an automatic, specific, one-dimensional, narrow, sense. For example, there are Hobbesians who think humans by nature are uniquely selfish. There are also Freudians who think that the single driving force behind all human behavior is the sex drive.

Such positions occasioned a reaction. At its most pronounced the reaction was embraced in Sartre's slogan "existence precedes essence." There is no human nature, no "essence," no fixed definition imposed by an outside designer. A knife, a pair of shoes, a coffee mug—these have essences in the sense that their makers had a predetermined idea of aim and function before bringing them into existence. They have no flexibility, no say in the matter. Humans, though, are without such a designer. And, if God does not exist "there is at least one being in whom existence precedes essence—a being whose existence comes before its essence, a being who exists before he can be defined by any concept of it. That being is man, or as Heidegger put it, the human reality." As such the individual man will "not be anything until later, and then he will be what he makes of himself." The only possible conclusion: "Thus, there is no human nature" (Sartre 1996, 22).

This presents an attractive take on human life. It offers a needed counterbalance to the narrow sense and oppressive use of human nature. But is it an overreaction? Isn't it a position better suited for disembodied spirits than for physiological, social, affective, historically, and culturally conditioned humans? Once again, the sensible, balanced position is articulated by Mary Midgley. In a dramatic pronouncement, she asks: "Why is no one living in the Republic of Plato?" (Midgley 1978, 56). One explanation is that humans are not disembodied minds who can define themselves in any way they envision. As affective and physiological beings, humans, for example, manifest special feelings and affection for their own children. Plato's ideal state, seeking the most efficient way to create leaders, disallowed parents from even knowing who their own children were.

The flaw in this arrangement is a version of what Camus called ideology triumphing over psychology, a utopian scheme riding roughshod over the human condition. Humans as physiological-affective creatures have special feelings, "like our strong and special affection for our children." These, Midgley continues, "are not just loose facts about us; they are the sort of thing that constitutes our central good" (Midgley 1978, 76). Midgley is here engaging in important claims about human beings. Are her assertions absolute, universal, apodictic, infallible? No, there will always be exceptions, always qualifications and distinctions to be made. Within an all-or-nothing framework, exceptions would discredit, entirely discredit, the general claim. That framework entails what might be called the "tyranny of the counterexample"—one exception (say a longtime smoker who remains healthy) and the entire claim is dismissed.

When we move to *razón vital*, thinking gets loosened up. A particular claim is not perfectly universal? There are exceptions? In that case, an examination and an explanation are called for. The fact of exceptions does not warrant dismissing entirely the assertion. A disembodied mind, treating Euclidean geometry as the unique model, can insist on absolutely certain, exception-free claims. *Razón vital* opens up a large swath of middle ground. Statements that are generally true or true for the most part are now welcomed as helpful in achieving an adequate take on things. That articulations can be contested does not mean they are to be unconditionally dismissed.

Moving beyond the all-or-nothing mandate also means leaving behind the fixation with a single, unitary trait which, Hobbes and Freud-style, is thought to identify *the* feature which defines human nature. But, *pace* Hobbes and Freud, there is no need to fear pluralism and multiplicity. Humans are complicated creatures. Why insist on oversimplifications? Midgley suggests thinking more in terms of clusters. Pure minds might prefer the purity of a foundational unit. The lifeworld is more generous. "Natural states," Midgley explains, "evolve as part of a whole."

> They do not, unless something has gone wrong, compete to take over entirely; each of them has some limits. What is *natural*, in fact, is never just a condition or activity—inquiry, say, or a space around one, or sexual activity, or playing with children—but a certain *level* of that condition or activity, proportionate to the rest of one's life. (Midgley 1978, 79)

Midgley's formulation overlaps with what Camus has envisioned under the symbolism of *Nemesis*. Midgley's way of phrasing it insists that (a) the components of the cluster have "some limits," and (b) the appropriateness of any activity is relative to a "certain *level* . . . proportionate to the rest of one's life."

Camus did not formulate his position as carefully. He did, like Midgley, draw attention to the notion of "limit." He did this with great rhetorical persuasiveness in his 1948 essay "Helen's Exile." The same motif formed, a few years later, the intellectual spine of *The Rebel*. Camus had serious qualms about anti-essentialism as too extreme a position. When he wrote *The Rebel*, much of the intellectual establishment would have disagreed. Today, things are different. In the field of psychology, for example, Jonathan Haidt has criticized the once dominant, overly rigid either/or stance. That stance pronounced a fixed dilemma: innateness versus social construction. The metaphorical formulations, "not wired" versus "hardwired," left no room for a third position. But it is just such a third position, thinking in terms of being "prewired," that best resonates with human experience. "Prewired" suggests some organization "in advance of experience." At the same time, it highlights how, unlike "hardwired," it does not mean "fixed and immutable." "Prewired" evokes some initial preconditioning but a preconditioning with plenty of room for flexibility and change (Haidt, 130).

Camus's own take is rooted more in ethics than in psychology. Specifically, his perspective grows out of a very concrete repugnance toward injustice and evil. An individual in revolt can be *righteously* indignant. Indignation need not be thought of as *merely* subjective. It can result from attending to evidence. That evidence can provide ingredients for a reasonable account supporting the judgment that the lifeworld falls short of conditions that promote more fulfilling, flourishing, significant lives. And "more fulfilling, flourishing, significant" are meant to be terms with substantive heft, a content correlated with an admittedly loose, tentative, somewhat vague yet still normative notion of human nature.

Sade, as Camus realized, offers a good test case. When a Sade insists that it is always wrong for a female to refuse him, that he can enact his freedom and force himself on her, the indignant man's reaction need not be random and based on some version of "I personally don't approve of what you are doing." It can be justified by providing an account that is intelligent, reasonable, and accepts the dignity of the female and the difference between desired and desirable. Such an account, Camus believes, will involve accepting that, integral to the human condition, some modes of behavior are better than others. Those modes, as Midgley indicated, will typically involve a balanced exercise of dispositions in proper proportion to one another. The better modes, better balanced ones, promote culminations constitutive of human well-being. They recognize how humans are social. At the same time, humans, as history reveals, don't always get the commendable/abominable distinction right. The temptation in that case is to go the lazy route, seek a path that minimizes effort, go for a totalizing pronouncement. Come up with a snappy slogan: existence precedes essence. This is the temptation Camus's book urges us to resist.

Camus's specific target, absolute freedom, could blossom in a landscape dominated by the disembodied *cogito*. Persons were no longer characterized as embodied, historically, and culturally situated beings who must work out the best, most measured combinations. In attempting to achieve such optimal combinations, embodied, situated, encultured individuals do not take the attitude of "thus I will it." They invite the cooperation of intelligence. For the disembodied *cogito*, such cooperation is tantamount to denial of autonomy and self-determination. Instead of conceiving of persons as integrated selves, the *cogito* prefers descriptions in terms of separate, buffered units. It favors a "faculty psychology." Differing modes of functioning are reified as separate faculties: intellect and will being the most prominent. Such a hypostatization prepares the ground for setting the two in opposition. The ability to select among options becomes *free will*, and free will becomes what St. Augustine called the *liberum arbitrium indifferentiae*. The "will" maintains a detached, indifferent stance to external factors. That is what makes it free.

As aware as he was of the limitations and dangers associated with absolute freedom, Camus could not take the necessary next step: set up a new paradigm. Pointing out anomalous instances associated with the old paradigm was about as far as he could go. His Mediterranean self, the one which luxuriated in lived experience, moved him in one direction. His academic, philosophical training (Michel Onfray pejoratively called philosophical education "formatting") drew him in another (Onfray, 87). In *The Myth of Sisyphus*, the two tendencies ended up in a draw. In *L'Homme Révolté*, the experiential, lived sensibilities begin to take the upper hand. Camus is not yet capable of articulating a philosophical position which will do what needs to be done: remap the territory in a way that breaks with the Great Bifurcation and moves toward a more ecological, interactive, sensibility. Still, while hanging on to his Mediterranean temperament, he begins to take important steps toward an altered framework. Those steps begin with an important realization: partial truths, false dilemmas, simplifications, and shortcuts do not match the complex richness of the lifeworld.

Worries about an Overdone Plot

What results is Camus's Mediterranean-inflected *pensée de midi*. This represents his attempt to move beyond the mismatch between his Mediterranean sensitivities and his academic formatting. Seeking a third way, Camus tries (a) to provide an account of the challenges, limitations, and dangers associated with nihilism and (b) to defend how overcoming nihilism requires embracing something like "human nature." This is the conceptual side of his argument.

There is also another side, one attentive to how humans situate themselves within certain plot lines. One specific plot line needs to be addressed and be altered. The plot in question offers a special challenge. (1) It is so taken for granted that it goes unnoticed. (2) It serves to impede the kind of criticism Camus needs to undertake. One of its major defects is how it reinforces the triumph of nihilism. What is the plot line? It's a scenario made prominent by an earlier North African, St. Augustine. The pivot around which the scenario turns is a theme Camus will highlight in his later work: *The Fall*.

The plot is straightforward enough. History can be divided into three epochs: an initial idyllic state, a Fall, and the subsequent need to reestablish the initial state. In terms made famous by John Milton: Paradise; Paradise Lost; Paradise Regained. In Camus's time, the most prominent manifestation of the pattern could be found not in a religious setting but in a political one, that of communism. The final, communist, stage of history was to be one which overcame the previous eras and their flaws. History moved in a progressive direction. The necessary final stage had been identified by Marx and Engels.

Despite differences as regards religion, Camus insists that Communism and Christianity share something in common. At the same time, the overlap is what separates this unlikely couple from the ancient Greeks. The dividing line is the progress-assuming, tri-partite reading of history. Such a reading considers human life and the "course of events as a history that is unfolding from a fixed beginning toward a definite end" (R, 189).

Camus might also have added that the Greeks were polytheists. This discouraged them from seeking always a single source or single foundation or a single goal. It encouraged rather a sense of inevitable multiplicity and the coordinate ideal of harmony rather than unity. Plotinus (205–270), it is true, would both emphasize a primordial unity and be a great influence on St. Augustine. In turn, Augustine would have a great influence on the trajectory of Western thought. Plotinus might be considered a Greek philosopher since that was the language in which he wrote. Still, he lived well after what is called the classical era associated with Athens. He was born some 600 years, yes 600, after the deaths of Socrates (470–399 BCE) and Sophocles (496–406 BCE). In the older climate of opinion, the one bathed in polytheism, multiplicity, and plurality were just givens to be taken for granted in grasping how things were. In the post-Plotinian, Augustinian-influenced world, unity was apotheosized in ways that made multiplicity and difference automatically pejorative.

Golden age stories would always be around, but for polytheists it was difficult to envision the process of history as that which began as an original unity, got contaminated as it fell away from this unity, and was in the process of an eventual, necessary restoration of unity. By contrast, worship of a single divinity, whether Jehovah or History, tended to encourage two interrelated simplifications that concerned Camus: (a) history is headed in a definite, preordained direction, and (b) if you are not with us, you are against us. "a" and "b," taken together, provide ample justification for the persecution of heretics and counterrevolutionaries. Those two groups are obstructions that must be eliminated as history moves to its pre-appointed goal.

All of this can be wrapped in an unspoken and unacknowledged blanket, what Camus called, reinforcing the Marxist-Christian connection, "collectivist messianism" (R, 70). It is important at this point to keep in mind how Camus followed Nietzsche in identifying Christianity as a locus of nihilism. It had situated all values in a transcendent realm, annihilating the value dimensions embedded in lived experience. "Christianity believes that it is fighting against nihilism because it gives the world a sense of direction, while it is really nihilist itself insofar as, by imposing an imaginary meaning on life, it prevents the discovery of its real meaning" (R, 69).[2] Such an evisceration of the ordinary remains a point of overlap between Christianity and Communism. Both have to be messianic. The opportunities and possibilities for here-and-now reform are rejected out of hand. In practice, this justifies a chase against "heretics," the elimination of those who "objectively" are in error and "objectively" are preventing the purified/rarified community from attaining its realization.

This is where a nuanced understanding of human nature plays an important role. The nuanced understanding would include the following: (1) humans come into existence with many dispositions; (2) unlike animals with innate abilities, human dispositions come to full realization only via cultural practices (i.e., humans are not hardwired but rather prewired); (3) cultural practices, at their best, aim at bringing to culmination those dispositions most conducive to flourishing; (4) the phrase "most conducive to flourishing" indicates a range that allows for variations but has boundaries; (5) the phrase "most conducive to flourishing" is real but never perfectly understood or articulated. This means finally that (6) it serves a constant prod to ever-ongoing reflection.

Such a cluster is why "philosophy" means the *search* for wisdom. It has to be an ongoing quest. It does arrive at helpful formulations. William James (1842–1910) metaphorically referred to these as bird-like "perchings." Such perchings, though, will soon be realized as inadequate in some ways. Philosophy will, once again, have to engage in "flights" (James 1890, 243). One reason the search arrives only at tentative, not perfect, "perchings" is the complexity of the *what* in question. *That* there is a human nature offers the lure which makes of philosophers ongoing searchers. Or, more exactly, the combination which accepts a *that* yet realizes how the *what* is too complex for any philosophical formulation to be perfect and final. Such a that/what combination brings out the importance of Ortegan irony. "Human nature," in its nuanced sense, thus serves as an ongoing prod to reflection. In this way it differs from both the extreme positions: "human nature has already been figured out" and "there is no such thing as human nature." Each of those tends to thwart rather than encourage thinking. Shortcuts and simplifications are always tempting, but "human nature" will always remain a prod to questioning and reflection.

In a similar vein, a nuanced notion of human nature need not be opposed to freedom. A thinker like Sartre can make the dilemma-driven pronouncement that freedom can only be present in the absence of essence. For him, the absence of essence, of human nature, has a unique meaning. It signifies that there is no preordained mold into which one is expected to fit. Without such a single mold, humans, unrestrained by limits, are radically free. The notion of a range which allows flexibility while retaining limits is not considered.

Camus, on the contrary, links total freedom with totalitarianism. Totalitarians need the assumption of complete malleability. The notion of human nature is, for them, inhibitory. Camus says it directly. Totalitarians combine "a negation and a certainty, the certainty of the malleability of man and the negation of human nature" (R, 237). When humans are understood as little more than raw material, "political realism" takes the form of an "unbridled Romanticism, a romanticism of expediency" (R, 237). Expediency, not constrained by having to think about what is consistent with human thriving, is then released from all bounds. "If there is no human nature, then the malleability of man is, in fact, infinite" (R, 237).

It is one thing to criticize overly narrow, restrictive, and conservative notions of human nature. It is quite another to deny its validity altogether. Such a denial provides a wonderful gift for dictators: individuals as pure plasticity, just raw materials to be shaped as directed by those in totalitarian control.[3] In general, the positions Camus is criticizing are those with a penchant for grandiose, totalizing generalizations. His differences with Sartre go deeper than disagreements about Soviet communism. Camus challenges the philosophers who escape to the more neat, more clear, realm of conceptual abstractions.

They are more comfortable in the realm of neat conceptual abstractions than in the complicated world of ordinary life. From their lofty perch they send down grandiose pronouncements: existence precedes essence; freedom is total or it is nothing. In the world of ordinary life, liberations of talent, enhancements of justice, relief from suffering, result from a particular combination: (1) an understanding of human nature that gives guidance to liberation, justice, and the relief of suffering; (2) reformist actions which actually make a positive difference in the lives of people; (3) solidarity, working with others; and (4) a realization that such activities take place in a mixed, not a pure world, one in which clusters of values must be properly balanced, not one in which a single value imperialistically overrides all others.

The disembodied *cogito* can readily think of itself as a mirror. Absolute certitude is then envisioned as a perfect, direct reflection in the mirror of what is the case in the external world. Unalloyed reflection guaranteed by the absence of interference between the external world and the mirror becomes the guiding ideal. When the "initial Paradise; Paradise lost; Paradise regained" template is added, the totalitarian drive is well in place. The new high priests, in direct contact with the Truth, are then justified in eliminating all obstructions to the foreseen ideal condition. Truth as only accessed via intermediaries, signs, hints, clues is dismissed as anxiety-producing and certainty-evading. Direct access to truths skips over the role of mediating instrumentalities.

Camus, once again going against the Modern grain, wishes to rehabilitate the notion of mediating agencies. This is a point that can be missed by reading only the English translation of *The Rebel*. In a major misconstrual, the translation does not recognize the French word *médiations*. For "mediations" it substitutes a word with an additional letter. The one letter change is quantitatively minor but semantically major. The translation renders a key passage as "a world and a method of thought without *meditation*" (R, 288, my emphasis). Camus is not suggesting that his *pensée de midi* is allied to "meditation." This could reinforce the detachment of the disembedded *cogito*. Rather his *pensée de midi* accepts embeddedness. Such embeddedness is characterized by the prevalence of *mediating* intermediaries. The thought at midday does not dream of a perfect, final, definitive matching of image in mirror and object in world. That scenario has little to do with everyday life. In the realm of the here and now adequacy of ideas works via mediations. Direct presence is a dangerous fantasy. What has to be struggled against, for Camus, is "world and a thought without *mediations*" (HR, 356, my translation, italics added). A world in which mediating factors will always be present is one of approximations, of better and worse, of spectra and continua.

An intellectual landscape which envisions direct presence and absolute certitudes will resist accepting a notion of human nature and what it brings with it: physiology, embodiedness, mutual dependencies, subjection to factors outside our control. "Human nature" also brings with it the constraint of limits. Going against the grain of what was prominent in the philosophy of his time, this combination of human nature and limits is exactly what Camus sought to revive. "If, on the other hand, rebellion (*la révolte*) could found a philosophy, it would be a philosophy of limits, of calculated ignorance, and of risk" (R, 289). The dream of absolute certitude is replaced by human inquiry and the fallibilistic (calculated ignorance), revisable (risk-accepting) conclusions it reaches. The flight from responsibility is now much harder to undertake. The disembodied spirit could take refuge in absolute certitudes modeled in Euclidean geometry. The Mediterranean, more natural, self accepts the middle position, neither that of absolute certainty, nor that of ignorance. Risk-taking, accepting responsibility for decisions that could be mistaken, becomes part and parcel of the middle realm, one in which humans make do with the best, most reasonable accounts.

Disembodied cogitos favor shortcuts, simplifications, direct access to certitudes (which are then confused with truths). Camus's expression *pensée de midi* is unfortunate in one way. It suggests via its highlighting of the midday sun, a perfect, enlightened, discovered once-and-for-all realm. It suggests a standard bifurcation: either the darkness of night or the full sunshine of midday. Camus would have done better to stay with his emphasis on mediations as defining the concrete experience of which philosophy must take account. *La pensée de médiation* would better bring attention to the living realm of mixtures, complexities, and contraries that must be held in tension.

Mediation brings us back to physicians and the intermediate role they play. For the physician it makes little sense to think in terms of the tri-partite plot: initial paradisiacal state/Fall/utopia of paradise regained. To invent an initial condition free of diseases is to engage in pure fiction. As *The Plague* insists in its last, anti-utopian, paragraph "the plague bacillus never dies or disappears for good" (Pl, 308). Dr. Rieux could have added, in an anti-Eden formulation, that "the plague bacillus *has always been with us, will always be with us.* There is no final resting point. There has always been, there will always be a demand for *hommes révoltés*." Along the way there will be reprieves, fragile times when human effort brings together a situation in which harmony, justice, freedom, health, and other central ideals achieve some conjoint realization. Those, however, will be fragile and imperfect. Reform will always be called for. There was no initial paradise. There will be no utopia. There can, though, be "better than what we have now," a better only made real if indignation is transformed into the right kind of action.

8

The Fall

The Plate Glass of Indifference

The Myth of Sisyphus contains a memorable image: a man in a phone booth. From the outside, Camus explains, his gestures offer little more than a "dumb show" (MS, 15). Camus uses the image to illustrate the "denseness" and "strangeness" that characterize the absurd (MS, 14). The phone booth scenario, memorable as it is, does not really offer the support Camus envisioned. It succumbs to an easy criticism—open the door, listen to the conversation, get to know the man, and he will seem less dense and strange. Regardless of its weakness, the image remains crucial for Camus's characterization of the absurd. We have already seen how the transformation of humans into epistemological subjects, spectator-minds standing apart from the push and pull of the life world, is a preliminary move. Its appropriate image: a glass partition separating the onlooker from the world. Once so separated, the world can seem dense and strange.

In addition to a metaphor involving the eyes, Camus also adds one involving the ears. Humans long for "happiness and for reason." That longing is met by "the unreasonable silence of the world" (MS, 28). Such is the contrast that defines absurdity. Camus's metaphors (pane of glass, silence) reinforce each other. If we envision ourselves as outside spectators separated from life events by an imaginary pane of glass, then what is beyond that partition will remain silent. More accurately, and as a criticism, the world *will have been silenced* by our self-transformation from participatory co-actant to detached spectator.

Camus's Cartesian heritage makes it difficult for him to give up this spectator-scenario. It will always remain something basic, a starting point for reflection. He remained committed, as I keep emphasizing, to a philosophical landscape which promotes sharp divisions. The ear-related imagery identifies a major one. Humans speak; the world does not. Indeed, this is the case. But it is the case in a very narrowly limited way. A false dilemma is made central: either *human* language or *silence*. If such were the choice, there would be little work for scientists. Their efforts are motivated by a different assumption. True, the world does not speak human languages. This does not mean total silence. In more positive and more formal terms, the world is pan-semiotic. "Semiotic" here indicates a milieu abounding in various forms of signs, signalings, indicators; in short, a world replete in information. A pan-semiotic setting is one in which humans participate in communicative networks of multiple sorts.

Let's take a simple example. Planning to make mushroom risotto I start by foraging. When I find mushrooms, they do not, in good English, say, "no, don't pick us, we're poisonous." At the same time, thinking in semiotic terms, the mushrooms are not completely silent. With the help of mycologists I can identify hints, indicators, clues, signs that these are not the kinds of mushrooms my family and I should be ingesting. Switching the image, something similar occurs when females (of the mosquito sort) are drawn to me out for a morning walk. Moving along jauntily, I breathe. Carbon dioxide sends a signal: blood supply nearby. If the walk is vigorous, I sweat. Another tip-off. My very movement also sends a signal. The mosquitos and I do not speak a shared language. Nonetheless, I'm a veritable font of semiosis, sending out signals, differences that make a difference to mosquitos needing blood for their eggs. Pronouncing the world to be silent can make sense. But it makes sense if and *only* if we think strictly in terms of human languages. The world is not silent in the sense that it is completely outside the realm of communication. Quite the contrary. It is, as the philosopher Michel Serres has put it, a vast interlocking system of communication, a vast *messagerie* (Serres 1995b, 12).[1]

We miss all of this when we set up some kind of plate glass between ourselves and the rest of our habitat. We tend to forget that our habitat is the living world *in* which, *by* which, *with* which, and *on account of which* we survive. When such prepositions are ignored, our habitat becomes little more than a literal "surrounding" or "setting," even "environ-ment" if used etymologically. Such terms indicate a kind of separable backdrop, that which is around yet disconnected from the subject who is at the center. The status of our milieu as a kind of atmosphere in which and by means of which we live is forgotten.

Without the plate glass divider, the lifeworld is abuzz with semiotic energy. With the plate glass divider, we get a Meursault. Mattering, semiosis, salience, differences making a difference—all of that gets bracketed. The result: a subject on one side and, on the other, the "external" world. With the partition in place, the semiotic dimension, prioritizing situatedness, inter-dependence, participation, and information, is excised. Once the semiotic dimension is eliminated, meaning gets severely restricted, a restriction that extends, ultimately, even to human language. A young woman asks, "Do you love me?" A neighbor asks, "Will you write a letter for me?" Neither utterance, for the disengaged self, carries much meaning. Initially and basically, they are sounds uttered by one subject and received by the other.

To enter a different philosophical landscape, the entire situation (I-engaged-in-dealings-with-my-circumstances) would have to be recognized as having ontological primacy. As soon as that primacy switches away from lived situations and turns instead toward "spectator-subject" receiving impressions from external units, meaning fades away. The insulated subject, as if behind a pane of glass, is free to treat the received impressions as indifferent, free to impose his own meaning on them. The utterances are not calls for which there are better and worse responses.

If we switch the context and introduce something dramatic, say a plague, then it is not so easy to preserve the glass partition. Events (I-engaged-in-dealings-with-my -circumstances) are not neutral occurrences in an external world. Nor, despite my reformulation, is "I" central. Any actual situation is characterized by "we." When the basal conditions of human existence are characterized by "we-engaged-in-dealings-with-our-circumstances," it becomes harder to envision indifference and the *ça m'est égal* attitude as prominent. Responses to indicators from the world are not all *égal*. Better and worse mean something substantive (think here of the mushroom example). *The Plague*, in this way, draws readers away from the realm of generalized indifference that was depicted in *The Stranger*. Would the next fictional work split the difference? Would it side with one or the other of the previous novels? Would it move in an entirely new direction? Much is at stake as we approach *The Fall*.

Moral Fallibilism Is Real

When we get to *The Fall*, we are presented with an individual who, Meursault-like, treats all signals, indicators, and clues as neutral. They are not calls occasioning a better or worse response. At the same time, Clamence is no Meursault. He willingly plays the social game. He is a lawyer who helps the downtrodden. Yet he has no respect for them. His mantra is straightforward: "I, I, I" (F, 50). He admits, openly, his self-love (F, 58). When he crossed the glass partition, it was in order to pretend goodness. Afterward, he returned to his insulated security as a subject standing apart from the outer world. From that setting, others are little more than objects for his use ("I used to mobilize so many people in my service" (F, 68). Any goodness is just pretense. Cries for help, conveniently blocked by the partition, go unheeded.

Until one night. That night, the assiduously preserved partition does not hold. It's midnight. Clamence has just left a female companion. He feels good. He is happy. Crossing a bridge he notices someone staring into the river. Having gotten to the other side, the silence is broken. He hears something. It sounds like a body splashing into the water. Then comes a cry, repeated over and over, fading in the distance. Now the silent world returns, but the silence seems painful, interminable. He feels the urge to do something. Then, rationalization kicks in: "Too late, it's too far . . . or something of the sort." He keeps to his path home. He tells no one (F, 70).

His external silence cannot, however, quiet his internal thrum. The event shakes him, haunts him. His rigidly disciplined life, one dominated by aloofness, safeguarded by the glass partition, has been disturbed.

Comfortable in self-enacted detachment, he should be cushioned from calls of distress. His name may be "Clamence," but for him the only clamoring that counts is his own. Any other clamoring is upsetting—especially if it takes the form of a call or an appeal. Calls or appeals disturb. They raise the level of anxiety. They clamor for a response. Responding is not only annoying and disturbing. It also requires differential evaluation. Some responses will be better, others worse. For the indifferent spectator, insulated behind his partition, "better" and "worse" are subjective impositions. For someone in the midst of things, someone who hears the cries of a young woman drowning, it's different. Now it's harder to go the *ça m'est égal* route.

So long as the universe does not speak, aloofness is protected. No responding, that is, no responsibility, is called for. When calls abound, when one is an enmeshed, involved participant, then detachment and equanimity are replaced by disquiet. The plate glass divider does not really create a neutral world. What it creates is one in which there is a highest value: undisturbedness. The plate glass of indifference brings, for the subject, a great benefit: equanimity, quietude. Remove the partition and responsiveness (accompanied by perturbation, interest, care, and risk) becomes rule rather than exception. The bridge scene as crafted by Camus is masterful in the way it indicates how difficult it is to maintain the illusion of indifference.

In the preceding novel, Camus had forced the hands of his characters. A plague becomes everyone's business. Camus created a different context for Clamence. There is no plague. It's a pleasant night. When the call comes, he is the one within earshot. He ignores it. What's the big deal? Within the confines of the Great Bifurcation there is no big deal. The universe is silent. Sounds, even human words, might be transmitted, but nihilism has leveled them, transformed them into neutral sounds. A plea for help? Just phonemes floating through the air. Such data bits are not calls demanding a response. Global equivalence, general leveling, and thus universal indifference rule.

Still, it's not that simple. Clamence, now outside the self-isolating barrier of indifference, confronts options. What is he to do? Call emergency services? Try to help directly? Ignore the sound and move on? Each of these options, within the framework of nihilism, is equivalent to any other. Opting for one or another, for an individual committed to absolute freedom, is up to the *liberum arbitrium indifferentiae*. There are no good reasons, certainly no compelling ones for opting one way rather than another. If there were, they would only mitigate, limit, downgrade one's freedom of choice.

Neutrality of evidence and subjectivity of choice together create what turns out to be a highly valued condition for the epistemological subject: preserving both undisturbedness and absolute freedom. The bothersome, burdensome work of figuring out the best response can be set aside. What we can call "nihilistic moral infallibilism" becomes operative. Whatever option is selected becomes, by virtue of being selected, appropriate. The very word "choice," now situated in the semantic landscape of nihilism, alters its connotation. It once meant "election among options guided by good reasons." Its semantic center now becomes "thus I will it." There are *no reasons* which guarantee the superiority of opting one way or another. Because absolute certitude is absent, one choice is as good as another. Armed with this notion of "choice," one understood as "thus I will it," the notion of erroneous response disappears. Clamence should be free of disquiet.

Yet Clamence cannot shake the distress occasioned by this event. Should he have responded differently? Could "better" and "worse" actually mean something? The philosophy of his time says "no." It's all just "boo" and "hurrah." Although this story is not called *L'étranger II*, it could be. Clamence envisions himself as an outsider. All around him, life seems like little more than a game. His calling card identifies him as a "play actor" (F, 47). This simplifies things. He can make his way in the world without worrying about better and worse. All he needs to do is undertake the role he chooses to play today. "Thus I will it," in other words, should sustain him. Today, generous helper of the oppressed. Tomorrow, defender of the status quo. Nothing is serious in any deep sense. Life is mostly a game (F, 86, 87). It's all role-playing. All options are on the same level. And why not? There is no infallible guarantee that one mode of comportment is better than another. Nihilistic moral infallibilism is both well-sedimented and self-satisfying.

Theoretically, at least. But there is a major difference between Clamence and Meursault. The plate glass of indifference was, in the bridge scene, shattered. Despite what should, given his philosophical plate-glass presuppositions, be the case, Clamence continues to be haunted by the woman in the Seine. He refers to the scene as the evening when he was "called" (F, 84). This particular call and his response mean that he will be troubled in two ways that will upset his highest ideal of undisturbedness. First, the inevitability of judgment (F, 76–7). Second, he will have to reconsider whether freedom is more a chore than a gift (F, 132). Freedom, as *liberum arbitrium indifferentiae*, once served as license to opt however he pleased. Now, as a mode of responding, it has morphed into something fearful (F, 136). Absolute freedom, accompanied by nihilistic infallibilism, was comforting. It disallowed the judgment of others. Now, having experienced a moment outside the walls of self-protective indifference, things have changed. Fallibilism is real. His ideological predilections and his scheme of values might proclaim that he should not be bothered by his actions. Nonetheless, he is bothered.

Recapitulation: Building up to *The Fall*

Who is Jean-Baptiste Clamence? His name reveals much. He is a prophet (John the Baptist) in the wilderness. His clamoring ("Clamence") is meant to announce something in the future. At the end of his narrative, he longs explicitly for a "gospel," or, as he literally puts it, for "good news" (F. 145). At the same time, he wishes his clamoring to be the center of everything. He's all clamoring and no listening. Listening to others would be a form of servitude. He identifies with Lucifer, the one who rejects any type of dependence. "I sit enthroned among my bad angels" (F, 143). His self is neither consistent nor integrated: do-gooder by day, debauchee by night. He lives a neatly compartmentalized, thus simplified life. This fantasy of simplification helps relieve the burden of responsibility. It also reinforces other tendencies associated with the Great Bifurcation: the "all or nothing" attitude; formulations in either/or terms; a primordial neutrality; the neo-Stoic ethical ideal which identifies a good life as one of maximal equanimity.

Some commentators, notably Olivier Todd in his Camus biography, have read *The Fall* as Camus coming to terms with his own life. The focus here is on his marriage, one in which he was far from a faithful, attentive husband. For Todd, Camus is admitting his flaws and regretting the way he treated his wife who had bouts of severe depression for which she was hospitalized. The woman in the Seine, in this telling, is Francine (Todd, 342). *The Fall* can then be read as an allegory, offering a kind of one-to-one parallel between fiction and life. Such a reading is suitable when the task is autobiographical. It is less so when, as in this book, the task is philosophical.

Attentiveness to Camus as a searcher after wisdom is my focus. Such a focus is why my analysis explores how each work contributes to the search. For Camus the quest revolves around, apologies to the reader if this is getting too repetitive, challenging nihilism. Camus, as he stated in his Nobel address, allied himself with those who rejected nihilism and had undertaken "a quest for legitimation" (ESS, 1073).

That quest was made difficult for Camus because he continued to work on the dyadic foundation provided in his *Myth of Sisyphus*. That foundation presupposed something he never quite set aside, the Great Bifurcation. Unpacking the elements implicated in this bifurcation would allow recognition of its guiding orientation: set up a plate glass of indifference; pretend the universe is silent. In a more detailed fashion, this orientation is built around several key claims: (1) the primacy of "I am" (rather than "we are"); (2) the separation of the "I am," the subject, from the "external" world of objects; (3) the "I" in "I am" is mostly a mind seeking absolute, irrefutable answers (a flesh-and-blood type would be satisfied with well-documented, well-reasoned beliefs); (4) the world is silent (rather than a dense network of call and response semiotics); and (5) humans are thought to be outsiders, alien-like, strangers in a strange world (rather than beings who are where they belong, in the habitat which is their proper home).

The "we are strangers" construal both underlies and pervades the early stage in Camus's thought. It provides an image which supports (a) the diagnosis of absurdity, (b) the acceptance of nihilism, (c) the silence of the world. This silence is consistent with the belief that nothing (*nihil*) in the world provides signs, indicators, clues, hints for intelligence. The outsider then looks onto a world that is both "external" and "unintelligible." Such an outsider, as an epistemological subject, feels "wild longing for clarity." But as an alien, he is disappointed in finding that he has been deposited in "this unintelligible and limited universe" (masculine pronouns preserved to capture the Camus position) (MS, 21).

How are we, in the twenty-first century, after the advent of ecology, to take this blanket claim of a world that is "unintelligible"? The very word "ecology" points us in a different direction. And doubly so. Its two components indicate an intelligent way of speaking (*logos*) about our home (*oikos*). It neither thinks of humans as aliens nor of the world as unintelligible. As is often the case in evaluating Camus, the problem is with a partial truth passed off as a complete one. The main flaw in Camus's exaggerated claim can be identified by attending to the suffix "ible."

Possibility ("potentiality") was, for Greek and Medieval thinkers, an integral constituent of existence. Post-Renaissance thinkers, seeking to streamline things, thought rather, here is a familiar theme, in terms of either/or. In this case, it would be *either* full clarity *or* total absence of meaning. The middle ground of experimentation, working with our surroundings to get a better sense of how they work, is left out of the mix. Such a middle ground would violate the rules of the Great Bifurcation. It would insist on the primordiality, not of subject set over against objects, but of the interplay between engaged and therefore curious inquirers and the world replete with information which the inquirers seek to explicate.

A successful experimental scientist, for example, seeks to move from the puzzling to the settled. Take the biologist Claude Bernard. He worked within a context in which there was much puzzlement about sugar, blood, diabetes. In response to one popular hypothesis, Bernard jotted into his notebook: "Is this true?" This question prodded him to undertake experiments. Those experiments led to a surprising outcome: sugar need not be ingested to be present in the bloodstream. The liver is glycogenic. It produces sugar on its own (Jörgens).

What counts in relation to Camus is that Bernard does not say: no one knows, no one can know with absolute certitude, therefore, the world is unintelligible. Quite the contrary. His assumption is that the world is intellig*ible*. The investigator/world setting is an in-between one. Livers do not come with placards on which is written: "we are glycogenic." At the same time, the investigator/world context is rife with possibilities. Movement from the puzzling to the settled is achievable. But only (1) if there is lots of interplay between investigators and their surroundings, and (2) there is a prior belief that the world is, to a great degree, at least, intelligible. To proclaim, as does Camus, that the universe is not intelligible is to ignore the efforts of people like Bernard. It is to accept the ideology of all-or-nothing.

To claim that truths do not parade around in self-evident fashion is one thing. To proclaim that the universe is not intellig*ible* is quite another. Running the two assertions together, as does Camus, is an occasion for confusion. It is also what keeps the hypothesis of absurdity locked in place. Rethinking the full ramifications of intelligibility does not appear to have been on Camus's radar screen. The baseline set in *The Myth of Sisyphus* (a pure mind demanding self-evidence, set off against a universe that does not provide immediate and total apodicticity) is one which endured.

To his credit, as he moved on from his earliest works, he grappled with difficulties associated with this assumption. Chief among them was an incompatible combination: making value judgments as if they were meaningful, yet believing that such judgments derived only from subjective preferences. As indicated in Chapter 5, *The Plague* is the narrative in which this tension is most forcefully presented. It suggests that Rieux and his volunteers are acting in a manner that is worthier than others. Such a suggestion was as far as Camus could go. At least, he could go no farther so long as he remained committed to his base position: the human-in-this-world setting is "absurd." Perfect awareness is demanded but not provided. Thus, the world is not intelligible. If this is indeed the case, then the work of intelligence is stunted. When it comes to evaluative judgments, all that remains are "boo" and "hurrah."

L'Homme Révolté attempted a bold step. Camus there made the case that we must accept something like "human nature." There is some teleological nexus at the heart of being human. We are not free-floating spirits whose good can be constructed in any way we wish. The morphology of the human condition is such that some activities and projects are better for human flourishing. Aristotle, as mentioned in Chapter 6, was willing to claim that even a rich man needs friends. His *Nicomachean Ethics* devotes lengthy sections to friendship as a key (not arbitrary, not just subjective) ingredient for a good and fulfilling life. That humans need friends is, for Aristotle, not an adventitious comment about us. Such a claim is both defens*ible* and intellig*ible*. It is defensible if there is something like human nature. It is intelligible if the world is not a surd.

The Fall: Something Is Amiss

This is the point where *The Fall*'s place in the Camusian corpus can be grasped. *The Plague* depicted generous-spirited, compassionate individuals working in solidarity to repair a broken world. In theory, they may well have been bathed in the nihilistic atmosphere which makes one response as good as another. In practice they acted as if better and worse provided real qualifiers. The theory/practice inconsistency is both recognized and left (theoretically) unresolved.

The Stranger, by contrast, had depicted a main character who lives out, as much as possible, a theory/practice consistency. The general atmosphere, again, is one in which differences do not *really* make a difference. All value judgments are matters of subjective predilection. Indifference is basal. Living this out, Meursault's behavior is anything but admirable. Reading *The Stranger* in the twenty-first century, we can, as I suggested earlier, read it as a *reductio ad absurdum*. It might be an inadvertent *reductio*. Still, reading it after the major philosophical, historical, scientific changes in the late twentieth and early twenty-first centuries, we can be excused for seeing it as a wake-up call. For those of us who are no longer bound by the Great Bifurcation, who recognize the limitations of authenticity ethics, who recoil at the evil of Auschwitz, who accept that this world is the proper home for humans, and who then judge Meursault to be defective in important ways, the story urges us to take a good look at the ingredients of an intellectual climate that would culminate in a character like him.

In *The Fall* we get a purposeful, not inadvertent, *reductio ad absurdum*. The story blends components of *The Stranger* and *The Plague*. Like characters in the latter, Jean-Baptiste Clamence engages in good acts. Like Meursault, Clamence has no real moral compass. Any such compass would constrain and limit his *liberum arbitrium indifferentiae*. Unlike Meursault, Clamence is willing to play society's games. His good actions, though, do not emerge from a consistent axiological nexus. His heart is not really in it. Unlike the heroes of *The Plague*, he has no real compassion for others. He accepts the value leveling associated with a nihilistic outlook. To get along in society, he has become quite good at pretending commitment and concern. What results in the end is a kind of inconsistent mess. Jean-Baptiste veers between behavior that is admirable and behavior that is deplorable. And why not? Without a moral compass, without any tug toward a moral *polaris*, one option is as good as any other. Why not go one better than Meursault? Recognize the social game as a game, and yet play it to the hilt.

Like Meursault, and unlike *The Plague*'s volunteers, Clamence is an isolated unit, a solitary self. Conjoint projects demanding solidarity are not for him. He is a bubble-wrapped self, disconnected and insulated from his surroundings. His notion of freedom entails release from all constraints. It demands complete autarchy. "Me, me, me" is an ongoing theme. "It is not true, after all, that I never loved. I conceived at least one great love in my life, of which I was always the object" (F, 58). Social solidarity of any sort is superficial, transitory, contrived. More importantly, it brings with it a kind of responsibility, a freedom-limiting responsibility. When he is going to have sex with the wife of a friend, Clamence merely tells himself that the two are no longer friends (F, 58–9).

It's not only that solidarity is minimized. Clamence is someone for whom solitariness has been hypertrophied. You want radical disconnection, Camus is saying, you want radical autonomy as freedom, okay, you will get it. How? The entire text is a monologue. The narrator has supposedly fastened onto an interlocutor, but even this auditor may be nothing but an imagined double, the simple projection of Jean-Baptiste himself. The "interlocutor" is about the same age as Clamence. Both are "sadducees" (F, 10). Jean-Baptiste, toward the end of his narrative, confesses a special affection for the "other," who, as it turns out, mirrors him in occupation, both being Parisian lawyers (F, 147). When the "other" "speaks," it is typically in indirect fashion. Most of what we learn about what the interlocutor supposedly said comes from Jean-Baptiste's rephrasing. One of the final commentaries is especially telling. Clamence admits that often we simply engage in speaking, "constantly talking and to no one, forever up against the same questions" (F, 147). The entire novel is an exercise in solipsism, a monologue whose speaker just does not listen.

As such it is also an exercise in evading obligation. The word "obligation" carries within it the root verb *ligare* to bind. Conversation, especially listening, heightens a sense of connection. If listening is blocked, then so too are connection and obligation. One result: escape to a realm of pure self-satisfying autarchy. Listening can only upset the undisturbedness sought by the autarchic individual. It messes with the fetish of absolute autonomy as freedom. The one who only clamors, who does no real listening, is one who spends his life burnishing and thickening the lamination that encapsulates him.

With *The Stranger*, Camus, based on his own comments, aimed at depicting someone admirable in his authenticity. We, today, might judge him as deplorable, as a *reductio ad absurdum*. With Clamence, things are different. Clamence is the work of an author who is engaged in ongoing reflection. As I have tried to indicate, Camus was caught in a bind. He had serious qualms about nihilism. At the same time, he continued to maintain attachments to the general context which gave rise to nihilism: the Great Bifurcation. What results is, in philosophical terms an *aporia*, a setting from which there are no exits. All Camus can do is draw a character living within the inherited landscape. With *The Fall*, he sends a clear message. Something is amiss. A prophet is clamoring. There needs to be change.

Why the need for change? Clamence is the poster boy. His world is that of "boo-hurrah" ethics. Help the downtrodden? Sure, why not? I feel like doing that now. Plus, it makes me look good. Engage in debauchery. Sure, why not? I feel like doing that now. Plus, it brings me immediate pleasure. The world, after all, revolves around me. I speak, the world does not. I utter monologues. Dialogue is not for me. Listening, for sure, is not for me. Autarchy and undisturbedness are the highest goods. If absolute freedom takes me in conflicting directions, well, that's fine because my preferences change. All around me, everything is little more than a game. I can remain aloof, undisturbed.

Manipulanda, Indifference, Call and Response

Clamence is honest about his zig-zagging. He's a be-true-to-yourself, *adequatio-mentis-secum* type after all. The role of noble humanitarian pleased him for a while. Then, a shift: time for demolishing that image. He continued to use the word "justice," but publicly inveighed "against the humanitarian spirit" (F, 92). Then, another reversal support for the humanitarian spirit. What's going on? Society demands role-playing, and Clamence is willing to oblige. This works fine if one is nothing but a play actor. Otherwise not every role is suitable. Unless one's main guiding principle is absolute freedom as *liberum arbitrium indifferentiae*. Then, one is liberated to undertake any role one wishes. What counts is that they must be understood strictly as roles being played.

Take love. Society and its games give pride of place to love. This one is particularly dangerous if it is not kept within the bounds of game-playing. Love involves interdependence and commitment. It identifies one particular individual as special. In other words, it stifles freedom. It curbs the exercise of desires. It requires removal of the laminate, the protective barrier that protects against entanglements. It makes difference, not indifference central. It necessitates listening. It's not for him. His life, monologic and insulated, is one in which he loved no one and nothing but himself (F, 100).

Debauchery, by contrast, is consistent with total freedom. Nothing about it endangers the lamination. "Debauchery," Clamence says, is "liberating because it creates no obligations" (F, 103). Nothing about it entails constraining entanglements and accountabilities. Debauchery thrives on indifference. This particular individual or that one, the differences are irrelevant. One trait counts: suitable partner for an orgasm. The bubble-wrapped self is a detached subject, seeking with maximal freedom to satisfy impulses. Beyond the bubble-wrap, there are only objects. Objects become, in turn, *manipulanda*, things to be manipulated, used, and then, in good consumer-society fashion, discarded.[2] Clamence gives utterance to the fantasy of others as *manipulanda* via a telling image: individuals stored in a refrigerator. They are thus always at hand if he wishes to use them (F, 68). Since the subject is the only one who speaks, there is no listening. Maybe the "things-stocked-in-the-refrigerator-for-my-use" are not all that happy with this status. Maybe, if the autarchic self took time to listen, he would realize this. But this would stymie what a simplified understanding of freedom demands: escape from responsibility and obligation. The "I alone speak" orientation is self-serving. The plate glass of indifference remains in place. Commitment, entanglement, along with differential response, that is, responsibility, are minimized. Conversation is optional.

At the same time, there is a problem. What underlies it all, what makes it liberating is indifference. But indifference soon reveals its negative side. Generalized, it deadens life, sclerosis sets in. Using an image with major personal implications, Camus describes it in terms of tuberculosis. The spread of indifference, along with the concomitant marginalization of emotions, follows the pattern of tubercular lungs. They react protectively by drying up. As a result they kill off the human whose lungs they are (F, 106).

The situation created by the laminated self can, in a similar way, prove self-defeating. Freedom comes to mean *liberum arbitrium indifferentiae*. Such a "free will" functions best in a context of isolation and encapsulation. Some familiar themes intersect here. Freedom could mean the ability to set a path for oneself, a path selected for good reasons. It could indicate commitment and the responsibilities that accompany it. It could, in other words, be understood as a human capability, one that is integrated with other capabilities. Far from being a separate faculty locked inside a bubble-wrapped subject, it would be understood as a function of the entire person. In that case it would not be considered as a separable pod sequestered within a self. It would, rather, be operational within an event or occasion, a situation in which interaction (with natural surroundings, with other humans) is primordial.

Camus creates a challenge by putting Clamence in just such a situation, one in which the sedimented, isolationist ideas which guide his life will be of no avail. What if, instead of a promiscuity that uses women for personal pleasure, there was a cry for help from a young woman drowning? This is the wake-up call. This is the haunting scene that Clamence just cannot, try as he might, eliminate. His life was well suited to freedom as indifference, to being always the speaker, never a listener, to others as *manipulanda*, to being a laminated self. Then came the cry from the river. In an intellectual milieu guided by assumptions associated with nihilism and absolute freedom, all possible responses should be equivalent. After all, the cries were just sounds, part of the world's meaningless din. Clamence walks on, neither calling for help nor seeking directly to render aid.

As someone endowed with a *liberum arbitrium indifferentiae*, as someone in possession of autonomous free will, unimpacted by surrounding events, this response was as valid as any other. Why then, should this scene haunt him so? Here, in a nutshell, we find the predicament in which Camus was caught. His philosophy background situated him within a particular theoretical context. His practical sense pushed him toward another landscape. As honest and reflective, Camus could not avoid the predicament. What he could do: make clear there was a predicament, sound an alarm. This is just what *The Fall* does.

The Myth of Sisyphus, prototypical for Camus's first cycle, ends on the positive declaration that "we must imagine Sisyphus happy." *The Fall*, late in the second cycle, ends with an ill Jean-Baptiste. It is also a Jean-Baptiste who continues to "hear the laughter" occasioned by his indifferent response, who is "happy" only so long as he is "soaring above this whole continent" (F, 144). There are also longing and hope in the final pages: longing for a new gospel, "good news" (F, 145); hope that there is justice and he will be arrested for his theft (F, 146); and most of all hope for a "second chance" at responding to the cries from the young woman. At the same time, there is also a note of defiance. It's too late for a second chance. "Fortunately" as the last word of the book pronounces (F, 147). This word is *Heureusement*, "happily" an echo of how we are to imagine Sisyphus *heureux*. This time, though, it's not clear that the claim is to be taken seriously. It might be voiced in a mocking manner. Clamence, we know, is not happy. Maybe he really would like another chance.

Judge-Penitent: Living in a Pan-prosecutorial World

None of this, however, is about to happen. It will always be, the book's ending indicates, "too late" (F, 147). Thus, the aporia, the stalemate. Doves hover overhead. They never land. The spiritual remains sequestered from the everyday. The life story of Clamence may be unsatisfactory, but that is all we have.

The Plague had opened another path, that of solidarity in the service of good. But, in a world where all values have been leveled, there is no substantial, reasonable case to be made for favoring Rieux over Clamence. *The Fall* gives readers the obverse of what was depicted in *The Plague*. Both stories grow out of a shared intellectual landscape. Its main contours are familiar: the Great Bifurcation, the primacy of "I am," the leveling of all values, autarchic freedom. In *The Plague*, freedom to choose goes toward solidarity, repairing a broken world, devotion to a cause bigger than self-interest. In *The Fall*, it goes toward satisfying impulses. These often conflict. What if Clamence's choices as a humanitarian lawyer are out of sync with those of Clamence engaging in debauchery? Well, it's not really a problem. *Liberum arbitrium indifferentiae*. Personal, immediate inclination represents the final word. The same could be said for the differences between Clamence and Rieux. Given the sedimented intellectual landscape, no value decision can receive a well-justified warrant. It's just "hurrah" for Rieux, "boo" for Clamence.

Moving beyond "boo" and "hurrah" is, for Camus, just not possible. "Thus I will it," and "thus I will it" alone, provides the final theoretical word. Final, maybe, but problematic nonetheless. Camus worried that indifference writ large leads to a kind of practical sclerosis. Since responses are equivalent, the habits associated with humane responsiveness can wither away from disuse. Why keep alive the challenging combination (intelligence, experience, emotion, differences that make a difference) that defines humane responsiveness? Much easier to follow the "thus I will it" route. Not only easier, but also fallibility-free. So long as the monologic "thus I will it" remains the final word, the choosing subject becomes infallible. Misjudgment is precluded. Risk and anxiety are eliminated. Decisions are not reached on the basis of seeking properly to read clues from the world. That world is, after all, silent, not intelligible. "Choosing" is no longer understood as selecting among options for good reasons. It becomes, to use an outmoded word, vagarious, not guided by anything apart from internal, personal predilections. Whatever the subject selects becomes, by definition, the end point beyond which there can be no discussion. Strange as it may seem, nihilism and personal infallibility are joined at the hip.[3]

We are now in a better position to appreciate how the theme of judgment comes to play such a dominating role in *The Fall*. Nihilism and its infallibility are firmly in place. At the same time, differences, disagreements, conflicts do not disappear. In a philosophical landscape that prizes dialogue, listening, and intelli*gibility*, discussion would offer one approach to conflict. This would involve, minimally, examining reasonable accounts given for one option or another. Final agreement will hardly ever be foolproof and universally applauded. Perfect proof is the exception rather than the rule, but dialogue keeps intelligence in play. Fallibility and risk are expected accompaniments to dialogue. *Razón vital* is doing its work.

In another context, a religious one, selection and risk would take on a different form. The model would be more penitential than dialogical. Error would mean having strayed from the path of righteousness. Having strayed, a penitent could admit "sinfulness," resolve to stay on the approved paths, seek to make amends. Fallibilism and dialogue go together as do sin and forgiveness. Camus makes things difficult for Clamence by placing him in a setting in which the paths of dialogue/fallibilism and penitence/resolve are both blocked. It is, though, one in which differing views, conflict, and opposition are very much in evidence. How does it all hold together? In the absence of dialogue and penitence, not too many options are left. One remaining scheme: a society built around judgment and prosecution.

This is just the kind of society depicted in *The Fall*. It's a pan-prosecutorial one, a realm of incessant finger pointing and condemnation. Society becomes a gigantic courtroom. Everyone is on trial all the time. And why not? If personal preference is the final word, then it's just my opinion versus yours. In Medieval Europe people would have trembled at the thought of the last judgment, well exemplified in the tympana beneath which the religious passed as they entered church. Now, says Clamence, there is no need for such a far-off threat. Humans do plenty of condemning all by themselves (F, 110). In fact, with the paths of philosophical dialogue and religious grace closed, the best way for individuals to feel good about themselves is to point the finger at others. We cannot, Clamence claims, echoing the St. Augustine take on original sin, "assert the innocence of anyone, whereas we can state with certainty the guilt of all" (F, 110).

Clamence's profession, a lawyer, is telling. Accusation, prosecution, putting others in the docket, these become common social sport. The process, quite literally, is "satanic," since "satan" in the Hebrew scriptures means the "accuser" (Meeks, 752). Accusation as opposed to dialogue and reflection become the default mode of being. Indeed, within the semantic landscape of nihilism, thinking is discouraged. After all, the world is unintelligible. Within a setting pervaded by intelligibility, judgments would be made within a system of values and priorities accepted for good reasons, reasons which could be articulated and explained. In such a case the accused, even if found guilty, would at least have to admit a kind of reasonableness to it all. An adherent of the law, Clamence asserts, does not fear judgment (F, 117). In that case there are rules. Infractions can be situated in relation to the rules. Take away that sense of law, recognize "boo" and "hurrah" as the final words, and accusation takes on an excessive role. At the same time, judgment becomes the "keenest torment" (F, 117).

Judgment, *krisis* in Greek, then emerges as a real "crisis." It creates a realm of unending torment. This is the realm inhabited by Clamence. It explains why, near the end of the book, he actually wants to be arrested (F, 130). He is in possession of a stolen painting. Thus far, law enforcement has not found him out. If he were discovered and found guilty, the judgment would be painful, but understandable, that is, be rooted in more than "boo/hurrah." Arrest and punishment would fit into an overarching pattern. Such a pattern, however, makes sense only in a world in which valuation has more to support it than the vagarious "thus I will it" pronouncement. Judgment would be painful, but not the highest torment. It would be framed within a context which made sense.

Without that dimension of sense-making what is one to do? How, living in the world of Clamence, avoid the highest torment? Clamence has identified a solution. Become a "judge-penitent." In a "boo-hurrah" world, assertions of innocence can always be rejected. Someone can always be found who will proclaim "boo" for almost any behavior. With proclamations of innocence meaningless, can there be another strategy for eluding one's tormentors? Clamence's answer is "yes." Don't proclaim innocence. Much better: accept the universalization of culpability. Turn it to one's advantage. How? First, admit guilt. That way no one will accuse you of inauthentic pretense and self-deception. Second, allow your authenticity in admitting guilt help you rise above others. Finally, indicate how being in such a superior position provides a warrant for judging others. The strategy turns out to be somewhat simple: bring oneself down, proclaim oneself a sinner, and use that self-abnegation as a way of standing above others.

It's all pretense, but what counts is raw efficacy. Admission of guilt, self-criticism can serve as a strategy for (1) deflecting external criticism before it comes, and (2) situating oneself in a position of "I'm avoiding bad faith" superiority ("practice the profession of penitent to be able to end up a judge") (F, 138). Not only that, the strategy brings a psychological advantage. Pointing at others, judging them, makes him feel better about himself (F, 137).

Nihilism and total freedom were once thought to be emancipatory. No submission to outside authority; no imbroglios of entanglement, no bothersome, judgmental, moral scolds; plenty of room for tolerance and broad-mindedness. *The Fall* suggests otherwise. Judgment is neither minimized nor eliminated. Quite the opposite, it becomes pervasive.

Not only that, judgment, properly contextualized, can actually have a positive side. It can situate an individual in a world that makes some sense. As things stand, Clamence is in possession of stolen goods; he is someone who did nothing to help a woman drowning. He would welcome a judgment on the order of "you could have done better." He has regrets, even though, given his assumptions, there are no good reasons for such regrets. Jean-Baptiste Clamence is, in the end, what his name suggests, a prophet in the wilderness. His message is loud and clear: "something is amiss." All he can do, though, is clamor. He cannot take the needed step of rethinking the philosophical paradigm responsible for things being amiss.

Hints for a Paradigm Shift

Camus gave several talks while in Stockholm to receive the Nobel Prize. One of them offered language which, if fully elaborated, would occasion a paradigm shift. It is a subtle, but significant point. Unfortunately, the point is made unintelligible by the standard English translation. The talk, "Create Dangerously," is about the roles and obligations of writers. In earlier epochs artists had the option of "remaining aloof" (RRD, 249). Today, the artist is, willy-nilly, impressed into service. Camus then adds an editorial comment: "'Impressed' seems to me a more accurate term in this connection than 'committed'" (RRD, 249). The key words in this translation are the two set in contrast to one another: "impressed" and "committed." The French terms are *embarqué* and *engagé* (ESS, 1079).

The ramifications of the two terms are major. To be *embarqué* is already to be on board. When Garret Hardin wrote a book introducing some early ecological ideas, he subtitled it *Voyage of the Spaceship Beagle*. The *Beagle* had been the ship on which Darwin sailed, and now Hardin wished to indicate that the whole earth was like a ship. We are passengers on the ship, and that ship is all we have. Camus's *embarqué* should be understood within such a context. There is no removing oneself, no situating oneself as an outside spectator.

We are living beings in a living world. We are already on board this particular ship at this particular time, with these particular people. If there is smoke on the ship, it's a matter of concern. Mattering is part of what it means to be already embarked. What happens on board is neither silent nor unintelligible. Excessive smoke is coming from somewhere? Smoke is a call that requires a response. Some responses are better than others. The "better" is neither merely theoretical nor subjective. A good, safe voyage depends on opting for better rather than worse. Think of an iceberg in the distance. This is not a bit of neutral data. One could imagine naval officers as epistemological subjects: "Iceberg sighted. We, with our *liberum arbitrium indifferentiae* can now subjectively decree what that means." Or, we could imagine someone, like the man moving peas from one container to another, proclaiming aloofness. Such attitudes can, of course, be undertaken. They even make some sense when the human subject is envisioned, not as within sight of an iceberg, not as in a city beset by a plague, but as someone set apart from the "external" world. For others, those already "embarked" on *this* journey in *these* circumstances, the attitude of *liberum arbitrium indifferentiae*, though possible, proves itself to be not only deluded but dangerous.

The image of being already embarked makes it difficult to define oneself as a detached spectator. A pan-semiotic situation, call and response, differences that make a difference, these are real. Mattering is not something superadded. It is aboriginal. Smoke is a call. An iceberg is a call. A plague is a call. Unbreathable air is a call. Depleted topsoil is a call. When we think of ourselves as already *embarqué*, indifference fades to the periphery as mattering moves to the center. Appraisal (listening to the *call*, seeking to understand its meaning) and electing among options (*response*) are arrayed along a spectrum of better and worse. The worse ones will lead to damage or even sinking of the ship. The better ones will leave the ship wholly or mostly intact. Intelligence, experience, and training can, and should, help guide the response. Better and worse in such cases are not mere matters of "boo" or "hurrah." The resultant course of action is opted for on the basis of good reasons, reasons allied to intelligence, experience, and training. Neither aloofness, a *liberum arbitrium indifferentiae*, nor nihilistic moral infallibilism will help ensure a safe, comfortable journey.

At the time Camus was giving his talk, there was much buzz about being an "engaged" writer. Camus's emphasis on the contrast between *embarqué* and *engagé* helps highlight an important difference. Whoever is already *embarqué* has little inclination to think in terms of being an outsider who would have to *take a special step* in order to become engaged. Being embarked means being already, as Camus puts it, "on the high seas" (RRD, 250). Mattering is present from the get-go. "Engagement" is a faulty way of representing this situation. It begins with the flawed assumption of being, aboriginally, an outsider. It assumes a starting point characterized by the plate glass of indifference. The primordial status of the self is envisioned as that of being disengaged. Such selves can, patting themselves on the back, decide to cross beyond the barrier and become "engaged."

Embarqué situates individuals in a quite different lifeworld. The pretense of being an outsider, always imaginable, is harder to square with lived experience. Humans start out already *in medias res*. The realm of *embarqué* is one in which humans are already and primordially situated in a web of mattering. Such mattering fails to be captured by Modern philosophy's exclusive categories, "subjective" and "objective." It emerges, rather, from the network of interactions that defines the lived situation. Asking whether things have value "in themselves" is to situate oneself within the semantic landscape of the Great Bifurcation. Apart from that bifurcation, it is situations and interactions that are primary. Disengagement, far from being fundamental, is the result of strenuous abstractive effort. It's a contrived stance, fabricated by separating ("abstracting") oneself from the physiological, affective, social, natural, historical, cultural dimensions that characterize human being-in-the-world. There is nothing basal and fundamental about the spectator self. It is a manufactured position supported only by the most strenuous abstractive oversimplifications.

The Myth of Sisyphus, following in the tradition of Descartes, rejected the ordinary as a starting point. Instead, it imagined a very abstract ground zero, one that, as an initial step, erected a pane glass of indifference between human beings and the habitat, which is their home. Indifference and detachment were crucial to the framework within which the young Camus was working. *Embarqué* and mattering offer alternatives that would necessitate major adjustments to the intellectual map Camus took for granted. Thinking of humans as already implicated in the goings-on of their habitats, thinking of them as already implicated in situations of mattering, offers an alternative paradigm, one that erases the preconditions for the diagnosis of absurdity.

Camus was sensitive to many difficulties associated with his target, nihilism. He does not seem to have realized how what he assumed as a starting point, the diagnosis of absurdity, was joined at the hip to nihilism. Because of this, he never combined the ingredients he was gathering into a new philosophical recipe. Those ingredients, as we have seen, included (a) dissatisfaction with nihilism; (b) a defense of "human nature"; and (c) the *embarqué-engagé* contrast. Although his own project envisioned him moving from *Sisyphus* to *Prometheus* and, finally, to *Nemesis*, his journey could not come to a proper culmination. He was good at pointing out flaws in the received framework, good at tinkering with its components, even good at indicating what could have opened pathways to new intellectual landscapes. The ingredients were there, but he never put them together in the form of a new groundmap.

What he could provide is what he does in *The Fall*: a keen sense of problems with the inherited paradigm. Clamence, given the nihilistic picture, *should have* been able to shake off the bridge memory. Why? Caring or not caring, deciding which action to undertake, these are up to the *liberum arbitrium indifferentiae*. That he ends up haunted by the bridge scene, ends up ill, longing for a second chance, these are indications of his status as a prophet or seer. It is also an indication that he has not risen above human nature. His clamoring is loud and clear: the inherited assumptions are flawed. His life serves as a test case. Where to go from here? Clamence hasn't a clue.

The Fall ends on a pessimistic note. Clamence wants another chance, but it's too late. It will always be too late (F, 147). So much for the character. How about the author? Camus as a searcher kept growing, reflecting, exploring. What comes next will be somewhat different from what came before. Until now, Camus has followed the pattern identified in his review of Sartre's *Nausea*: first, ideas, then fiction. First a philosophical position and then its exposition in story form. In more technical terms he has remained true to the tradition which accepted the primacy of thought over being.

His next literary works will, tentatively, begin to reverse the process. They will start to prioritize being over thinking. Ideas will not come first. When they do come, they will grow out of the lived experience represented in the stories. Pluralism, multiplicity of perspectives, complexities lived out in practice—these will now take center stage. The theme of absurdity will not disappear, but more and more, its grip will be weakened. It may even be that by the end, the doves will actually have landed. Lots go on in Camus's next work, the short stories gathered under the title *Exile and the Kingdom*.

9

Exile and the Kingdom, I

The Backward-Looking Stories

"Better Sometimes to Remain Confused"

Was Camus's creativity finished in the years approaching his 1960 death? The short story collection *Exile and the Kingdom* (1957) provides a test case. Many critics think the stories do not match up to the better-known novelistic trio, *The Stranger*, *The Plague*, and *The Fall*. As we saw in the introduction, even an astute reader of Camus like Ron Srigley thinks that the period after the publication of *The Fall* was a "dry" one. It is certainly true that *Exile and the Kingdom* garners less attention than the three popular novels. One critic referred to the stories as "hermetic" and noted how their appearance occasioned puzzlement (*incomphréhension*) (Baldi, 91). A website listing Camus's major works does not even include *Exile and the Kingdom* (Fiches). Micheline Tisson-Braun's commentary was categorical: "Camus's last years offer no major work after *The Fall*." She specifically references the short stories as belonging outside the category of "major work" (Tisson-Braun, 54). Conor Cruise O'Brien was unimpressed: "The manner of the short stories is generally flat and grating, suggestive of painful effort" (O'Brien 1969). Others emphasize how, if the stories have significance, it has nothing to do with any light they might shed on the human condition. It's a political significance relating to the Algerian independence movement. The stories' relevance turns on how they represent "an evolution in his [Camus's] representation of North Africa" (Erickson, 74). Apart from political issues, positive commentary emphasizes style over substance. Susan Tarrow, for example, indicates how Camus is "experimenting with narrative techniques." In this way, she echoes Camus himself who mentioned to Jean Grenier his intent "to change the writing style with each novella, and work out something original" (Todd, 350).

Overall takeaway: the stories are like remnants. They were, it has to be admitted, written by Camus. Still, they remain decidedly inferior to the triumphant triad of novels. The main problem with such an analysis has been hinted at earlier: it remains *Sisyphus-centric*. That is to say, it judges Camus on the basis of his earliest production, not in terms of someone who was growing and changing. My examination seeks to follow Camus as he developed. It also takes account of how the wider intellectual climate of opinion for readers of Camus has changed. Lots has happened since the middle of the twentieth century, changes in philosophy, in society, in the sciences.

The central theme of this book thus comes into focus: Camus was heir to a philosophical legacy which painted him into a corner. It was a corner with no escape, or, at least, no escape without altering the philosophical presuppositions he continued to assume. Even though his developmental trajectory did not culminate in a paradigm shift, the journey is still worth following. Why not, then, allow Camus to struggle with this challenge, to grow, develop, explore, and seek ways of dealing with the positions he held as a young man? Why assume that his greatest contributions were the narratives with the most philosophical heft? Or, stated differently, why assume that the apex of Camus's achievement is identified by those novels which start with philosophical ideas and embody them in narrative flesh? Why not give proper due to a serious artist as he continues his exploration? Why always privilege philosophy (ideas) and relegate literature (lived experience) to a secondary status?

It is possible, and in the case of Camus interpreters, common, to prioritize the works that exemplify preestablished philosophical positions. This "philosophy provides the soul, literature the body" approach is but one take on the literature/philosophy relationship. Camus, it is true, did, in his review of Sartre's *Nausea*, identify literature as a handmaiden of philosophy. True also, his three novels reveal him as someone who could embody philosophical ideas in literary fiction. This provides great fodder for academic commentary and a straightforward line of interpretation.

When it comes to the short stories, this mode of approach can only lead to a judgment of inferiority. They don't follow the "philosophical idea first, literary expression second" mode. As such, they automatically fall outside the category of "major work." What I have tried to suggest is that the Sisyphus-centric take is misguided. This is so in two ways. It freezes Camus in time, identifying his overall trajectory with where he was at the time of his earliest triumphs. It also judges literary works on a questionable scale. On that scale, one that parallels soul/body dualism, the most commendable narratives are those which provide fictional flesh for a preordained philosophy.

Exploring how Camus is someone engaged in an ongoing search means rethinking this scale of valuation. It means, for one thing, that when Susan Tarrow claims that Camus was "experimenting with narrative techniques," he was doing so in order, properly, to deal with the changing appreciation of reality he was seeking to articulate. A binary-fixated philosopher might insist that style and content are to be compartmentalized. A creative artist will seek, instead, interpenetration, will, while still a seeker, experiment with narrative techniques.

The reality with which Camus was struggling had to do with having inherited a philosophical legacy which limited his options. The diagnosis of absurdity, if followed out consistently, led to practical consequences which Camus abhorred. The heritage he absorbed was like an ellipse with two foci: Descartes and Nietzsche. From Descartes came the Great Bifurcation, the notion that humans and the world stood over against each other. Humans were like detached spectators, and, as such, were like strangers or aliens in a strange world. From Nietzsche came a follow-up on the Great Bifurcation: it led straight to nihilism. The gap is so great between subject and objects that all meaning, now removed from the latter, is located exclusively in the former.

The resulting challenge: how to set about construing a life trajectory within this framework? The framework is not just that of admitting how life is characterized by difficulties that, in a loose, nontechnical sense, can be labeled "absurd." Camus, influenced by a philosophical tradition that favors trafficking in abstractions, moved "absurdity," in *The Myth of Sisyphus*, to a new level. Highlighting everyday, ordinary, routine vexations would not have made much of a splash. Rather, the orientation had to be formulated more dramatically. "Absurd" would no longer be understood as characterizing some dimensions of existing. It would now define *the* basal condition of humans as beings confronting an external world.

"Absurdity" postulates a primordial, unqualified, unbridgeable frustration. Such an unbridgeable frustration, not as one characteristic among others, but as *the* solitary, exclusive descriptor, was, in turn, the product of inventions associated with the spectator self. These fantasies led to expectations, epistemologically, of perfect, apodictic certitude. In ethics they led to expectations of perfect conditions for realizing ideals. Such expectations were bound to be thwarted. Unreal expectations came to occasion an inevitable letdown. This is the soil which transformed ordinary inanities, ordinary absurdities into a totalizing philosophical claim: life is absurd.

At this point the more traditional understanding of philosophy as seeking an orientation that allows for meaningful lives in an intelligible world is automatically ruled out. The imperialistic claim about life's absurdity pronounces that the world is unintelligible. It is joined at the hip to nihilism: our milieu provides nothing (*nihil*) along the lines of guidance, signals, or indicators to aid intelligence and experience as they seek to provide help for living. The ancient understanding of philosophy grew out of a particular intellectual landscape, one rooted in a particular belief: ordinary life offered the possibilities and opportunities for arriving at constructive positions about living meaningful lives in an intelligible universe. Nihilism and the diagnosis of absurdity render this assumption untenable. Together, they managed to devalorize the quotidian. Such total devalorization is clean, neat, and total. It's a logic-chopper's dream. But perhaps it is a fiction-writer's nightmare.

What if the complexity of human life is distorted when characterized in terms of the bifurcation: *either* unencumbered realization *or* nihilistic frustration? Philosophies and the stories that illustrate such a dilemma may be provocative, but the provocation comes at an expense: they contract and streamline human life. Such simplifications work well for a philosophy that retreats into a realm of pure ideas. It does not work so well for literary artists attempting to divulge the density of lived experience.

Iris Murdoch, both novelist and philosopher, worried that trafficking in the realm of rarified, purified, simplified abstractions represented a betrayal of the storyteller's art. The *roman à thèse*, she might have said, stands as just such a betrayal. It oversimplifies the vast complexity of human experience. Her positive archetype is the nineteenth-century novel associated with names like Dostoevsky, Eliot, Dickens, Tolstoy, and Austen. That novel took for granted the thick, gnarled, multifarious, motley domain of human life. The newer novels, ones tightly controlled by a philosophical outlook, may be neat and coherent. Such coherence is bought at high expense, the deflation of experience. These novels necessitate, as one commentator put it, "the forfeiture of the enormous territory of human experience that the nineteenth-century novel took to be its proper inheritance" (Jacobs).[1] The fullness of lived experience will always spill over the boundaries established by abstract thought. "Coherence," Murdoch claims, "is not necessarily good, and one must question its cost. Better sometimes to remain confused" (Jacobs).

No better shorthand description could be provided for what is going on in *Exile and the Kingdom*: "Better sometimes to remain confused." For the *Sisyphus-centric* reading of Camus, confusion, enigmas, frustrations *should not* be part of what the disembodied mind (the *cogito*) confronts. It demands a setting whose components can be grasped in ways that are clear, neat, rational, distinct. The detached spectator-mind revels in purity, clarity. It aims at certitude, not truth. It thrives in a world of exclusive absolutes and rigid either/or formulations: absolute lucidity or absolute unintelligibility. It is not just frustrated but undone by lingering confusions, enigmas, surds. Such surds simply do not match its projections about how the world should be. From its perch, such inconveniences mean that he (possessor of mind) really does not belong there. He is more like an alien, an outsider, a stranger. That perch, as I have tried to show, is both artificial and fabricated. It has little to do with the abundant, replete, at times turbid, experience explored by the nineteenth-century novel. It has, instead, everything to do with a specious, manufactured redefining of human being-in-the-world.

Changing the Paradigm

This being-in-the-world is the exact locus where any serious alternative to nihilism can begin. Humans will have to be understood in concrete, inclusionist terms, as living beings in a living world. The gap between humans and the world, a world which the spectator self envisions as "external," will have to be recognized as artificial. Ordinary life will have to be reinvested with possibilities for goodness. In the lovely phrase from W. H. Auden's "Lullaby," the aspiration is that the cradled child will "find the mortal world enough." Given the intellectual inheritance of Camus, this is precisely what could never happen. The mortal world was "absurd," that is, never enough, never adequate to the demands of the *cogito*.

Camus, in *The Myth of Sisyphus*, was harshly critical of escapisms. He couldn't, however, offer a positive alternative. As a result, his take could best be symbolized by the stubborn determination of Sisyphus. In other words, *The Myth of Sisyphus* did nothing to challenge received philosophy. It actually reinforced the basic separation of, on one side, the mind-endowed, meaning-hungry self and, on the other, an indifferent, value-free world. His only recommendation: posit, rather against common sense and logical consistency, that, regardless of the evidence, humans should nonetheless follow the example of Sisyphus. Such advice went against the grain of evidence. It proposed a strategy that was just plain irrational. As we saw in Chapter 1, Susan Sontag had recognized this, pointing out how Camus, "solely by the power of his own tranquil voice and tone," moved readers "to humanist and humanitarian conclusions in no way entailed by his premises." Then, disregarding how most individuals would feel, Camus insisted that we have to "imagine Sisyphus happy."

Let's face it, this is the best Camus could do. The best he could do, that is, given the philosophical presuppositions to which he remained committed. Those presuppositions, however, are far from obvious, necessary, or written in stone. They arose because of a philosophical fabrication, a move that extracted humans from their status as living beings in a living world. Then, and only then, could it appear that humans are set off against the world, a world that is not their proper home. Once humans are envisioned as aliens, it makes sense to highlight a sharp contrast between their demand for meaning and a world which, in that regard, is neutral and indifferent. Camus's major novels are bathed in such an atmosphere. They may be engaging, coherent, and provocative, but they (1) treat literature as if it were just bodily housing for a preexisting philosophical soul, (2) are based on faulty philosophy, one whose main flaw is that it (3) distorts and simplifies human life.

Times have changed since the era when Camus was a student. Many philosophical movements have emerged which no longer function within the guiding framework of the Great Bifurcation. Some of the change has been influenced by the sciences. The Cartesian dispensation, the one in which humans, as minds, stand over against a world which is external and alien, turns out to have little in common with post-Darwinian biology and contemporary ecology. It also has little to do with everyday lives. It does, however, bring one big advantage: it flatters the being who would (a) like to be in the center of things and (b) envision himself as radically free (i.e., unencumbered by dependence and the need for adjustment to conditions not of his own making).

The Cartesian dispensation was the general orientation inherited by Camus, an inheritance which, despite some uneasiness, remained mostly intact in his fiction. At least until *Exile and the Kingdom*. And, even there, what we witness are only tentative moves toward a different take. It's a take that I call "rehabilitation of the ordinary." The short stories begin this process. It's a process moving toward a paradigm shift, one which Camus could never quite make. The Great Bifurcation was to remain a constant presence. In theory, at least. In practice, Camus realized how individuals would need to rebel against its ramifications The six short stories in *Exile and the Kingdom* exemplify this tension.

Camus's major novels were, whether he wished to admit this or not, *romans à thèse*.

Exile and the Kingdom breaks with this pattern. The six stories develop along the lines of what Iris Murdoch suggests literature does best. They do not read as exemplifications of a philosophy They read more like phenomenological explorations, attempts to get at the manifold, multifarious dimensions accommodated by the lifeworld. In general, it's a move away from "man" as an epistemological subject and lonely being-unto-death. The hinted-at new focus is one that pervades Camus's lyrical essays: humans as beings-welcoming-life. The Cartesian-inspired position began with the isolated male, alive but deposited in a world described, for all intents and purposes, as an alien land. It was not a home but an arena filled with indifferent, neutral stuff. Instead of live beings in a living world, the understanding depicted a statue-cogito in a "mineral" world.

This statue-cogito, mostly an embodied mind, was, in turn, flummoxed by the inevitability of death. Once freed of bodies, spirits are not supposed to die. "Man" as "being-unto-death" became a central philosophical concern. This focus has a lengthy history. Michel de Montaigne got lots of attention with his 1580 piece entitled "To

Philosophize is to learn to die." Montaigne was situated in a lengthy tradition. In *The Phaedo*, Socrates claimed that those who "apply themselves in the right way to philosophy are directly and of their own accord preparing themselves for dying and death" (*Phaedo*, 64a in Hamilton, 46). If Socrates was a predecessor of Montaigne, Martin Heidegger was a successor. Had Montaigne been able to peer into the future, he could have envisioned how, for Martin Heidegger, "being-unto-death" (*Sein-zum-Tode*) was central to achieving authenticity (Heidegger, 307). While concern with mortality is certainly understandable, it can be overdone. (As someone in the Aristotelian stream, I'm always on the watch for excess and deficiency). In the case of a fixation on mortality, excess is encouraged by a philosophical landscape which (1) accentuates isolated individuals and (2) forgets a crucial dimension of being-in-the-world: birthing.

This is where the shift to "we" becomes significant. The "I" of the Cartesian "I am," despite self-delusions, does not just appear out of nowhere. We are beings who result from the union of sperm and egg, gestate in a female, are born,[2] grow, live, age, die. Within this trajectory many of us, in conjunction with another, leave offspring. The pattern of human existence is more complicated than that of a lonely spirit facing a death that should not be. Our post-ecological sensitivities add to this complication. We are not aliens in a world that is just indifferent, neutral, mineral. We are living beings. This means we live *in*, *with*, and *by means of* the habitat of which we form a part. We are the culminations of begetting and birthing, agents who breathe, eat, live in communities, privilege certain attachments, recognize interdependence, and either beget or witness the arrival of the next generation. When the fuller ramifications of "we are" come into play, it is harder to disconnect ourselves from the physiological, biological, affective conditions which form part of an integrated habitat. It is, by contrast, a whole lot easier to understand ourselves as already *embarqué*.

Our existential condition is one which, far from segregating us from the rest of the biosphere, integrates us within it. The basic element of existence is not "I am." It is not even Ortega's "I am I and my circumstance." That phrasing still highlights an "I" in some ways not dependent on "circumstance." Such a formulation does not go far enough in emphasizing how the elemental constituent of existence is, rather an event or occurrence, an entanglement of elements enduring for a span of time. Within such occurrences, there are organisms, persons, activities, and natural conditions, all engaged in interactions. There never is an absolute "I," a detached, laminated unit.

These multiple, interacting constituents can, via abstraction, be bracketed. Such bracketing was the major move in post-Renaissance, "Modern" thought. Bracketing is not a problem so long as it is recognized as such. It should be understood for what it is: a specific and artificial eliminationism. Such eliminationism can be undertaken for particular purposes, as when a molecular biologist leaves aside the biosphere, the species, the organism and concentrates on chemical activities within the nucleus of a cell. What counts is that the eliminationism be recognized when it occurs. If not, the isolated units that result from the purposeful exclusionary move can come to be understood as somehow more real than the concrete event or occurrence. The resultant isolated human can then highlight "Being-unto-death" as the major concern. Such phrasing is dramatic and attention-grabbing. The alternative combination—having-been-born, living-in-a-habitat, being-part-of-a-human-temporal-chain, overlapping-with-the-next-generation—is less marketable as a slogan. Its ramifications, though, bring out the fuller, multilayered dimensions of existence.

Here is where *Exile and the Kingdom* takes on special importance. Its stories move in the direction of situating humans in the complicated lifeworld. Camus's three novels were all bathed in the atmosphere of *Thanatos*. Meursault is a murderer facing execution. Rieux finds himself in a situation dominated by death. Clamence's life was exemplified by disconnection and sterility. He is sick and dying. In that trio of works *The Plague* stands out as the work in which *Thanatos*, though pervasive, is not triumphant. *Eros* hovers over the entire novel, highlighted by its absence. Painful separation from loved ones is a major theme. Rieux's wife is away at a treatment facility. Rambert's love interest is in Paris. A mother and father lose a child to the disease. The plague had generally enforced a "life of separation," one disconnected from companionship's "living warmth." It had meant "exile" and "yearning for a reunion" (Pl, 298). Such longing was so strong that Rambert's love-partner had secured a ticket on "the first train" allowed back into the quarantined city (Pl, 294). Instead of *Thanatos*, *The Plague*, alone among Camus's three novels, ends on a note of *Eros*: "They knew now that if there is one thing one can always yearn for and sometimes attain, it is human love" (Pl, 300).

As we saw in the Introduction, Camus envisioned a three-cycle trajectory for his work. One way of describing the last cycle was to stress the theme of love (Ess, 1610). *The Stranger*, *The Plague*, and *The Fall* belong to the first two phases, the ones dealing with absurdity and revolt. They remain within a context in which *Thanatos* is dominant. *Exile and the Kingdom* represents a shift, a tentative move in making room for life and love. It embraces the context of living and rings several changes on the theme of love. It's an earnest exploration, not a translation of already fixed ideas in story form. Because it is exploratory, the shift is partial and tentative. Nonetheless, it represents an opening for new possibilities.

Several traits accompany the recalibration. (1) The first-person narrator shows up in only one of the stories, and it is one which looks backward. (2) Children make an appearance. (3) "We are" takes center stage. (4) "Being" recovers its precedence over thinking. Finally (5) an important metaphorical dimension appears. Camus has generally associated liquidity with happiness, as when Rieux and Tarrou "take an hour off—for friendship" (Pl, 245) a time-off which culminates in a joint, relaxing, enjoyable, deeply satisfying, swim (Pl, 257). In *Exile and the Kingdom*, liquid metaphors serve as central images for a new direction. It's a direction that highlights fluidity, blendings, soft edges, flow; in other words, life. Their antitheses take the form of images associated with minerality: solidity, rigid boundaries, coldness, stones.

Camus's early death prevented readers from knowing exactly what direction his mature explorations would have taken. The unfinished autobiographical novel *The First Man* is (1) a draft, and, (2) as we shall see in Chapters 12 and 13, only takes us through Camus's youth and early adolescence. The last of Camus's revised works is the short story collection. What we can do in trying to understand Camus is enter into a conversation with it. As we begin to do so, one more preliminary remark is in order.

In my use of *Eros* and *Thanatos*, I am borrowing from Sigmund Freud (Freud, ch. 6). His term for the life instinct, *Eros*, was but one of the Greek words that can be translated as "love." The best exploration of ancient Greece's multiple terms can be found in the well-known study by C. S. Lewis, *The Four Loves*. Lewis's text is kind of dated, but the central point remains valid. When the ancient Greeks spoke of "love," they understood it to be a cluster term, with at least four thematic templates. There was (1) *storge*, the kind of affection parents and children have for each other; (2) *philia*, friendship—a kind of love much celebrated by the ancient Greeks; (3) *eros*, sexual attraction along with the partnering and childbearing that accompanies it; and (4) *agape*, a term that was given a place of honor in Christianity. Lewis refers to it as "gift-love," the free, generous donation of self, a relationship in which reciprocity is not a central element. (5) To this list I would add a fifth term, also borrowed from ancient Greece, *xenia*, guest-friendship, the attitude of generous welcome extended to foreigners, strangers, guests. The stranger is understood to be a kind of gift, a living revelation of how varied and complicated is human life. Keeping these five manifestations of love in mind will be helpful when examining the specific stories that make up *Exile and the Kingdom*.

The six stories can be divided into three groups. Two of them are backward-looking. They are concerned with either the impossibility of *eros* or the predominance of *Thanatos*. Two stories open an exploration of love in several of its forms: *philia*, *storge*, and *eros*—friendship, family affection, and spousal attachment. Finally, two of them revolve more around love as *xenia* and *agape*. Each of these loves involves a free gift whose impact is to break down barriers. With the breakdown of barriers comes a kind of conversion. It's a transformation that reshuffles both inherited ideas and the ways of life that accompanied them. The reshuffling is so dramatic that, in the end, continuity replaces sharp divisions, going so far as to emphasize a continuum between the mineral and the living.

The Backward-Looking Stories: 1

The opening story, "The Adulterous Woman" may, at first glance, seem to explore *eros* as a life-enhancing, nihilism-denying force. It could then be classified not as backward- but forward-looking. Taking a close look at "The Adulterous Woman" reveals how this is not the case. What emerges is how the story continues to breathe in the atmosphere of the Great Bifurcation. It's a story whose characters are isolated units thrown together. Much of the imagery involves mutual gazing, spectating. Such gazing among laminated selves is set within a natural world dominated by minerality. The more interactive realm of speaking/listening is minimized. The hotel manager is "taciturn" (EK, 11); Janine is "almost deaf" to human voices, more attuned to "the murmur of a river coming from the window" (EK, 11); at dinner with her husband Marcel the conversation tacks between the utilitarian "It's [the water] not boiled. Have wine" and self-serving "We French, we know how to cook" (EK, 12).

Ordinary, everyday life is characterized by alienation. Sterility (a *Thanatos* affiliate) dominates. The life world is not fertile and fecund. It is devoid of the possibilities for connection and harmony. The story continues to traffic on the all-or-nothing highway.

Ordinary love, fertile, enduring connection with another is not possible. Difference is real, but it is not a call to harmony. Rather it serves as a reinforcement to separation and detachment. There is, though, an escape mechanism. Alienation can be overcome. But such overcoming must follow a path different than that of *eros*. It is the path of quasi-mystical fusion of the self with the cosmos. Only then can the *cogito*-centered isolation of humans from the world be overcome. Ruled out ahead of time are harmony, concord, accord, love-tinged aspirations that recognize the inevitability of difference.

Looming in the background is the notion of an initial oneness and its "decay" (read also "fall") into multiplicity and differentiation. The aboriginal oneness represents the kingdom of undifferentiated homogeneity. The realm of differences is one of exile. *Eros*, as a force for concord within difference, is an illusion fostered by those stuck in exile. It thus represents, for the characters, a faulty ideal. The real aspiration is longing for the mystical moment, one in which the aspiration is to overcome difference and return, even if only temporarily, to some state of undifferentiation.

In terms of imagery the move involves leaving behind the realm of minerality, that of exile, and turning toward the realm of liquidity, the lost kingdom. The setting for "The Adulterous Woman" is the state of exile, alienation, and minerality. The story opens with a bus ride. The bus is battered by a "sandy wind" (EK, 3). It is winter. Even the fog is described as "mineral." There are palm trees, but even they seem "cut from metal" (EK, 4). The surroundings offer little more than "stone, stone everywhere" (EK, 8).

A mineral world is lifeless, "stone, stone everywhere." It is governed by *Thanatos*. Particles bump and crash into one another. Fecundity, liquidity, mixing, and blending are the exceptions, not the rule. The central couple Janine and her husband have settled into a mineral-like arrangement. *Eros* has no place in such a realm. *Eros* thrives in a realm characterized by liquidity: flexibility, porous boundaries, possibilities for genuine confluences, combinations, and culminations.[3] The interpenetration associated with *eros* often culminates, as the result of moist, lubricated intercourse, in pregnancy, a fetus completely bathed in liquid, followed by a birth, marked by a profusion of wetness. Janine and Marcel, twenty-five years into their marriage, have settled, instead, into a predictable, mostly mechanical coexistence. There were negative signals early on. Janine realizes that Marcel "probably did not love her." She, in turn, desperately needed to be needed, and "Marcel needed her." Besides, loneliness is a powerful motivator. Only unusual people can "always sleep alone" (EK, 22).

Even though Janine is childless, she feels a certain kind of symbolic pregnancy. Her heart, she senses, had been dragging around an "immense weight." It was a weight from which she wished to be "delivered" (EK, 22). This "delivery" is not that of a child conceived via *eros*. It is liberation from an alienated condition, that of a mind cast into bodily existence. Janine feels the unhappy weight of "exile." She seeks escape ("delivery") by making contact with a "kingdom," a realm in which the differences, contingencies, and frustrations of this lifeworld will all be dissolved. Love, which works within the realm of differences, contingencies, and frustrations, just will not do. Love cannot leave behind the weight of everyday life. Real escape requires deliverance from the here and now, even if the deliverance is only temporary. It's an all-or-nothing setup: encapsulated isolation or total fusion. The in-between path of *eros* falls miserably short. Its sad state is not altered by changing partners, literal adultery. The players will be different, but so long as complete union, moving beyond difference, is envisioned as the ideal, the path of *eros*, which always involves differences, will prove deficient.

Janine's need for delivery from self-enclosure is motivated by a powerful "call." She feels drawn to a realm "where life stopped, where no one grew old or died" (EK, 23). She is drawn, in other words, to a kingdom apart from this life. This life, after all, is considered to be one of permanent exile. She answers the call by ascending to a parapet where she is surrounded by a "garland of stars" (EK, 23). Her climb distances her from the heavy, corporeal, material realm. The world of burdensome embodiedness recedes as she perceives "everything swimming before her eyes" (EK, 24). Losing more and more of her insularity, her differentiation, she can commune with that which is her "deepest being" (EK, 25). The heaviness of exile fades away, as does "the anguish of living and dying" (EK, 25). She catches a glimpse of, or, more accurately, becomes one with, the kingdom which is her real home. The wonders of that realm, like sweet waters, "fill Janine" (EK, 25). As was the case with St. Theresa of Avila in the throes of a mystical experience, the best descriptors come from analogy with sexual climax. Janine lies on her back. The sky stretches above her. She is filled with the "waters of the night," an experience which occasions her to respond with a "moaning mouth" (EK, 25).

Janine has succeeded where a biological adulteress would have failed. She has left behind the burdensome realm of leaden, weighty, material, bodily separateness. All difference has been dissolved in a grand undifferentiated fusion. Camus had, in *The Myth of Sisyphus*, claimed that the entire issue of absurdity would not arise if he were "a tree among trees, a cat among animals." In those cases "I should belong to this world" (MS, 51). For a brief moment Janine loses her differentiation, that which defines exile-status. Camus's imagery describes the experience in plant-like terms: "At the same time, she seemed to be recovering her roots, and the sap rose anew in her body, which was no longer trembling" (EK, 25). The realm of absolute undifferentiation is her proper home, the abode of her "deepest being." The world of quotidian, ordinary life is a realm of differences, and thus exile. It is one in which differences are always signs of defect. Only a flight from finitude, an escape, even if temporary, can bring about contact with the "kingdom," envisioned as a realm of atemporal, undifferentiated, all-encompassing, one-ness.

Back in her room, Janine has to face reality as an exile. In an all-or-nothing framework, the ideal state can only be characterized in terms of unity beyond differentiation. A reformulation in terms of harmony which always admits, and even necessitates, differences cannot appear on her radar screen. A setting in which harmony (as opposed to unity) offered an appropriate aspiration would make room for the primordiality of difference and the ingenuity of *eros*. As far as Janine is concerned, there is an unbridgeable gap between lowly quotidian existence (which is the only home *eros* could have) and the lyrical mysticism which allowed her, for a brief while, to overcome divisions and commune in perfect, undifferentiated fusion with the kingdom that, as ultimate source of her being, she conceives to be her real home.

Having achieved such mystical union, the memory is sweet. It comes, however, with a realization that is bitter: achieving the kingdom is the exception; living in exile is the rule. Marcel notices she is "weeping uncontrollably" (EK, 26). Hers are tears of someone who has tasted Paradise Regained but lives within Paradise Lost. More specifically, she is someone who still lives within a paradigm that posits an initial Paradise now lost and can only think in terms of escaping the here and now in order to enter Paradise Regained. Within such a scheme, *eros*, harmony-within-difference, is just not operative.

In *The Myth of Sisyphus*, Camus criticized religious escapism. Inventing a transcendent realm which would correct all the flaws, alienations, and frustrations of the here and now, was to engage in illusory thinking. Janine's naturalized mysticism changes this a bit, but only a bit. The intellectual air she breathes has simply de-theologized certain basic elements. The world is not "fallen." It is a place of "exile." Either way, the main emphasis is the same. This world is not our real home. Religious mysticism may be rejected, but a secular version is alive and well. Janine simply tweaks the ingredients. The out-of-the-ordinary fusion is no longer unifying with the divine. One out of which everything comes. It is still, however, an experience of direct fusion, a move that is not possible within the humdrum, blemished world in which differences cannot be eliminated. Nihilism, religious or secular, remains intact: the here and now is not a realm of *dunamism*, the Greek term for possibilities. It is devoid of energies such as *storge*, *eros*, *philia*, energies that could serve to help transform possibilities into realizations. The "kingdom" must always lie elsewhere. The everyday is nothing but earthbound, material, that is, "mundane" in the most pejorative of senses. The divided domain of Clamence, doves above, earthbound life below, with no interweaving between them, lives on.

The Backward-Looking Stories: 2

The other backward-looking story, "The Renegade," features someone else seeking to escape the mundane. His is the traditional religious escape. The fallen world provides no guidance. The transcendent realm makes up for this. It is replete with absolutes and commands. The main character is a priest, devoted to a Catholicism which, as a mentor once told him, is "the sun" (EK, 28). Escaping the mundane is one side of nihilism, the refusal to recognize possibilities for goodness and sacredness in the here and now. It's an escape highlighting what could be called "un-carnation." The story's title, "renegade," identifies the protagonist as a nay-sayer, a negator. Despite being officially part of a religion centered on incarnation and *agape*, his trajectory is driven more by resentment, arrogance, and antipathy.

An ancient Greek pun characterizes the world of our prelate. The terms in question, *eris* and *eros*, although close in sound, differ in meaning. *Eris* was strife, combativeness. The Romans called her *discordia*. *Eros*, much better known to us, signaled love, harmony, concord. Though lesser known today, *eris* was once considered to be a formidable presence, one powerful enough to have caused the Trojan War.[4]

The renegade, as a priest, should live a life guided by the kind of love known as *agape*, a "gift-love" that does not mandate mutuality. Such love is nowhere to be found in the story. The only "love" the priest refers to is *eros*, and then it is merely to indicate how he has explicitly repudiated it. When, as a young seminarian, he saw girls, he did not make an effort to turn away. Doing so would be to accept that, though *eros* is good, he has committed to a life that, for a greater good, requires the sacrifice of *eros*. Instead, he overtly despises the young women (EK, 29). He seeks, constantly, to disincarnate, to rise above that world where *eros* maintains such power.

The *eros*-inclusive world is defined as fallen. It is a realm of exile, one from which he longs to escape. When he is insulted and mistreated by the girls, he thinks of this as a good thing. They worship, while he repudiates, *eros*. By abandoning *eros* and ignoring *agape*, the renegade is left in a Clamence-like state. For Clamence, it is a pan-judgmental domain of constant finger pointing. For the prelate, it's a realm dominated by *eris*. The renegade's world is one of difference, dissention, discord. It is a place of unending combat. Guided by *eris*, he does worship a divinity. It is not the one to which he is officially committed. It is, more accurately, *Nike*, goddess of victory.

The "renegade" tells us that he leads a life dominated by a "single idea." That idea is allied to Clamence's notion of universal guilt (in traditional religious terms "original sin," in later Calvinist terms the wretchedness of all humans who cannot be saved except by divine grace). The "single idea" is neither contextualized, qualified, nor carefully explained. Instead, the "single idea" is one that, as a rarified, purified abstraction, he will take to "its logical conclusion" (EK, 29). Speaking to Dominicans in 1948 Camus had complained about a dangerous notion within Christianity. It was the Augustinian diagnosis of *nemo bonus*, a ramification of original sin, "no one is good." As a blanket claim, it encompassed not just the "damnation of unbaptized children" but also the pessimistic teaching that "man was incapable of saving himself by his own means and that in the depths of his degradation his only hope was in the grace of God" (RRD, 72). Given such an understanding, *Nemo bonus* and nihilism work well together. More specifically, nihilism is just, as Nietzsche recognized, *nemo bonus* after the death of God. Nihilism and a particular kind of religion form a symbiotic couple. The postlapsarian realm is one in which ordinary life is so depraved that only external grace can redeem it. Take away grace, and what is left? The belief that ordinary life offers *nihil*, nothing to assist the quest for a good life.

The renegade carries this attitude, in its pure Calvinist form, to "its logical conclusion." The first implication is to divide the world into those who have received grace and those who have not. The second is to assume that he is on the side of the saved. The third is that others have to be saved and he, alone, possesses the path to salvation. This understanding brings with it an immediate obligation: he must "evangelize," impose his mode of salvation on the poor, deprived heathens. Conversation, which involves listening, is a waste of time. The effective task is conversion. Forget *agape* and *Abba*. It's all about *eris* and *Nike*.

If Camus had wanted to provide an image for what it means to live out nihilism thoroughly and exhaustively, he could not have improved on "The Renegade": set the story in a "city of salt"; relate a tale about one whose behavior (and title) signals a great and definitive "no" to life. The renegade does not emerge from nowhere. He inhabits an intellectual landscape whose interlocking traits should, by now, be familiar. (a) All distinctions between good and bad result from divine commands; (b) nothing in the here and now, a realm given over to nihilism, can provide indications that certain actions are more abominable or admirable than others; (c) judgments are not to be made on the combined basis of experience, intelligence, and reasonableness; (d) combat (*eris*) aiming at total victory (*Nike*) becomes the default mode of life. The renegade, following out this logic, admits that he "dreamed of absolute power" (EK, 31). He heads for the city of salt with one goal in mind: "subjugate those savages" (EK, 31).

Fired up in his enthusiasm, the renegade has sidestepped an important reality check: those he seeks to subjugate may have absolutes of their own. They too may think in terms of *eris* and *Nike*. They may automatically and unequivocally categorize outsiders as enemies. It may be that he is the one who will undergo conversion. After he has been captured, beaten, his tongue cut out, his allegiances are indeed transferred. What remains the same is the structural pattern: the one that revolves around an exclusive (and exclusionary) divinity, a divinity that requires a neat classification of people into in-group and out-group. This is the central irony of the story. The priest's allegiance changes from Catholicism to Fetishism, but his central (us versus them) take remains unaltered.

When the combat mode of existence dominates, love, in all its forms, is absent. *Agape* is not even given lip service. *Xenia* is replaced by xenophobia. *Philia* is ignored. *Eros* is either dismissed, as with the renegade, or transformed into violent rape as with the fetish (EK, 38). The villagers taught him, says the priest, that "you must settle accounts with love" (EK, 32). The phrase *régler son compte avec l'amour* could also be rendered as "settle your score with" or "finally get revenge on" the (false) teaching that made so much of love. It is not surprising that the renegade switches his allegiance to the new high priest and his religion of power. The renegade, fan of *eris* and *Nike*, was already in that mindset. The object of worship remains power. Only the representative symbol has changed.

The city of salt perfectly represents the realm of rigidity rather than love. It's all about minerality and *Thanatos*. There is nothing soft, liquidity, or welcoming about it. Harshness is everywhere. Inflexible rules dominate. The city itself is "closed to outsiders" (EK, 30). The entire environment suggests arid barrenness, not the lush abundance of life. The setting is that of an "endless sea of brown stones, shrieking with heat, burning with a thousand mirrors bristling with fire" (EK, 32). The villagers seem to have "cut out their white and burning hell with a blowtorch of boiling water just to show they could live where no one else could" (EK, 33).

The alternative, a world more of love than power, is better suited to liquid metaphors: supple boundaries, reciprocity, confluence, fertility, inter-communication.

Camus's descriptions indicate how liquidity is completely absent. He does so by using terms resonant of liquidity and turning them against themselves. There is, for example, a "sea." But it is a sea of "brown stones" (EK, 32). There is water, but it is a "blowtorch of boiling water" (EK, 33). At the same time, rain, real rain bringing a wonderful gift to a fertile land, is here identified as a threat. It would dissolve "the ghastly city" which would then "shrink slowly, irresistibly, and dissolve entirely in a viscous torrent" (EK, 34). Minerality dominates: in surroundings, in thought, in mode of living. There is a "kingdom," but it is a perverse one, "a sterile city sculpted from a mountain of salt, separated from nature, deprived of the rare and fleeting blooms of the desert" (EK, 42). It's a cold, stone-like realm of power and domination. The city is not only distant from nature and flowers but also "shielded from those chance or affectionate gestures--an unusual cloud a brief and raging rain" (EK, 42).

One of the renegade's literary precursors, Faust's Mephistopheles, had described himself as a re-negade, one who always says no, a force of perpetual negation, one who denies, negates (*verneint*) (Goethe, ll 1339–44). Does goodness exist? No, it's an illusion, a "daydream" (EK, 42). Can perfection (as opposed to improvement) be attained? No—don't even try. But why the wild pendulum swings? Why not hold on to the complex plenitude manifest in the lifeworld? Aristotle, a more biologically sensitive, down to earth, type made much, especially in *Metaphysics* book 9, of *dunamis* (from which we get "dynamic" and "dynamism"). *Dunamis* signals something important about the lifeworld: it is latent with potentiality, opportunity, capability. Instead of nihilism, an Aristotelian would speak of *dunamism*, the capacities, opportunities, potentialities as yet unrealized in experience. *Dunamism*, unlike nihilism, welcomes yea-saying. Or, more accurately, it recognizes the need for the proper blend of nay and yea-saying: saying no to the possibilities for evil and yes to the ones whose culminations are beneficent. Such *dunamism* allows an affirmation of the here and now. It sanctions a yes-saying (1) to the opportunities in the lived world; (2) to sorting out which opportunities are worthy of realization; (3) to assuming responsibility for such a sorting out; (4) to working within those conditions to bring possibilities to realization

Such a *dunamism*, it is true, would make life more onerous. It would interfere with shortcuts and simplifications. It would admit the inevitability of frustrations, fallibilism, imperfect, and flawed achievements. The easier path is definitely the one of nihilism. Just say no to the effort of converse and commerce. Go with a neat, either/or, rationality. Avoid the need to deal with nuance, fallibility, distinctions, moderate successes; the need, always, to sort out possibilities, to evaluate differential responses (responsibility). Rigid legalism makes things easy. Simplicity gives rise to much less anxiety than does complexity. The static world of minerality can be self-serving. Worshiping *Nike* makes people feel good about themselves.

Saying "No" to Ordinary Life

Where does it all lead? *The Stranger* can be read as an inadvertent *reductio ad absurdum*. *The Fall* can be read as an explicit *reductio*. My take is that "The Renegade" is similar to *The Fall* in this regard. After all, the renegade himself says he would take his basic assumption, his single idea, to "its logical conclusion" (EK, 29). In a powerful manner, "The Renegade" draws harsh implications. Those implications, unchallenged, make us all dwellers in a city of salt, always in a combat mode, always devoted to the idol *Nike*.

It's all neat, clean, pure, and held together by force. It's akin to the "Being" of the pre-Socratic philosopher Parmenides (b. 515 BCE): whole, complete, unchanging. The world outside the city of salt, the greener one, can never be as clean and pure. It is a web of complications, subtleties, irreducible differences, mixtures. It is well captured by Walt Whitman's phrase "I contain multitudes." It is not Parmenidean Being. Nor is it Nothingness, sheer lack, emptiness, just a blank page. The lifeworld's status is more like that of a language: neither absolutely fixed, nor infinitely malleable. The lifeworld's status is precisely the one despised by clear-and-distinct types: that of the in-between.

It is not just abstraction-friendly philosophers who dislike the in-between. A force of evil like Mephistopheles realizes that the concrete lifeworld provides the biggest obstacle to his aims. The in-between, the mixed and mongrelized, offers poor territory for the great negator. He prefers the pendulum at its extremes. He doesn't mind utopian thinking because, once achieved, it proclaims a blanket "no" to reformist sensibilities. It might appear to be a "yes," but such a yes is nothing more than a disguised "no," since what is says "yes" to is an ideal which shall never be ("u-topia" means, literally "no-place").

In a similar vein, the negator doesn't mind the contrary of utopianism, blanket pessimism. This option openly embraces stasis (nay-saying to reform). The all-or-nothing attitude continues to dominate. The biggest threat to Mephistopheles, as he knows, is the in-between, the realm of yes-and-no, the one which says "no" to defects and "yes" to repair. That realm is a throbbing, ever-renewing, and, yes, clumsy, place. It stands in the way of someone who negates creation, someone fixated on an*nihil*ation (Goethe, ll. 1362–78).

That kingdom of salt, in a similar vein, has annihilated whatever might be associated with vibrancy and life. It's a place permeated by the "blows of the iron sun" (EK, 35). The renegade prays for relief: "Rain, O Lord, one real rain, long hard rain from your sky!" (EK, 34). The city of salt has its own lord, one who rules over a "city of order, finally, right angles, square rooms, stiff men" (EK, 42). This place is a city of "no." It is devoid of life in the fullest sense. Free play, give and take, novelty, vulnerability, variability, difference, and beauty have been suppressed. They have been replaced by homogeneity and regimentation. There is no place for love. Waiting to assassinate his successor, the renegade prays to his new God: "may hatred reign mercilessly over a world of the damned" (EK, 45).

The prayer grows out what his new masters have taught, how he must "settle accounts with love" (EK, 32). Love, a risk-related attempt at connection, depends on a preliminary "yes," even a definitive series of "yeses." The most important of these is a yes to love for life, for this life, here and now. The quotidian world would then be not one of nihilism but of *dynamism*. It would be one in which creation and connection began with a welcoming "yes" to possibilities within the ordinary. Unlike Janine, it would accept that love is possible in the here and now. It would abandon the dream of escape via total fusion. It would seek rather a harmonious working together within differences. Unlike the renegade it would not despise *eros*.

In neither of the two stories just examined is there a move toward rehabilitation of the ordinary. It is other stories in the collection that begin this trajectory. The next chapters will deal with them in pairs. Chapter 10 will deal with two stories that loosen the grip of thinking in terms of exile and kingdom. The final pair, examined in Chapter 11, opens pathways toward a new paradigm. This new paradigm would be "dynamic" rather than "nihilistic." Maybe, the stories suggest, there are real possibilities and opportunities latent within the quotidian. Maybe it's time to jettison the entire pattern of exiles dreaming of a perfect kingdom. Maybe we are ordinary residents who can make our home a better place.

10

Exile and the Kingdom, II

The Transitional Stories

Liquidity and Minerality

"The Adulterous Wife" and "The Renegade" represent very different trajectories. The general background, though, is the same: nihilism's denigration of the ordinary. Two other stories in the collection begin moving outside of this orbit. Mephistopheles, as we have seen, worried about one major obstacle. It stood in the way of establishing the realm of "nothingness." The obstacle was surprising in its banality: this world. When we say "no" to the here and now, we help the spread of nothingness. This spread encourages skepticism and despair, exactly the seeds that Mephistopheles sought to sow. The "negate the ordinary" scenario then can become an impenetrable self-reinforcing loop.

The two Camus stories already explored are situated within this loop. Janine finds everyday life marked by ennui, boredom, frustration. The only relief: liberation via escape, an escape involving contact with some other, nonhuman, realm. The renegade seeks a perfectly unified, homogeneous world, one in which differences have been abolished. He wants liberation from the demands of love, wants, as he puts it to "settle his score with love." Accordingly, he rejects conversation. He aims, instead, at conversion. Love requires listening, some attentiveness to the other. Once the aim becomes liberation from love, dialogue is replaced by monologue, conversation by conversion, harmony by domination.

Underlying all of this is a familiar inheritance from the Great Bifurcation: thinking in sharp either/or terms. Nihilism cannot abide nuance. *Either* the world is perfectly rational, answers fully to our needs, can be fathomed by infallible formulas, OR we live in a relativistic muddle where ideals are just human inventions. Life can then be characterized as uniquely frustrating. Skepticism becomes the ruling mode for intellectual life. The in-between realm, the actual lived world, with its clumsiness, and its opportunities, is one that Mephistopheles, friend of de-creation via nay-saying, cannot abide (Goethe, ll. 1364).

It is one from which Janine and the renegade seek an escape. Both ignore what is right in front of them. For flesh-and-blood persons, the lived word is (a) home, and (b) it's not all bad. True, it has its challenges. True, it demands responsibility and effort.

True, achievement is accompanied by risk and anxiety. But effort and responsibility, along with real risk and genuine achievement, are what make it a proper abode for *Homo sapiens*. The mystic and the friend of absolute domination may dream of escaping to a realm where uncertainty, contingency, differences, ennui, risk, and ongoing effort have been eliminated. They aim at stasis. Stasis, however, comes at a great cost, the elimination of struggle and achievement, the turning away, as the renegade avows, from love.

The here and now, the proper home for humans, is decidedly not a realm of easy formulations, rigid fixities, neat legalisms. It's a realm that allows for fluidity, flexibility, and interchange. Boundaries exist, but they (1) always involve fuzzy limits and (2) allow for some porosity. Differences are irreducible, but "other" need not mean "enemy." Mixings and blendings are at once inevitable and welcome. Being "confused," as we saw from Iris Murdoch, is not always a bad thing. This is especially true when confusion is mostly an admission of how complicated reality is.

Taking this notion further, and emphasizing mixing and blending, the philosopher Michel Serres has sought ontological rehabilitation for the term "confusion." Instead of imagining ourselves and other entities on the model of a block of granite, why not think in terms of organisms, of complicated entities whose different components can work well together. Why assume that a deeper unity underlies mixture? Why not think in terms of mixtures going all the way down? When we begin to think this way, then combination, blending, commixture, "con-fusion," becomes the safest general claim about all things (Serres 1985, 181–3).

Living beings in a living world are composite creatures in a variegated habitat. The shift proposed by Serres got a boost with the inception, in 2007, of the Microbiome project. It turns out that a human individual is not just a blend of organs but also a commingling of entities. Without the symbiosis of microorganisms, microorganisms whose cells outnumber those with our own DNA, humans would be stunted. "The bacteria in the microbiome help digest our food, regulate our immune system, protect against other bacteria that cause disease, and produce vitamins including B vitamins B12, thiamine and riboflavin, and Vitamin K, which is needed for blood coagulation" (Hair).[1] What we call an individual is a unique person, but the uniqueness does not derive from components that are homogeneous in their DNA or even belong to the same species. The individual's distinctness is that of being a unique host/guest mixture, a mixture in which different entities are commingled. When the interactions taking place in this realm of amalgamating work well, health results. There's an ethical corollary to this, one that runs counter to the attitude of the renegade: ideals need to be formulated in terms of harmony and concord, not in terms of unity as rigid homogeneity.

Rehabilitating "confusion" allows room for a positive take on a topic central to Camus's third cycle: love. Either/or, by contrast, represents an attitude consistent with combat and with the image of minerality. When, fearing confusion, we define freedom in terms of autonomy, we turn away from what it means to be a living being in a living world. The "individual" then becomes an entity that, for survival, does not require ongoing conversations between (a) all its organs, (b) the micro-entities that help constitute it, and (c) the milieu by which it survives. The model that rejects commingling insists that self-identity and non-dependence go all the way down. The mixing and blending that make us who we are is denied. Not just denied but turned into something pejorative.

In a context ruled by the notion of pure self-identity and characterized by rigid boundaries, mixing and blending can only signal impurity, degradation, pollution. Purity, unity, segregation, imposition of a single model, in other words, de-creation, tend to dominate. Creation, allied to fertility, and thus to novel blendings and mixings (con-fusions), is disparaged. Liquidity and minglings come to be understood as agents of contamination. What results is described by the term that has become inherently derisive: "mongrelization." But why should mongrelization be an automatically pejorative term? Because of an antecedent semantic landscape shaped by a philosophy that prizes unity and purity. The contesting metaphors pervading Camus's work are thus set in place—on one side, purity, control, domination, that is, minerality; on the other, blendings, fluency, hospitality, that is, liquidity.

The Quotidian Almost Rehabilitated: 1

In one way, the story called "Les Muets," the "Ones Who Do Not Speak" or, as it is translated "The Voiceless," could be seen as continuing in the tradition of "The Renegade." The absence of the speaking tongue is central in both cases. The stories, though, are quite different. "The Renegade" features zealots, individuals whose dream of domination necessitates the silencing of all others. Difference is inherently dangerous. It's "us" versus "them." The aim: imperialism's homogeneity. Make everyone over in a single image.

"The Renegade" focuses on only one tongue, the one that talks. Even then, the talk is not for conversation but for conversion, to enforce submission. Conversation requires give and take, talking and listening. Important as this is, the tongue that talks is only one of our tongues. There are also the tongue that tastes and the tongue that loves.[2] *Les Muets*, unlike "The Renegade," takes us into a more familiar setting, one populated by more ordinary people. It is a realm where the three tongues (talking, tasting, loving) intersect. Intersection does not mean absence of tension. As with "The Renegade," "Les Muets" is built around its own *us* versus *them* enmity. In this case, it is not religious conflict but an employee strike that is central. *Us* versus *them* is labor versus management.

What most differentiates "Les Muets" from "The Renegade" is a thicker description of human feelings. In "Les Muets" the us/them opposition is mitigated by points of overlap, shared interests, common sympathies. The story's title refers to what is commonly known as "the silent treatment." It's a self-imposed silence, silence used by the laborers as a weapon for those who are otherwise powerless. But the tongue that speaks represents only one dimension of complex individuals. The tongue that tastes and the tongue that loves are also operative. Their presence leaves open the possibility of conjunctions even where conversation has been stifled.

The story is also framed by liquidity. The sea, especially, is prominent. Minerality, so dominant in "The Renegade," is mostly absent. Importantly, children make an appearance, as does family life. Hospitality, a theme present in each of the *Exile and the Kingdom* stories, becomes more central. Finally, there is no isolated city of salt. The inhabited locale is situated within a wider, interconnected world, one of technological innovation and marketplace transformations. Neither management nor labor is immune from the impact of such factors. The context, in short, is a composite, "confused" one. The generalized "no" of walled-off sequestration is not viable.

The technological innovations along with coordinated changes in market demand are real. They represent a kind of call to which various responses are possible. Escape from the here and now is not an option. Nor is total conquest. In a barrel-making enterprise, management needs labor and labor needs management. Both need a market. The here and now stands as the only real there is. It's got problems, but also possibilities. As persons who recognize their situatedness in the lived present, the story's characters are not given to grandiose, absolutistic pronouncements. They do not seek refuge in another realm. They simply want to make a living. This is so in two senses: (1) the economic sense of having enough resources to live comfortably and (2) the desire to chart a meritorious life path.

Accepting, rather than negating, their situatedness makes a difference. Their affirmation of ordinary existence means they take heed of the complexities involved with multiple tongues and multiple kinds of love. Three dimensions of the tongue and three sorts of love stand out in the story. The three lingual dimensions have already been mentioned: the tongue that talks, the one that tastes, and the one that loves. Love itself is manifested in ways that take us back to the Greek multiplicity. There is *philia*, friendship and solidarity among workers. There is *storge*, affection for children. Finally, there is *eros*, spousal relationship.

The tongue that talks becomes a weapon in the management/labor dispute. In "The Renegade" the main character's tongue had been torn out so that he could no longer speak. The workers in *Les Muets* consciously and purposely halt their speaking. They adopt the silent treatment. Silence is, for them, a weapon in the service of *eris*. Their action is not arbitrary. They choose silence as an appropriate response to demeaning behavior directed toward them. The workers are not Parisian intellectuals who dismiss all social standards as merely conventional. There are standards of human-to-human comportment. Even if these are unwritten, they remain functional. When breached, a serious offense has occurred. M. Lassalle is the boss. Times are tough. Artisanal barrel making is an industry in decline. The company's bottom line is suffering. The boss does not wish to diminish his profits. He freezes workers' salaries. They protest. Against the advice of their union, they strike.

So far all of this takes place within standards governing worker-management interplay.

Tensions between workers and management are neither surprising nor avoidable. The strike comes about as workers organize using the tongue that speaks. They enter into negotiations with their employer. After a few discussions, the boss, as the workers see it, crosses a line. He violates a principle that should remain relevant even in the midst of a strike. The offense: lack of respect. Tired of negotiating, asserting his position of superiority, ignoring many years of built-up relationships, the boss abruptly shuts down dialogue "Take it or leave it," he proclaims. In doing so, he renders the workers voiceless. He had no need of physically and violently ripping out the tongue as in "The Renegade." Nonetheless, the result was similar. The workers were appalled: "A man doesn't talk that way" (EK, 52). From their point of view, the boss, by abandoning dialogue, had given up on treating them as fellow human beings.

Making matters worse, the boss taunts his employees, saying that when the factory is closed he saves money. Not only is this not true, "but it hadn't helped matters since he was telling them to their faces that he only gave them work out of charity" (EK, 53). The owner and the workers need each other. Between them, though, a great gap has opened, a gap signaled by suppressing the tongue that talks. First, the owner's ultimatum silences the employees. Then, retaliation: the workers adopt a strategy of enforced silence.

Even after the strike has failed, and operations have resumed, the silent treatment continues. The boss tries to reopen conversation with a morning greeting. A sense of solidarity keeps the employees united in their punitive silence. What can they do? Their strike has failed. They have no leverage. They need work. They realize that forces outside their control will soon render their skills obsolete. Options for manifesting displeasure are limited. The silent treatment is powerful. It is also, as M. Lassalle's anger reveals, effective.

The workers also have little to say among themselves. Even Esposito, the most radical of them, keeps quiet when the senior and most generous-spirited employee rebukes his co-workers for "behaving like children" (EK, 61). Another tongue, though, the tongue that tastes, begins to reopen lines of linkage. In the past, those lines, characterized by a table with shared food and shared talking/listening, had included the boss. He had, at times, "invited them to eat at the barrel works; they would grill sardines or sausage." They were even known to break open some wine (EK, 52). The linkages, though, were limited and one-sided. The boss was always the host, never a guest. The boss "had never gone to their homes" (EK, 53).

The tongue that tastes fosters worker-to-worker solidarity. Yvars, the story's central figure, shares his sandwich with Said, the only Arab employee (EK, 60). Esposito also unveils a special taste-centered treat. His grocer, feeling bad about the strike's failure, has donated coffee. In a sort of industry-site communion, the coffee cup is passed around (EK, 61). The tongue that talks is still mostly quiet. The tongue that tastes, though, has been loosened. Yvars begins to relax. After sharing his lunch, "his feeling of uneasiness since the interview with Lassalle suddenly disappeared, leaving in its place only a fine warmth" (EK, 60).

That warmth is soon dissipated by a ringing bell. Ballester investigates and, using the tongue that speaks, announces solemnly "The girl had an attack" (EK, 62). The "girl" is the boss's daughter. One worker has his tongue spontaneously loosened: "Perhaps it's nothing" (EK, 63). In *The Renegade*, difference is understood one-dimensionally. "Different" translates directly into "enemy." In *Les Muets*, one layer of difference-as-enemy is real and prominent: boss and laborer. M. Lassalle is "other" and enemy. He has broken the strike. This is one layer. At the same time, he is a father. He is an enemy of the workers in the first context. In the second, he is harder to classify as "enemy." There is an important overlap with some of the workers: fatherhood.

The strike did much to reinforce a straightforward "us versus the enemy" attitude. In *The Renegade* the story ended there. Sympathy and its close relative, empathy, were nowhere to be found. The main relationship between the two camps was war. *Eris* set the tone and *Nike* was the guiding divinity. In the more complicated setting of a small company, relations are multilayered. Employer and employee frequent each other day in and day out. This makes more evident the multiple facets of people's characters. Everyday familiarity changes the other from a "type" to "this particular person." The social interchange that takes place is multidimensional and more fluid. Barriers, such as those of class, do not disappear. At the same time, there are layers of affection, shared concerns, sociality, even solidarity that can make those barriers more supple.

"The girl had an attack." It's a brief phrase, but it changes the dynamics. No longer is the labor/management split front and center. Worried-parent-with-a-sick-child becomes a point of overlap. Despite the self-imposed silent treatment, the workers feel a humane concern for M. Lassalle and his daughter. The tongue that speaks is even loosened. There's the spontaneous "Perhaps, it's nothing" from one worker. "Sick child" is an experience that cuts across class lines. It confuses things, softens boundaries, reemphasizes points of interconnection. Although a child's illness has somewhat released the tongue that speaks, that relaxation is limited. The pain and sense of injustice associated with the strike run deep. In general, the silent treatment remains. The workers feel an urge to speak. Yvars is typical. His body is aching from work. His heart is aching from the news. "He would have liked to talk," but he says nothing (EK, 63).

Sadness characterizes the mood of the employees, "sorrow and a kind of obstinacy." Yvars senses the word "misfortune" bubbling up within him, but it disappears (EK, 63). Then, as closing time arrives, Lassalle enters the work area. The employees are embarrassed. There is a general sense that someone should speak. Obstinacy keeps them silent. The only word uttered, a simple "goodnight," comes from Lassalle. As the boss walks away, Yvars "thought they should have called to him," but they do not (EK, 64). When the workers say goodbye to each other, the tone is different. Yvars's utterance is delivered "with all his heart." The others reply "with the same warmth" (EK, 64). It is highly unlikely that any of them would some day own a factory. Any one of them, though, could, any day, be confronted with a sick child. This shared fear solidifies a bond of rapport between them. As Yvars bicycles home, he cannot get the little girl out of his mind (EK, 65).

The days when wooden barrels made by skilled craftsmen were in big demand are over. A way of life is changing. There are no utopian solutions. The writing is on the wall. The workers' way of life will soon be silenced for good. It's kind of hopeless. It is hopeless, at least until children, a new generation, enter the picture. If their children can stay healthy and grow into adulthood, perhaps life will be better for them.

Yvars is typical. He returns home to the family associated with *eros*, the tongue that loves and *storge*, affection for offspring that are the product of *eros*. The story's final scene takes place in the family home. That is a venue where the various tongues, the one that loves, the one that tastes, and the one that talks, intersect. At first, the silence from work spills over to silence at home. Fernande, Yvars's wife, asks if all is well. He maintains his self-imposed muteness. Then, an evening ritual settles in. The tasting tongue is activated. Fernande brings "the anisette, two glasses," and "the jug of fresh water" (EK, 65). At this point the talking tongue is liberated. "He told her everything, holding her hand, as he had done early in their marriage" (EK, 65). If time could be reversed, they would go away "across the sea." But time cannot be reversed. No fantasy-based dreaming will bring back artisanal barrel making. Still, their child is healthy. He wants to be a teacher. The here and now offers some hope.

The last word is mine, not Camus's. It does, though, reflect the temperament as the story ends. It signals a contrast with *The Myth of Sisyphus*. That essay was all about purified, stripped-down concepts. "Hope" meant one thing only: the desire for an afterlife that would make all well. It offered, for those with a religious sensibility, a realm of escape. The absurd hero who rejected such escapism had not only to embrace a quotidian life but to embrace one that was hope-free. Both the religious type and the absurd hero agreed on one point: everyday life offers nothing that could encourage hope.

Les Muets minimizes concepts that are abstract, purified, stripped down. It takes us into the thick, variegated, manifold experience that is everyday existence. Here "hope" need not be aligned with a future transcendent state. "Hopes," as Gabriel Marcel explained, are *not* most commonly of the grandiose sort. They are ordinary ones suited to the kind of creature we are (Marcel, 29). We enter the attitude of hopefulness on a regular basis. We hope that our friend's journey will be a safe one. We hope, as does Yvars, that our children will succeed in life. In this there is very little escapist utopianism. John Macquarrie, in a study of the human condition, reinforces the point. Hope, he claims, is not at all the same as a "brash and shallow optimism" (Macquarrie, 243). Instead, hopefulness is an indicator. It suggests how the quotidian conditions of life provide possibilities which allow for fruitions and culminations. Hope is an in-between sentiment. Shallow, utopian optimism says "yes" to dreams of an ideal future realm. Pessimism utters a definitive "no" to ordinary life conditions. Utopian dreamers and pessimists have one thing in common: denigration of the here and now. Typical hopefulness, by contrast, accepts how the lived world offers a mix of yes and no. It is neither so fixed that all changes are impossible. Nor is it so wide open that we can impose on it any utopian formula we envision. Hopefulness, as Macquarrie notes, avoids totalizing temptations. It "implies belief that the world has some openness in its texture, some space for freedom and creativeness" (Macquarrie, 245).

Commitment and effort on our part identify an important ingredient in taking advantage of "some openness" and using "freedom and creativeness" in order to bring certain possibilities to fruition. It also indicates a way out of the semantic limitations associated with the Great Bifurcation. "Commitment and effort" need not mean merely "subjective" and "relativist." "Some openness" does not translate into infallible certitude. The situation is better understood holistically, as a participatory nexus in which call and response can be properly calibrated. This position had already been hinted at in *The Plague*'s closing sections. A situation marked by death is one in which humans are left with only memories. "How hard it must be," Rieux editorialized, "to live only with what one knows and what one remembers, cut off from what one hopes" (Pl, 292) Rieux's efforts were in part motivated by a hopefulness that the plague would eventually be beaten back. Optimal states are fragile. Creativeness, what comes from the proper yea-saying/nay-saying blend, is precarious and easily lost. It is also, as Rieux recognized, sustained by hopefulness.

Everyday hopes allow us to recognize our setting as one that is in-between. Though limited by many factors outside our control, we are not confined within the rigid determinism of fate. At the same time, ours is not a condition completely adrift. We partake of a semiotic environment, one in which there are hints and indications about how best to chart our lives. These hints are clues or signals. They are not "signs" in the clumsy sense of dramatic Damascene moments like being knocked off one's horse by a blinding light. Shortcuts, de-complications, simplifications always represent a temptation. Ordinary hopefulness helps deflect the attraction of oversimplification. It recognizes the necessity of challenge, struggle, fallibility, and creativeness. It lives within the dynamic relevance of possibilities. It accepts the opportunities of (real but not unlimited) openness and freedom. It welcomes the combination of responsibility and effort. It does not make the absence of risk and anxiety the major desiderata of life.

The simplified, purified, monosemic concept "hope" dismissed in *The Myth of Sisyphus* is indeed spurious. But rejecting one kind of hope is not the same as rejecting hopefulness altogether. Everyday, concrete hopes remain. They offer motivations for repairing what has been rent. They encourage undertaking the sustained efforts needed for such repairs. They motivate creativeness. They represent the sorts of hopefulness well suited to flesh-and-blood humans, persons participating in concrete, overlapping, living webs of communicative interaction.

The Quotidian Almost Rehabilitated: 2

Camus continues a move toward rehabilitating the ordinary in the collection's funniest story. Significantly, like "Les Muets," it is also a story that includes children. The protagonist has great talent as a painter and very little when it comes to dealing with people. One of the themes that runs through *Exile and the Kingdom* is hospitality, the proper roles for hosts and guests. The couple featured in *The Adulterous Woman*, Janine and Marcel, are Europeans in Algeria. As representatives of colonial power, however, they do not think of themselves as guests. *The renegade* features someone who is also a European in Algeria. In that story, the priest is a bad guest and the villagers are awful hosts. *Les Muets* offers a more multifaceted conjunction. There is, as we have seen, food and drink, commensality among the workers. There is even a description of food and drink sharing, one that involves the factory owner, acting as a good host to his workers. Still, as we also saw, mutuality is limited. A strong asymmetry vitiates the guest/host relationship. M. Lassalle has shared food and drink with his workers. In this way he behaves as should a good host. However, he rejects the correlative status of guest. He never sets foot in the homes of his workers. He is always the host in control, never the vulnerable guest.

The story entitled *Jonas, or the Artist at Work* gets much of its comedic effect from a simple fact: Jonas is an overly generous host. He is a reverse Mephistopheles. Mephistopheles always says no. Jonas cannot say no. This leads to consequences: his house is overrun, his art suffers, and, by the story's end, he has overreacted by retreating to the lifestyle of a cloistered monk. With the dismissal of prudential judgment associated with the right yes/no combination, absolutized yea-saying turns out to be as bad as unconditional nay-saying.

Camus once complained about readers failing to grasp the humor in his fiction. It would be hard to read *Jonas* without at least a smirk, if not an outright guffaw. The story pokes fun at painters, at sycophantic acolytes, at landlords, family life, and art critics. At the same time, the story examines different kinds of love. *Storge* makes an appearance. Jonas is a father. Jonas and his wife Louise, living *eros*, are making a life together. Jonas has a good friend, Rateau, one whose *philia* is contrasted with the false friendships of various hangers-on.

The story takes a theme from *The Stranger* and turns it from catastrophe to farce. The theme: someone who floats above the ordinary concerns of life. Meursault's disengagement grew out of generalized indifference. Jonas is, rather, a *que será, será* type. He simply goes with the flow, allowing circumstances to determine his activities. His is a life characterized by an unconditional, unlimited "yes." As a result, his life, this may seem counterintuitive, has little room for hope. Hopefulness is inherently allied with freedom rather than fatalism. It admits some openness in the fabric of things. It encourages instituting changes via free election among options. Fatalism discourages all of this. It accepts an already-set trajectory. There is no space of openness, no room for selecting among possibilities, no way to bring about a genuinely altered outcome.

The hope/freedom/effort mix (con-fusion?) also deflects the shortcuts much beloved to proponents of both the absolute no and the absolute yes. Once shortcuts and simplifications are set aside, what counts is an effort at getting the mix right. Success is never guaranteed. Seeking, in terms of actual conditions, to achieve the proper response (responsibility) will always be accompanied by anxiety and risk. When a major goal becomes not achieving good but avoiding anxiety and risk, then the Jonas strategy defines one resulting path: adopt a "what can I do?" fatalism; proclaim that your life is guided by a "star."

Jonas's fatalism, soft and easygoing as it may be, is nonetheless real. This emerges in self-reflections about artistic talent. Jonas does not associate artistic creativity with Tarrou's "vigilance that must never falter." He does not think of it as (1) the recognition of some endowment, one (2) needing to be explicitly embraced, and that (3) cannot be brought to culmination outside of strenuous effort. Such a process is not only onerous and anxiety producing, it also (4) entails an additional component: filtering certain goods. A writer, for example, might have to sacrifice pleasant socializing with friends in favor of time at a desk cranking out a fixed number of words per day.

Jonas has found a way to minimize anxiety and avoid awareness about sacrificing human goods. How? *Amor fati*, just say yes to whatever happens; claim it is the result of his "star." The story opens by describing Jonas. He is characterized as someone of "trusting modesty." But "modesty" turns out to be selectively understood. What he means is that he simply gives credit to his "star" (EK, 87). In *The Stranger*, Meursault was fond of a grandiose ontological pronouncement about the indifferent nature of things. This indifference translated into an attitude of *ça m'est égal*, "it's all the same to me." Jonas favors the more deferential *comme vous voudrez*, "as you like" (EK, 104). In both cases an important evasion takes place. The need for selecting among options, saying yes to some and no to others, is sidestepped. Meursault, committed to *liberum arbitrium indifferentiae*, says, in effect, I'm radically free, all options are the same, why bother troubling myself with responsibility. Jonas, in effect, says, it's already in the cards, so why should I trouble myself selecting among options and responsibility. His "yes" is thus a yes to whatever happens. It is *amor fati* in the strongest sense. It is not a "yes" to the actual human condition. Such a "yes" would, ironically, be a "yes" to the need for making "yes/no" distinctions. His "yes" is a more abstract, universal, purified one.

This is where the *leitmotif* that runs through all of the stories, hospitality, plays an important role. As a virtue, hospitality urges being a good host and a good guest. In an Aristotelian context, virtues are subject to perversion via either excess or deficiency. Virtue, in other words, requires balance, or as Camus called it "measure." Humans manifest many possibilities for good and bad. Selecting the right cluster and cultivating, in proper combination, the components of the cluster present real challenges. Even good actions like hospitality, generosity, forgiveness, and tolerance can be pushed too far. Jonas's excess is that he always says "yes." Anyone who wants access to him or his home has that wish granted.

Faust's Mephistopheles was an absolutist in the direction of "no." Camus's Jonas is a Mephistopheles in reverse, an absolutist in the direction of "yes." Jonas does not take charge of his life. The specifics, as described by Camus, are humorous. The culmination is not. There is not really a "star" leading inexorably to the point at which Jonas ends. Belief in some version of fate is both a pervasive temptation[3] and one that can, as with Jonas, lead to isolation and sterility. Jonas is the poster boy for those who succumb to fatalism, even of the soft sort. He's not a bad person. He reveals himself as having no nasty or deplorable inclinations. His guiding motto, "as you like," is inoffensive enough. The resulting life, in Camus's description, is more humorous than malevolent. Clutter, distractions, people falling over each other dominate. It's a comedy of both manners and errors.

Beyond the humor there is a serious side. Jonas's unwillingness, in practice, to say "*this* is more important, and, as a result, *that* must be sacrificed," leads him, in the end, to the kind of withdrawal usually associated with an anchorite. Living in the real world with all its complexities and responsibilities is just too much. His reaction is a totalizing one. Withdrawal is, for him, the only way out. The resultant state of self-imposed isolation is one in which love, whether *storge*, *eros*, or *philia*, cannot germinate. Like painting, love requires effort, commitment, and personal involvement. It cannot burgeon and flourish if the highest ideal is elimination of risk and anxiety. It cannot happen without a determination to chart out a course that will, as time develops, progressively realize some accomplishments and, at the same time, leave others in abeyance. The move toward actual accomplishment can be aided, even motivated, in the ordinary sense of the term, by hope. There needs to be a sense that life offers real flexibility, a belief in genuine possibilities over which we have some control. When ordinary hopes are operative, something recedes to the periphery: the passive quiescence associated with *amor fati*, submission to one's "star."

In a real sense, Jonas is an innocent. He is both naive and endowed with great artistic talent. In another sense, Jonas is also someone who shirks responsibility. "As *you* wish" is telling. He lets outside forces take control. Although endowed with great promise, he fails to bring that promise to its culmination. Actualization would require a "promise" of a different kind, the kind that makes a commitment. Both "promise" and "commitment" draw on the Latin verb *mittere*, send forth. A commitment and a promise, when lived out, require a particular yes/no combination. Selecting this specific path means parting with advantages that come with alternatives. The promise of being a faithful husband brings with it a commitment to making a life with this particular spouse. Commitment to being a good father requires special attentiveness to these particular children. Commitment to being an artist means taking responsibility for the effort, time, and challenges that are required to produce works of art. Commitment to being a husband *and* father *and* artist requires an even more complicated mixture of yeses and noes. The potential alone, for example, being a promising artist, father, or husband, remains a utopian illusion without the active carrying out of the activities associated with the promise. It stands apart from the neat alternatives: "I mean well, but will not carry through" and "I'll just wait for my star to guide me."

Jonas has talent, a wife, children, and a friend. The narrator describes Jonas's relationships in terms of love: Jonas "loved his painting, and Louise, his children, Rateau, and a few others as well" (EK, 105–6). This is "love" in theory, an inner feeling, not a full-fledged, lived realization. Fulfilling the promise of love would require differential appraisal allied to deferential conduct. It would necessitate some naysaying to the unending stream of visitors; would require constancy when distractions of all sorts arrived; would entail living out, in practice, selective valuation, arriving at the right mix of time with family, time with guests, time for a friend, and time for painting. There are no ready-made formulas for getting the blend right. That's why the Greek emphasis on moderation or balance was so important—because it was hard to achieve.

The story's narrator, after describing the loves of Jonas, adds an editorial: "But life is short, time goes by quickly, and his own energy had its limits" (EK, 106). Our lives are bounded by a span of time. There is no avoidance of evaluative culling. Our limited lifespan means that some yes/no combination is inevitable. Humans, though, are never in short supply of self-deception. They can pretend that such sorting out is avoidable. Jonas's commitment to his "star" offers but another twist to the grip that nihilism has on our consciousness. Belief in fate, that is, any of the various forms of determinism, offers a disguised manner of voiding (and avoiding) responsibility. It opens the way to a great simplification: always say "that's just how things are." Ignore (really "annihilate") the genuine possibilities in the here and now. Follow the more lackadaisical, more risk-free path of always affirming a single formula.

Jonas lives out such a single-formula life. Camus, telling the story, offers a negative evaluation. After a while, Jonas no longer really feels alive. The narrator says Jonas loved his children "as much as his painting because they alone in the world were as alive as it was" (EK, 112). So far so good. The twist comes with the limited range of what is "alive." Just before this, Rateau had asked Jonas bluntly, "Do you exist?" to which Jonas had answered, "No, I'm not certain I exist" (EK, 110). Even when it came to painting, Jonas was detaching himself from the realm of the quotidian, the realm of concrete existence in the fullest sense. Jonas, seeking to escape the maelstrom that surrounds him, begins a process of detachment and disconnection. Being a living being in a living world is not for him. His attempt to rise above it all reveals itself in a new take on his craft. He worked less, "thinking about painting" rather than painting (EK, 112). When he does paint, he concentrates on otherworldliness. His canvases contain mostly skies (EK, 113).

Life, as Jonas conceives it, *should not* entail selection among options, selections which necessitate surrendering some goods in favor of others. Intellectually, Jonas has inherited a theoretical outlook that oscillates between extremes. The extremes (within this scheme) are (a) live with others and be constantly distracted, or (b) withdraw, live alone, free, and unencumbered. The notion of achieving the right mix is banished from the start. Having excluded the option of achieving an appropriate blend, Jonas can only seesaw between extremes. At first he is someone who can never say no. By the end, he has become someone who only says "no." He transforms himself into a sort of cloistered monk. He builds a shelter within his apartment, a kind of cave into which he can withdraw. Just as the anchorites sought saintliness by serving the spirit separated from the body, so Jonas now believes he can serve his art best by disconnecting himself from the everyday world. After all, for him, the quotidian realm meant nothing but interference and interruption. He ends up as a sort of Jonas from the Bible, albeit a Jonas sequestered in a whale of his own making.

His escape does not follow the religious path criticized in *The Myth of Sisyphus*. Nor is it the Janine-inspired escape via a naturalized form of mysticism. Still, it remains a very real form of escape, one with damaging consequences for those who love him. From the self-sequestered location, the only utterance heard is "Leave me alone. I'm working" (EK, 122). The second part of this assertion, we come to find out, has not gone well. At one point he turns a canvas against the wall, vows that he will never work again, and is described, Sisyphus-style, as "happy." As far as the first part of his claim, "leave me alone," he comes to realize its drawbacks, especially the family togetherness he is missing. From outside his hovel he can hear "children shouting, water running, dishes clinking, Louise talking." "The world was still there, young, lovable: Jonas listened to the lovely murmur of humanity" (EK, 122). Sadly, even though the murmur may have been lovely, it is one from which he had purposely sequestered himself.

From his insulated perch, the sounds of wife and daughter prompt a reaction: "He loved them! How he loved them!" (EK, 122). The impact of that judgment lies in the word "how." Jonas always loved them, in theory, in spirit, inside, "really." What he could not do, what required promise, commitment, and effort, was to love them in practice, to give up the nonsense about his star, abandon his unlimited "yes" saying. Only then could he chart out a life that would have provided the time and effort to make *eros* and *storge* enduring attainments. To realize the promise of being a husband and a father is to make promises about presence, actions, effort. Such promises cannot be kept if, by falling back on fate or a "star," Jonas drifts along, allowing himself to be drawn and tugged by whatever immediate tendencies surround him. Without a promise that will live out a blend of yes and no, the possibility of making love a reality disintegrates. Theoretical love may be imagined from an isolated cave. Real love-making can only occur within the murmur of everyday living.

Instead of the Greek exhortation "nothing to excess," Jonas's guiding principle becomes "only excess." His last canvas says it all. Well, it would say it all if it were legible. Rateau, examining the work, realizes it is blank save for one word. Even that word is hard to make out. It could be *solidaire* or *solitaire* ("solidary" or "solitary"—a contrast whose full force is missed by the English translation as "independent/interdependent" (EK, 123). Excess rules. *Either/or* defines life. Set aside are balance, alignment, calibration, the onerous dimensions of responsibility. Within such an *either/or* frame of reference, the ordinary, everyday lifeworld, the one of "children shouting, water running, dishes clinking, Louise talking" will always be lost.

In the end, Jonas has, in effect, said "no" to the flesh-and-blood world. He has affirmed, as much as is possible, a state of disembodiment. He is less like the Biblical prophet Jonas and more like a Christian hermit. The prophet, after all, was unwillingly trapped inside the beast. Once released, he returned to his assigned mission. The hermit/monk purposely withdraws from the world. His life follows pathways charted by the road map of the Great Bifurcation. That map only shows passages defined as segregations: self from society, fact from value, and, in fancier Latin terminology, *vita activa* from *vita contemplativa*. Such oppositions are inherent within the inherited intellectual landscape. Jonas, thinking he is merely following his star, has no clue that he is guided by a lengthy intellectual tradition. He thus has no inclination that, instead of trying to follow the inherited and sedimented map, what is needed is a new map allowing a different take on the territory. Jonas, stuck with the vintage map, can only work within the alternatives defined by it. The *vita activa* is too much of a mess. He opts for a more secure, anxiety-minimized version of the *vita contemplativa*. He is unlike Yvars, not depicted as sharing, face to face, an aperitif with his wife. Jonas has become more like St. Simeon Stylites, who spent three decades perched on a pole. Like St. Simeon, Jonas has to have food sent up to him. Like a flesh-hating anchorite, like someone who is more a detached spirit than a full-fledged human, Jonas hardly touches his food (EK, 120).

Ordinary life for Jonas is both close and far away. It is close enough that he can hear "the lovely murmur of humanity." Its affirmation (saying "yes" to the responsibility for sorting out "yes" and "no") was a real opportunity. Yet, in the end, nihilism along with its sharp either/or, rules. Or, saying the same thing in a different way, asceticism rules. Jonas turns his back on the quotidian and the possibilities for love that lie latent within it.

Rejecting the affirmation of yes/no responsibility means that all possibilities for the affiliations associated with love come to be severed. Jonas has explicitly adopted the role of a laminated self. His existence is better defined by self-enclosed minerality than porous liquidity. There are calls to connection. *Storge*, for example, beckons. He is drawn to his children. But, he turns away. Rateau, good friend, representative of *philia*, is true to the end. Jonas does not distinguish between Rateau and the sycophants who fill his apartment. Louise, forgiving and loyal, emblem of *eros*, is left to fend for herself. All around Jonas the fecund opportunities of everyday existence are available. These will be missed so long as he uses as his guide the groundmap that depicts a subject set over against objects.

A genuinely different groundmap would not highlight dyads at all. It would instead, thinking in more concretely descriptive terms, emphasize events. "I am I and my circumstance" or, even better, "we, involved in multiple interactions" would more adequately identify the elemental patterns of existence. This would be even more fruitful if the "we" included the nonhuman (biological and natural) realm. Such a map would, instead of a dyadic structure, make room for confluences ("con-fusions") of interacting components. As counterintuitive as it may seem, there are, on this map, no discrete, detached, autarchic units. Transactions, coactions, communicative relationships of call and response are every bit as basic as are the coacting participants. Jonas, on the hoary map, can think of himself as a separated self. The newer map would draw him in a different direction. He would be encouraged to understand himself as someone both dependent upon and contributing to overlapping and intersecting events. Only abstract eliminationism segregates contributors from the conditions to which they contribute. It's as if someone who needs to breathe could be separated from the atmosphere which makes breathing possible.

For those living in a milieu of "events," life becomes (drawing on the etymology associated with the verb *venire*) that of an "ad-venture." Responding to possibilities by accepting adventure brings with it risk and anxiety. Life as an adventure does not privilege the goals of quietude, equanimity, absolute rest, mystical escape. Responsibility means responding properly. This in turn means undertaking the difficult quest of arriving at the proper mix of nay-saying/yea-saying.

Adventure and responsibility can, of course, be avoided. The path of sequestration, the secular version of a *vita contemplativa*, offers one means of avoidance. Such avoidance comes at a price. As the narrator tells us, Jonas no longer feels fully alive (EK, 110). Having rejected the adventure associated with flesh-and-blood fullness ("solidary"), only a harsh, abstract isolation ("solitary") remains.

The other transitional story, *Les Muets*, ended on a note of connection. Yvars and his wife hold hands. They share a drink. Jonas ends on a note of disconnection. It is not a disconnection resulting from chance or from necessity. The disconnection results from a consciously assumed isolation. Yvars, his wife, and their son present a picture in which love is brought to a limited but genuine realization. Some of the positive dynamism latent in the lifeworld has been actualized. Connection and love are accompanied by hope, if not for Yvars and Fernande, at least for their son. Jonas, by contrast, is a lot like the doves mentioned by Clamence. Ordinary life is, for him, hopelessly fallen. He seeks to hover above, not to be situated within, ordinary life. In that way he ensures that however abundant the womb of quotidian life may be, that abundance will never see the light of day.

11

Exile and the Kingdom, III

The Forward-Looking Stories

Xenia and *Agape*

In some of the stories about Sisyphus, his crime, a serious one for the ancient Greeks, involved harming guests to his city. He was thus guilty of violating the ancient Greek obligation of hospitality (see "Greek mythology" in the Bibliography). The intersecting themes of hospitality and love have been present in the stories so far discussed. In each, the shadow of nihilism looms large as the move toward rehabilitation of the ordinary barely figures. The Great Bifurcation remained a controlling presence for the two stories ("The Adulterous Wife" and "The Renegade") examined in Chapter 9. As with Medusa, a disconnected head turns everything into stone. The renegade takes up residence in a city of salt. Janine finds herself in a landscape that is "only stone, stone everywhere" (EK, 8).

Without a paradigm shift, there can be only an "absurd" opposition between the living human and the world described as essentially mineral. Perfection rather than appropriate culminations, totality rather than harmony remain as guiding ideals. In "The Adulterous Wife," Janine's mystical experience reveals how she can never be fully at home in the here and now. For her, life here in this world is one of exile. The realm of non-alienated perfection, the "kingdom," is situated elsewhere. "The Renegade" exemplifies how awful the ramifications of nihilism, when allied to a totalitarian attitude, can be. It depicts a climate of opinion in which spiritual perfection can only be attained by turning away from the "fallen" realm. Within the fallen realm, others, representatives of difference, are inherently understood as enemies. There is no room, in such a fallen state, for the virtue of hospitality.

The Renegade is a really bad guest. His malignancy is only matched by the villagers in the city of salt who are terrible hosts. There is no human interaction between them, no sense of shared humanity, of curiosity, of desire to learn from one another. Those would require some sense of positive possibilities among already existing communities. Without this shared assumption, guest/host generosity is replaced by the dialectic of domination/dominated. Dialogue is rejected out of hand. Neither *philia*, *storge*, nor *agape* are anywhere in sight. *Eros* is present only in the perverted forms of celibacy and rape.

One of the stories studied in Chapter 10, "The Silent Ones" (*Les Muets*), offers possibilities for *philia*, *storge*, and *eros*. Comradeship exists among the workers in the barrel factory. Affection for children offers an opening for empathy. A couple holding hands, engaging in a heartfelt conversation, provides the culminating scene of the story. The hospitality element, though, highlights the basic, unhealed rupture in the tale. M. Lassalle can be generous toward his workers, people who are like "guests" coming to his place every day. Like a good host, he has been known to share food and drink with them. However, it's a one-sided affair. Hospitality invariably involves him as host in the sense of someone who is in charge. He never visits the homes of his workers, never undertakes the more vulnerable role of guest. This basic asymmetry signals the impossibility of a satisfactory resolution as labor and management face economic and technological challenges that will harm both of them.

The other story from Chapter 10 indicates how the various sorts of love can be close at hand yet rejected. For Jonas, hospitality is perverted by being pushed to an extreme. His fatalism makes it hard for him to enact a healthy balance of yes and no. Since he cannot really say "no," his home is overrun by guests, guests who make life intolerable and work impossible. *Eros*, *philia*, and *storge* should be within Jonas's reach. He says he loves his wife, his children, and his good friend. But *eros*, *philia*, and *storge* are not just states of mind. They come to life, realize full manifestation, only in practice. Jonas, as someone who thinks that fate will take care of everything, simply fails to realize how effort on his part needs to be an important ingredient. He lives in an abstract realm populated by purified, oppositional, concepts like *solitaire* and *solidaire*. The messier, lived world, one in which yes and no need to be properly blended, is not for him. He escapes via a well-trodden path: that of the ascetic.

The two remaining stories, the subjects of this chapter, emphasize two additional manifestations of love: *xenia* (guest/host friendship) and *agape* (gift-love). Both *xenia* and *agape* work in settings where differences are more prominent than similarities, and where relationships develop outside of a context which is inherently egalitarian and reciprocal. This separates them from *philia* and *eros*. These two are typically rooted in an explicit attraction, a kind of reciprocal connection that is of background, shared interests, or sexual passion. *Xenia* and *agape* involve greater risk-taking. This is so in several ways. First, differences are taken for granted as irreducible. Second, reciprocity is not required. Third, as a result, although all the loves involve risk, the risk is, for them, heightened. The chances of things working out badly are more prominent than with the other loves.

The paradigmatic scenario in both cases, a scenario that includes irreducible difference, risk, and generosity, is the guest/host relationship. Guest and host, in the most prototypical case, must be strangers, those who are different. At the same time, there is an overarching, shared element: humanity.[1] In other ways, it is difference that stands out. Such a combination (similar-yet-different) is hard for the iron-clad, coldly logical mind to hold together. It prefers the realm of either/or, prefers the neat distinctions made by what logicians call excluded middles. It insists that only one of the totalizing claims, "the other is different" or "the other human is identical," can be true. There is no middle ground.

Xenia and *agape*, by contrast, require holding together both the reality of difference and the reality of kinship. They also demand holding together another in-between position: humans are neither constantly roaming exiles nor fixed home-dwellers. They are, by nature, wanderer-inhabitants. Earth is where they belong, so they are not exiles in any radical sense. At the same time, if they trace their ancestry far enough, they will realize that they came from a place that was not the one they now call home. Humans are, in some ways, like exiles, and in some ways like home-dwellers. In terms of old Hollywood Westerns, they are both the cattlemen and the ranchers.

Since they are at once wanderers and residents, their challenge is (1) to make good homes in the here and now; (2) recognize how, in an important way, everyone is a wanderer or stranger; (3) how otherness and difference are not deviations from a single norm; and (4) how the resultant aspirational condition should be that of concord or harmony. Love, which Camus was to make central in his third cycle, offered pathways to such concord. The forms of love highlighted in the two stories to be examined in this chapter are *xenia* and *philia*. Like *eros*, *philia*, and *storge*, these forms of love only manifest themselves fully in the here and now. Because they take for granted both stranger status and difference, they require preliminary realizations: how difference and existence overlap, and how we are all wanderer-homebodies.

The pattern of initial Paradise/Paradise Lost/Paradise Regained is foreign to them. That pattern brings with it a particular kind of baggage, one which denigrates the here and now. The truths associated with labels like "exile" and "kingdom" are perverted when framed in the scenario of Paradise Lost/Paradise Regained. Within that plot line, "exile" means being in a land that is totally alien, one where we do not at all belong. "Kingdom" comes to mean that status we can recapture only if we have escaped from this land of exile. Exile and kingdom, along with spirit/matter and sacred/profane, are turned into abstractions set automatically in opposition to each other.

The wanderers-home-dwellers, by contrast, are those who are neither completely exiles nor fully at home. They are hosts/guests. Their main challenge is to make the here and now, the only home we have, more like an aspirational one. The main strategy for those wishing to undertake this task, one not typically accepted by colonizers, is taking a free and risky first step: greeting strangers as if they are long-lost relatives, children of God heretofore unknown. In this way they hope to encourage a particular cycle of behavior, one modeled on being good hosts and good guests. If all goes well, a cycle of mutual involvement and harmonious entanglement can be inaugurated. Such a cycle, in turn, would provide a counterbalance to its evil twin: a cycle highlighting suspicion, violence, and vengeance.

Accepting the Responsibilities of Xenia

The story translated as "The Guest," *L'hôte*, is set in a context of *eris*. Suspicion, violence, and vengeance are all-pervasive. It's the beginning of the Algerian War for Independence. Lines are drawn. "Wartime" is evoked early in the story (EK, 72). A character makes clear the us versus them scenario: "If they rise up, no one's protected" (EK, 74). Besides the climate of impending war, there is also the harsh geographical climate. The area has been suffering from drought. Water, as we know, was important as both reality and symbol for Camus. Its absence is never a good thing. Instead of lush liquidity, there is snow, cold, and harsh. And there is minerality, lots of it. The setting is one of "merciless lands inhabited only by stones" (EK, 76).

In "The Renegade" characters and the landscape reflected one another. In "The Guest," the fluid warm solvent of humanity contrasts with the icy, mineral surroundings. This is the case with the main character, Daru, a school teacher. It is also the case with two other characters who could have been thinly drawn: the policeman who delivers an Arab prisoner to Daru's residence and the Arab prisoner himself. Possibilities for one-dimensional depictions abound. The police officer could be cruel, corrupt, officious, domineering. The Arab, a murderer, could be vicious and heartless, could hate the colonial oppressors, could be a constant threat, could require unending surveillance.

The story has a simple structure. Someone has committed murder. He is being brought to justice. Police officers, given the impending insurrection, are stretched thin. Ordinary citizens are asked to pick up some slack. One consequence: a police officer delivers his prisoner to an isolated school teacher. There is to be a transfer. The prisoner will be handed over to the teacher who will then deliver him to authorities in a nearby town. Admittedly, such use of a civilian is unusual. Without the context of insurrection, it would be out of the question. Nonetheless, the straightforward situation remains: there is a murderer who needs to be delivered to the proper authorities; there is a police officer who would, if conditions were different, undertake the task; there is the school teacher, a good, loyal, upright citizen, who is asked to help out.

The teacher should normally acquiesce. He is no fan of murderers. The narrator describes him as actually feeling "a sudden anger toward this man" (EK, 73). Subsequently, he thinks that the crime was "idiotic" and that the "man himself revolted him" (EK, 82–3). At the same time, the prisoner is a guest. Daru, the teacher, is a host. In this context, a whole new moral code kicks in. There is a lengthy tradition both in the Greco-Roman philosophical inheritance and within religious traditions of "theoxeny." Guests are to be given special treatment since they could be gods in disguise. In a more mundane sense, we are all, potentially at least, guests who might be in need of a hospitable welcome. The French word *hôte* resists a neat, binary, either/or categorization. It can mean both "guest" and "host." It's a rich term for describing the human condition. As I tried to indicate earlier, humans are wanderer-residents. Humans are wanderers (if we go back far enough in time, we will find ancestors who came from elsewhere). Humans are also sedentary homesteaders (we are situated in a particular place at a particular time). Neither status is fixed and final.

Home-dwellers ("hosts") can, given certain circumstances, become strangers and wayfarers ("guests") once again. The ambiguous connotation of the French *hôte* is actually rich and telling. Strangers and wayfarers can, in time, find themselves in reversed conditions. All of this takes place within everyday experience. There is no need for dramatic, grandiose pronouncements about our existential status being that of "exiles" from another realm, a transcendent "kingdom" which we dream of re-inhabiting. F. Scott Fitzgerald is famous for saying that "the test of a first-rate intelligence is the ability to hold two opposed ideas in mind at the same time and still retain the ability to function." Some terms, like *hôte,* make it easier to be a Fitzgerald-style "first-rate intelligence."

The *combination* of being both wayfarer and settled dweller highlights the importance of the guest/host relationship. In ancient Greece, the chief god had, as one of his titles, *Zeus Xenios,* Zeus, champion of hospitality. As late as 1923, Buster Keaton's movie *Our Hospitality* took a humorous look at the ancient virtue. Keaton's character is in love. He visits his beloved's family. Soon, those relatives make a discovery. The beau belongs to a family involved in a generations-old feud. He is, in other words, an enemy. They are sworn to kill members of this clan. However, he is a guest. Hospitality places certain demands even on sworn enemies. The family members simmer because they cannot exact proper revenge. The Keaton character wants to escape, but, once outside the house, he is fair game. The comic possibilities abound and are well mined. That such a plot could exist is a sign of how powerful, as late as the early twentieth century, was the tug of hospitality.

Daru, the teacher, is not especially ideological. Nor is he prone to philosophical disquisitions. He is, though, rooted in the heritage of hospitality. As a result he is firm. Baldacci, the policeman, becomes exasperated. He makes clear that what he has asked is not a polite request, "it's an order, son" (EK, 75). Daru's response is equally blunt, "I won't turn him in" (EK, 75). Such a situation is often labeled "tragic." A character is caught between conflicting demands. In this case it's the law of hospitality and the law of the land. They cannot both be satisfied. Daru is no friend of murder or murderers. Justice is important. At the same time, there are the demands of hospitality. The wider sociopolitical context complicates things. The battle for Algerian independence will draw clear lines: those of European descent on one side, the indigenous population on the other. The policeman knows this. He chides Daru by saying, "If you want to break with us, go ahead" (EK, 75). Daru would rather avoid the dilemma altogether. Alone with the prisoner, his spirits are raised by the thought that the Arab might escape. This would be an anxiety-freeing relief since Daru would be "once more alone with no decision to make" (EK, 77). The prisoner, though, does not run off. This leaves Daru in a situation in which he is forced to choose. Given that mandate, he opts for the law of hospitality.

There are hints from the beginning that the old virtue is neither arbitrary nor conventional. The teacher considers it to be, as with the ancients, coextensive with the human condition. He warmly welcomes both the policeman and the prisoner, offering them hot tea, asking, even, if the rope tying the prisoner's hands can be released. When alone with the prisoner, Daru, as a good host, prepares a meal. There are layers of difference between the two of them: European versus Arab, outside colonizer versus indigenous subject, teacher who distributes grain to starving locals versus ill-educated murderer.

Nonetheless, they share some things in common. The need for nourishment is one. "Are you hungry," says Daru, signaling an indicator of human overlap (EK, 77). Surprised at being treated as an ordinary guest, the prisoner asks, "Why are you eating with me?" Daru's straightforward answer, "I'm hungry" (EK, 78). In other words, don't make a big deal out of it. You are a guest, I am a host. We are now seated across from each other, just two hungry individuals sharing a meal. We have our differences *and* we have our similarities.

There is, as the narrator points out, some recognition of brotherhood. There's a parallel with soldiers sharing the same sleeping quarters. In those quarters a kind of bonding occurs. It's as if, having shed weapons and clothing, "they were joined together each evening beyond their differences, in the ancient community of dreams and fatigue" (EK, 80–1). The differences are real. They are not to be minimized. So are the overlaps: hunger, dreams, fatigue. A steel-trap mind, a rigorous logic-chopper would insist that the concept "similar" and the concept "different" are mutually incompatible. They must be kept rigorously apart. A Fitzgerald-type "first-rate intelligence," more in line with *razón vital*, would recognize the error of forcing lived experience into the neatly compartmentalized molds of logic chopping. Maybe an ambiguous term like *hôte* actually reveals something. Maybe it is the models of steel-trap, logic-chopper thinking that should be overcome. Maybe the overcoming could occur in ways that bring intelligence and experience more in line with each other. If this means accepting that a particular individual may be *both* different and similar, then so be it.

In ancient Greece, the practice of hospitality included parting gifts. Unlike what we might expect, the gifts were not offerings from the guests. Rather, the gifts were from the hosts, a sign that it was the guests who had brought something good to the home. Daru, as we have seen, would rather have avoided the entire guest/host scenario. Still, true to the demands of hospitality, he prepares some food and brings money as he and the prisoner head out. At a crossroads, always an obvious symbol, Daru hands over the packet of food and a thousand francs. He then points the way to the city where prison awaits, *and* another way, a road that will lead to nomads, a people for whom the tradition of hospitality continues to be alive and well. They will, Daru says, "welcome you and give you shelter, according to their law" (EK, 85).

Since the story highlights the celebration of hospitality, along with the triumph of virtue, the prisoner, on his own, takes the path toward the prison. Or at least it might seem that the story celebrates how virtue is triumphant. This is only so if virtue is its own reward. Daru's actions, it turns out, follow the adage: "no good turn goes unpunished." Upon returning, he finds a threat on his chalkboard: "You turned in our brother. You will pay" (EK, 86).

The dynamic of "us" versus "them" has not disappeared. Soon, with the full-blown war for independence, it will dominate. But, thanks to Daru, the hospitality alternative to the vengeance cycle remains a live possibility. In the end, caught in an impossible situation, one has to choose. Daru accepts that responsibility. He selects the way of the ancients, one that privileged the cycle of hospitality. Algeria will soon fall prey to this cycle's evil mirror image: that of vengeance.

Life brings with it an inevitable tragic dimension, situations in which perfect resolutions are no longer possible. *The Guest* sort of exemplifies Camus's own position vis-à-vis Algerian independence. He was no friend of colonialism. At the same time, he realized that, like Daru, he and his family were, despite European ancestry, Algerians. It was the only home they knew. He also rejected the terrorist tactics of the insurgents, tactics that could have led to the killing of his mother. Confronted by a supporter of the Algerian Liberation Front about why his moral outrage seemed muted in the case of Algerian liberation, Camus's response was heartfelt, personal, and directed at those who would commit violence against civilians: *En ce moment, on lance des bombes dans les tramways d'Alger. Ma mère peut se trouver dans un de ses tramways. Si c'est cela, la justice, je préfère ma mère.* ("Right now people are planting bombs on tramways. My mother could find herself on one of those trams. If that is justice, I prefer my mother.")[2]

Camus wanted justice. At the same time he wanted no part of terrorist tactics that targeted civilians. As the us versus them situation worsened, Camus opted out. At one point he decided to stop speaking about Algeria. The kind of resolution for which he hoped, an independent Algeria with room for the descendants of European colonists, was out of the question. He was a Daru-type: committed to simple human decency but caught in circumstances where important compromises with such decency seemed requisite. We don't know what happened eventually to Daru. We do know that his commitment to an ancient code made him, like Antigone, an enemy of the state. Unlike Antigone, Daru was also caught in another web. His commitment to the ancient code made of him not just an enemy of the state but, due to a misunderstanding, also an enemy of the insurgents.

The stalemate suggests a rigorous realism settling in on Camus. For those who view Camus through a single filter, it could be explained away as another dimension of absurdism. Poor Daru is caught in an absurd world, one whose contours he did not invent but whose contours place him in an impossible situation. Caught between two loyalties, he has to decide which is the more pressing. He makes his selection. The code of hospitality prevails. In a setting dominated by absurdism and its backdrop of nihilism, no option would, in any substantive way, be superior to any other. But Daru is no Meursault. He does not live out, in practice, the ramifications of absurdism. Even in a difficult situation, even where loyalties are divided, he rejects the way of indifference, even though it would relieve some of the burden associated with responsibility.

He refuses to shirk responsibility. He does not minimize its burden by telling himself that all the options are the same anyway, or that by choosing, he invents the standards to be followed. He accepts how the options have to be weighed, and how one of the paths is better than the other. Evaluative decisions are unavoidable, fallible, and anxiety-inducing. They matter. And, if they matter, then the lifeworld is more complicated than what nihilism allows. Like Clamence, Daru's voice is prophetic. There is a contradiction between nihilistic assumptions in theory and a mode of living that insists on some selections being, in a substantive way, better than others. Though prophetic, Daru's voice is a lonely one. The cacophony of social violence around him will dismiss his isolated call. The harshness of his surroundings serves as an apt symbol. His soft hopefulness for a more liquid world simply has no place in the high desert.

Guest/Host Reciprocity

When we get to the final story in the collection, Camus situates the reader in a particular environment. It's an aqueous one. This is important since the tension between the mineral and the liquid identifies contrasting life options. The story in question has, first of all, a paradoxical title, one that would be welcome by Fitzgerald: *La pierre qui pousse*. This is translated as "The Growing Stone" but could also be "the stone that grows" or "the stone that pushes, or maybe even 'prods.'"

Minerality and life, opposites, are here conjoined. The story's setting is, from the beginning, bathed in liquidity. Two people are in a car. They have left behind "the long, long navigation across a red desert" (EK, 131). They arrive at the bank of a river. When the engine is shut off, they hear "the sound of the water." A "fine rain" had fallen earlier. Traces of it "still floated in the humid air." The sky, now clear, is populated by "misty stars" (EK, 126). The forest which surrounds them is "a sea of vegetation." As they drove toward their destination, "a damp breeze, warm and slightly sharp, blew through the car window" (EK, 131).

The opening sections also signal the prominence of guest/host interaction. The main character is an outsider brought in to help control flooding. He is described as larger than life, someone with a kind of supernatural aura. He has a "colossal body" and a "huge back" (EK, 125–6). His movement in and out of the shadows is described as a "resurrection." With each "resurrection," he seems "taller and more massive" (EK, 126). On the ferry coming to transport him, there is a lantern surrounded by a "yellowish halo." Once arrived, the stranger is greeted by a judge who describes him, Biblical style, as someone who can "command the waters" and "conquer rivers" (EK, 133).

We are in a very different realm from that of "The Renegade." Minerality and death have moved to the margins. The main character, although described in religious terms, is not in any way a representative of religion. He is, though, as with the renegade, an outsider. The Renegade came as a conqueror. He defined what it meant to be a bad guest. D'Arrast comes as a friend bearing gifts. He is an engineer ready to share the fruits of science and technology. The story indicates that he will be a good guest. As a good guest, he is interested in the people he meets. In "The Silent Ones" M. Lassalle had never been a guest in the homes of his workers. His relationship to them was always that of host, that is, always the superior one. D'Arrast, although the bearer of superior technology, follows a different tack. He displays an active interest in the town's inhabitants, going so far as making a special effort to visit their homes. Not just any homes. He wishes to befriend the most dispossessed, to enter the "huts" of the town's poorest residents. Once inside, the destitution is obvious. He absorbs the odor of "smoke and poverty" (EK, 139).

Still, poor as they are, the inhabitants are good hosts. A young woman offers D'Arrast a drink. It's not champagne as with the mayor's reception. It's cane liquor. Still, offering a libation is what good hosts do. D'Arrast, as a good guest, accepts. There are no crystal glasses, formal dining rooms, or well-dressed participants. Still, the host/guest exchange begins to build linkages, what the ancient Greeks called *xenia*, guest-friendship. The stranger comes bearing various gifts. Some gifts are offered as part of the work which has been commissioned. He is an engineer. He bears the gifts of technology. Other gifts are freely offered. These are the ones associated with his character, principally the gift of friendship. As an attentive guest, he makes a first move toward what, if the proper culminations result, will be a setting dominated not by *eris*, "discordia" but by harmony "concordia." The gift of *xenia* is both a free offering on the part of the stranger and an initial move in the direction of creation, the direction of bringing to birth new affiliations, new lines of intersection among people whose differences could easily lead to de-creation as isolation and estrangement.

Despite his name, which indicates aristocracy, D'Arrast does not lord it over the locals. He meets a cook who tells him that the driver has identified D'Arrast as a "lord." Those days are in the past, D'Arrast explains. "Now there are no more lords in our countries" (EK, 142). He could have said that there are no more "lords" of inherited aristocracy. There might still be other kinds of "lord," those whose prominence is based not on inherited titles but on expertise and behavior.

D'Arrast's presence, unlike that of the renegade, does not come with the mission to subdue and dominate. He is here to help, to help real people. He has an official task, it is true. He could, preserving his distance from the locals, carry out his work. He chooses otherwise. Beyond the externally imposed obligations, he is also a visitor who, freely, takes additional steps. Chief among these is recognition. The village inhabitants, no matter how poor or how different, he deems worthy of friendship. The gifts he bears, both the ones resulting from professional obligation and the ones freely offered, converge on one point: they bring liberation, not domination. He will, as a result of his profession, help free the villagers from the ravages of the river. Then, as we shall soon see, he will free them from associations of lordship. Solidarity, friendship, building connections, these are his guiding principles. He is no longer a "lord" in the aristocratic sense. He preserves, however, a sense of "nobility" in a different and wider way. There is no denying his superiority in terms of engineering skills. In other ways, he is dependent and needy. He is a guest genuinely interested in the members of the community in which he finds himself.

The renegade had set out with a specific goal: conversion of the heathens. D'Arrast arrives as someone attentive to the needs and ways of the community members. By the end he will have effected a conversion, but it will be quite different from the one envisioned by the Renegade. The latter's model was that of power and domination. He worshiped a transcendent divinity who served as a divine dictator. The alternative model envisioned by D'Arrast: having power and being restrained in the use of it. Ancient lords and kings modeled themselves on the Renegade's kind of divinity, one of power and might. Such power and might was neither contextualized nor limited. The godlike, in such an understanding, was above the quotidian and was one whose use of power was unrestrained. D'Arrast will occasion a particular spiritual transformation in the community. It will suggest a new take on godliness: the sacred is neither transcendent nor primarily understood in terms of power.

A key moment indicating the transformation has to do with D'Arrast being offended by the police chief. The chief, making a spectacle of himself, accuses D'Arrast of carrying a flawed passport. He, the chief, effectively ruins the engineer's welcoming ceremony. Old, *lex talionis* patterns immediately kick in. There has been an offense. A score must be settled. Reprisal is the order of the day. The judge (always a favorite target for Camus) is the spokesman for the path of retribution. He insists that D'Arrast, having been offended, must determine the "punishment to be inflicted on this dreadful character" (EK, 136). It's like Zeus punishing Prometheus or, closer to Camus's works, Sisyphus. The punishment is an automatic attempt to set a skewed balance aright. It's all very straightforward, legalistic, and instinctual. It's as if *Nemesis* were a machine without any flexibility or mercy.

D'Arrast stands for an entirely different approach. Although he is the aggrieved victim, "he did not want any punishment" (EK, 136). The judge, thinking in more formal, straightforward, legalistic, terms, is categorical: "punishment was indispensable" (EK, 136). When they meet on a later occasion, the judge once again pursues the question. D'Arrast, as is his wont, demurs. He goes so far as suggesting clemency. D'Arrast's admonition, "you should just let him go," is completely incomprehensible to the judge. His world is that of rigid, mechanical balance. There is no liquidity about it at all. An offense has occurred. It must be met by punishment. Leniency is out of the question. "The judge said that this was not possible, and that he had to be punished" (EK, 140). D'Arrast and the judge live in completely different moral/intellectual landscapes. Meeting again at a subsequent reception, the judge is insistent. D'Arrast, this time, is ready. He replies that he has indeed thought about how to deal with the police chief. The result of such thinking is lengthy and deserves to be cited in full:

> He would consider it a personal favor, and an exceptional gesture, if they would be so good as to pardon this thoughtless person in his name, so that his stay here—his d'Arrast's, as he was taking so much pleasure in getting acquainted with the lovely town of Iguape and its generous inhabitants—could begin in a climate of concord and friendship. (EK, 147)

On one side, the sedimented code of *lex talionis,* that of honor/offense/punishment: justice as cold, impersonal, settling a score, vengeful. On the other, having power without using it; justice balanced by mercy manifested as warmth, forgiveness, harmony, and friendship. The language employed by Camus is replete with religious and classical overtones. The word translated as favor is *grâce*, a free gift. D'Arrast is a special kind of gift-bearing guest. He comes as someone offering an alternative to the rigid cycle of crime and punishment. The offended one, in this latter context, must enact a punishment on the perpetrator. The free gift of grace, by contrast, takes another path, one that takes a risk by leaving behind the cycle of vengeance and mathematical balance. Some freedom must be provided for *agape,* another name for the gift-love that is *grâce.*

The gift-emphasis also brings D'Arrast into the moral landscape of ancient Greece and *xenia.* When he asks that the police chief be forgiven, the word he uses is *pardonner.* Both the English "forgive" and the French *pardonner* are related to the offering of a gift. To for-give is to break with the cycle of retribution. It opens the possibility for another relationship, one based on the cycle of gift exchanges. The French *pardonner* similarly contains the word for gift, *don.* The one who exercises freedom by bringing gifts seeks, as D'Arrast explicitly states, to "begin in a climate of concord and friendship."

He is one who, first and foremost, seeks to break with the heritage of *eris.* He comes in the spirit of *agape* and *xenia,* gift-love and guest-friendship. He takes pleasure in making the acquaintance of Iguape's residents, especially the most downtrodden. A few sentences after his reply to the judge, D'Arrast says that he has been invited "by friends" to the huts and a dance ceremony. Although an aristocrat by name and by profession, he does not think of himself as a "lord" in a universal manner. In some ways, he is superior. In others, he welcomes human solidarity. On the basis of his superior skills, he will help prevent future flooding. On the basis of solidarity, he will meet the villagers as friends.

He is a gift-bearing stranger. As an engineer, he will alleviate the town's problems with the river. He also brings another gift, that of social transformation. One demonstration of this is his request relating to the police chief. D'Arrast asks the authorities to grant him the right to "pardon." As we have just seen, "pardon" literally means to offer a gift (the "don" part comes from the Latin *donare*, to give or bestow gifts). D'Arrast's plea is so heartfelt that even the judge is converted. Continuing the guest/host dynamic, the judge says that, given the pardon, the chief will even be invited, as befits *xenia*, to dinner.

D'Arrast's ancestors represented one meaning of "lord." He represents another. Older lords brought domination and oppression. He brings emancipations: liberation from the local river's ravages; liberation from rigid class and racial distinctions; liberation from the cycle of vengeance. There is also a major liberation involving the stone of the story's title, a stone assumed to have magical powers. In all of these respects D'Arrast is a special kind of visitor, a heroic one.

A "hero," as Margaret Visser explains, is first of all somewhat larger than life. D'Arrast's physical description certainly fits this bill. More importantly, the hero is a "boundary crosser." In particular, a certain hero brings about a kind of conversion, a transformation in thinking. The constituents of a particular setting may remain the same, but the way they are understood has altered after the hero's visit. This is not change for the sake of change. Rather the heroic figure brings transformations meant to "deepen and broaden the best in us" (Visser 2002, 109). Some transgressions serve to de-create, to bring rupture, divisiveness, and isolation. Boundary crossings can also serve to create, to build linkages, connections, and affiliations. Both hero and villain are boundary crossers. A stranger may be a friend or an enemy. It depends on what transformations emerge from interactions with the newcomer.

The straightforward transformation, the one for which D'Arrast was hired, has to do with the river. His engineering expertise will see to this transformation. By his presence and comportment, he occasions other transformations. His presence results in "conversion," but a conversion unlike that envisioned by the renegade. D'Arrast stands as a model for mutual recognition among various ethnicities, races, nationalities. Hardly anything is easier, more tempting or more natural than erecting walls around racial, ethnic, national identities. "Us" versus "them" is a quite easy to indulge sentiment. It's natural to think of difference in terms of deviation. Outsiders are enemies. Natives are primitive, backward, superstitious. Such a combination, in its fullest force, was depicted in "The Renegade." Within that framework there remains no place for either *xenia* or *agape*. *Xenia* disappears. It is replaced by *eris* in the service of *Nike*, enmity, and the drive for domination. The visitor, "Renegade" style, even while a visitor, self-identifies as always a host, always the one in a superior position. From that elevated perch, there is no real interest in listening to the denizens of the newly entered territory. They are only and always "other," never long-lost, hitherto unknown, relatives.

The key moment that contrasts D'Arrast with the renegade is the moment of hospitality. D'Arrast first asks to visit the poorest members of the community. He is then offered and accepts the gift of a beverage. The setting is one in which differences which would make it easy to erect barriers are obvious and plentiful. D'Arrast is white.

The community members are black. He is well educated. They are not. He can control the river. They can do little about its regular flooding. He is financially successful. They are desperate for work. Differences do not disappear. Nor does D'Arrast ignore them. It is his response to differences that is transformative.

Instead of building walls that reinforce otherness, he acts as a generous-spirited guest. He does some serious building and some serious listening. Sometimes building by listening. His building projects do not primarily involve erecting walls. Rather what he builds are relationships and affiliations. There is no question that he is superior in some ways. His expertise will minimize the river's ravages. Such superiority, though, is context-sensitive. He understands the villagers to be fellow human beings. Superiority in engineering does not negate general human solidarity.

Rehabilitating the Ordinary

The locals, well installed in their own "us *versus* them" landscape, are initially suspicious. They too fall into the pattern of resenting the outsider. D'Arrast's presence at a festival is tolerated only for so long. At a certain point they ask him to leave (EK, 154). "Us versus them," hardly anything could be more natural. But it is precisely because the attitude is so common that the transformation (conversion?) occasioned by the visitor takes on importance. There will always be outsiders, strangers, others. Religious, ethnic, racial, cultural differences are not about to disappear. Still, some conversions can take place, especially as regards the practices we undertake within those conditions. Take the stock approach to justice as tit for tat. The model here is clean and neat: a crime upsets the balance. Punishment restores it. What could be more obvious? More natural? More satisfying? *Nemesis*, acting mechanically, would approve.

Yet, as with the judge and the police chief, this most natural, obvious, and satisfying response is exactly the one D'Arrast seeks to modify. The situation with the judge is limited in the sense that only a few people, the judge, D'Arrast, and the chief, are directly involved. There is a wider transformation that can be effected. It has to do with the very categories of "exile" and "kingdom." It's never made explicit that the inhabitants of Iguape think of themselves in terms of exile. What is clearer is that, given their religious beliefs and practices, they associate the "kingdom" with another realm. Here is where the sacred stone plays an important role.

It is housed in a special and appropriate place. Its home is the church, a locale separated from the neighborhoods in which day-to-day life is carried out. The stone belongs in the building that stands for the transcendent kingdom. That kingdom, in the popular consciousness, is also the realm of final judgment, itself envisioned as strict, fixed balance. The main religious practice is not that different from economic exchange. Praying is not about awe, gratitude, reverence. It's more like subjects asking a king for favors. Religion comes to be understood as a combination of power, a kind of magical power combined with contractual reciprocity. Humans petition to have their desires satisfied. To help persuade the divinity, they promise something in return. The cook's promise exemplifies this power-cum-contract pattern: "you do something for me, and I'll do something for you." The cook, fearing death by drowning, made a promise to Jesus: save me and I will carry the stone.

Sometimes, though, the contractual arrangement breaks down. The cook, having drunk and danced too much at the previous evening's celebrations, simply cannot keep up his end of the bargain. He is too tired and weak to carry the stone for the entire prescribed path. D'Arrast, described as resembling "some bestial and reassuring god" (EK, 150), has yet another conversion in store. He, in a free (i.e., noncontractual) act of generosity, replaces the cook, picks up the stone, and continues the procession. However, true to his role as encouraging conversion, he does this with an important difference. As he nears the church, D'Arrast abruptly changes course. In so doing he ignores the implorations of the crowd. They want him to continue on the path leading to the church. Instead, D'Arrast heads for the poorest part of town. Locating the cook's hut, he enters and drops the stone onto the glowing fire at the center of the room. D'Arrast feels a tremendous "wave of joy surging inside him" (EK, 165). He is filled with a "tumultuous happiness" (EK, 166). Unlike the totally subjective and, let's face it, irrational, happiness of Sisyphus, this is one connected to actual achievement. Life after D'Arrast will no longer be an unending repetition of the same. The villagers believed in magic, in a stone that could actually grow, a stone set apart. D'Arrast disconnects the stone and magic. The villagers separated the realm of transcendence and that of ordinary life. D'Arrast uses the stone to instantiate another kind of *pousse*, to push, foster, reconciliation.

What has happened? D'Arrast has loosened the iron grip of either/or thinking. He has naturalized the spiritual (and, at the same time, spiritualized the natural). He has, literally, engaged in "sacrifice" (a term which means "making sacred"). He has brought Clamence's doves down to earth. More literally, D'Arrast has blurred the line between immanence and transcendence. There is no longer a need to endow the mineral with magical properties. Spiritual possibilities are already latent within the everyday. It is in ordinary homes that those possibilities can be brought to culmination. The earlier understanding, a magic stone stored away in a special temple, is just a distraction from the realization of the wholeness that characterizes holiness.

"Exile" and "kingdom'" no longer need to provide the oppositional context within which the villagers orient themselves. The here and now can be considered a proper home, not a place of exile. The "kingdom" no longer needs to be envisioned as located in another realm, one symbolized by a church set apart. In *The Myth of Sisyphus*, Camus had identified a moment in which the absurd reveals itself. It is a moment which is in no way momentous. A deep, irreparable rupture has opened between ordinary life and meaningfulness. Everyday life comes to be recognized at nothing but a "stage set" (MS, 12). Beauty, in the "stage set" world, seems to surround us in the form of nature's wonders. Eventually, though, humans come to "lose the illusory meaning with which we have clothed them" (MS, 14).

D'Arrast's depositing the stone in a humble home says otherwise. Maybe the problem is that the stone was moved to the church in the first place. Maybe the sacred/ordinary rupture resulted from an arbitrary segregation dictated by the imposition of neat, rigid, logical categories on a world that is more liquidy, more complicated than rigid logical categories allow. Translated into religious formulations, the Great

Bifurcation came to be articulated in terms of this life as a place of exile. It became a "fallen" realm into which humans were cast. It was not their real home.

D'Arrast occasions a conversion. The newly located stone provides an impetus, a "push" or "prod" toward a new way of taking things. Aristocracy is not annihilated. D'Arrast represents a new kind of aristocrat. Kingdoms, similarly, must be rethought. No longer need they be envisioned as set off in either a transcendent or utopian realm. It's time to set aside the pattern of Paradise Lost and Paradise Regained. The whole contrast which leads to a major exile/kingdom bifurcation needs to be put into question. No longer should "kingdom" be automatically associated with that which is higher, purer, removed from ordinary life. The sacred is present here, in ordinary life, even in the huts of the desperately poor. The possibilities for a good kingdom are latent within the here and now. It is up to us to make them real

When we dream of a kingdom that is elsewhere, we are encouraged to act in certain ways. Like Janine, we may seek a mystical union with what is different from the everyday. Like the Renegade, we, believing ourselves to be the conduits to the kingdom, may seek to dominate and convert. Like Jonas, our frustration with the state of exile may occasion isolation and withdrawal from the everyday. Like M. Lassalle, there is a resistance to entering the homes of the lower classes. Such modes of being occupy a realm of sharp divides. Each says "no" to the here and now. Each reinforces walls. By bringing the stone into an ordinary household D'Arrast has modeled a different approach: a circle in which the outsider is greeted with an invitation. The final words of the story are instructive: "sit down with us" (EK, 166).

C. S. Lewis, seemingly thorough in his exploration of Greek terms indicating love, had ignored *xenia*, a model pattern for guest and host, for those who are strangers to each other. That pattern: start by assuming both difference and common humanity; reach out with food, drink; listen; engage in the sharing of stories. Camus's explorations of love were only just beginning with *Exile and the Kingdom*. By the end of the collection, the very notions of "exile" and "kingdom" have been put into question. More specifically, key themes from *The Myth of Sisyphus*, the denigration of the here and now, insistence on its "silence" and unintelligibility, no longer seem as solidly grounded as they once did. Camus, the literary artist, has taken important steps in the direction of complicating ordinary life experience. There are hints, as with "The Growing Stone" ("The Stone which Pushes"), that new directions can be envisioned. Camus's premature death means that we will never really have a sense of how he might have charted the new directions.

12

The First Man I, What Is "First"?

A Work in Progress

After *Exile and the Kingdom* no finished text of Camus, at least not one revised and reworked for publication, remains. When Camus was killed in a car crash, he left behind a satchel. Its contents were a passport, some photos, a paperback *Othello*, a copy of Nietzsche's *The Gay Science*, and a handwritten manuscript. The manuscript's 144 pages were the beginning of a work tentatively entitled *The First Man*. *The First Man* was to be a major literary accomplishment, the first for Camus since winning the Nobel Prize in 1957. The pages left to posterity are tantalizing in the promise of what will forever remain unfulfilled. Still, what remains is something from Camus's hand. With proper sensitivity about its preliminary state, it can take its place as a *bona fide* part of his legacy.

If we are to believe Agnès Spiquel, Camus had envisioned a major contribution, a kind of *War and Peace*. The plan was to interweave Camus's personal story with the world events that marked his lifetime.[1] And what events they were: the First World War, the Russian Revolution, the stock market crash, the Second World War, the Nazi occupation of France, Hiroshima, the Algerian War for Independence, not to mention major changes in the arts and the sciences. Camus himself had hinted at a work to come in his 1958 preface to a reissue of *L'Envers et L'Endroit* (translated as *The Wrong Side and the Right Side*). That preface mentions "a work I dream of." That work, he continues, will "be like *The Wrong Side and the Right Side* and that it will speak of a certain form of love" (LCE, 15). How the project would have succeeded is anyone's guess. We have to content ourselves with the manuscript that remains. The narrative is autobiographical. "Jacques Cormery," the protagonist, is forty years old, but the events related, with the exception of references to the Algerian War of Independence, all revolve around Camus's early years. The story ends when the young man is entering the *lycée*.

Thanks to Camus's enormous talent, the text, even in its rough form, is rich and captivating. So much so that it has received excessive praise. The philosopher Alain Finkielkraut proclaimed that *The First Man* was Camus's "*Chef-d'oeuvre*" (Finkielkraut, 122). Why? Finkielkraut celebrates how Camus is true to himself, especially as regards a warmly positive attitude toward the world. It is a work rich in its capacity "to seize and represent tastes, colors, odors. It's both an affective and olfative memoir" (Finkielkraut, 127–8, my translation).

Although *chef-d'oeuvre* is over the top, Finkielkraut does capture a particular dimension emphasized by Camus. The narrative stays close to the concrete, to the multi-textured experience of living. The side of Camus's character which tended toward *yes-saying* rather than toward revolt is a controlling presence. This side was always real for Camus. It formed part of his *amor vitae*, his embrace of life. Typically, though, it emerged in relation to the natural world. His *amor vitae* was mostly an *amor mundi*. This *amor mundi* involved a deep "yea-saying" because it was felt. Once rationality, that is, the human realm, entered the picture, Camus's personal response shifted more in the direction of "nay-saying," manifested in the themes of absurdity and rebellion.

In the sections of *The First Man* that he left us, Camus's focus is on a child and adolescent. The intellectual dimensions within which a "no" would be operative do not yet occupy center stage. It is perhaps not surprising that a recollection of these years would be generally characterized by an attitude of yea-saying. After all, it is the time covering formative and rather innocent years, a time which left a permanent, and positive, deposit in the man who is writing. As befits a work which starts with a birth, Camus has been quoted as affirming that he saw this manuscript as a new beginning. He hoped, despite already being a Nobelist, to get a new "start" with this manuscript.[2]

From what remains, we cannot predict whether the envisioned re-naissance would actually have materialized. Nonetheless, even in its present form the story remains richly textured and ripe for commentary. These occasions for commentary fall into two major categories. Each will be the subject of this and the next chapter. Chapter 13 will concentrate on the theme that was to mark Camus's third cycle: love. Regarding this topic, there are serious lacunae, especially regarding *eros*. The story ends with adolescence, just when *eros* would begin to make itself felt. Still, when it comes to love, the manuscript, as it stands, offers explorations of *storge*, family affection, and *philia*, friendship. It provides some hints as regards *eros*.

This chapter will explore the book's title *The First Man*. It's a title rich in social and philosophical resonances, resonances in need of exploration and elaboration. As a result, the present chapter will examine various ramifications of what it means to be "First."

The "First," or the Father-of-Oneself Fantasy

In his notebooks, Camus mentions a secret that will be revealed in *The First Man*: "he is not the first. Every man is the first man, no one is" (*il n'est pas le premier. Tout homme est le premier homme, personne ne l'est*) (C3, 165). With such phrasing Camus seems to be engaging in purposeful paradox. Sorting out the claim's components, we can say, to begin with, how history validates the initial claim "he is not the first." An absolutely first man might appear as a necessary hypothesis for some, but recorded history takes us back only to settings with multiple individuals already present. The second component, "every man is the first man" is thus historically flawed. Nonetheless, as we shall see, it articulates a powerful strand in human thinking, a partial truth that can become a self-serving illusion: belief in a completely autarchic start and total control over self-creation.

The illusion comes as part of a multifaceted package. The package is often accompanied by the desire for autonomy, defined as being an unencumbered self. In its fullest sense, the illusion envisions a self-enclosed unit (I hesitate to use the adjective "human"), a unit with no parents, no gestation, no birth, no past, no tradition. What is envisioned, in effect, is mostly a disembodied mind or spirit. It comes from nowhere and, beyond some constraints associated with materiality, thinks of itself as beyond other limitations, including those of situatedness in a particular time or place. Projecting such a disconnected unit requires quite a bit of abstractive eliminationism.[3] Its initial kernel of truth is worthy of attention: each human is unique. That truth then gets a particular emphasis when it draws its meaning from a semantic landscape which already privileges disconnection and self-sufficiency. At that point, eliminationism kicks in. The unique individual comes to be stripped of dimensions that are integral to it, especially the biological, the social, and the affective.

One result: a mode of speaking which overemphasizes the prefix "self." Thus we get a language replete with expressions like *self*-conscious, *self*-made, *self*-creating, *self*-actualizing. It's a partial truth, which, marginalizing context, gets blown all out of proportion. The exaggeration not only redefines humans but redefines them in a way that excises much that makes them human. John Dewey, one of the philosophers who helped move philosophy away from the framework in which Camus was trapped, phrased the matter directly: "Many good words," he emphasized, get "spoiled when the word self is prefixed to them: Words like pity, confidence, sacrifice, control, love. The reason is not far to seek. The word self infects them with a fixed introversion and isolation. It implies that the act of love or trust or control is turned back upon a self which already is in full existence and in whose behalf the act operates" (Dewey 1922/2012, 138).

The "fixed introversion and isolation" identified by Dewey is not just an imaginary fabrication. It can lead to an understanding in which humans (1) think of themselves as disconnected from their natural surroundings; (2) forget that they arrived as the result of (a) an egg/sperm conjunction, (b) gestation in a female, and (c) birth from that female; (3) define freedom, not as the ability to elect among options and undertake actions which work in conjunction with actual conditions, but freedom envisioned as complete non-dependence, *liberum arbitrium indifferentiae*; and (4) can actually reach a point where they envision themselves as "firsts," as having arrived in the world as inherently autarchic units. In other words, not flesh-and-blood humans, not physiological creatures, not part of a span which had a before and will have an after.

Because it came to be allied with important political moves associated with republican citizenship and enhanced freedom, the encapsulated self proved to be an attractive rendition of the human condition. Camus, as an early twentieth-century figure, remained within the orbit of this take on emancipation. This meant, as is often the case with him, that he was of two tendencies. The philosophical inheritance which gave rise to the first man illusion remained strong. At the same time, his sense of concrete situatedness, his love of nature along with memories of his childhood made him sensitive to the limitations of his philosophical inheritance. What results is the conflict exemplified in his notebook: a tug toward the first man illusion, especially as it emphasizes enhanced unencumbered freedom, but also an awareness that such notions of a first man are illusory.

Because what remains of *The First Man* is a draft, it is not clear how Camus would have worked through the tension. The book's working title, *The First Man*, indicates some leaning in the direction of there being such a thing as a "first man." Making such an understanding explicit, Camus had apparently toyed with the idea of calling the book "Adam" (Vanbonne, 118). In the notes left along with the manuscript, Camus sketched out a first part entitled "Nomads." It includes several telling sentences: "Trip to Mondovi. He finds childhood and not the father. He learns he is the first man" (FM, 308). Another note reiterates how the absence of a father made of the son a "first man." "At age forty, he realizes he needs someone to show him the way and to give him censure or praise: a father. Authority and not power" (FM, 297). Still another entry suggests using a classmate as contrast. Give Pierre, the note says, "a past, a country, a family, a morality?" (FM, 291).

The meaning associated with using a classmate as a foil is straightforward. Most people, like the classmate, are not "first." They come into the world as part of families. Those families, in turn, have their stories, their ancestors, their value systems. A newborn enters an already configured setting. What comes afterward is influenced by the acclimatization occasioned by the family situated in a particular culture at a particular time. The youngster is initiated into the lore, the habits, the value system of the preexisting community.

When the youngster is a male, the key figure in this scheme would be the father. Or at least that is how Camus, without a father, envisioned it. For him the situation was complicated by several factors associated with the missing father: a mother and grandmother who were both illiterate; family members so busy making a living that time for shared lore was nonexistent. This meant that, in a sense, young Albert was *like* a "first man," someone having to discover for himself, fend for himself, construct himself.

At the same time, the young boy, though without a father, was neither first nor isolated. The matrilineal presence, uneducated as it might have been, was there before him and there with him. In concrete, empirical terms, young Albert (1) did not come into this world from nowhere and (2) did not grow up in an isolation chamber. He had gestated in and been born from a mother who was still around. He had a place to which he could return each night, a place shared with a mother, a grandmother, several uncles, and an older brother. He may have felt like more of a "first man" than some of his friends. Literally, though, as he recognized in his notebooks, no one is a first man.

As he tells his story, however, the alternative take, one which emphasizes the first man, the "Adamic" dimension becomes more dominant. Adopting such an imaginative framework is both understandable and attractive. It gives the impression of total independence, that is, non-dependence. There is an absence of encumbrances. There is a sense of general openness as one charts a unique trajectory. There is the satisfaction of being self-made. At the same time, despite the imaginative projection of a completely self-made individual, the notion of someone who is literally a first man is, as Camus's notebooks recognized, a fantasy. It is possible, in imaginative eliminationism, to minimize, overlook, or conceal the biological, historical, social factors that are present. Literal truths can be overridden by illusions. The concrete, mammalian situation is familiar: all humans, as far back as we can empirically record, come after others. Those others had to provide (1) sperm and egg, (2) a womb for gestation, and (3) successful birth from a female. If there ever was a first man, or, as the first creation story in *Genesis* claims, a first man and woman ("So God created mankind in his own image, in the image of God he created them; male and female he created them"), that event is so far in the past and so shrouded in mystery as to be of little use as we orient ourselves within the concrete conditions of our existence.

Such empirical considerations, though, have not always thwarted first-man mythmaking. For the heritage within which Camus was situated, the Adamic illusion (associated with the Bible's second creation story) was alive and well. Its most prominent manifestation came from religion. The creation story involving Adam came to be the one most celebrated. Within the philosophical tradition, the seventeenth and eighteenth centuries helped foster a nonreligious revival of the Adamic fantasy. Some of its main articulations came from prominent thinkers like Thomas Hobbes (1588–1659), John Locke (1632–1704), and Jean-Jacques Rousseau (1712–78). By contrast, Aristotle, along with older thought in general, had assumed that humans were social animals by nature. This is what Aristotle meant by his claim that by nature man was a "political animal" (Aristotle, *Politics*,1253a).[4] They were not isolated units that had simply emerged. By nature, their proper abode was in communities. The post-seventeenth-century depiction changed this in an important way.

The newer philosophical anthropology emphasized the now-familiar depiction of humans as self-made men (the male aspect is important). Such individuals were envisioned as autonomous, fully rational adults who sort of arose out of nowhere. Hobbes went so far as to envision them as "sprung up out of the earth, and suddenly, like mushrooms, come to maturity, without all kind of engagement to each other" (Hobbes 1658/991, 205). Hobbes was typical in that his projection of originally isolated individuals was part of a project which, quite opposed to Aristotelian claims, envisioned an initial status of autarchic selves who then, via a contract, transformed the autonomous units into a community. This should not be confused with reformist changes which alter the conditions from one instantiation of community to an altered, revised one. The claim is more fundamental, asserting that there is a pre-community setting and that there is a definitive and initial community-creating act.

Part of the defense of social contract theories was the story about an initial "state of nature" where men sprung up like mushrooms. Such stories skipped over some obvious components of human life: conception, gestation, birth. Susan Bordo, critiquing this position, aptly referred to it as the "father-of-oneself fantasy" (Bordo, 452). The "father-of-oneself fantasy" is (1) rooted in a fixation on autonomy, which (2) translates interconnections and interrelationships into anti-autonomy "dependence" (a term which becomes inherently pejorative); (3) the fear of dependence comes to be associated with a fear of the female and a rejection of dependence on the female. (5) In the end the fixation on radical autonomy is self-satisfying for a particular group.

Guided by both the Adamic illusion and post-seventeenth-century construals of humans as autonomous units, an author could, understandably, come to represent himself in "first man" terms. Camus, whose *Myth of Sisyphus*, was shot through with the assumptions of Modern philosophy, was already attuned to the context for which the notion of "first" seemed natural. *The First Man*, composed decades later, is, despite its title, a more multilayered text. It is, to begin with, the work of a more mature Camus, someone whose reflective life has not remained static. Second, the text is neither a philosophical essay nor a literary expression of philosophical ideas. It is a memory-rooted, fictionalized autobiography. *The Myth*, solidly within the framework of the Great Bifurcation, could be built around a cerebral analysis, one in which the mammalian, biological, familial, cultural contexts could be bracketed. The themes readily bracketed in a concept-centered analysis (connectedness and dependence: biology, family, maternity, situatedness, cultural context) would be much harder to sideline in an autobiography true and attentive to actual occurrences.

Being from Nothingness

The First Man also differs in important ways from the earlier fictional narratives. Mostly, as just indicated, this is because Camus is retelling an actual story, his own. Whereas his other novels begin with death (dead mother, a plague, someone near the end of life), *The First Man* opens with birth. A full rendering of that story would find it hard to eliminate the familial, cultural dimensions of having (1) been conceived by a specific man and woman; (2) gestated in this unique female; (3) been born in a particular place, at (4) a particular time. The book's early narration indeed highlights just such an interrelated context. *The First Man* does not begin with a full-grown man, appearing, Adam-like, out of nowhere. It begins with a pregnant woman. She is about to deliver. The newborn will not be father of himself. He has a mother and a father. He is descended, via his parents, from Spanish and French ancestors. He arrives in a milieu which he has neither invented nor chosen. What all of this means is that he is not a "first." He is neither a new Adam, springing directly from God, nor a new denizen from the state of nature, entering the world free of connections, dependencies, and cultural situatedness.

In one sense, starting with a birth is quite normal and ordinary. In another, the choice of highlighting birth is important in terms of philosophical ramifications. The concrete, ordinary conditions of conception, gestation, and parturition are all taken into account. The Adamic illusion seems well forgotten or, at least, overwhelmed by phenomenological fact. Still, the lure of the Adamic fallacy is strong. The ordinary mammalian, temporally and culturally conditioned, circumstances, can seem kind of lowly for a creature who seeks to rise above the material.

A contrasting scene, envisioned by another novelist, indicates how the story could have been related in a different way. The other author is Vladimir Nabokov. His depiction can be characterized as within the lineage offered by the title of Jean-Paul Sartre's magnum opus: *Being and Nothingness*. Nabokov opened his biography with a stunning line far removed from ordinary birthing: "The cradle rocks above an abyss, and common sense tells us that our existence is but a brief crack of light between two eternities of darkness" (Nabokov, 19).[5] "Being," in other words, is an exceptional state, a surprising island in an ocean of nothingness. Such dramatic phrasing is impressive. It also reinforces a "first man" understanding. It does so for an obvious reason. It favors abstract theorizing over a concrete description. The abstract formulation, typically, is eliminative: the ordinary, mammalian processes of conception, gestation, and birth are quite simply ignored.

Here is where we get a slight variation on the theme of "first." When the concrete particulars of a newborn's arrival are transformed into an abstract tale about "being" emerging from "nothingness," each new entity can be recognized as a "first." He (the gender specificity is important) comes from nowhere, makes something of himself, then fades away into another nothingness. All of this, the pattern should now be familiar, depends on a great forgetfulness, most likely a purposeful forgetfulness: occluding whatever is associated with the female.

The Adamic myth, the state of nature fantasy, the Nabokov theorizing, all provide backdrops against which the claim of being a "first" man would make sense.[6] At the same time, they all suffer from an identical flaw. Humans are born of someone with a uterus, at a particular time, in specific circumstances. No one is literally a "first." *Omne vivum ex vivo*, proclaimed Pasteur. He was dismissing the notion of spontaneous generation, the biological version of the "father-of-oneself fantasy." Just so, *omne humanum ex humano* serves as an important, nitty-gritty reminder, pulling us back from the abstract, eliminative, neat, self-serving, but faulty, fantasies of over-rationalistic intellectuals.

Relato, not Isolato

Although Camus, as we have seen, often falls prey to such fantasies, the opening scenes of *The First Man* are situated in the nitty-gritty, concrete world. They make clear that, when an actual birthing scene is attended to, "first man" has nothing to do with the "being-and-nothingness," "emerge-out-of-nowhere," "gynephobic" "father-of-oneself" understanding of the human condition. The text places flesh-and-blood individuals front and center. They are a pregnant woman and her husband. Their setting is not just anywhere. It's a journey to a new home, a place where the husband will, the very next day, begin his new job. It is raining. They are in a horse-drawn cart. The woman is having labor pains. The newborn is no Adam, no denizen of the state of nature, no instance of being arising from nothingness. Little Jacques has specific parents. He is born in a spare, rural building. His mother's contractions were painful. A local woman was brought in to help.

Whereas Nabokov's story followed a philosophical trajectory, Camus's is more in line with the gospel narration of a birth in Bethlehem. It's not clear if there is intended either a religious or a self-inflating aspect to this parallel. With the incomplete state of *The First Man*, we will never get to determine if either of these or yet another dimension was to be emphasized. Based on the text we have, we can say that the birth scene is far from the Nabokov-style flight to abstraction. It's a down-to-earth depiction of a poor couple, a pregnant woman, and the birth of an infant.

The birth, as is typical, was characterized by moisture: blood, water, afterbirth. The meteorological conditions in which the birth takes place are also dominated by moisture. The weather accompaniments situate us far from "being and nothingness" abstractions. They also move us away from the inside-the-head perspective dominant in Camus's novels. The story's opening describes clouds, heavy and water-filled. Having traveled from the Atlantic, they were now shedding large drops on the wagon carrying the pregnant woman (FM, 3–4). Instead of the perspective occasioned by the Great Bifurcation, "humans here—world there," the description is now one of intertwining. The human, watery, birth is interwoven with nature's forces of moisture swirling about.

We get a sense here of the epic dimensions which were to mark *The First Man*. It was not to be an abstract attempt to unravel or exemplify philosophical concepts. It would also not be another spare, bare, narrative à la *The Stranger*. In that early novel, the natural world and even other people were more like props on a stage than co-participants in a living world. For the opening section of *The First Man*, Camus, by contrast, draws on his inner Balzac. He presents people as situated, enveloped really, within specific surroundings.

For the younger Camus, relationships were described in I-and-other terms. The starting point was an encapsulated self who would come to encounter others. That representation was consistent with the social contract tradition. It envisioned an original setting composed of disconnected units. It did not think of the aboriginal condition as that of humans already implicated in natural and social circumstances. Instead, a particular self-centered projection was invoked: initially isolated entities fated to encounter (as if this were unusual) others. The isolated individual's "encounters" are described (1) as if individuals were not initially in a social context, (2) in terms that depict the event as not personal but rather as that of a subjective consciousness receiving objective data, and (3) one that brackets dependence on natural circumstances, for example, air to breathe, water to drink, food to eat.

The birth scene in *The First Man* thus represents a major departure from Camus's usual narrative rendering. Camus now emphasizes, as primordial, a more interpersonal context, one marked by care and concern rather than by disengaged consciousness. In addition, this interpersonal context is itself woven into a natural environment. The story, instead of being abstract and eliminative, is concrete and inclusive. Camus's previous literary productions had worked with a buffered understanding of the human condition, one in which the human was a stranger to the world beyond the buffer. *The First Man*'s opening sections situate us in a person/nature/society milieu that is more copious, ample, plentiful, and interwoven. The human is no longer a stranger set off against a backdrop that is separate. The central character is intertwined with not just the social factors but also the meteorological and biological ones that make up the lifeworld. The newborn, in other words, is neither a "first" nor, borrowing a term from one of Camus's favorite novels *Moby Dick*, an "isolato" (Melville 1851/1956, 137).

The Stranger gave expression to Modern philosophy's fascination with the "isolato," someone conceived as an ahistorical, acontextual, detached, individual. By contrast, *The First Man* emphasizes what we might call the "relato" or "inter-relato." The newborn's situatedness is actually attended to. As such, it cannot be separated from biological, social, cultural, and historical factors. Together these provide the lifeworld in which this particular child was born to these specific people, on this date, in this place. The result, more inclusive than eliminative, interweaves not just the anthropological conditions of biology, family, culture, history, economics, and politics but also those of meteorology and geography. The shift is breathtaking in both its scope and its challenge to the Great Bifurcation which pervaded Camus's earlier works.

Countering Nietzsche's "Last Man"

In this sense the "first" in *The First Man* could be understood ironically. No one, despite Adamic or state-of-nature delusions, is "first." Camus, as we saw, had noted how no one is a first man and everyone is. In one sense, everyone is unique and thus a "first," that is, not simply a duplicate of someone else. Such a unique person also will work out a unique trajectory and, again, in a quite usual way, be the first to do so (in all its specifics, at least). Such a person will neither simply be reducible to a general type nor be the mere plaything of historical patterns. An individual, in concrete practice, can, in principle at least, resist such reductionism. At the same time, it remains true that large numbers of people might fall into a particular pattern, one that plays out the general trajectory of their time. As the nineteenth century came to a close, Nietzsche had expressed a fear about this latter path. He worried that, given its intellectual inheritance, the contemporary European age would be characterized by the appearance of what he identified as a "last" man. Camus, in choosing a title for his book, would have been sensitive to the resonances associated with Nietzsche's label.

Nietzsche's rendition of a "last" man resulted from his concern about a particular direction in Western thought: a move away from standards of excellence and their replacement by ones favoring a lowest common denominator. The end result would be nothing-ism, "nihilism." Religion had been a major force in both fomenting (via the language of a "fallen" realm) and then disguising nihilism by promoting a divine rule giver. Once this divinity was removed ("God is dead") the nihilism it kept hidden would be brought to light. Once such nihilism became firmly entrenched, norms and criteria would be understood as merely arbitrary. Such a loss of criteria would represent a genuine cultural crisis since healthy cultures need standards of excellence.

Nietzsche envisioned only two directions which could follow upon the death of God. Both were problematic. One was hopeful, if not utopian; the other, realistic and pessimistic. The hopeful alternative was evolutionary. A new intellectual climate, one radically changed by the death of God, would require a new kind of human. This would be a creature radically different from the run-of-the-mill types that more and more were coming to predominate. The new man, Nietzsche's famous *übermensch*, "superman," or literally "overman," would be necessary to cope with the ramifications of nihilism. A new philosophical landscape required a new kind of human, someone who, despite general nihilism, could preserve excellence.

The need for an overman becomes clear when we recognize what would happen if this new man could not be engendered. It's not a pretty picture. The alternative could be summarized in the title of a book by José Ortega y Gasset, *The Revolt of the Masses*. Instead of excellence, humans, giving in to the leveling tendency inherent within nihilism, would opt for the leveling of taste. Absent independent standards, two guideposts would move to the center: pleasure and popularity. Whatever most people thought best would become, by definition, best. Of course, "best" would then be devalued. It would be relativized (since popular tastes are both fickle and guided by instant gratification). The result would be a great move away from excellence. Ease and comfort would dominate as guiding ideals. The ethics of "petty people" would be one seeking lives characterized not by excellence but by longevity and pleasure (Nietzsche 1885/2008, Section LXXIII, 3). Higher aspirations would no longer tug at the human character. Superior and inferior would be replaced by blanket equality. There would be a descent toward lowest-common-denominator lifestyles. Such a descent would be symbolized by the figure whom Nietzsche labeled the "last man" and described as "contemptible" (Nietzsche 1885/2008, prologue, 2). A banalized sense of equality dominates. Leveling becomes the order of the day. Risk-taking is avoided. Quality is now defined by popularity.

Camus, with the title he gives his book, seems to be offering a more sanguine take on things. In the notes left with his manuscript, he alludes to a popularized version of the Nietzschean standpoint. "We are the first men," says the note. Then comes a contrast: "not those on the wane as they shout in the (illegible word) newspaper, but men of a different and undefined dawn" (FM, 319).

We need to make careful distinctions here. In countering Nietzsche's dystopic vision Camus is not insisting on a utopian one. His position, as was made clear in *The Rebel*, is free of revolutionary messianism. He welcomes aspirations, hopefulness, and disappointments. Such a combination, though, is rooted in the here and now. Transcendental dreams, including those of achieving an "overman," are set aside. Still, Nietzsche was onto something. In a world which, consciously or unconsciously, embraces nihilism, the trajectory will be toward a great leveling, or, as Camus preferred to put it, toward a denial of measure and limits. The resulting democratization of taste and ethics will then involve substituting quantity for quality. Better and worse, as evaluations, will not disappear. They will be retranslated in terms of popularity. The inevitable result: a society in which, as Nietzsche put it, the "petty people" will be "master" (Nietzsche 1885/2008, LXXIII, 3). As far as Nietzsche could tell, the resulting mass man will be the "last" man, the one who is bound to emerge, given the intellectual tendencies of the age. The last man, sadly, would stand as the logical end toward which Western intellectual history has been heading.

When we think of Camus's "first" man, we should think of it in terms of multiple resonances. One of these would be as a response to Nietzsche. It is not that Camus dismissed the diagnosis of nihilism and its dangers. As we have seen, responding to the challenge of nihilism was central to his entire effort. It is rather his sense that nihilism could be answered apart from either the *übermensch* or the *letzter Mensch* of Nietzsche. He was inclined, though he never followed through in a thorough way, to fashion a response around *amor vitae*, a celebration of life which would incorporate the rehabilitation of the ordinary. And "ordinary," for him, would mean people like the poor, illiterate members of his own family, people far removed from Nietzsche's nobility-inspired notions of an *übermensch*.

In many ways Camus's family could be pigeonholed into the Nietzschean category of "last." Their abode was devoid of books. Their language skills were rudimentary.

Cinema represented the highest of the arts to which they were drawn. Their preoccupations were mundane and lowly: scraping together enough resources to get by day to day. If history is linear, the generational trajectory is inflexible. No one in the future will stand as a counterexample to such "last" men. Within such a deterministic frame, young Albert, rooted in such a soil, would be doomed to exemplify Nietzsche's last man.

From Nihilism to Pan-Semioticism

Much of this is abstract and academic, "philosophical" in the worst sense. Life is teeming with variety. General patterns allow for exceptions. Individuals who fall into a particular category often tend, in some ways, to overflow the category. Camus's life story offers a good example. There is a kind of quiet heroism in the ordinary lives described by him. The relatives that make up his household are not exceptional in ways that would be celebrated by society. They are uneducated, often violent, lower-class people. "Poor," "crude," "illiterate," "proletariat," "exploited," "colonizers"—there are many labels that could apply, many ways in which the individuals could be indexed. What Camus reveals, by taking us into this world, is how indexing does not really get at the concrete plenitude, the not fully indexable nature of his family.

Although it might be tempting to do so, the relatives cannot neatly be gathered under the heading of Nietzsche's "last" man. In many ways they do represent the leveling down indicated in Nietzsche's prediction. But "many ways" is not the same as "all ways." An illiterate mother can be proud of her son's academic prowess. A desperately poor, mean, violent grandmother can be persuaded to give up a source of extra income by letting her grandson attend the *lycée*. The grandson might even become a leading intellectual, a defender of elevated standards. At birth the odds might be strong that the child will exemplify the path of "last" men. Nonetheless, he might break with the pattern and be the "first" to be educated, the "first" to become an intellectual, the "first" in his family to make a major mark on culture. What *The First Man* does is attempt a full-bodied characterization of a poor family, making sure not to depict them as mere instances of any general type, certainly not as the "last" manifestations of philosophical and cultural decay.

Philosophical orientations and general historical claims are unavoidable. The Nietzschean diagnosis of nihilism and the trend toward the "last" man captured something real about the West's tendency toward a general value leveling. Still some qualifications are called for. First, European Modernity is not to be confused with all cultures across the globe. Second, even what is called the Western tradition is itself multiple. The dominance of a particular strand within it need not be identified with the tradition as a whole. Third, this means that what has been diagnosed as a tendency toward the "last" man may result from the historical dominance of one strand within the tradition. Finally, if that is the case, a reform is possible from within the tradition, a reform which will recover some constituents which the dominant strand has moved to the periphery. This last step is exactly the one proposed by Camus.

Looking with fascination to ancient Greece, he understood himself to be shifting the marginal/focal mix and offering ways to a new Renaissance. Grandiose claims such as proclaiming the era of "last" men can be helpful by indicating how one particular trajectory has reached a dead-end. Perhaps that dead-end offers an opportunity for a major new take on things. Perhaps, that new take can find its inspiration in dimensions of Western thought relegated to the margins by Modernity.

Camus, though he engages in the project of renaissance only haltingly, is doing what is needed for a reworking of inherited assumptions. He is not just going back to ancient Greek texts. He is also seeking to reestablish the importance of lived experience. Nietzsche's writings highlighted how the heritage from post-Cartesian philosophy, especially the sharp separation between humans and the world, had come to one kind of end (as logical culmination): nihilism. Articulating a new climate of opinion, one which would move in a different direction, would not be easy. Such a project would require jettisoning an ingrained assumption that Camus had fully assimilated.

This is the baseline I have often mentioned: the divorce of humans from their surroundings. It is, first of all, a "view," and one that envisions a particular primordial setting: "man here," "*external* world, there." This easily morphs into "subjective, value-imposing, realm here," "objective, value-free realm there." When accompanied by an Adamic story about a first man showing up out of nowhere, the emphasis on disjunction gets even stronger. When the death of God becomes an additional element, the ground is prepared for a trajectory which culminates in the "last man." The individual for whom valuation is subjective, who draws on neither nature nor tradition, who lives in a context without secure foundations for value, is someone who can easily succumb to laziness, pleasure, popularity.

But what if, instead of beginning with contrasting abstractions, like "man" and "world" or "being" and "nothingness," we begin with a lived experience, say a real birth. What if the biological conditions of human existence were not bracketed? What if gestation in a mother were taken seriously? This would move the human understanding in a different direction. It would, to begin with, challenge the basic bifurcation (man versus world) that underlies much of Modern philosophy. At the same time, it would focus on what has been a great occlusion: birth. When we start with a concrete birth, the disjunctive assumptions of Modern philosophy become harder to defend. Interdependence, interaction, interweaving tend to become more central, tend to be recognized as more rule than exception.

In a setting which admits the primordiality of interdependencies and interactions, evaluation can take on a more ordinary meaning: the attempt at reading signals properly, at marshaling interactions so they culminate in proper fulfillments. A newborn offers a helpful example. A newborn is hungry. A source of nutrition, the lactating mother, is nearby. If situated on the mother's stomach, the infant will, on its own, move toward the source of milk, a phenomenon known as the "breast crawl" (see "Breast Crawl: A Scientific Overview"). The infant is not a subject surveying objects. Nor is the infant an alien or outsider dropped into a foreign land. The infant is where it should be. This world is its home. That home, in turn, is not "silent." It is replete with signalings. A washed breast, observation has shown, does not draw the infant to the degree that does an unwashed one.

Is the value of milk "subjective"? The very phrasing of the question reveals its limitations. It's a question born of the Great Bifurcation. Life experience suggests that, yes there is a personal dimension, the infant is hungry. This does not make the value of milk "subjective" as if the properties of the milk were irrelevant. There is a correlativity at work. Breast milk is valuable to the infant for specific reasons and on account of specific properties. It even contains "human milk oligosaccharides" which the infant cannot digest. These are really, but indirectly, helpful to the newborn's thriving. They provide nutrients for the gut bacteria which the infant needs for good health (Yong). The newborn arrives in a world to which it is well suited. To speak in terms of "subjective" or "objective" is to miss the key interactive, correlative point. There is a personal dimension along with a property-based dimension to value. Breast milk is valuable for the infant. It is valuable in this context at this time. The coordinated scenario can, via abstraction, be dismembered. The complementary components can be artificially separated. Then, and only then, that is, after considerable conceptual elimination of inter-relationality, will the simplified "subjective" or "objective" approach seem like an appropriate one.

As just mentioned with the "breast crawl" example, the newborn finds itself in a complicated context, but neither a silent nor a completely obtuse one. There are signals. "Converse," which, according to the *Oxford English Dictionary*, once meant "familiar engagement or occupation (with things)" is primordial. Some engagements as responses to signals are better than others (not every newborn in experiments achieved a successful breast crawl). Still, the overall pattern is established: every setting is one of call and response. Optimal responses will draw on interactivity.

For mature individuals, these will depend on intelligence, experience, and the properties of the interacting components. Will this combination inevitably lead to perfect certitude and infallibility? Not at all. Judgments of better and worse will always be subject to missing the mark. This is especially so since the right mix of personal factors and situational properties offers a difficult target. Once again, it's about *measure*, about getting the mix right. A hungry adult may desire to load up on sugar-rich foods. Chocolate bars and cream puffs, it seems, will do the trick. But will they really? The properties they bring with them might not make their choice a nutritionally optimal one. If personal preference does not do it, how about fixed formulas? Guidelines help, but idiosyncratic attributes can mean the guidelines need to be customized in terms of this particular individual at this particular time in this particular setting. Better and worse are real. The paths to their establishment, however, are difficult and require effort.

For those who prefer shortcuts and oversimplifications, the language of subjective (personal preference) and objective (rigid formulas) is a great boon. For those who wish for a description adequate to the thick, complicated, interactive character of life experience, the case is different. Responsibility, as judgment which responds appropriately to actual conditions, cannot be avoided.

One instance of this centrality of judgment emerges when *The First Man* turns its attention to Camus's beloved grade school teacher. M. Bernard has the opportunity to select candidates for scholarships to the *lycée*. He needs, in other words, to make judgments. This particular person will be deciding. Still, the selection cannot properly be described as "subjective" in the sense of arbitrary. Nor is it "objective" in a coldly mechanical, impersonal fashion. The teacher, M. Germain, called M. Bernard in *The First Man*, has had to exercise judgment. There are reasons why Albert and the others were selected. It's not that they carried labels saying, infallibly, "we are the ones to select." Evaluation is not that simple. They had shown talent, and when M. Bernard opts for this particular group, he is responding to evidence accumulated over the years. Other students could have been chosen. Selecting for reasons does not eliminate fallibility. Nor does it eliminate borderline cases. The teacher's selections were neither arbitrary ("subjective" in a strong sense) nor the result of following a rigid formula ("objective" in the strong sense). There was room for factors like a personal "hunch" or an inclination based on experience.

The final determinations, risky and fallible, resulted from a particular sort of interaction, one which prized evidence, personal experience, awareness of what it would take to succeed, and acquaintance with the students in question. This required effort, deliberation, and discrimination. The selected group was heterogeneous. Jacques (Albert) and his friend Pierre were selected. There was also "Fleury," "a kind of prodigy who did well in all subjects." Another, Santiago, was "a handsome boy who was less gifted but succeeded by virtue of diligence" (FM, 159). M. Bernard, doing the best he can, is not a calculating machine. He draws instead on experience and intelligence to arrive at his evaluation of who are the students he should nominate for the scholarship competition.

M. Bernard and the French schooling system play roles that move away from the trajectory that leads in the direction of "last" men. Aiming for excellence, humans do not always hit the mark. Nonetheless, the aim and the effort can be recognized as both worthwhile and requiring some particular cooperation. Evaluators, when things work well, avoid shortcuts and simplifications. They bring to bear a combination of intelligence and experience as they examine evidence. Using terms with etymological family ties, we can say that *desiderata* result from *considerata*. The ends ultimately desired come about as a result of reflective consideration. In this way humans once again become live beings in a living world. They do not redefine themselves as minds geared to absolute infallibility. Integration rather than eliminationism becomes the order of the day. Nihilism is no longer so appealing. It is replaced by what could be called *semioticism*, the realization that the conditions within which humans find themselves provide some intimations, hints, suggestions, clues, that is to say, ingredients for a decision-making process. Such indications call for consideration before *desiderata* are finally settled upon.

Such *semioticism*, or better, *pan-semioticism*, requires a major shift in philosophical anthropology. Interaction has to be recognized as having primacy over detachment. The Great Bifurcation has to be set aside. Here is one way in which Camus's search for his father could have paid important dividends. The elder Camus worked in a vineyard. Viticulture challenges the overly abstract philosophical inheritance in multiple ways. To begin with, it reminds us of our status as living beings in a living world. We are not isolated "firsts." We come into an already existing situation, one which we did not create. Second, viticulture emphasizes human-and-nature interpenetration. Third, it embraces rather than dismisses the ordinary. Finally, semioticism, paying attention to indicators, signs, clues, is crucial. Decisions about when to harvest, for example, are neither arbitrary nor infallible. There will always be a personal dimension when it comes to figuring out the significance of indicators in a context. Whatever decision is taken might be improvable.

Within the form of life that is viticulture, nihilism is pushed to the margins. Similarly, viticulture presents a setting in which the formal diagnosis of absurdity is put into question. Frustrations, challenges, obstacles, difficulties abound. These, however, do not mean that there is a fundamental, unbridgeable disconnect between the aim of a vinter and the vines being tended. To make a blanket pronouncement that the vines are "silent," that is, provide no indicators or clues, would be a hyperbolic distortion. Qualifiers like "somewhat," "in some ways," and "partly" would remove the lure of abstract purity. They would help bring out the recognition that the diagnosis of absurdity as a general, universal qualifier for human existence depends, as we have seen, on some preliminary, artificial, demands (1) that the world be made for us, (2) that knowing is either infallible or arbitrary, (3) that our surroundings are simply neutral, devoid of indicators or signs calling on us for understanding.

Practices like trimming, irrigating, controlling for bugs and fungi are not just subjective in the sense of imposing arbitrary values. The particular strategies constituting those practices emerge from attempts to figure things out, to improve quality and quantity of the harvests. "Figuring things out" has a personalized dimension, but one that partners with operative conditions in the nature of things. It's more a matter of properly reading signals than it is of imposing structures. The signals, say particular amounts of rainfall, the absence or presence of pests, sunshine, frost, do not lend themselves to perfect mathematical precision. Harvest now, given this year's climate, or harvest next week? Some judgment call will inevitably be present. But it will be a judgment based on experience, learning, and operative conditions. It will neither be a subjective imposition nor just an incontestable conclusion that is the result of directly perceiving clear-and-distinct objective data.

What counts, philosophically, is a description which most fully captures humans as concerned actants, people engaged in practices within a context of concern. Viticulturists worry about lots of things. Given their setting and their goals, they have to. What they don't worry about is nihilism. Or at least their practices do not embody the implications of nihilism. The natural setting within which grape vines grow is (a) one which includes not just vines but people who savor wine and (b) anything but indifferent. The climatic and geological variations between Burgundy and Algeria represent differences that make a difference. Vinters must heed local conditions. There is regularly a need to make judgment calls. As engaged participants, they realize the necessity of working in conjunction with natural surroundings. Embracing nihilism, that is, saying that there is nothing (*nihil*) on the nonhuman side of things that serve as indications for valuation, is of course possible. It is even attractive to a certain kind of egghead approach to things. It does little, however, for bringing about a successful harvest.

Camus's father was neither an intellectual, a scientist, nor a major economic player. The kind of work in which he engaged, though, was significant for rethinking the guiding assumptions that led to nihilism. If Albert felt troubled by nihilism, then the search for a father which drives the early sections of *The First Man* would have offered a rich opportunity. Regular practices of those engaged in agriculture re-situate humans away from the city-dweller, spectator model that has been dominant since the seventeenth century. Camus wrote *The First Man* from the perspective of a son who felt the loss of his missing father. What he does not seem to have appreciated is how much his nonphilosopher father, as someone involved in agriculture, could have offered important lessons for the intellectual elite.

13

The First Man II, What Is Love?

The *Aporia* of Love

The Roman colonizers of the area we know as Algeria loved wine. They planted the grapes whose posterity would be worked by Camus's father. The love of wine, though, was not what Camus had in mind when he identified "love" as a topic to be explored in his third cycle. That "love" would be the one for which the term is most commonly used: spousal love among humans. There's an anecdote, possibly apocryphal, which has Camus discussing his proposed third cycle. His wife, Francine, overhearing the conversation, has an immediate reaction: "You, you are going to talk about love ... but you have never been capable of love."[1]

The anecdote is telling in several ways. (1) It reinforces what is known from other sources, that Camus was moving on to his third cycle. (2) It indicates how the term "love" is generally understood within the context of *eros*. (3) It identifies a challenge for Camus. Conjugal love, a prominent arena for the theme, was not his strong point. Olivier Todd's biography highlights both his infidelities and the emotional/psychological toll they took on Francine. (4) Francine's comment touches on a theme already made central in *The Fall*, the inability to love.

This fourth point provides a clue for approaching *The First Man*. In that autobiographical work, Camus makes a point of distinguishing himself from Jean-Baptiste Clamence. He does this by setting up a contrast between himself and Clamence. The major difference: emphasizing his ability to love. In *The Fall*, Camus, by his own admission, had created an empty, unattractive character. Clamence loved no one. *The First Man* would indicate how Camus was someone capable of love. Because the text only covers early years, the kind of love mostly dealt with is *storge*. Readers will be left forever in the dark about how Camus, given his history with women, would have dealt with *eros*.

From earlier texts, especially his lyrical essays, we get a sense that Camus was most at ease when discussing love outside the human context. A general attitude of *amor mundi* was manifested most fully in his general affection (he even called it "nuptials") for the natural world. When it comes to the human context, the one in which the word "nuptials" is most often used, things are different. The essay "Return to Tipasa" is significant in this regard. In it he explicitly raises the theme mentioned by Francine. Not being loved is one thing; "there is only misfortune (*malchance*, literally "bad luck") in not being loved." The more important deficiency, echoing *The Fall*, is "not loving."

Not being loved results from *malchance*. The inability to love, by contrast, is not simply a matter of *malchance*. It's a *malheur*. "There is misery in not loving" (LCE, 168).

The inability may be a *malheur*, but here is a reality humans have to confront: "In the clamor we live in, love is impossible" (LCE, 168). But how literally did he take the claim that love was "impossible"? As we shall see, this claim is most relevant when it comes to *eros*. *The First Man* opens with descriptions indicating how *storge* is real and possible. The *Lyrical Essays* had already indicated how love of nature was possible. Such *amor mundi* is a love that does not disappoint. Indeed, it can serve to restore our energies. The failings of person-to-person relationships are inevitable. To counteract their burdensomeness, it is helpful to unite with the wonders of nature. "Here, once more, I found an ancient beauty, a young sky, and measured my good fortune as I realized at last that in the worst years of our madness the memory of this sky had never left me. It was this that in the end had saved me from despair" (LCE, 168).

Camus is here articulating a position that he consistently held, one exemplified in "The Adulterous Wife." The interpersonal realm is one of frustrations and disappointments. The natural one is a source of beauty, satisfaction, refreshment. We can speak of "love" as regards both nature and humans. As regards nature, love culminates in an almost mystical sense of oneness. When it comes to humans, the most real love is *storge*. *Eros*, by contrast, is more illusory than real. In this regard, Camus does not seem to have changed his views since *The Myth of Sisyphus*. He there complained that love was an invention of poets. "We call love what binds us to certain creatures only by reference to a collective way of seeing for which books and legends are responsible" (MS, 73). *Eros*, Camus is saying, is not, by nature, operative in human life. It is a contrivance of culture. *Storge*, by contrast, is rooted in biology, in maternity and paternity. It, unlike *Eros*, thus has some mooring in the workings of nature. Once the conventional, that is, irreal source of *Eros* is exposed, it becomes easier to understand its "impossibility."

But this impossibility also presents a problem. It introduces yet another facet of how absurd human life is. Love may be impossible, but it is felt to be exigent. The inability to love, as Camus put it, was a *malheur*, an affliction. This inability, as a deficiency, was made prominent in *The Fall*. It had earlier been identified as a major failing by one of Camus's favorite authors, Fyodor Dostoyevsky. Father Zossima, the saintly priest in *The Brothers Karamazov*, delivers a sermon in which he describes the real meaning of "hell." Hell, he insists, is the inability to love (Dostoevsky, 301).[2] Camus echoed this sentiment not only in *The Fall* but also when making specific comments about Dostoevsky. In an explanatory note (1959) accompanying his stage adaptation of Dostoevsky's *The Possessed*, Camus makes some important admissions. First, *The Possessed* is one of the four or five books which, for Camus, rank "above all the others." Second, Dostoevsky's characters are "neither strange nor absurd." Finally, *The Possessed* interweaves nihilism and the bane of being unable to love. "And if *The Possessed* is a prophetic book, it is not only because it proclaims our nihilism, it is also because it highlights souls torn apart, or dead, incapable of loving and suffering from this inability" (TRN, 1877, my translation).[3]

Love thus represents what philosophers identify as an *aporia*, a contradiction from which there appears to be no escape. It is both fundamental and impossible. Such a quandary makes of love a rich topic for someone with Camus's talents. This is especially so since, as we have already seen, Camus did not think his quest was complete. He continued to be a seeker and searcher.[4] All of this suggests that the still searching Camus, concentrating on the theme of love, would make that theme focal in *The First Man*. It thus makes sense to examine that work in light of the *aporia* and ask whether Camus has made any movement beyond it.

Love as Debt

When Camus linked loving and admiring in his lyrical essays, he was expressing his deep *amor mundi*. He was uttering a generous, Nietzschean, *Ja sagen* to life. Such ardor, though, here is the *aporia*, seems interrupted at the nature/human boundary. *Amor mundi* is one thing. *Te amo* is quite another. On one side, love and admiration are responses continuous with nature's processes. On the human side, disruption rather than continuity rules. There, love (*eros*) is thought to be an artificial, cultural, imposition.

Amor mundi originates in an experience such as the one described by Camus at Tipasa, or one experienced by Janine in "The Adulterous Wife." The originating context is finding oneself in a natural setting that is not of one's making. This is followed by attentiveness to what is the case, an attentiveness that, when fully lucid, grows into wonder-filled admiration and affection.

The human-to-human situation is quite different. The originating context is now a choice. Freely made selection replaces insertion in a context not of our own making. Sheer givenness, as in a natural setting, is minimized. The emphasis goes, rather, to the side of liberty. The only givenness is that of too many options, a multiplicity which makes election among options all the more precarious.

This is a point at which the fuller meaning of *Ja sagen* comes into play. Saying "yes" might at first be understood in a *que será, será*, fatalistic, sort of way. This is an exaggerated neo-Stoic take, one that Nietzsche, with his *amor fati*, and Jonas with his "star," came to embrace. The yes-saying, however, can also be understood differently. The different understanding is more complicated, but life itself is complicated. In the more entangled understanding, yea-saying would involve an embrace of life *along with the responsibilities* that accompany it.

In the brief essay "The Almond Trees" Camus identifies a special human responsibility, that of repairing the world. As we shall see in the conclusion, Camus explicitly identified repairing the world as a human responsibility: "We must mend what has been torn apart" (LCE, 135). If some repairing is needed, then saying yes to life, to human existence, need not mean *amor fati* fatalism. It can also mean affirming how the human context involves, willy-nilly, a combination of yes and no saying. Yea-saying, in this more substantial sense, affirms the need for responsibility. It acknowledges not just the inevitability of challenges and difficulties (*amor fati* goes this far) but also the need to work, Dr. Rieux style, at changing what needs to be changed. Dr. Rieux's "yes" to life is a "no" to the plague.

This fuller yea-saying attitude accepts the human condition as it is, including "yea-saying" to the responsibility for repair that comes with it. Nay-saying, by contrast, says "no" to the actual human condition. It does this by redefining humans either as beasts or angels, as completely determined by nature or as belonging to another, higher, realm. The yes-saying that is disconnected from fatalism is an affirmation of the human, that is, in-between condition. Such a "yes-saying," here is the sticking point, brings with it a need for deciding when nay-saying is called for. The finite world is one which, in many respects, stands in need of repair. In such situations it is important to say "no, that's not the way it should be." A generous-spirited yea-saying to existence is neither unqualified nor formulaic. It is a "yes" which affirms the need to get the yes/no mixture right.

The contrasting attitude, dominated by a general *nein sagen*, was pervasive in Camus's *Myth of Sisyphus*. That text was characterized by the absence of in-betweens. *The Myth*, as we have seen, traffics in stunningly abstract all-or-nothing territory. Everyday life must *either* provide perfect answers *or* there are no answers. The all-or-nothing attitude is encouraged by an initial nay-saying: a dismissal of ordinary, everyday, mundane existence. In the latter realm, resolutions, even when imperfect and conditioned by time and place, are possible. The more humble realm of everyday life is both a realm of enigmas/obstacles and a realm of opportunities. That humble, quotidian realm is thus, in an important sense, "true," as in "true to life." As such, it is one that can be affirmed with a generous multifaceted *Ja sagen*, one which includes a *nein* dimension. It is also one that can be explored by a literary artist, an exploration begun by Camus in *Exile and the Kingdom*.

In that regard, *The First Man* is continuous with the short story collection. The narrative in *The First Man* seeks phenomenological comprehensiveness. There is, as with the short stories, a break with the novels. Each of those was a *roman à thèse*, an attempt to articulate, in story form, some philosophical perspective. *The First Man*, as autobiographical, moves in a different direction. Camus seeks not to illustrate a philosophical position but to retell a life story. It redresses the balance by emphasizing lived experience first, philosophical reflection later. The theme of the third cycle, exploring love, is present. But now it is not the philosophical idea of love but the concrete lived narrative that takes center stage. Coming after *The Fall*, and in line with how Camus understood Dostoevsky's *The Possessed*, we can expect that instead of an antecedently accepted philosophical position, the narrative will move along the lines of genuine questioning. And a major question will involve whether the main character is capable of loving.

The ability to love, if demonstrated, would move Camus outside the orbit of Clamence. It would also move Camus outside the orbit of Meursault. In *The Stranger*, love is treated, if not as an impossibility, at least as an artificial, unreal illusion. Meursault agrees to marry a young woman. "Do you love me," she asks. His reaction: he probably "didn't love her," and after all it was a question which "didn't mean anything" (S, 41). A similar phrase is repeated in relation to Meursault's mother. This time he says he probably did love her. It's a claim discredited by the immediate follow-up, "but that didn't mean anything" (S, 65).

The First Man separates the two contexts, that of *eros* and that of *storge*. Camus will present himself as someone capable of love, at least in terms of *storge*, and especially in relation to his mother. This will be a love that means something. *Eros*, on the other hand, will remain problematic. What separates the two contexts? A lingering nature/

culture split. The context for *storge* is closer to the natural realm, one more dominated by necessity, by situations which are given, ones which have not been freely chosen. The context for *eros* is quite different. There, it is the voluntary, not the inevitable that dominates. Within the realm of nature, the dominating tendency is that of necessity, the inexorable workings of physical processes. Within the realm of culture, the dominating tendency is freedom.

The two realms also help explain the gap between *storge* and *eros*. *Storge*, modeled on parent/child affinity, is unavoidably implicated in layers of necessity. No child has selected its particular parents. They stand as an unchangeable given. So are date and place of birth. *Eros*, on the other hand, is situated within a context of freedom. We may have no say about who our parents were, but, outside the arena of arranged marriages, we, exercising complete liberty, elect erotic partners. This distinction will bear important fruit for Camus. Love as *storge*, with some roots in the realm of nature, will be accorded substantive heft. Love as *Eros*, inseparable from freedom, will not.

The opening section of *The First Man* is entitled "Search for the Father." Camus's reflections surrounding *storge* begin with a major absence: the father who died in the First World War when Albert was nine months old. The issue about the ability to love arises immediately. Since he had never known his father, Camus had to admit that he could "not muster a filial devotion he did not feel" (FM, 24). When the topic of love arises, it emerges more prominently in relation to substitute fathers. A prominent figure in *The First Man* is a friend/mentor, a stand-in for Camus's influential philosophy professor, Jean Grenier.[5] The name Camus gives him "Malan" is strikingly similar to *malin, a descriptor* signaling not just academic brainpower but also intelligence combined with astuteness and shrewdness. Malan, the descriptive signals make clear, is a font of wisdom and cleverness. He also served as a substitute father. Malan actually addresses Cormery, colloquially as "my son." These are words, *mon fils*, which Camus had never heard pronounced by his biological father.

With this friend/mentor, the topic of love arises naturally. Cormery says that though he is often arrogant, arrogance is an attitude he cannot adopt in the presence of Malan. Malan asks "why?" Cormery's response: "because I love you" (FM, 32). It's a love, Cormery goes on to explain, based on admiration and gratitude. When Cormery was "young, very foolish and very much alone," Malan had paid attention to him. That attention "opened for me the door to everything I love in the world" (FM, 33).

At another point, addressing specifically Cormery's ability to love, Malan asserts: "Yes, you love life." He then goes on to explain, "You have to, since that's all you believe in" (FM, 35). Jacques, as this interchange already makes clear, is no Clamence. He is capable of love. He even repeats his vow of affection for Malan, "with all your faults I love you" (FM, 34). Cormery's capacity for loving is thus trumpeted clearly, even as he admits, that this ability, in him, is limited. After declaring his affection for Malan, Cormery continues, "I love or revere very few people" (FM, 34).

The opening pages of the book set an important pattern. It is one which will contextualize much of what Camus says about love. Two important dimensions stand out: (1) Love arises most naturally in settings more dominated by necessity than by freedom. (2) Camus mixes together love/gratitude and love/admiration.

The dimensions come together in Cormery's love for Malan. The element of necessity arises because a particular individual happened to be teaching at a particular university. It also arises because this particular individual paid attention to a young man in a way that culminated in a much-appreciated kind of flourishing. When Malan tries to minimize his influence, saying that Cormery was already "gifted," Cormery responds in a way that both reinforces the theme of necessity and adds that of gratitude/admiration. First, he emphasizes gratitude/admiration: "But even the most gifted person needs someone to initiate him." Then comes the necessity/love connection: "The one that life puts in your path one day, that person must be loved and respected forever, even if he's not responsible. That is my faith!" (FM, 33).

The "faith" in question is a fundamental belief about responding to one's circumstances. It's not free choice that stands out. Exigency, not liberty, sets the pattern. The person whom life "puts in your path" and whose actions are both admirable and generous is one who *must*, as Cormery insists, "be loved and respected forever." This last phrase which conjoins love and respect indicates the way in which Camus fuses, in perhaps an overly hasty fashion, terms which, though they often intersect, need to be carefully distinguished.

Camus apparently loved pets. He named them for historical figures. One dog got the moniker "Kirk" in honor of the Danish thinker Søren Kierkegaard (1813–55), One of Kierkegaard's fables is instructive in relation to the Camusian intertwining of love and gratitude. It's the parable of the king and the maiden which is found in chapter 2 of Kierkegaard's *Philosophical Fragments*. The story's general outline is familiar: a powerful, wealthy king falls in love with a young woman from an impoverished background. He could proclaim his love and win her heart. That direct approach would leave lingering doubts. Would she accept his overtures only because she admires his position and accomplishments? Would she accept only out of gratitude for being lifted out of poverty? If the king wants both to love and be loved, if he wishes the love to be genuine, one path above all others is recommended. The king must renounce his position. Merely disguising himself as a poor peasant will not suffice. Only when the king has actually become an ordinary person on the same level as the maiden can he rest assured that her attraction to him is due to love and not to either admiration or gratitude.

The story is a bit ham-fisted in its obviousness. It is also, as originally told, meant to serve Christian apologetics, explaining the centrality of the Incarnation. Still, ham-fisted or not, situated within Christian apologetics or not, it bears an important lesson for the human condition. Admiration and gratitude may encourage affection. They are, though, not the same as love. There is a kind of love whose presence is most fully active when it is clear that it cannot be identified with either admiration or gratitude.

Kierkegaard's parable brings forward an important distinction. For him love was *sui generis*. Its generative center was neither gratitude nor admiration but something more like a free gift offered to what is attractive, that is, worthy of attentiveness. Camus works within a different semantic landscape. For him, the generative metaphor through which love can best be understood is that of debt. A free gift, it is true, can be a response, specifically a response to that which is "attractive" in the fullest sense as an acknowledgment of value in another person. Nonetheless, the presence of "response" in both the cases of free gift and of indebtedness does not mean that the two situations should be considered interchangeable. The former is best described, as Plato did in *the Symposium*, as attraction to what is "beautiful," a word which, in Greek, combines the good and the valuable.

In the case of debt, the setting changes. The general conditions are not those in which there is some sensitivity to how the "beautiful" resonates in this other person. Rather, there has been some kind of bestowal or remittance. In return for the favor, the recipient now owes a debt to the donor. This is so even if the donor did not engage in the activity purposely to enlist the recipient in an entanglement of indebtedness, "even if," as Camus put it, the donor is "not responsible." What counts is an interrelated triad: (i) receipt of a benefit, (ii) lucidity about having received the benefit, and (iii) the appropriate response of gratitude. Within this exchange model a certain inexorability dominates. There is, first of all, finding oneself in a situation that is not of one's own making. There is then the reception of a benefit which one did not orchestrate. Finally, the sequence of benefit received/debt owed is not a negotiable, discretionary one. The causal sequence culminates in obligation. The benefactor, Camus insists, *must* "be loved and respected forever."

It's not clear why Camus adds "loved" in this formulation. Insisting that benefactions be recognized, that gratitude be the appropriate response, represents the instantiation of an old code. Adding that "love" "must" be part of the package is puzzling. Puzzling, at least, if love as *eros* is the primary analogue. If, instead, love as *eros* is simply a cultural construct, then it makes sense to emphasize another kind of love, the one that is an offshoot of admiration/gratitude. In this regard Camus is a kind of inverted Kierkegaard. For the Dane, *eros* can be made real, but only if the elements of gratitude and admiration are removed. For Camus, if love (now separated from *eros*) is to be real rather than illusory, it requires mooring in admiration and gratitude.

The debt scenario and the free gift scenario differ, especially as regards the topic mentioned earlier, the contrast between nature in which necessity dominates and culture, more characterized by liberty. Necessity makes its presence doubly felt in the debt context.

1. There is the necessity associated with a givenness over which an individual had little or no control. Students arrive at a school where some specific instructors are employed. Those teachers are already in place. At the grade school level, there is absolutely no choice. At university, there might be more possibility for election among options, but the selectivity is severely limited. It's necessity that rules. The same holds true for favors received. If we ordered them in advance, they would not be favors.
2. There is also the ethical imperative of showing gratitude. This necessity is closely linked to straightforward factual knowledge. There is lucidity, and intellectual honesty when activities of others are acknowledged. This lucidity, in turn, can trigger a particular response, that of gratitude. It's like a causal sequence that, once set in motion, continues to a specific end. Failure to stay with the sequence represents a deficiency, a break in the natural pattern. When it is not impeded, the pattern moves through several stages. (i) A situation which just is, that is, has

not been chosen. (ii) That situation involves favors received. (iii) Then comes the response of gratitude. (iv) Such gratitude can then be transformed into affection and affection into love. Love thus is understood as continuous with the realm of natural processes.

When we enter the realm of freedom, things, for Camus, change dramatically. Instead of a process which is continuous with a natural causal sequence, the move to the arena of freedom represents a break. Not only is it a break, the move is accompanied by a heightened sense of anxiety. Where necessity predominates, the anxiety associated with free choice is reduced. If I had nothing to do with selecting who was my grade school teacher, I am relieved of anxiety on several fronts. The possibility of error is gone. So is the inevitable yes/no mix that accompanies all selections among options.

This brings us back to Buridan and his hungry donkey. The donkey can identify no difference among the haystacks. His move toward one rather than the other, a move demanded by hunger, results from an isolated act of will, one for which a reasonable account cannot be given. At first, such a situation may seem liberating. The one choosing is unfettered by external constraints. There exist no mandates compelling obedience to factors separate from one's will. Eventually, though, this sense of liberation comes to be accompanied by a dramatic increase in anxiety. If there were a difference between the haystacks, then an election in favor of one might be mistaken. Fallibility is always, in such conditions, possible. At the same time, election brings with it the possibility that the choice made was, in some substantive sense, a better one. There is unavoidable risk. There is always the possibility of error. But the general setting is one in which reading signals aright is a possible outcome.

If, by contrast, there are no differences that make a difference, then the categories of better and worse fade away. There is no work for intelligence, attentiveness, or sensibility. The absence of differences that make a difference transforms "error" into a meaningless term. At the same time, it eliminates the possibility of having made a selection that is fitting. Such an elimination, seemingly liberating, brings with it another consequence, a heightened sense of anxiety.

The more traditional setting is one in which selection among options is guided by intelligence and experience. The newer setting is closer to the image of staring into an abyss. It's an abyss because there are no differences that make a difference. Buridan's ass looks out onto a situation which has no indicia at all, no clues, hints, signs. When such indicia are present, intelligence and experience can attend to them. Then, such attentiveness can be utilized to guide the culling and selecting that will ensue. Without such clues, Buridan's ass acts on blind faith. It chooses without good reasons. When such a notion of freedom dominates, Modern man, radically free in a universe that is "silent," is condemned to unlimited and life-dominating anxiety.

Such anxiety is only heightened by the awareness that any selection will involve an excision. The yes/no mix cannot be evaded. A young man wishes to be a painter. His father insists he will be a lawyer. If the individual, his name could be Paul Cézanne, opts for painting, then he is leaving behind the world of being a lawyer, and vice versa (see Cézanne entry in the Bibliography). So long as one accepts ordinary, finite life as the kind that is appropriate to humans, then the yes/no mix is recognized as part of the tragic-comic situation. Fallibility and some degree of anxiety are part of the condition to which someone says "yes." If someone says "no" to the human condition, thinking that the embodied, encultured human life is inherently defective, then a higher level of anxiety kicks in. Somehow, a philosophical orientation arose, one in which humans should (1) have access to absolute certitude, thus avoiding the anxiety accompanying decisions that have to be made via a sheer act of will, and (2) should find themselves in a logic-chopper's world of neat separations, one where yes is just yes and no is just no, avoiding the inevitability of a yes/no mix.

Since it is unlikely that humans will achieve superhuman cognitive capacities and since selecting among options means just what it says, there seems no avoidance of higher-level anxiety. No avoidance, that is, so long as selecting in the context of unencumbered freedom maintains a domineering presence. Eliminate or minimize this notion of unencumbered freedom and higher-level anxieties can be reduced. The more a setting is dominated by necessitarian elements, the less someone has to choose. The lower level of voluntary choice also lowers the level of anxiety. One's father is just one's father. Ditto for mother and teachers. The only decision to be made, when the situation has been favorable, is whether to accept the obligation of gratitude and, for Camus, to allow the transformation of gratitude into feelings of affection. Love, within such conditions, is achievable. Otherwise, love is mostly a society-induced illusion. In situations of raw freedom humans find themselves in a Buridan's ass kind of situation. Since, as with Buridan's haystacks, there are no real differences among possible love partners, *eros* is completely irrational. When it comes to *eros*, all choices are arbitrary.

I am the Sum of My Affections

This is where the situation stands after *The First Man*'s initial exploration of love. As an autobiography *The First Man* is also exploring another issue: who am I? The issues are related. To the question "who am I," the general answer might well be "the sum of my affections." "Affections," in such a context, should be understood both passively and actively. On the passive side the key questions are "who has loved me, cared about me, made efforts that reflected concerns about me?" On the active side, "where, in my practices and activities, have my dispositions, inclinations, pursuits, led me?" In short, chronicle my attachments and you will have a good sense of who I am.

The First Man, indeed, does something like this. Its narrative offers a tracking of affections. When it comes to an understanding of love, we have seen how the exchange with Malan identifies key ingredients for Camus. The guiding metaphor is indebtedness. Such obligation is, first, recognized but then allowed to grow into a feeling of genuine affection. Given this initial introduction, it would seem that *storge*, love for family members, would fit most comfortably within the debt model which blends love, indebtedness, gratitude, and necessity. And indeed it does.

The verb "to love," *aimer*, shows up regularly in relation to family. The most pointed, direct use of the term is in relation to Camus's mother. In a touching letter Camus describes how, upon hearing he was a Nobelist, his first thoughts were of his mother (FM, 321). This immediately sets a contrast to the tone conveyed by Meursault in *The Stranger*. Meursault was depicted as someone who adopted an attitude far from affection. It was an attitude of radical neutrality and objectivity. So dominating was this attitude that it even applied to the relationship between son and mother. *The First Man*, less concerned with illustrating a philosophical position, more in line with bearing witness to lived experience, follows a very different tack. In the earlier book, "mattering," despite its etymological roots in *mater* (mother), is rigorously excised. By *The First Man*, things are different. The *mater* is someone who matters.

Regarding love, Camus does not gloss over the fact that, if there was endearment, the general atmosphere in the small apartment was not especially affectionate. When C. S. Lewis described *storge*, he drew on specific images: a mother nursing, pets huddled together with their litter (Lewis, 32).[6] Huddling together emphasizes the sense of touch, and touch, accordingly, holds a place of importance in descriptions of love. This is especially true of *storge* and *eros*. Hugging and kissing are signs of affection directed from parents toward children, children toward parents, and lovers toward each other. It is in regard to storgic touch that Jacques Cormery's recollections are far from idyllic. Camus's mother's maiden name was Sintès, and in the Sintès household, touch most often meant a beating by the grandmother. During those beatings, Cormery's mother remained silent. She did nothing to prevent her own mother's violent methods for disciplining her grandchildren.

Does this dominance of beating rather than hugging mean that *storge* was absent? Here is where nuance plays a role. Affection is important. Young Cormery craves it. He needs to know he is loved, especially by his mother. The adult Camus looking back also needs reassurance that he is someone capable of love. In retelling his story, the narrator recalls instances of affection. They are, conspicuously, described in the absence of caresses of hugs. Young Jacques in need of feeling loved had to make do with looks and words from a distance. In the aftermath of beatings by the grandmother, the mother, not having intervened, would turn toward the child the face he "so loved" (FM, 53). Such a glance, combined with the exhortation "Eat your soup. . . . It's all over. It's all over" might have been all the mother could do, but at least she did it. The mother, Jacques could feel, was not indifferent. She cared. He mattered.

At times, this son-to-mother interaction is described matter-of-factly. At others, the narrator adds some editorializing. The household, he has made clear, was not particularly warm and fuzzy. Had it been, regular hugging would have sent clear signals of love. In their absence, the child harbored doubts about being loved until one significant day. It began with an overheard conversation, the mother is praising him to an aunt. The praise is accompanied by an especially warm, loving look. Although physical contact remained absent, Jacques experienced an important revelation: "she loves me, then she loves me." Until that point, by Jacques's own admission, he had not been sure (FM, 93). The revelation was immediately implicated in reciprocity. He realized his mother loved him and, as for himself, "he realized how desperately he loved her" (FM, 92). Jacques is neither a Meursault nor a Clamence. Speaking of his mother and uncle, Jacques is unequivocal. He had never "stopped loving them." Then, in a coda harking back to Francine's complaint, he adds a self-evaluation. Love for his family, he says, specifically "his ability to love them," was all the more significant "when he had failed to love so many who deserved it" (FM, 129).

Eros as Problematic

Success with *storge*, Camus is explicitly admitting, did not mean that all would go well with the love called *eros*. In a note left with the manuscript, Camus acknowledges that, as regards women, he was guilty of excess, *démesure* (FM, 316; PH, 362). In those reflections, his self-evaluation is frank. He articulates the contradiction between what he demanded, that his ideal woman be virginal, "with no past and no men," and his own behavior, which found faithfulness to be impossible (FM, 315). His promiscuous ways, he admits to having four women at the same time, left him with a life that he judges to be "empty"(FM, 296). In this way Cormery is like Clamence. In notes left with *The First Man*, Camus, tantalizingly suggests the need for a response to *The Fall*. The suggestion, unfortunately, is isolated and undeveloped (FM, 293).

It is undeveloped because the narrative ends before the allure and experience of *eros* would displace *storge* as the dominant locus for experiencing love. This is sad because, in the absence of *eros*, Jacques's expressions of love for his mother do not find their place within the wider network of loves. Isolated from this multilayered context, love for his mother becomes sharply focused and exclusive. In school, having to identify his mother's occupation, pangs of embarrassment develop because he has to write "domestic." Nonetheless, the sense of embarrassment is a transient one. His mother was his mother. He harbored no desire "to have a different family or station in life." The connection to her was unbreakable: "his mother as she was remained what he loved most in the world, even if that love was hopeless" (FM, 205).

Love is often opposed to hate, but it could just as well be opposed to indifference. In this regard, it's Cormery versus Meursault. The former simply cannot take up the attitude of a detached spectator. He is talking about his life as it was concretely lived. Others might index the mother as little more than a "domestic." The son's loving attitude has little to do with cold rationality's predilection for indexing, placing an individual into a category. Love allows an awareness closed off to abstract rationality. It responds to the specific cluster that is this particular person. For an abstraction-minded intellect, Camus's mother could be classified as a "domestic." A loving son would recognize how the particular person, Catherine Hélène Sintès Camus, overflowed such a limited categorization. The abstracting mind is fond of categories. It can dismiss Ortegan irony. The loving person, by contrast, is sensitive to individuals. It lives Ortegan irony in practice.

The epistemological subject traffics most comfortably in the realm of categories and classes. Pesky individuating differences that make a difference can be ignored. For an example of someone who traffics in categories, we can turn to a figure from *The Myth of Sisyphus*, Don Juan. Don Juanism treats the differences between women as irrelevant. What counts is the category: "possible sex partner." Since each member of the category shares this trait, and since this is the essential trait, the members of the group are interchangeable. There are no good reasons for isolating a single person as special in ways that make a significant difference. Multiplying partners becomes an honest way of living what it means to be an epistemological subject. As a kind of bonus, it also serves as an avenue of revolt. Don Juan rejects the illusions fostered by society, illusions sedimented in bourgeois life.

Besides the context of abstract categories, there is another, related, path that encourages Don Juanism. For the abstract mind committed to neat, separate, clear, and distinct ideas, the messiness of everyday life represents an annoyance from which one needs to be liberated. But liberation, though a proper goal, needs to be adequately understood. If freedom means "free will," and this in turn means *liberum arbitrium indifferentiae*, then indifference, insensitivity to difference, becomes an emancipatory attitude. It frees an individual from the risk associated with selection. Haystack 1 or haystack 2? It's all the same to the chooser. Intellectually at least. Practically, choosing, say, haystack 2, means saying "no" to haystack 1. When the alternatives are many and attractive, and when differences do not make a difference, opting for one alone entails a difficult renunciation, losing all the others.

In fiction, the painfulness of loss can be minimized by the ingestion of a love potion, as with the medieval story of Tristan and Isolde. The potion eliminates uncertainty and the need to elect among options. It creates infallibility. A potion so exaggerates the "yes" dimension as to render the "no" dimension invisible. Love potions, though, exist only in imaginative fantasy. Are there other ways to lessen anxiety? Don Juanism offers one: forego selection. Risk and fallibility are thereby minimized. So are the responsibilities associated with commitment.

Both versions of Don Juanism, that which deals only with types and that which rejects the yes/no mix, overlap in an important way. Both admit how incompatible is the mix of love and freedom understood in a particular way. In the first case, freedom as indifference precludes committing to a particular person. In the second case, the desire to escape the risk associated with selection precludes committing to a particular person. The relation between *eros* and liberty comes to be understood as an inverse one. When one waxes, the other wanes.

The First Man's exploration of love is best understood within such a context. When the dimension of necessity is more prevalent than that of liberty, love is possible. But this is love as *storge*. The prototypical case would be a family into which, willy-nilly, an individual is born. It can also occur with instructors to whom a student has been assigned. Because its origins are in an implacable given and because its movement follows a pattern that resembles a causal sequence, love as *storge* is real. Things change drastically when we enter an arena where freedom as free will dominates. There, without the rootedness in an inevitable given, love as *eros* can be understood as an illusion fostered by poets.

When it comes to *eros*, *The First Man* does provide some evidence of movement away from the template set in *The Myth of Sisyphus* and *The Stranger*. The work's general tenor is worlds apart from the pervasive indifference manifested by Meursault. With *The First Man* we are drawn into a concrete setting in which differences are significant. Jacques (young Albert) does not take on the role of disengaged spectator. His embeddedness in this particular family makes it hard for him to stand aloof from a harsh grandmother, an illiterate, silent mother, friends who love soccer, a classmate who insults him, a teacher who shows him special regard. Jacques does not deal in abstract types. He reconstructs what it was like to be this particular child in this particular context. He is always a participant in the doings and undergoings that characterize his life. Indifference, for such an active participant, would require a special effort at disconnection. The more natural attitude, the one he manifests, does not treat either his surroundings or the individuals who populate them as spheres of indifference. Quite the contrary. His memoir keeps highlighting differences that made a difference.

The move away from detached spectatorship allows room for admitting other means besides cold rationality for gaining access to the concrete reality in which we are immersed. It does this by removing the plate glass of indifference, the partition that deprives care, concern, discriminating judgment, and preferential attentiveness from their roles in gaining a fuller sense of how things are. The eliminationist wall simplified things. At the same time, it was an artificial construction. Instead of offering a special path to the "really real," it encouraged a distorted understanding of lived experience. Even something so basic as description, Mary Midgley helpfully reminds us, is an act of "selecting what matters" (Midgley 1978, 110).[7] The very act of describing, far from being comfortable within the glass partition model, indicates how evaluation and ascertainment of facts go together. Emphasizing the "glass partition" approach, as the most neutral, eliminative one, is itself a prioritizing move, an evaluative, non-neutral stance. By highlighting the actual experiences of growing up, *The First Man* recreates situations in which differences, not indifference, dominate. In this way, *The First Man* seems poised to undertake a serious rethinking of love.

This, though, does not occur. Part of the problem is the unfinished, unpolished version of the text. Still, working only with the manuscript that is available, a by now-familiar pattern emerges. No longer is indifference the major obstacle to love. Now, the major obstacle is liberty. We are brought back here to the model of debt/gratitude that emerged early in the text. Love, for Camus, arises within a sequence patterned on causality. Necessity and gratitude are its key components. "Necessity" identifies a dimension not freely selected. Jacques, for example, has found himself in a milieu and has been the recipient of a teacher's largesse. The givenness, this is crucial, identifies facts of the matter over which the participant had no control. The sequence is *not* set in motion by a free choice. The sequence, once initiated, follows a typical pattern: (a) the initial givenness, (b) some benefaction, (c) awareness of the benefaction, (d) gratitude, and (e) a feeling of love toward the benefactor.

The sequence may sound odd, but Camus's thinking is consistent. If love is something that goes deep in our being, then it is best rooted in the inexorability of natural processes, not the arbitrariness of human choice. If all loves involved a merely discretionary choice, one could opt either in or out, and such an opting, being arbitrary, would carry no evaluative valence. Jean-Baptiste Clamence could then not be judged as morally wanting. His inability to love would simply result from an understandable restraint: avoiding error by not making a commitment.

If, as Dostoevsky thought, and as Camus thought, the inability to love represents a real deficiency, then the kind of love in question cannot be a simple matter of personal discretion, a choice of the free will. Dependence on a mother does not derive from free will. It simply is the case. It can be ignored or denied, but such moves betray that which is obvious and evident. Similarly, one arrives at school and is assigned this particular teacher. If, in addition, this individual does one a favor, then there is a double inevitability. A loving relationship to mother and teacher is an appropriate response. That response has a basis in the nature of things, in the inexorability of one's situation. This rootedness is real. It is also a rootedness that is absent when love, as *eros*, originates in an act of free will.

What It All Means

Because all we have of *The First Man* ends with adolescence, readers do not get a detailed reflection on *eros*. An interpreter thus faces a quandary. It is one which, because the manuscript was cut short, will never be resolved. As we have seen, in the extant manuscript Camus suggests strongly, even says explicitly, that the conditions for the emergence of love are those of dependence, inevitability, and beneficence. These are mostly located in "nature," in the world characterized by the objective, ineluctable working out of things. Such factors would be identified by logicians as "necessary," though not "sufficient." It's sort of like clouds and rain. Clouds alone may not be *sufficient* for rain, but they are a *necessary*, that is, a requisite condition. With them—maybe rain, maybe not. Without them—definitely no rain. Camus's position is that necessity, dependence, and beneficence are love's "necessary" conditions. Love simply cannot come to realization without them.

Here is where a problem arises as regards *eros*. Outside the world of arranged marriage, *eros* is considered to be most operative in a context dominated by voluntary choice. Thus we face the Camusian quandary. If a dimension of what philosophers label as "facticity" is a necessary condition for love, the possibility of love disappears when facticity is replaced by a setting in which the dominating factor is free choice. There then results an inescapable muddle. Unfreedom is a necessary condition for love. The form of love known as *eros* cannot, however, exist apart from freedom. Thus the muddle: *eros* is widely celebrated, but as a form of love that requires freedom, it is at best an illusory social construct. Camus, it appears, remained, even in the late 1950s, attached to this notion which was first suggested in *The Myth of Sisyphus*. The position identifies an inverse relationship between liberty and *eros*. As one rises the other falls.

Once again we are brought back to what Camus was never fully able to shake off: the Great Bifurcation. Refusing depictions which take account of mixtures, in-betweens, continua, or degrees of difference, its *modus operandi* is to divide whatever can be neatly separated in the mind, even dimensions which, in ordinary circumstances, might seem to belong together. An example: on one side, the objective realm, the natural world dominated by the laws of physics, chemistry, biology; on the other, the subjective realm, inhabited by the radically free being who exercises freedom. Such a neat division, one which remains with Camus in *The First Man*, makes it difficult to situate *eros* anywhere outside the fanciful realm celebrated by troubadours. Storgic love has a certain substantiality because it is anchored in a setting whose original condition has nothing of the voluntary in it. When we switch to a setting in which voluntary choice is predominant, the substantiality of love tends to fade. It becomes a product of culture divorced from nature.

Because the autobiography ends with adolescence, the draft which remains is mostly silent about how Camus would have dealt with this topic. What we do have, and what Camus's editor-daughter has helpfully included, are notes relevant to *The First Man*. One of those notes is particularly significant. It appears to be a sketch for passages to be included in a future work. The contents reveal a consistency in Camus's thinking about love. Specifically, they indicate how, for him, the love/necessity link was not peripheral but central.

The passage begins with a familiar theme: a clear indication that the character in question was capable of love: "He had loved his mother and his child." This is immediately contextualized by a telling commentary: "everything that it was *not up to him to choose*" (italics added). The subsequent sentence only intensifies the point: "And after all he, who had challenged everything, questioned everything, he had *never loved anything except what was inevitable*" (italics added). The passage repeats themes developed in *The First Man*. Love, in its fullest, most actualized manifestation, cannot emerge in a setting dominated by what is voluntary. Necessity, not freedom, provides the most fertile soil within which the plant of love will emerge. The realm of freedom, by contrast, is one characterized by multiple options and unfettered discretion. Such a realm encourages not *eros* but the free multiplication of experiences. It refuses the yes/no complementarity. It discourages the encumbrances that come with enduring commitments.

Camus's language is categorical. The envisioned fictional character had "never loved anything except what was inevitable." Then, helpfully, comes an explanation of what falls into the category of "inevitable." This includes "the people fate had imposed on him," "the world as it appeared to him," whatever had been unavoidable, including "his illness, his vocation, fame or poverty." He subsumes all of this under a metaphor that had been central to the short story *Jonas: The Artist at Work*: "in a word, his star" (FM, 311).

These texts reinforce a Camusian position. Outside of inevitability there can be the simulacrum of love, an artificial, assumed pose, but not the real thing. "For the rest, for everything he had to choose, he had made himself love, which is not the same thing" (FM, 311). Being human, he had felt passion and tenderness. These, though, as felt, were (1) on the order of unchosen, inevitable reactions to stimuli; (2) capricious and transitory. These feelings came and went according to circumstances. Because they were fleeting and changeable, they would be inconsistent with a subsisting, growing, enduring relationship. Such moments of passion and tenderness must be recognized for what they are, real *and* transient.

The moments of passion and tenderness had actively discouraged commitment to one specific individual. They had sent him "to others." Not surprisingly, the upshot of such reflections reinforces the basic paradox: the necessity and incompatibility of combining liberty and love. The character in question admits as much: "he had loved nothing he had chosen except what was little by little imposed on him by circumstances" (FM, 311). In the end, summarizing the inverse relationship between *eros* and *libertas*, he makes a great generalization. "The heart," he insists, "the heart above all is not free" (FM, 311).

How can all of this be subsumed within the central theme for Camus's third cycle: love? Several strands come together. Mostly they fall within the heading of an *apologia pro vita sua*. There is, first of all, the vindication "I am not Clamence." In *The First Man*, Camus, as we have seen, describes himself as someone capable of love. The second dimension is also part of vindication. This one, though, is more hypothetical. *The First Man* does not extend into the years in which Camus would be retelling his polyamorous love life. From the texts we do possess, he seems to be preparing the ground for such narration by insisting on the, by now, familiar theme: love and liberty exist in inverse relation to one another. Love, as a genuine presence, emerges best when necessity predominates. *Eros*, as a result, is nothing more than a cultural game. Outside the game it is an unrealistic impossibility. Third, *The First Man*'s discussion of love only got so far as discussions involving *storge*.

Based on the remaining draft, that's about all a commentator can say. Camus's third cycle, the one focused on love, must remain, for fans of Camus, both truncated and disappointing.

14

Conclusion

Literature Is Not the Handmaiden of Philosophy

Isabelle Huppert is one of France's leading actresses. In an interchange with the philosopher Simon Critchley, she made this pronouncement: "Of course, what theatre is about is aliveness, a certain experience of aliveness. That's all that matters. The rest is just ideas." The philosopher Critchley was initially taken aback. He then came around: "She was right. Theater is not just about ideas" (Critchley, 279).

Critchley's generous attitude is what could be called a post-Modern one, a perspective that no longer follows the Modern (Renaissance to World War I) playbook. For many centuries, philosophy had proudly worn the mantle "queen of the sciences." It assumed an automatically superior position vis-à-vis other disciplines. Why? Its province was ideas. Ideas were primordial. They could be incorporated, embodied, expressed via words or stories. What counted was their primacy. They were like souls inserted into bodies. Stories, like bodies, were, as vehicles, secondary. In such a setting the very expression "storytelling" takes on a derivative, secondary connotation. The storyteller is considered to be engaged in diversion and entertainment. Even when taken more seriously, the task remains derivative: make ideas palatable. The pattern is dyadic: ideas are foundational; stories exist to exemplify the ideas.

Even if, as Camus wished to do, we take inspiration from ancient Greece, there is no need to identify the ancient views with those of Plato, whose *Republic* contrasted philosophers with poets and banished the latter. Plato's own teacher, Socrates, believed that philosophy itself begins not with ideas but with wonder. "This sense of wonder is the mark of the philosopher. Philosophy indeed has no other origin" (Plato, *Theatetus*, 155d). "Wonder" identifies an attitude of astonishment and fascination, often accompanied by some bewilderment. The combination arises because wonder does not occur in a vacuum. The milieu in which humans find themselves is one that is fascinating, astonishing, bewildering. Wonder-based inquisitiveness, that is, philosophical reflection, represents one response to such prompting. If wonder is the originating context, and if wonder is a *response* to one's milieu, then ideas are not primordial. Ideas offer modes of coming to understand the milieu which prompted wonder in the first place. They are like maps which, while helpful, always (remembering Ortegan irony) fall short in some ways.

Readers, having come thus far, realize how my guiding orientation is one which favors Huppert's claim. Expressed straightforwardly, it's the priority of life over ideas.

The reading of Camus I have been defending suggests how the life-and-ideas tension was a defining aspect of his character. His academic training had emphasized the dominance of ideas over life. His youth in Algiers suggested the opposite, the primacy of life over ideas. There was Camus, student of philosophy, and there was Camus, directly savoring life. In his most well-known works, philosophy student Camus tended to dominate. Ideas came first, lived experience second. His earliest essays, that is, pre *Myth of Sisyphus*, had, by contrast, been more celebratory of lived experience. The works by which he is best known, by contrast, emphasize ideas over life. With *Exile and the Kingdom*, this at least is my thesis, there is an attempt to restore primacy to lived experience. Stories and the lived experience they detailed are prioritized over ideas.

In the era of *The Stranger* and *The Myth of Sisyphus*, Camus retained what he had absorbed at school: a ruthlessly dyadic and eliminationist Cartesianism. It overemphasized the dimension of disengaged rationality. While doing so, it marginalized other aspects of human life, dimensions like physiology, affectivity, sociality. Humans, or "man" as Camus would have said, might reluctantly be recognized as physiological, social, and affective, but these were associated with the lower end of the dyadic composite that was the human being. Mind was what defined "man." "Man is a rational animal" became the guiding principle of a whole era. The adjective "rational" was a loaded, because exclusionary, one.

The meaning was no longer the "animal in possession of speech," which was how Aristotle had phrased it (*Nicomachean Ethics*, 1098a, 1–3). The meaning was stronger and oppositional. The more Aristotelian, continuity-with-some-differences model was set aside. That model envisioned a flourishing human life as one resulting from the harmonious culmination of the physiological, the social, the affective, and the intellectual. In place of the Aristotelian harmony-centered approach, there developed an isolationist model. Since man = mind, the more one rose above the physiological/social/affective dimensions, the more one approached the purely "rational" ideal.

Such a man-as-mind could readily identify himself as an outsider or stranger in the world. Reveling in a realm of pure thought also encouraged totalizing pronouncements, viz. *either* there is perfect certainty *or* we don't have rational understanding at all. Camus, in *The Myth of Sisyphus*, stated it straightforwardly: "I want everything explained to me or nothing" (MS, 27). This "cry from the heart," as Camus phrased it, was (because of the Great Bifurcation) bound to be frustrated. As we have seen, this frustration, the gap between what humans seek and what the world provides, serves as the focal point for the diagnosis of absurdity.

But why assume that this particular cry of the heart, emerging within a sharply dyadic context, is normal and natural? Why privilege man-as-mind and its accompanying all-or-nothing expectation? We come back here to Huppert's assertion and the philosopher Critchley's eventual agreement. Lots has changed since Camus was a philosophy student. The Cartesian model, especially its embrace of a Great Bifurcation, no longer dominates. Within that model, it made sense to expect that the lived world should match up perfectly with the purity of ideas. If, by contrast, we accept Huppert's position, life takes priority. Lived experience can be understood as always thick, rich, complicated, superabundant, full of surprises, surprises that will often reveal the shortcomings of whatever philosophical formulations our minds have articulated.

Within the Cartesian framework, literature was relegated to a specific role: handmaiden of philosophy. It gave embodiment to ideas, making them accessible. Huppert reverses this. Literature, closer to life, helps divulge the conditions that occasion wonder and, subsequently, philosophical reflection. Huppert spoke from the perspective of an actor. From a more formal academic perch, the literary critic Lionel Trilling had, in the first half of the twentieth century, defended the primacy of literature in similar terms. The role of literature was that of taking "the fullest and most precise account of variousness, possibility, complexity, and difficulty" (Trilling, xiii). The novelist, Trilling asserts, engages in the process of "searching out reality" (Trilling, 213). Hupperts's "aliveness" and Trilling's "variousness, possibility, complexity and difficulty" identify the concrete plenitude of which philosophical reflection must take account. Reversing things, giving Cartesian priority to ideas, opens a passage for oversimplifications, non-nuanced, totalizing pronouncements. It reinforces the faulty notion that the life world must match the neatness of ideas.

Though Camus considered himself primarily an artist, a literary artist, *The Myth of Sisyphus* and *The Stranger* reveal the degree to which he remained committed to Cartesianism's insistence on the primacy of ideas over life. He even made the point explicit. We saw how in reviewing Sartre's *Nausea*, Camus had insisted that "A novel is never anything but a philosophy put into images" (LCE, 199). Sartre himself, indicating how this was a common assumption, reviewed *The Stranger* by treating it as if it were ancillary to Camus's first philosophical treatise. Meursault, Sartre wrote, was "constructed so as to furnish a concerted illustration of the theories expounded in *The Myth of Sisyphus*" (Sartre 1947/1962, 113) Sartre's depiction made sense since Camus had planned specifically to compose a philosophical work (*The Myth of Sisyphus*), a play (*Caligula*), and a novel (*The Stranger*) as various modes for expressing absurdity. *The Stranger* can thus properly be called a *roman à thèse*, a story meant to provide a narrative illustration for the understanding of absurdity laid out philosophically in *The Myth of Sisyphus*. Literature, thus conceived, is a body into which can be poured ideas conceived in the mind.

Philosophy without the Great Bifurcation

Such a dyadic model had already been challenged at the time Camus was writing. To get a sense of what a paradigm change would look like, it is helpful to start with English and a term at the center of the older paradigm, "mind." Colloquial English offers a good point of departure. It uses the word in several ways. There is, of course, the Cartesian sense of mind as a substantive, as a unit that forms part of the body-mind combination, specifically a container for ideas. English, though, also uses "mind" as a verb. In that case the entire, undivided, person is implicated. We might ask someone "to mind" the store while we go out, ask people whether they "mind" us taking a seat at their table, or admonish children to "mind" their language. In those cases "mind" is not a container. The mind-as-substantive model not only limits the scope of intelligence, it also leads to questions being formulated in certain ways. One of the most prominent asks whether the "external" world matches up with the ideas enclosed in the mind. When the wider usages of mind are taken into account, its connotations become more inclusive, more interactive. The verbal use, for example, highlights attentiveness ("mind the store"), consideration for others ("do you mind if I sit here"), care about propriety ("mind your language"). One huge difference: "mind" the verb does not, as does "mind" the noun, reinforce the Great Bifurcation. Instead, it suggests the primacy of reciprocal interplay and, importantly, the centrality of concern rather than neutral objectivity.

In terms specifically relevant to evaluating Camus, to "mind" involves paying attention to differences. By contrast, "indifference" is the assumed position of the noun "mind." It thinks of itself as a neutral eye impacted by data coming from the other side of a neutrality-inducing partition. The other uses of "mind," as a verb, and even as the gerundive "minding" are, in this regard, theorized out of existence. Such a narrowing of what is involved with mind and minding brought forth an important philosophical offshoot. It culminated in a significant redefinition of humans. They became neutral recipients of indifferent data. They became, in other words, entities defined by "mind," more than persons for whom "minding" as attentiveness to differences that make a difference was central.

What to do when such neutrality is at odds with ingrained human dispositions? Camus's resolution: rebel. Admit the objective accuracy of mind as neutral eyeball but refuse to go along with the implications of meaninglessness. No other options presented themselves. Or, more accurately, no other options except rebellion presented themselves so long as the main lines of Cartesianism remained intact. Still, given his philosophical commitments, Camus did well to embrace what was an inconsistent position. He preserved what needed to be preserved, *both* the substantive and the verbal/gerundive senses of mind. He could not, because of his philosophical inheritance, hold them together in any integral way. Still, a great part of his appeal derives from his awareness that neither dimension was to be jettisoned altogether.

Though willing to embrace a tension, Camus, as we have seen, was explicit about where to draw a line: nihilism. That nothing guides human valuation, that judgments are, in the end, arbitrary, is a position too much at odds with human experience. What he failed to recognize is the straight line that can be drawn between the Great Bifurcation and nihilism. Once mind-as-noun is set off against the world, the latter too easily becomes nothing but a realm of mere neutral data, just an alien setting, little more than raw material ripe for manipulation and control.

Given such a background, yet preserving humanistic inclinations, Camus crafted a resolution: admit the general meaninglessness of the external world, but shape a life in opposition to it. In this way Camus was not unique. The collapse of meaning in the nineteenth century had occasioned analogous reactions in other fields. One of the most prominent came from biological science. It was best formulated by T. H. Huxley, someone so articulate and so avid in defending evolution that he gained the nickname "Darwin's bulldog."

Huxley's predicament was typical. How to confront the crisis in meaning occasioned by the unbridgeable gap between a world, described as meaningless by science, and human life, desperate for meaning and value?[1] What was a sensitive intellectual to do? Hold on to what was precious in human life *and* hold on to what contemporary biology taught. How? Huxley's response, proclaim the existence of two realms. On one side, the "cosmic process" (struggle for existence, survival of the fittest); on the other, the "ethical process." In drawing this division, Huxley was encouraging his version of rebellion. The "ethical process" would have to go its own way, even if it meant rebelling against the dominant trends within the "cosmic process" (Huxley).

Since the time of Camus and Huxley, the groundmaps they took for granted have been tinkered with and revised. Ecological science has emphasized interconnections and interdependencies as primordial. More importantly, it also has come to recognize how, in addition to competition, natural processes are marked by cooperation in light of a well-balanced whole.[2] Within philosophy, the last years of the nineteenth and first decades of the twentieth centuries were marked by serious remappings of the territory, a remapping associated with names like Charles Sanders Peirce, Alfred North Whitehead, and Martin Heidegger.[3] These remappings, while proceeding in divergent ways, overlapped in some respects. (1) They sought to redraw and thus replace the Cartesian map centered on the Great Bifurcation; (2) in so doing, they emphasized how humans were living beings in a living world (especially Peirce and Whitehead; Heidegger retained a strong sense of separation between human and world); (3) they tended to replace bifurcation by continuities and integrations; and (4) they restored selective attentiveness in a caring environment to its proper place. Another philosopher, Ludwig Wittgenstein would make prominent the centrality and pervasiveness of lived experience in a lifeworld, the *lebenswelt*.

The shift in paradigm proposed by such thinkers was one Camus would never make. He continued to chart a course guided by the Great Dyad. As I explained in the Introduction, Ron Srigley expressed the quandary best. Any comprehensive attempt to move beyond modernity's conclusions was frustrated because Camus remained "faithful to its premises" (Srigley, 8). Because Camus never engaged in a paradigm switch, his options were limited. The one he chose, rebellion, both grew out of and served to reinforce the Great Bifurcation: recognize absurdity and engage in a free act of defiance against it.

It pains me, a philosophy professor, to say so, but Camus's main weakness was his philosophical inheritance. If the literary artist had not digested a bellyful of (Modern, dyadic, Great Bifurcation) philosophy, he might have been less predisposed to grandiose claims about the world being "silent." He might have lived out Trilling's role for novelists: helping to bring out, as regards reality, "the fullest and most precise account of variousness, possibility, complexity, and difficulty" (Trilling, xiii).

Achieving such a thick "translation" of lived experience does not require that the world "speak." If we accept, as accurate descriptors "variousness, possibility, complexity, and difficulty," room is opened up for a world alive with semiotic density. When geologists, for example, "investigate" the earth, its components and processes, they do so with a particular hopefulness: that their investigations will bear fruit. To "investigate" is, etymologically, to study "vestiges." For geologists, these *vestigia* are the marks or traces that provide information. *Vestigia* as marks, indices, or other sorts of evidence stand apart from human languages. A mountainside does not utter, in Mandarin, Tamil, English, or Spanish, "glaciers shaped me." It is nonetheless replete with vestiges whose meanings investigators can come to discern. Such discernment, when taken seriously, avoids shortcuts and simplifications. It requires effort: proper procedures must be followed. Hypotheses have to be crafted. These have to be examined and critiqued by peers. As such processes come to culmination, the conjectures can be justified as secure and well-warranted beliefs. They are fallible and revisable but nonetheless warranted. They are, in other words, trustworthy, truthful.

The Great Bifurcation distorts such a semiotic setting. It encourages shortcuts and simplifications. One strategy: impose an either/or grid on inquiries. Proclaim, for example, that communicability can be reduced *either* to human languages *or* nothing. Since the geological, plant and animal components of the world do not speak human languages, the world, once the either/or framework is accepted, can be described as silent. There is also a further incentive for declaring that the world is silent. It is an incentive that Camus seems to have ignored, but that others did not. A "silent" world can then be treated as a realm ripe for exploitation, ripe for the imposition of meanings from without. The resultant picture is congenial to self-centered, indolent types whose main concern is not truth but domination.

Insisting that the world is silent works well for those inclined to shortcuts and simplifications. There is, though, one major problem: the lifeworld, *of* which humans form a part, *in* which, and *by* which they live, is more multilayered and information-dense than this. It's more a milieu of interest and concern than it is a setting partitioned off by a plate glass of indifference.[4] Simple, ordinary, taken-for-granted activities help highlight this point. Take breathing and eating. The quality of air and the fertile possibilities of topsoil are not matters of indifference.

Beyond breathing and eating, there is the presence of children. Locke, Hobbes, Rousseau, the entire "father-of-oneself" crowd, emphasized isolated, adult, autonomous males. By contrast, Aristotle brought children up early in his *Politics* (1252a, 25–31). His general approach was at odds with the one which was later to theorize "isolatoes" into existence. Aristotle began with more everyday observations: humans are social beings by nature. Interdependence is correlative with existence. As a prime example of interdependence he mentions that of males and females if there are to be any children. When philosophers marginalize children, when all the focus goes to a (male) isolato, a particular concern arises in a particular manner. The concern: being-unto-death, that is, the autonomous unit, now living, confronts singly and in isolation his inevitable death. A major question then comes to the fore: how can there be meaning for an individual life that is fated to death? This is not a new issue. It was already central in the religious tradition which offered a ready answer: we don't really die. Camus both continues in the tradition of religion (taking the death of an individual as a problem) and opposes that tradition (denying life beyond this earthly one). The starting point, though, is shared: me and my death, or, the isolato will not live forever.[5]

All of this overlooks, theorizes out of existence, something important: historical process, childbearing, having-been-born, the continued existence of humans after an individual has died. Humans come into existence via birth, at a particular time, in a context which has a history. The newborn is an isolato neither in social terms (there are always others who share time and place with us) nor in historical terms (others came before us, and others will come after us). Perhaps, as an Iroquois saying has it, a crucial question is not one focused on the fact that the individual will die. Rather the crucial issue is one of responsibility regarding the historical stream in which we find ourselves. "Our every deliberation," so goes the saying, "must consider the impact of our decisions on the next seven generations."

Michel de Montaigne once famously uttered that "to philosophize is to prepare for death." He might, given a different perspective, have suggested that "to philosophize is to reflect on how to live so as to leave a fecund legacy for those who will follow." Such a reflection, though, would have required that children be taken seriously, something which European philosophy, at a particular stage, the stage fascinated with the "father-of-oneself" fantasy, tended not to do. As we have seen, children make a brief appearance in Camus's short stories. Similarly, *The First Man* starts with a birth. Otherwise the emphasis is on the "isolato" and specifically on the isolato face to face with death. The alternative understanding, that humans are part of a continuum, that others have come before us, and others will come after, is not taken seriously as a fundamental ingredient as we seek wisdom about our being-in-the-world.

It takes a lot of conceptual eliminationism to arrive at a point where the human condition is best characterized via the lens of a single individual confronting his death. Such a concern, along with the odd seminar-room friendly question about whether there really is an "external" world, became widely accepted modes of discourse once a particular semantic landscape was set in place. The landscape inherited by Camus, one shaped by the Great Bifurcation, had mostly run its course by the time Camus was composing his works. As I mentioned earlier, philosophers, sensing this, began to articulate alternatives. Such paradigm shifts took many forms as the nineteenth century transformed into the twentieth. To give readers a more detailed sense of what the altered landscape would look like, I offer a sketch based on the tradition I know best, that of American Pragmatism. As a representative figure, I will cite William James, who, in one of his offhand comments, accepts Montaigne's challenge by coming up with a response fully in line with Iriquois folk wisdom: "The great use of a life is to spend it on something that will outlast it" (Perry, 237).

The Great Bifurcation begins with, well, a cleavage. It's quite artificial. So are the resulting components. On one side, humans have been redefined. Skipping over physiology, sociality, affectivity, they become minds. Such minds can no longer be living beings in a living world which is their home. They are more like strangers set off against the other side of the rupture, what now becomes an "external" world.

Setting aside this artificial rupture, and all fanciful, eliminationist, purified, initial states, Pragmatism issues from a context, as Socrates explained long ago, of wonder. And wonder, in turn, is occasioned by the concrete, actual, multidimensional context of ordinary life. That life is one in which humans are engaged in various dealings and interactions with things. Praxis, not disengagement, is primordial. Philosophy's aim, within this altered groundmap, is to make "praxis," practices, customs, norms, as flourishing as possible. Progress in the effort of making practices more flourishing requires avoiding any sort of fantastical, Adamic, move. Artificial starting points need to be guarded against. Life practices, habitual patterns of action, whether sharing a table with others, developing an occupation, courtship, or community activities, do not emerge from any tabula rasa initial state. They emerge within historical, cultural, natural settings. And those settings are where a philosophy occasioned by wonder and aiming to make practices more wisdom-informed begins. In other words, begin where humans are, *in medias res*. Don't artificially project a simplified initial state. Recognize that *res*, in Latin, has a wide semantic range, covering not just "thing" but "affair," "circumstance," "condition," "benefit," "interest," even, with *publica*, a "state" or "commonwealth" (Lewis 1879). The *res* of which we are in the midst describes a realm of interactions, one of humans involved in various sorts of dealings within their milieu.[6]

Several passages from William James indicate key ramifications when compared to Camus. To begin with, not only can the world no longer be described as "external," but it can no longer be understood as neutral or indifferent. When we are engaged in dealings, when we seek to come to grips with our surroundings, we (1) pay attention to differences and (2) do so because we are concerned. For James, such a resituating of humans-in-the world sounds the death knell for philosophies that erect a mind/world separating plate glass of indifference. James goes so far as to characterize "mind" as caring, rather than as a neutral, indifferent recorder of inputs. Any philosophy, which transforms its objects "into terms of no emotional pertinency," he warns, "leaves the mind with little to care or act for" (James 1890/1950, 313).

This claim parallels Mary Midgley's remark that straightforward "description" is not so straightforward. It involves an evaluative move: paying attention to what matters. Most settings overflow with givens. Attending to all of them simultaneously is not possible. The "facts" are both *real* and *selected*, that is, attended to because of their relevance. And relevance depends on the kind of dealings in which participants are involved. Salience is both crucial and context-dependent. Such dependence, though, is misrepresented as "subjective" when interaction and context are bracketed.

Recognizing how *dealing* with things is primordial occasions an important change. The substantive "mind" is no longer basal and isolated. A fuller understanding can come to the fore, one that incorporates the verbal and gerundive forms "to mind" and "minding." This conjoint emphasis allows for a more fully human understanding of how intelligence works. No longer are we tempted to isolate "mind" from other important modes of being-in the-world. "Minding" becomes a complex, integrative, activity.

"Rational" then comes to be understood not in terms of logical purity but in terms of the entire, temporally conditioned, cluster. As a corollary, "irrational" changes its meaning. What formerly identified "rational," the operations of a detached, disengaged "mind," now come to identify a paradigmatic case of the "irrational." After all, it was this detachment which "irrationally" cast the very existence of the world into doubt. The more integratively "rational" approach becomes the one which is involved and concerned. The entire loop (context in which issue arises, selection of what counts as facts, concern for results, hypotheses, supporting evidence, consequences for praxis) provides the basal frame of reference, and it is the circuitry as a whole that determines the degree of rationality.

The shift to a paradigm which emphasizes dealings with things bears significantly on the most famous works of Camus. The human/world bifurcation and the temptation to envision humans as outsiders are two sides of a single coin. Together such a setting inhibits the possibilities for making practices more intelligent and thus more flourishing. On this point James is categorical. We can lay it down as a rule, he says, "that a philosophy which utterly denies all fundamental ground for seriousness, for effort, for hope, which says the nature of things is *radically alien to human nature*, can never succeed" (James 1897/1956, 88–9, italics added).

"Succeed" here is a word with multiple meanings. A philosophy can, *pace* James, "succeed" in the sense of becoming popular. A talented writer like Camus, or an influential science writer like T. H. Huxley can fuel its wide appeal. James intends a different sense of "succeed." What he wishes to impress on his readers is the sense of a philosophy succeeding because it is adequate to the fullness of human experience. Understood in this way, a position like that developed in *The Myth of Sisyphus* has little chance of success. Why? It begins by claiming that the "nature of things is radically alien to human nature." A philosophy which begins by theorizing away interconnections while theorizing into existence a plate glass of indifference is one ill-suited for encouraging a wisdom that culminates in enhanced practices. As James phrases it, the "heroic" ages have one thing in common: a sense that this world is our home. "If we survey the field of history and ask what feature all great periods of revival, of expansion of the human mind, display in common, we shall find, I think, simply this: that each and all of them have said to the human being, 'The inmost nature of the reality is congenial to *powers* which you possess'" (James 1897/1956, 59–60).

This last claim, no surprise here, is exactly what Camus denies in *The Myth of Sisyphus*. More importantly, the lingering influence of this "absurdist" starting point will forever remain with Camus. He will always believe that the powers of humans and the nature of reality are inexorably *uncongenial* to each other.

As I have tried to indicate, there are fictional works, some short stories, and *The First Man* which offer movement away from the Great Bifurcation. Camus here leaves behind the mandate to produce *romans à thèse*. Instead, these works are replete with scenarios best suited for an intellectual map built around concrete practices. Those scenarios might involve an engineer building a dam, a couple with hopes for their child, a cooling swim, a game of soccer with friends, a pregnant woman and her husband desperate to find a suitable setting for an imminent birth. Taking such examples as paradigmatic results in an important awareness: the Great Bifurcation is nowhere to be found. No sharp line is drawn between individuals, the projects in which they are involved, and the milieu which incorporates them. Dramatic pronouncements on the order of "I demand perfect clarity but the universe remains silent" are marginalized. A new groundmap seems to be in the making. The abstract "universe" would become *this concrete place*; my "absolute demands" would become *factors needed here and now to bring this situation to a proper culmination*; the "silence of the universe" would be replaced by a *multiplicity of sign systems*, which, on the model of dendrochronology, have lots to communicate.[7]

Such communication, taking place within a context that is not just polyglot, but polysemic, would occasion the need for interpreters and translators. The older mind/world opposition encouraged thinking of mind as a mirror whose ultimate goal was perfect, final, unchangeable reflection of reality. The altered paradigm makes inquirers more like translators. Translations, despite their degree of excellence, always, in some ways, fall short. Some aspects of the original just elude translation. In *The Myth of Sisyphus*, there is no room for "somewhat" or "mostly accurate." Only two categories are allowed, perfect mirroring or, to use an out-of-date but appropriate term, nescience. The territory occupied by translation, a middle, in-between, realm, one of degrees and levels, approximations and asymptotes, simply cannot be accommodated. However, once the groundmap is altered, translators become the norm.

Three (Potentially) Paradigm-Shifting Essays

Camus's extended essay *The Rebel* stands as a lengthy development of how he challenged nihilism. *The Rebel* was published in 1951. During the late 1940s and early 1950s, he had published essays which are rich in the ways they suggest how he came close to adopting a philosophical orientation which would embrace the world as the proper home for humans. Each essay is worth highlighting as we rethink Camus in the twenty-first century.

"The Enigma"

The side of Camus, closer to what Lionel Trilling associated with literary artists, made an appearance in those essays. The three I will highlight, from the 1954 collection *l'été*, are especially significant: "The Enigma," "Helen's exile," and "The Almond trees." In them Camus formulates an understanding both distant from and at odds with the orientation articulated in *The Myth of Sisyphus*. Drawing on his understanding of ancient Greece, and contrasting it with what he believes is the current intellectual state of northern Europe, he charts out a kind of middle way needed to break from the Great Bifurcation.

The title of one essay, "Enigma," highlighting a term Camus borrowed from Aeschylus, sets the tone. It offers a more adequate description of the human condition than does the label "absurd." The "absurd," as we know, occasions a reaction of rebellion. "Enigma" encourages reflection, and reflection of a particular sort, one that implicates life experience. "Enigma," in this sense, is not a mere brain-teasing cognitive riddle. In philosophy, the stock example comes from Socrates. The oracle at Delphi, in an enigmatic pronouncement, declares Socrates to be the wisest of all men. Upon hearing this, Socrates is led to investigate. He knows that, as an utterance of the priestess, it must be true. He also realizes that its meaning is not at all obvious. It takes years of experience and reflection for Socrates to arrive at an understanding: in only one sense is he "wisest." He has an awareness that is missing in the professional and more famous teachers of his age. He is cognizant of his limitations, is aware of what he does not know. This makes him "wiser" than those who loudly proclaim their "wisdom" defined as omnicompetent expertise. The initial enigma-utterance did not occasion cold logic. Instead, it encouraged life activities in order for its formulation to be adequately translated.

The Modern, Cartesian-inspired, era fled from enigmas. It aimed at that which was more congenial to a pure mind seeking absolute certitude. It championed clarity, distinctness, apodicticity. It liked clean edges. It favored transforming living enigmas into mind-resolvable puzzles. It insisted on resolutions that left no loose ends. When the demand for clean edges and certitude was not met, the situation was diagnosed as "absurd." Lived experience, though, is replete with enigmatic situations, situations with fuzzy edges, the need for distinctions and qualifications, and a requirement that experience cooperate with intelligence. Lived experience, in short, may be ill-suited for a pure, rational mind, but it is congenial to *razón vital*.

Seeking reasonable resolutions, inquirers have no need to theorize away the enigmatic dimensions of our situation. A milieu within which inquiries take place, if enigmatic, will manifest both intelligibility and opacity. The opacity aspect, recognized in Ortegan irony, means that one need not expect pure, perfect, no loose ends resolutions. Such an ideal distorts the human condition by placing it outside temporality, outside finitude, and, yes, also outside truth as well-justified belief. It succumbs to a typical Modern temptation: seeking certitude rather than truth.

Camus does not contrast "enigma" to "absurdity." What he does is explain how the exploration of absurdity was but the beginning of an ongoing inquiry. "The Enigma" opens with a plea that commentators not turn a vibrant, searching self (i.e., Camus) into one whose trajectory is finished, fixed, and frozen. Commentators may want his search to be over, but he is someone still seeking. *Celui qui cherche encore, on veut qu'il ait conclu* (N, 142). The goal of the search remains consistent: how to move beyond nihilism (N, 149). This search had led him, early on, to reflect on an idea prominent in his time: absurdism. Such an early reflection does not represent a final resting point. He thought of it, rather, as offering a point of departure, even if lingering elements continued to inform his later work.[8] What the more mature Camus has come to realize is a logical flaw within the very pronouncement of nihilism. The very utterance "everything is meaningless" is an assertion wanting to be taken seriously. In other words, wanting to be treated as meaningful. In addition, and in line with the trajectory encouraged by William James, there is a contradiction between a theoretical position which rejects the validity of value judgments and the way in which people live. "But living and, for example, eating, is in itself a value judgment" (*Mais vivre, et par exemple se nourrir, est en soi un jugement de valeur*) (N, 148).

Once we reach this point we have come a long distance from *The Myth of Sisyphus*'s youthful cry: "I want everything to be explained to me or nothing." That is the demand not of a temporal, finite searcher but of a pure mind demanding absolute certitude. The temporally conditioned, admittedly finite searcher would have to undo the damage wrought by eliminationist theorizing. Specifically, he would embrace, not dismiss, the circumstances in which he found himself. Stated otherwise, he would rehabilitate the ordinary.

Rehabilitating the ordinary would draw attention to how much the quotidian setting of human life is Jamesian, that is, one of association, involvement, doings, undergoings, and undertakings. In such a setting, selective attentiveness, concern-conditioned awareness, is everywhere. Even determining facts relevant to a case requires a selection among all the possibilities. This does not make it subjective or arbitrary. The demand for certitude wanes as the demand for truth waxes.

Camus's eating example helps sort out interactive from subjective. Healthy eating is important for all persons. What constitutes healthy eating, though, is not subjective. Healthful eating requires a sensitivity to the ways in which various plants and animals provide nutrition rather than toxins or empty calories. Once we step aside from the high perch assigned to disembodied minds, once we regain our place as living beings in a living world, our milieu comes to be recognized as meaning-ful. Nihilism is then revealed for what it is: a problem invented by eggheads (certainly not by egg eaters).

Having arrived at this point we can now turn to Aeschylus and the pre-Modern map which he took for granted. It is one that did not make a fetish of clean edges. It allowed plenty of room for middle ways, for in-betweens, for blends and mixtures. Pre-Modern thought might recognize dualities, but it had not formulated them as a Great Bifurcation. Plato is not Descartes. Pre-Modern thought could, along with Aristotle, admit varying degrees of precision for varying types of subject-matters.[9] Human intelligence was not dismissive of degrees, of more and less. It was comfortable with the way human intelligence arrived at its achievements. There was no felt need to exclaim: "Now, everything has been explained." The Aeschylus favored by Camus could welcome a more fluid character of existence. He articulated this via the adjective "enigmatic." At the center of his universe, "we find not fleshless nonsense but an enigma, that is to say, a meaning which is difficult to decipher because it dazzles us" (LCE, 160) "Enigma," Camus is careful to point out, is not the same as saying life is "fleshless nonsense," that is, meaningless. Nor, we could add, is it the same as saying the human condition is absurd.

"Helen's Exile"

Scholars can quibble over whether Camus's ancient Greeks were really a confabulation pieced together by him. What counts is his belief that the path for overcoming nihilism runs through ancient Greece. Nowhere is this stated more explicitly than in "Helen's Exile" (1948). "The Enigma" substituted the realistic notion of "enigmatic" (somewhat obscure, never-perfect-once-and-for-all comprehension) for the utopian ideal of a final resolution. "Helen's Exile" complements this by linking intelligence and "limit." "Limit" counters nihilism by acknowledging dimensions of our context to which we need adapt. A world without meaning, one in which nothing (*nihil*) constrains us, is one empty of limits. For the nihilistic mindset, limitations are considered to be, universally, artifacts of convention and of freedom-limiting oppression. They, following the great either/or mandate, represent lived factors as one-dimensional constraints, not as what emerges from intelligent attentiveness. Because of the inherited, bifurcation-friendly, framework, they cannot be understood as integrally human commitments, that is, results of selections made *in conjunction with* and *on the basis of* experience-based inquiries.

We find here a familiar pattern and a familiar theme. The Great Bifurcation spawns a particular progression: (1) a mind that expects perfect clarity and certitude, (2) a world that disappoints, (3) the proclamation of absurdity because of (1) and (2). Step outside the initial imposition of a Great Bifurcation and things change. Accepting, for example, a more Jamesian primacy of praxis in conjunction with an ecology-friendly appreciation of interconnections would alter the Camusian progression. The alternative would be more sensitive to concreteness and life experience: (1) live persons seeking to come to grips with how things are, (2) surrounding conditions full of (a) signals that help, along with (b) frustrations and impediments that disappoint, (3) appreciation for the tragi-comic status of human beings in the world that is our home.

The two patterns can be differentiated via the Camusian notion of "limit." Limit disappears within the absurdist dispensation. Its contours are recognized, and there needs to be an effort at establishing them, in the Pragmatist one. It disappears within the first because the conditions outside of mind have nothing to offer as guidance. Limits have to be taken into account within the second because, aiming to make practices more flourishing, it is important to understand the possibilities and restrictions operative in the world. Camus's ordinary example of eating, once again, proves helpful. Humans need nutrition. Getting a handle on which plants and animals will best serve nutritional needs becomes a matter of concern. There are many flora and fauna that will serve. There are, however, limits. If one is an Agrippina wanting to murder husband Claudius, poisonous mushrooms will do the trick. For the rest of us what counts is the ability to recognize the (large but not limitless) range of edible fungi. As a corollary (this is what people do not like about "limit"), it is important to attune our activities so that they resonate harmoniously with the boundaries inherent in our situation.

When understood solely within the landscape of the Great Bifurcation, an insistence on limits becomes one-dimensionally a freedom-impeding burden. Limit then identifies nothing but a restriction on *liberum arbitrium indifferentiae*. The denial of such limits then becomes a temptation for someone wishing to maximize autonomy. That is to say, the philosophical position which denies limits does not simply arise for ontological or epistemological reasons. There is also, as Aldous Huxley realized, some self-serving motivation at work. "The philosopher who finds no meaning for this world is not concerned exclusively with the problem of pure metaphysics; he is also concerned to prove that there is no valid reason why he personally should not do as he wants to. . . . For myself . . . the philosophy of meaninglessness was essentially an instrument of liberation, sexual and political" (in Klein, 96). We are brought back here to William James. Concepts have roots in experience, take a particular form, and issue into certain behavioral patterns. Adequacy, sufficiency, rationality are labels that should be applied, not just to the components taken in isolation, but to the entire cluster, including the behavioral patterns to which they give rise.

In Camus's reconstructed orientation, one inspired by the Greeks, freedom would remain important. But it would be recontextualized. First, in line with Greek pluralism, freedom would stand as one of multiple values that, properly blended, would culminate in a well-ordered whole. Second, freedom would no longer be understood as *liberum arbitrium indifferentiae*. Freedom would now mean the ability to select among options, a selection *guided by* an intelligent awareness of one's surroundings. In other words: goodbye to Buridan's ass. Freedom would best be exercised *in conjunction with*, not in the *absence of*, intelligent discernment. For those accustomed to the easy, self-indulgent notion of freedom as *liberum arbitrium indifferentiae*, the Camusian shift could only be understood as an oppressive restriction.

But the revival of "limit," or, more accurately, the reconceptualization and rethinking of limit, was exactly Camus's point. The ancient Greeks, sensitive to physiological reality, knew about *Nemesis*. They insisted on the need, first, to discern, as best as they could, limits, and then adjust comportment to them. The enigmatic character of our situation meant that limits could be misread. Oedipus, unknowingly, murders his father. At the same time, some limits are artificially narrow and need to be reformed. Societally imposed limits can mandate that Capulets are forever banned from marrying Montagues. Greek and Shakespearean tragedies overlap in their exploration of limits from various angles. What results is a triple realization: (1) limits are not always explicit and obvious; (2) limits as embodied in social codes can be flawed and overly restrictive, (3) reform can get carried away and overreact by denying altogether the existence of limits. Without the triple realization, familiar extremes can emerge: (a) boundaries too narrowly drawn; (b) the pretense that there are no boundaries. In either case the enigmatic dimension is ignored. Ortegan irony is overlooked. Both extremes, though, are alluring in several ways. They reinforce self-indulgence. They foster intellectual slothfulness.

The hard work of intelligence, searching, inquiry, investigation can now be shortcircuited. Transgressions are either considered as easily identifiable because of a rigid code or to be denied because there is no code. For Camus, the latter presented the more worrisome contemporary problem. The Europe of his time, he complained, had abandoned limit and moderation. Europe is the "daughter of excess" (*démesure*, literally rejection of measure, limit). What results is a move driven by the motive for achieving "totality." Then comes a theme more fully developed in *The Rebel*. "And, even though we do it in diverse ways, we extol one thing and one alone: a future world in which reason will reign supreme. In our madness, we push back the eternal limits, and at once dark Furies swoop down on us to destroy" (LCE, 149).

Nemesis, even when not taken literally, serves as a counterweight. When transgressions have occurred, balance must be restored. As Camus understands her, *Nemesis* is not primarily a goddess of vengeance. Keeping with his theme of recognizing limits, Camus describes her as "the goddess of moderation, not of vengeance" (LCE, 149).

Somehow, in his third cycle, Camus was going to weave together the themes of *Nemesis* and love. How he was going to pull that off will forever remain a matter of speculation. What we can say is that essays like "The Enigma" and "Helen's Exile" can be read as foreshadowing the analyses of *The Rebel*. He is moving toward a paradigm shift which would situate him in territory quite different from that articulated in *The Myth of Sisyphus*. It would be a territory marked not by a thirst for absolutes in knowing but rather one recognizing the tentative, enigmatic, character of human seeking. It would also be a territory no longer fixated on the single, isolated ideal of freedom as *liberum arbitrium indifferentiae*. The recognition of limits would mean that one task of intelligence would be to take differences seriously, to figure out which differences make a difference, when, and how. The raw willfulness of Buridan's ass would be replaced by intelligent discrimination.

"The Almond Trees"

There is a third dimension, also found in the *Summer* collection, that would help draw a new groundmap. Such a ground plan, this is no surprise to readers who have stayed with me thus far, would leave behind the Great Bifurcation. Instead, it would rehabilitate ordinary life, interdependence, and situated experience. This third component is most explicitly found in "The Almond Trees." Consistent with his repudiation of utopian fantasies, Camus urges a more concrete, limited, ongoing task as the work of humans. "We must mend what has been torn apart" (Literally, "sew together again what has been torn"; *Nous avons à recoudre ce qui est déchiré*) (LCE, 135; N, 112).

This task, repairing the world, was best exemplified in *The Plague*. That novel, though, remains within the framework of the Great Bifurcation. Were he to update the story, Camus would have to make a few changes. The original Dr. Rieux, taking the Great Bifurcation as inevitable, says that he works "against creation." More accurately, because more in line with the complexity of lived experience, the physician works both with and against the lifeworld. Healing the sick means, in part, working against a dimension of creation, that is, against the illness. At the same time, healing serves the aim of restoring another dimension: health. Health is not something invented by medicine in a vacuum. Body temperature, blood pressure, the level of sugar in the blood, these are benchmarks utilized by physicians. In the language of "Helen's Exile" they represent limits not to be transgressed. Not to be transgressed, at least, without a resulting state of illness.

A version of *The Plague* that did not orbit around the Great Bifurcation could also affirm the key place of semiosis. A diagnostician does not take an all-or-nothing attitude, that is, *either* the symptoms are textbook perfect and the diagnosis is, beyond any doubt, absolutely correct *or* it's just an opinion. Instead, learning, training, and experience are put to work in discerning what the symptoms are communicating. Symptoms are *indicia*, and it takes a special kind of skill to grasp what they mean.

Physicians, in their dealings with patients, are in no way nihilists. Nor are they subjectivists. In other words, they work outside the framework of absurdism. The universe, for them, is not silent. It transmits information. That communication, in turn, provides guidance for the work of repairing the world. It's not foolproof. There is lots still to learn. Commitments have to be made in the face of imperfect evidence. At the same time, there are successes. Enigma, limit, repair, and responsibility can form a coherent amalgam. The aim of reformation can be carried out apart from the dream of certitudes that lead to various forms of totalitarianism. When responsibility is taken seriously, it begins with an attempt at discerning ranges and limits. Then, based on the best warranted beliefs, it moves onto the next stage: committing to activities aligning practices intelligently with those beliefs. Taken together the cluster is bathed in an atmosphere of hope. There is a real possibility for repairing the world, for "sewing together what has been torn."

Evaluating Camus

What does the analysis presented in this and earlier chapters mean for an evaluation of Camus? First and foremost, it is a mistake to categorize him as the philosopher of absurdity. This judgment ignores his development as a seeker and turns him into a static figure, the young man who wrote *The Stranger* and *The Myth of Sisyphus*. A more accurate overview, one better warranted by Camus's own words and development, would be to think of him as someone who sought to repudiate nihilism by formulating a philosophy of limit and measure.[10] At the same time, it is important to admit how Camus never got around to articulating, in a comprehensive way, his myth of *Nemesis*, a philosophical orientation that would have reworked the initial conditions that led to nihilism.

He could not provide such a comprehensive reconstruction because he remained committed to the Great Bifurcation. In "The Enigma" he explains how, for him, the absurd provided a starting point, much like Descartes's systematic doubt. The point of departure, though, was meant to be just that. It was not to be confused with his final position. But selecting a point of departure is a fraught process. I once heard the distinguished historian of ideas Etienne Gilson make an important observation. Philosophers, he explained, can choose their starting points. What they cannot choose: where those starting points will lead them. By starting with the diagnosis of absurdity, Camus could never fully do what he wanted so desperately to do: articulate a position no longer contaminated by nihilism. In fixating on the absurdity of existence as his foundation, Camus accepted the Great Bifurcation as the center of a particular intellectual solar system. That solar system contained planets named "absurdity," "nihilism," and "rebellion." Camus struggled toward an alternative cluster with planets labeled "enigma," "limit," and "repair." So long, though, as the Great Bifurcation remained unchallenged, Camus could not really move from one solar system to the other.

In this regard Camus was not alone. The intellectual quandary he faced, how to preserve human values in an indifferent, neutral world, was a major concern by the end of the nineteenth century. I mentioned T. H. Huxley as someone else taking up an issue prominent at his time. Science more and more seemed to be claiming that the world was "merely" a province of atoms and molecules blindly following natural laws. Such a scheme left no room for human values, purposes, or meanings. Yet there was a strong pull in the direction of such values, purposes, meanings. Charles Taylor's detailed historical study *A Secular Age* uses the label "cross-pressured" to indicate the condition in which humans found themselves (Taylor 2007, ch. 16). When Camus wrote *The Myth of Sisyphus*, he was entering the discussion at a rather late stage. The intellectual climate of his time provided a receptive audience. Camus's contribution was to articulate the issue in a way that would resonate more widely than had works like Huxley's "Evolution and Ethics."

As we have seen, Camus wished to move beyond the "absurdist" starting point. He longed for a philosophical solar system whose center would be *Nemesis* (properly understood). Although he never got there, he made important moves along the way.

Philosophically, *Nemesis*, along with limit and measure, emerged in a real, if not explicit, manner when Camus defended human nature in *The Rebel*. The rehabilitation of ordinary life made only a spotty appearance, but it did so most prominently in the short stories. Some of them restore to ordinary life what Trilling identified as the contributions of literature, "the fullest and most precise account of variousness, possibility, complexity, and difficulty." In the language I have been using, this meant restoring what the Great Bifurcation had theorized out of existence: mattering within the quotidian. The very title of the final short story, "The Growing Stone" (or "the stone that pushes," "the stone that prods"), suggests moving beyond the annihilating mandate. A "stone that prods" points toward a context in which the material world and the living world need not be insulated from one another. The protagonist's sensitivity to difference, along with his aim to be a good guest, tended to soften the rigid, clean edges separating races and cultures.

When D'Arrast resituates the growing stone in an ordinary household, he is fomenting a special kind of reformation, one in which sacred and secular interpenetrate. The nihilism which had impacted religion such that the everyday came to be described as fallen could henceforth be set aside.[11] The here and now, that is to say, the ordinary, D'Arrast's move suggests, is not a realm of nothing (*nihil*). The ordinary is rehabilitated. It can once again be understood as rich with possibilities, possibilities that will reach their proper culminations only if, like Rieux and D'Arrast, humans accept the responsibility for repairing the world.

Notes

Chapter 1

1 Tony Judt properly recognized that, for Camus, nihilism was what needed to be acknowledged and addressed: "the *real* problem he [Camus] insisted, is nihilism, and until we have learned to recognize and name that for what it is we shall not find a way out of the impasse" (Judt, 103).
2 Srigley goes on to assert, quite rightly, that Camus's method "guaranteed that even his best critical insights would never be entirely free of modern assumptions and thus would continue to compromise his efforts in a variety of different ways" (Srigley, 8).

Chapter 2

1 One traditional introduction to philosophy text, published in the same year as *The Myth of Sisyphus*, put it this way: "It [philosophy] has normally culminated in the attempt to do intellectually what religion has always done practically and emotionally: to establish human life in some satisfying and meaningful relation to the universe in which man finds himself, and to afford some wisdom in the conduct of human affairs." "But whatever its precise relation to other kinds of knowledge, there is general agreement on the type of problems with which 'wisdom,' and hence philosophy, is centrally concerned. They are those which raise the question of the *meaning* of human life, and the *significance* of the world in which man finds himself" (Randall, 1, 5).
2 Another Nobelist and friend of Camus, Jacques Monod articulated a similar position: "If he accepts this message [of contemporary science] in its full significance, man must at last wake out of his millenary dream and discover his total solitude, his fundamental isolation. He must realize that, like a gypsy, he lives on the boundary of an alien world; a world that is deaf to his music, and as indifferent to his hopes as it is to his sufferings or his crimes" (Monod, 160).
3 A book exploring the friendship between Camus and the Nobel Prize-winning biologist Jacques Monod explains how contemporary circumstances, not just philosophical reflection, helped make central the theme of nihilism: "The terror and cruelty of the Occupation, the slaughter of tens of millions in the war (the second such war in a generation), and the horrors of the Holocaust that were coming to light had made many despair and abandon any hope for the future of humanity. Denial of any meaning or purpose in life—nihilism—was a widespread response" (Carrol, 7).
4 In his earliest work, *The Birth of Tragedy*, Nietzsche blamed Socrates as the originator of what became the scientific spirit and its guiding illusions: perfect knowledge and its application toward creating a perfected human condition. Nietzsche describes the

"profound *illusion* that first saw the light of the world in the person of Socrates" this way: "the unshakable faith that thought, using the thread of causality, can penetrate the deepest abysses of being, and that thought is capable not only of knowing being but even of *correcting* it" (Nietzsche 1872/1967, 95).

5 Nietzsche, a major influence on Camus, had faced the issue in his *The Birth of Tragedy*. Having a clear-sighted understanding of how things are "man now sees everywhere only he horror or absurdity of existence; now he understands what is symbolic in Ophelia's fate; now he understands the wisdom of the sylvan god, Silenus: he is nauseated" (Nietzsche, 1872/1967, 60). Ophelia succumbed to the temptation of suicide. Silenus is famous for having answered the question about what would be best and most desirable for humans with the phrase "not to be born" (Nietzsche 1872/1967, 42).

6 See his essay "*L'énigme*" in ESS. I discuss the essay in this book's conclusion.

7 Midgley supports her position by using the example of sex. "Anyone who today treated the general need for sexual activity of some kind as a shameful weakness would be resisted (rightly), by being told, first, that this is a basic condition of our nature, second, that it is not so much a weakness as an opportunity, a highroad away from the supposed state of sterile independence to the real vigorous activity of a shared world. Exactly the same is true of the need for continuity. The imagined state of isolation and ceaseless change would be possible only to some kind of solitary pure intellect, uncommitted to action in the world it watched—a machine (say) geared to respond on fresh principles to each change in the objects passing before it" (Midgley 1978, 205).

8 For an indication of how reluctant thinkers continue to be as regards "moral facts" or anything that suggests differential data in moral affairs, see Susan Wolf's *Meaning in Life and Why It Matters*. Wolf works hard at defending an objectivist-style position. The commentaries that follow indicate how ingrained is philosophical opposition to such a notion. Iris Murdoch's *Sovereignty of Good* likewise explicitly challenges the ground plan that culminates in emphasizing only "the solitary omnipotent will."

Murdoch goes so far as to explain how the kind of freedom that is a human good is not sheer arbitrariness but rather implicated in an attempt to use intelligence properly: "Freedom is not the sudden jumping of the isolated will in and out of an impersonal logical complex, it is a function of the progressive attempt to see a particular object clearly" (23).

Chapter 3

1 Certainly, the description of Odysseus who saw Sisyphus in the underworld does not suggest someone whose condition is a happy one. "And I saw Sisyphus too, bound to his own torture, grappling his monstrous boulder with both arms working, heaving, hands struggling, legs driving, he kept on thrusting the rock uphill toward the brink, but just as it teetered, set to topple over—time and again the immense weight of the thing would wheel it back and the ruthless boulder would bound and tumble down to the plain again—so once again he would heave, would struggle to thrust it up, sweat drenching his body, dust swirling above his head" (Fagles, 260, bk. 11, ll. 681–689).

2 "Vital reason" plays a prominent role in Ortega's critique of earlier philosophies. This is especially so in his book *El tema de nuestro tiempo* "The Topic of Our Time," a book whose English title *The Modern Theme* is misleading. The "topic" of our time is not to

reinforce Modern (Renaissance to the First World War) notions. It is to critique and overcome them.

3 "Just take for example Ortega y Gasset, whom you were right to mention. He is perhaps the greatest of European writers after Nietzsche, and yet it would be hard to be more Spanish" (RRD, 243).

4 A generation prior to Ortega, William James had also tried to bring philosophy back to its senses (and away from the realm of pure rationality achieving definitive, deductive-logic type certitude.) "Philosophy," James proposed, "lives in words, but truth and fact well up into our lives in ways that exceed verbal formulation" (James, 1902, 456).

5 An analogous case is made from within information science by Leslie Valiant in *Probably Approximately Correct*. Valiant emphasizes "ecorithms." These are distinguished from algorithms because they are self-correcting as a result of interactions with their environment.

6 René Descartes had gone so far as to dismiss the role of parents in bringing someone into being. What they provided was the material envelope in which the real self, the "mind" was enclosed: "All that, at the most, they [parents] contributed to my origin was the giving of certain dispositions (modifications) to the matter in which I have hitherto judged that I or my mind, which is what alone I now consider to be myself, is inclosed" (Descartes, Meditation 3).

7 See Butler and Plutarch in the Bibliography.

Chapter 4

1 Answering critics who described Meursault as marked by a cold neutrality (*équanimité*), Camus replied that indulgence (*bienveillance*) would be a more suitable term (Pingaud, 190). There are some exceptions among interpreters. Benedict O'Donohue, for example, challenges the standard reading and aims to "explode" what he calls the "messianic myth" surrounding Meursault (O'Donohue, 3). Even here, though, the Arab victim fades into the background. O'Donohue's real concern is Camus's "deeply ingrained machistic misogyny" (3). Instead of both murder and misogyny, the former is minimized as the latter is exclusively highlighted. The murder victim makes no real appearance in O'Donohue's essay and the murder takes a backseat to the charge of misogyny. "In conclusion, far from being innocent and exemplary, Meursault is guilty not only of manslaughter but also of systematic machismo and misogyny" (O'Donohue, 16). Whether "manslaughter" is the appropriate term for the killing is debatable.

2 Galileo here anticipates what, following John Locke, will come to be called "primary" and "secondary" qualities. The former are said to have real, objective existence in the world. The latter to be dependent on the live human being. Galileo expresses it this way: "To excite in us tastes, odors, and sounds [i.e. secondary qualities] I believe that nothing is required in external bodies except shapes, numbers, and slow or rapid movements [i.e. primary qualities]." "Having shown that many sensations which are supposed to be qualities residing in external objects have no real existence save in us, and outside ourselves are mere names, I now say that I am inclined to believe heat to be of this character" (Drake, 276, 277).

3 Joseph Laredo's translation for the Penguin Classics version of Camus's novel renders the title as *The Outsider*. British versions generally prefer *Outsider* to *Stranger*. Both translations emphasize the key point, someone who is more alien-like than homedweller.

4 A recent commentator John Foley, defending Meursault's consistency, puts it this way: "He is honest when he feels he can speak in honesty—that is, ultimately, in relation to his own feelings" (Foley, 15). Here, a Rousseau-influenced take on "truth," which we can only speak with certitude about that which is internal to us, manifests itself in Meursault.

5 Mental life becomes a hall of self-reflecting mirrors once the interaction with one's milieu is replaced by the sundering of mind from world. Søren Kierkegaard articulated it directly in *Sickness unto Death*. "A human being is spirit. But what is spirit? Spirit is the self. But what is the self? The self is a relation that relates itself to itself or is the relation's relating itself to itself in the relation" (Kierkegaard, 1849, 43). The main themes emanating from the Great Bifurcation are present here: (1) the de-biologizing of humans, now considered to be "spirits"; (2) the ignoring of biological interdependencies, relationships that undermine the notion of being an autonomous, nondependent self, for example, breathing, eating; (3) the resultant emphasis on internal mirroring; the new scenario in which spirits, "minds" in more strictly philosophical terms, reflect back only on themselves. The statue-cogito is here alive and well. It doesn't need to breathe or eat, only think; and the only thinking that counts is self-reflective.

6 What emerges from these and other comments is how Camus considered his main character to be somewhat of an innocent. Pingaud cites a passage from Camus's notes projecting a novel in which there would be a condemnation, and "this condemnation would befall an innocent" (Pingaud, 104).

7 Later, in a telling scene, Meursault specifically identifies himself as a reporter. After remarking how the journalists in the courtroom are characterized by an attitude of indifference, he notices one in particular. He gets "the odd impression of being watched by myself" (S, 85).

8 "At a time when he should be thinking of his dead mother, he observes and records trivialities" (Feuerlicht, 617).

9 "For two hours the day had stood still; for two hours it had been anchored in a sea of molten lead" (S, 58). "The sea carried up a thick, fiery breath. It seemed to me as if the sky split open from one end to the other to rain down fire" (S, 59).

10 Carl Viggiani, for example, just about loses sight of the fact that, in the beach scene, we have one individual, without much provocation, and with other options, murdering another real person. That the murderer is of European descent and the victim an Arab is admitted but brushed aside in favor of more metaphysical concerns. "Why Meursault kills and why he dies remains a mystery, however, just as for Camus, the universal and eternal murder of men, i.e., the reality of death, is a humiliating and incomprehensible phenomenon. In social terms, for Camus, murder, or death, is the door through which man enters history.... In metaphysical terms the murder is an explosion of revolt against the very forces that bring him to his act, and in particular against the sun. Everything that Camus has said about deicide, the implicit identification of sun and divinity in his works, all the sun symbolism in *L'Etranger* and most of his other works, and the imagery of the murder episode, in which the sun, and not the Arab, is the enemy, suggests this meaning" (Viggiani, 883). John Cruickshank simply takes Meursault's

description at face value. "Meursault really shot the Arab through an instinct for self-defence, an automatic reflex, and because he was momentarily deluded into believing that he was actually being attacked" (Cruickshank, 1956, 248). Carol Petersen has written that "in truth" the Arab "was murdered by the sun and not by Meursault" (Petersen, 48; cited in Foley, 180). An Algerian novelist has tried to redress the balance by publishing in 2014 a novel which tells the story of the victim (Daoud).
11 This reading differs from that of Louis Hudon, who neutralized the murder as a mere set of muscular movements, explaining the extra four shots as sort of an irrational explosion of aggravation. "The muscular contraction which causes the revolver to fire is an involuntary act, most carefully presented as such, an accident. At worst, it is involuntary manslaughter, not murder. The four other shots, those which condemn him, are simply an act of immense exasperation, exercised on what must be presumed at that point, to be an inanimate object" (Hudon, 61).
12 Such deficiency meant everything to the Chinese philosopher Mencius, who could assert bluntly "whoever is devoid of the heart of compassion is not human, whoever is devoid of the heart of shame is not human, whoever is devoid of the heart of courtesy and modesty is not human, and whoever is devoid of the heart of right and wrong is not human" (Lau, 73).
13 This claim is controversial. Some commentators like Edouard Morot-Sir positively embrace the Rousseau-style denunciation of bourgeois society found in *The Stranger*. Morot-Sir celebrates Meursault as the "universal man hiding in each of us." Evoking language reminiscent of Rousseau's statue of Glaucus example, the commentator goes on to indicate what is "universal" in Meursault: "man stripped of his cheap disguises (*oripeaux*) and of his lies" (Morot-Sir, 19).
14 A police officer, having brought Meursault to the trial chamber asks if he has the "jitters." "I said no and that, in a way, I was even more interested in seeing a trial. I'd never had that chance before" (S, 83).

Chapter 5

1 "*Car l'absurde est contradictoire en existence. Il exclut en fait les jugements de valeur et les jugements de valeur sont. Ils sont parce qu'ils sont liés au fait même d'exister. Il faut donc déplacer le raisonnement de l'absurde dans son équivalent en existence qui est la révolte.*"
2 "*L'homme révolté, c'est l'homme jeté hors du sacré et appliqué à revendiquer un ordre humain où toutes les réponses soient humaines.*"
3 One theme will be left out of my analysis: how *The Plague* was meant to be an allegory of the Nazi occupation of France. Roland Barthes pointed out how the story failed in this regard. Some parallels worked: here was the descent of an evil force onto a community and the need to resist. Otherwise there were just too many disanalogies. A disease is an equal opportunity agent, striking randomly. An occupying force comes with secret police, recruits informers, specifically targets resisters, engages in torture. Even though this allegorical dimension no longer carries much weight, the novel, as this chapter will make clear, remains significant.
4 "*La Peste* is about the problem of evil, and contains an explicit rejection of Augustine's free will defence" (McBride, 25). "The feature of the absurd which is particularly

emphasized in *La Peste*, and against which Camus revolts most strongly, is the problem of evil" (Cruickshank, 178).
5 At other places, he stated bluntly that there is no such thing as "total nihilism" (ESS, 865); insisted on his opposition to "romantic nihilism" with its rejection of rules (ESS, 801); reminded a hostile reviewer that *L'Homme Révolté* included a "critique of posthegelian nihilism" (ESS, 759); linked nihilism to conformity and servitude (ESS, 731); and introduced a collection of essays from the early 1950s with the claim "we are beginning to emerge from nihilism" (ESS, 713), a phrase repeated in an essay on artistic creation (ESS, 803).
6 Speaking to Dominicans, Camus prefaced his remarks with this assertion: "In the second place, I want to declare once again that, believing myself in possession of no absolute truth and no absolute message, I will never begin from the principle that Christian truth is illusory, but only from the fact that I have not been able to accept it" (*que je n'ai pu y entrer*) (ESS, 371, my translation).
7 Emmanuel Mounier makes a similar point, in relation to a faulty notion of religion to which he refers as "alienated religion." It worships the "God of philosophers and bankers." It is helpful, in relation to this "idol," to proclaim that "God is dead" (Mounier, 111).
8 The "fullness" of human life, Taylor asserts, "is something that happens between people rather than within each one" (Taylor, 1999, 118, 113).
9 "Before the reality of human shortcomings, philanthropy—the love of the human—can gradually come to be invested with contempt, hatred, aggression" (Taylor, 1999, 32). "The tragic irony is that the higher the sense of potential, the more grievously do real people fall short and the more severe the turnaround that is inspired by the disappointment" (Taylor, 1999, 33).
10 For a more in-depth analysis, see the Bibliography for works by O'brien and Said.
11 Robert Putnam's studies have shown that, in the formal language of social science, "diversity and solidarity are negatively correlated" (Putnam, 2007, 142). Stated more normally, where there is great social diversity, there is "lower confidence in local leaders . . . lower political efficacy, lower frequency of registering to vote . . . less expectation that others will cooperate to solve dilemmas of collective action . . . lower likelihood of giving to charity or volunteering . . . fewer close friends and confidants . . . more time spent watching television and more agreement that 'television is my most important form of entertainment'" (Putnam, 2007, 150).
12 "Nous sommes toujours dans le cercle, avec ceci de plus, toutefois, qu'il nous est possible de répondre affirmativement à la seule question qui nous paraisse de quelque importance: l'homme peut-il, à lui seul et sans le secours de l'éternel, créer ses propres valeurs?"

Chapter 6

1 "Camus the writer, not Meursault the character, Camus the humanist, not the existentialist, was preoccupied with our common humanity, our shared human nature, our essence rather than our existence." "Across his life and career as a thinker and writer Camus never discarded or discounted his focal concern with human happiness and human nature" (Meagher, 24, 48).

Chapter 7

1. Sartre keeps emphasizing "responsibility" but does so while trying to avoid fallibilism. In *Being and Nothingness*, he tells us that he is using the word "responsibility" in an ordinary sense as "consciousness (of) being the incontestable author of an event or object" (Sartre 2001, 529). The emphasis here is all on ownership of the decision and not on the possibility of choosing in error. It's kind of like someone who says "It's up to the individual" and fails to recognize two separable meanings associated with such a phrase. Meaning 1 is the self-ownership meaning: "I am the one, finally, who has to choose, to select, to make the decision." Meaning 2: whatever decision I take is, by definition, fine. It's as if someone were to say "my diet is up to me to determine *and* whatever diet I choose will, by definition, be healthy." This last implication is what Camus cannot abide. He wishes to emphasize how there are standards to which we need attune ourselves.
2. A few lines later, Camus added this passage: "Nietzsche's paradoxical but significant conclusion is that God has been killed by Christianity, in that Christianity has secularized the sacred" (R, 69).
3. Several decades later, the Camus position was reinforced, within a very different tradition, by, once again, Mary Midgley. "We are not, and do not need to be," she reminds us, "disembodied intellects. We are creatures of a definite species on this planet, and this shapes our values" (Midgley 1978, xxii). She criticizes those who believe that the notion of human nature threatens freedom: "I take this position extremely seriously; I believe it to be thoroughly misconceived and very dangerous to human freedom itself. The notion that we 'have a nature,' far from threatening the concept of freedom, is absolutely essential to it. If we were genuinely plastic and indeterminate at birth, there is no reason why society should not stamp us into any shape that might suit it" (Midgley 1978, xviii).

Chapter 8

1. Even if we remain within the human context, Walter Benjamin reminds us, it is a mistake to take the word "language" too narrowly. The telling title of his essay is "On Language as Such and on the Language of Man." It opens this way: "Every expression of human mental life can be understood as a kind of language, and this understanding, in the manner of a true method, everywhere raises new questions. It is possible to talk about a language of music and of sculpture, about a language of justice that has nothing directly to do with those in which German or English legal judgments are couched, about a language of technology that is not the specialized language of technicians. Language in such contexts means the tendency inherent in the subjects concerned—technology, art, justice, or religion—toward the communication of the contents of the mind. To sum up: all communication of the contents of the mind is language, communication in words being only a particular case of human language and of the justice, poetry, or whatever underlying it or founded on it" (Benjamin, 62). Victor Hugo offers support for pan-semiotism in his poem which celebrates living beings in a living world: "*Ce que dit la bouche d'ombre.*"
2. The label "manipulanda" comes from Erazim Kohak. A depersonalized world, one in which the general model is that of technology, that is, where objects are precisely

designed to serve a specific function, is one which will soon be overrun by the idea that whatever is outside of the self is there to be manipulated. "In a nature so conceived, from which the dimensions most crucial to lived experience, those of value and meaning, have been intentionally bracketed out as 'subjective,' there is no more room for a moral subject" (Kohak, 18).

3 For an analogous take, critiquing relativism while using the language of "infallibilism," see the bibliographical entry under Ward.

Chapter 9

1 This is a position echoed by the philosopher Martha Nussbaum. When we read philosophers, she explains, our "natural response is that this is not how it *feels* to be in that situation. It does not feel like solving a puzzle, where all that is needed is to find the right answer" (in Zaretsky, 111–12).

2 The *Stanford Encyclopedia of Philosophy* entry on Heidegger explicitly *disassociates* "birth" from its biological condition: "Here Dasein's beginning (its 'birth') is to be interpreted not as a biological event, but as a moment of enculturation, following which the a priori structure underlying intelligibility (thrown projection plus falling/discourse) applies" (Wheeler, sec. 2.3.4).

3 In his notebooks the year before he died Camus jotted down notes on how all life begins in a watery realm. He begins the reflections by referring to the sea as a divinity (*La Mer, divinité*). He goes on to describe the mineral world ("a land of stone" *un pays de pierre*), one without life ("with neither animal nor plant life" *sans vie animale ni végétale*). Such a realm is one filled with only the noise caused by rain and wind in the midst of an enormous silence (*un pays de pierre empli seulement du bruit de la pluie et du vent au milieu d'un silence énorme*) (C3, 311).

4 Having not made the invitee list for a wedding, *eris* is determined to wreak havoc. She does this by inserting a golden apple which was to be the possession of the most beautiful guest. The three contenders, Hera, Aphrodite, and Athena, all offered bribes to the human, Paris, who had been appointed judge. Aphrodite promised Paris that he could have the lovely Helen. This was the game changer. Paris awarded the apple to Aphrodite. Helen was indeed lovely, but also quite married, a fact that did not bother Paris. He visited the home of Helen and her husband Menelaus. Then, violating all sorts of rules about proper guest-behavior, left with Helen in tow. Menelaus with the help of his brother Agamemnon organized an army, and, in one thousand ships, the Greeks sailed for Troy to reclaim Helen. Thus began a decade-long war, a war rooted in a simple act of dissension by the one whose name means discord, *eris*.

Chapter 10

1 About ⅓ of human energy comes from bacteria, mostly due to the fermentation of carbohydrate materials we cannot break down on our own. (See Yong, *I Contain Multitudes*, in the Bibliography.)

2 The best development of this theme can be found in Serres, 1985.

3 Margaret Visser traces the various forms of fatalism in *Beyond Fate*.

Chapter 11

1. Robert Meagher's analysis of Camus understands this especially well (195–6). "The rituals of hospitality come down to the host assuring the guest that he wishes him to live. He wishes him well. He recognizes their human bond, their essential friendship. It is human sympathy and compassion in its purest, most primal expression" (Meagher, 195–6).
2. For a concise explanation of the exchange, including how it was misreported in *Le Monde*, see Zaretsky, 84–6.

Chapter 12

1. "*Camus parle beaucoup de son roman dans sa correspondance et dans ses Carnets, où on peut en suivre la genèse à partir de 1953. Il envisageait une grande fresque— un peu dans le genre de Guerre et paix de Tolstoï—où son personnage, Jacques Cormery, aurait traversé les événements majeurs de la première moitié du XXe siècle; il n'a eu le temps d'en écrire qu'une petite partie, puisque le protagoniste est encore adolescent quand s'interrompt le manuscrit ; pour le reste, nous en sommes réduits à des conjectures, appuyées sur les notes et les documents d'un abondant dossier préparatoire*" (Spiquel).
2. "'Je commence vraiment mon œuvre avec ce livre,' avait confié, en 1959, un Camus pourtant déjà auréolé du Nobel de littérature" (Dupuis; see also Todd, 744).
3. Plutarch emphasized the more concrete, more complete, dimensions of humanity: "For our soul having in it a natural inclination to love, and being born as well to love, as to feel, to reason, or understand, and to remember" (Plutarch 1898, 292).
4. The classicist Wolgang Kullmann has noted how Aristotle was already combating those who pictured the state as resulting from a social contract (Kullmann, 107). The thinkers who tended toward the illusion of a "first man" were typically those who fostered social contract theory.
5. The rest of the paragraph goes like this: although the two are identical twins, man, as a rule, views the prenatal abyss with more calm than the one he is heading for (at some forty-five hundred heartbeats an hour). I know, however, of a young chronophobiac who experienced something like panic when looking for the first time at homemade movies that had been taken a few weeks before his birth. He saw a world that was practically unchanged—the same house, the same people—and then realized that he did not exist there at all and that nobody mourned his absence. He caught a glimpse of his mother waving from an upstairs window, and that unfamiliar gesture disturbed him, as if it were some mysterious farewell. But what particularly frightened him was the sight of a brand-new baby carriage standing there on the porch, with the smug, encroaching air of a coffin; even that was empty, as if, in the reverse course of events, his very bones had disintegrated."
6. Nietzsche explicitly criticized such "cause of oneself" thinking, calling it a "self-contradiction" that holds sway "in the minds of the half-educated." "The CAUSA SUI is the best self-contradiction that has yet been conceived, it is a sort of logical violation and unnaturalness; but the extravagant pride of man has managed to entangle itself profoundly and frightfully with this very folly. The desire for 'freedom of will' in the superlative, metaphysical sense, such as still holds sway, unfortunately, in the minds

of the half-educated, the desire to bear the entire and ultimate responsibility for one's actions oneself, and to absolve God, the world, ancestors, chance, and society therefrom, involves nothing less than to be precisely this CAUSA SUI, and, with more than Munchausen daring, to pull oneself up into existence by the hair, out of the slough of nothingness" (Nietzsche 1901/2016, ch. 1, par. 21).

Chapter 13

1. The conversation was reportedly with Michel Gallimard. "*Après beaucoup d'insistance, Camus lui confie, qu'il travaille sur un roman, « un troisième cycle en quelque sorte, après l'absurde et la révolte, ce serait sur l'amour. » Francine, qui assistait à la conversation, rétorqua: « Tu vas parler d'amour toi !... mais tu n'as jamais été capable d'aimer"* (Tebbani, 256).
2. "'Fathers and teachers,' I ponder, 'What is hell?' 'I maintain that it is the suffering of no longer being able to love.'"
3. "*Les Possédés sont une des quatre ou cinq œuvres que je mets au-dessus de toutes les autres.*"
4. One of his most devoted interpreters, Roger Quilliot, complained about critics wanting "a man who is still searching to have reached his conclusions" (ESS, 861, my translation).
5. Chapter 3's title reads "Saint-Brieuc and Malan (J.G.)."
6. "The image we must start with is that of a mother nursing a baby; a bitch or a cat with a basketful of puppies or kittens; all in a squeaking, nuzzling heap together; purrings, lickings, baby-talk, milk, warmth, the smell of young life."
7. Midgley uses a helpful example (5–6): "*What counts as a fact depends on the concepts you use, on the questions you ask.* If someone buys stamps, what is going on can be described as 'buying stamps,' or as the pushing of a coin across a board and the receiving of paper in return—or as a set of muscular contractions—or one of stimulus-response reactions—or a social interaction involving role-playing—or a piece of dynamics, the mere movement of physical masses—or an economic exchange—or a piece of prudence, typical of the buyer. None of these is *the* description. There is no neutral terminology. So there are no wholly neutral facts. All describing is classifying according to some conceptual scheme or other. We need concepts to pick out what matters for our present purpose from the jumble of experience. There is no single set of 'scientific' concepts which can be used for every job. Different inquiries make different selections from the world. So they need different concepts" (Midgley 1978, 5–6).

Chapter 14

1. A contemporary physicist, Brian Greene, continues to work within the tradition of dyadic cleavage, one that automatically discounts intermediate positions, one that traffics only within a sharp either/or. "As we hurtle toward a cold and barren cosmos, we must accept that there is no grand design. . . . There is no final answer hovering in the depths of space awaiting discovery. Instead, certain special collections of particles

can think and feel and reflect, and within these subjective worlds, they can create purpose" (Greene, 325).
2. For details about how this shift in mapping applies to forests, see Wohlleben.
3. Peirce's "Some Consequences of Four Incapacities" appeared in 1868. Whitehead's *Science and the Modern World* was published in 1925. Two years later came Heidegger's *Sein und Zeit*.
4. The physicist John Archibald Wheeler has indicated how the plate-glass separator has no place in contemporary physics. "We used to think that the world exists out there, independent of us, we the observer safely hidden behind a one-foot thick slab of plate glass, not getting involved, only observing. However, we've concluded in the meantime that that isn't the way the world works. We have to smash the glass, reach in" (Wheeler, 19).
5. Heidegger's version is typically arcane: "The 'end' of Being-in-the-World is death. This end ... limits and determines in every case whatever totality is possible for Dasein" (Heidegger 1927/1962, 276–7).
6. Iris Murdoch has pointed out that even a unitary descriptor like "red," in order to have meaning, has to be uttered within a network of shared social practices. "'Red' cannot be the name of something private. The structure of the concept is its public structure, which is established by coinciding procedures in public situations." She indicates how this builds on Wittgenstein: "He limits himself to observing that a mental concept verb used in the first person is not a report about something private, since in the absence of any checking procedure it makes no sense to speak of oneself being either right or mistaken. Wittgenstein is not claiming that inner data are 'incommunicable,' nor that anything special about human personality follows from their 'absence,' he is merely saying that no sense can be attached to the idea of an 'inner object.' There are no 'private ostensive definitions'" (Murdoch 1970, 11, 12).
7. Besides the fairly familiar dendrochronology, there is the practice of osteology, the study of bone remnants. Here is an example from someone examining the secular/sacred distinction with regard to meat eating in ancient Greek religion: "In this paper, I will concentrate on what the bone evidence can contribute to our understanding of this issue. The osteological material, for long neglected within the study of Greek religion, can provide information different from that of the texts, inscriptions and images, which will make it possible to diversify various assumptions surrounding the status of meat" (Ekroth, 255).
8. "*A quoi bon dire encore que, dans l'expérience qui m'intéressait et sur laquelle il m'est arrivé d'écrire, l'absurde ne peut être considéré que comme une position de départ, même si son souvenir et son émotion accompagnent les démarches ultérieures*" (N, 147).
9. "Our discussion will be adequate if it has as much clearness as the subject-matter admits of, for precision is not to be sought for alike in all discussions, any more than in all products of the crafts" (*Nicomachean Ethics*, 1094b, 11–14).
10. Roger Grenier has the best single-sentence summary of Camus's trajectory: "A youthful Nietzschean, projecting for his work 'power, love and death, under the aegis of conquest' goes through the absurd and revolt, to end up with a philosophy of measure, the old nemesis of the Greeks." ("*Un jeune homme nietzschéen qui projette pour son œuvre 'force, amour et mort sous le signe de la conquête' traverse l'absurde et la révolte et aboutit à une philosophie de la mesure, la vieille némésis des Grecs*") (Fauconnier, 114).

11 Historically, this nihilism was given a great boost (and a crucial foothold in Western thought) by the movement, dominant in the first centuries of the Common Era, known as "Gnosticism." Central to Gnosticism was a drive to escape from the here and now. The *Internet Encyclopedia of Philosophy* describes its central thrust this way: "Chief among these elements is a certain manner of "anti-cosmic world rejection" that has often been mistaken for mere *dualism*" (Moore).

Bibliography

1. Works by Camus

C1. *Carnets, janvier 1942–mars 1951*. Paris: Gallimard, 1964.
C3. *Carnets III, Mars 1951- décembre 1959*. Paris: Gallimard, 1989.
Ch. *La Chute*. Paris: Gallimard, 1956a.
EE. *L´envers et l´endroit*. Paris: Gallimard, 1937; 1958.
EK. *Exile and the Kingdom*. Trans. Carol Cosman. New York: Vintage, 2007.
ER. *L'Exil et le Royaume*. Paris: Gallimard, 1957.
ESS. *Essais*. Bibliothèque de la Pléiade. Paris: Gallimard, 1965.
ETR. *L´Étranger*. Paris: Gallimard Folio, 1942b.
F. *The Fall*. Trans. Justin O'Brien. New York: Vintage Books, 1956.
FM. *The First Man*. Trans. David Hapgood. New York: Alfred A. Knopf, 1995.
HR. *L´Homme Révolté*. Paris: Gallimard, 1951.
LaP. *La Peste*. Paris: Gallimard Folio, 1947; 2008.
LCE. *Lyrical and Critical Essays*. Trans. Ellen Conroy Kennedy, Ed. Philip Thody. New York: Vintage Books, 1970.
LRB. Lettre d'Albert Camus à Roland Barthes sur "La Peste". 1955, janvier. https://etlettera.wordpress.com/2015/01/15/1s-es-l-lettre-dalbert-camus-a-roland-barthes-sur-la-peste-janvier-1955/.
MS. *The Myth of Sisyphus and Other Essays*. Trans. Justin O'Brien. New York: Vintage Books, 1991.
N. *Noces suivi de L'été*. Paris: Gallimard, 1959.
OC. *Oeuvres Complètes, vol. III*. Ed. Jacqueline Lévi-Valensi. Bibliothèque de La Pléiade. Paris: Gallimard, 2008.
PH. *Le Premier Homme*. Paris: Gallimard, 1994.
Pl. *The Plague*. Trans. Stuart Gilbert. New York: Vintage International, 1948; 1991.
PS. Preface to *The Stranger*. 1955. http://olenglish.pbworks.com/f/Preface+to+The+Stranger.htm.
RRD. *Resistance, Rebellion, and Death*. Trans. Justin O´Brien. New York: Vintage Books, 1995.
S. *The Stranger*. Trans. Matthew Ward. New York: Vintage, 1942a; 1989.
TR. *The Rebel*. Trans. Anthony Bower. New York: Vintage, 1991.
TRN. *Théâtre, Récits, Nouvelles*. Bibliothèque de la Pléiade. Paris: Gallimard, 1962.

2. Works by Others

Arendt, Hannah. *Eichmann in Jerusalem: A Study in the Banality of Evil*. New York: Penguin Book, 2006. (Original work published 1963).

Aristotle. *The Basic Works of Aristotle*, ed. Richard McKeon. New York: Random House, 1941.
Aronson, Ronald. "Camus vs Sartre." *Times Literary Supplement*, September 7, 2002. https://www.the-tls.co.uk/articles/private/camus-vs-sartre/.
Aurelius, Marcus. *Meditations*. Trans. Gregory Hays. New York: Modern Library, 2002.
Baldi, Maria Rosa. "'L'exil et le Royaume' d'Albert Camus: Une Lecture de la Nouvelle 'les Muets.'" *Francofonia* 24 (1993): 91–107.
Barthes, Roland. "La Peste, annales d'une épidémie ou roman de la solitude?"*Bulletin du Club du Meilleur Livre* (February 1955): 4–8.
Bateson, William. *Mind and Nature: A Necessary Unity*. New York: Bantam Books, 1979.
Bede. *Ecclesiastical History of the English People*. Trans. Leo Sherley-Price. London: Penguin Books, 1990. (Original work published 731).
Benatar, David. *Better Never to Have Been: The Harm of Coming Into Existence*. New York: Oxford University Press, 2006.
Benjamin, Walter. *Selected Writings, Volume 1: 1913–26*. Cambridge, MA: Harvard University Press, 1996.
Bloom, Allan, Trans. *Plato's Republic*. 2nd ed. New York: Basic Books, 1968.
Bordo, Susan. "The Cartesian Masculinization of Thought." *Signs* 11, no. 3 (Spring 1986): 439–56.
"Breast Crawl: A Scientific Overview." http://breastcrawl.org/science.shtml.
Brée, Germaine, ed. *Camus: A Collection of Critical Essays*. Englewood Cliffs, NJ: Prentice-Hall, 1962.
Butler, Shane. "Cicero's Grief." *Arion: A Journal of the Humanities and the Classics* 26, no. 1 (2018): 1–16.
Callcut, Daniel. "What are We? On Paul Gauguin, Authenticity and the Midlife Crisis: How the Philosopher Bernard Williams Dramatized Moral Luck." *Aeon*, 2018. Accessed October 14, 2021. https://aeon.co/essays/living-the-life-authentic-bernard-williams-on-paul-gauguin/.
Carrol, Sean. *Brave Genius: A Scientist, a Philosopher, and Their Daring Adventures from the French Resistance to the Nobel Prize*. New York: Crown, 2013.
Cézanne, Paul. "Paul Cézanne Biography." Accessed May 24, 2020. https://www.biography.com/artist/paul-cezanne.
Cicero, Marcus Tullius. *Cicero's Tusculan Disputations, Full Text*. Accessed February 16, 2022. https://archive.org/stream/cicerostusculand00ciceiala/cicerostusculand00ciceiala_djvu.txt.
Condillac, Étienne Bonnot, Abbé de. *Condillac's Treatise on the Sensations*. Trans. Geraldine Carr. Los Angeles: University of Southern California School of Philosophy, 1930. (Original work published 1754).
Cottingham, John. *On the Meaning of Life*. New York: Routledge, 2003.
Cottingham, John. *Why Believe?* London: Continuum, 2009.
Critchley, Simon. *Tragedy, The Greeks and Us*. New York: Pantheon, 2019.
Crossman, Richard, ed. *The God That Failed*. New York: Columbia University Press, 2001. (Original work published 1949).
Cruickshank, John. *Albert Camus and the Literature of Revolt*. New York: Praeger. 1978.
Cruickshank, John. "Camus's Technique in L'Etranger." *French Studies* 10, issue 3 (1956): 241–53.
Daoud, Kamel. *The Meursault Investigation: A Novel*. Trans. John Cullen. New York: Other Press, 2014.
Davidson, Sara. "Rolling into the Eighties." *Esquire*, February 1, 1980: 15–24.

Descartes, Rene. *Discourse on Method*. 2016. http://www.gutenberg.org/files/59/59-h/59-h.htm. (Original work published in 1637).
Descartes, Rene. *Meditations*, Meditation 2. 2001. http://www.classicallibrary.org/descartes/meditations/5.htm (Original work published in 1641).
Descartes, Rene. *Meditations*, Meditation 3. 2001. http://www.classicallibrary.org/descartes/meditations/6.htm. (Original work published in 1641).
Dewey, John. *Human Nature and Conduct*. 2012. https://www.gutenberg.org/files/41386/41386-h/41386-h.htm (Original work published in 1922).
Dewey, John. *The Quest for Certainty. In The Later Works vol. 4*. Carbondale: Southern Illinois University Press, 1984. (Original published in 1929).
Dewey, John. *Art As Experience. Vol. 10 in The Later Works: 1925–53*. Carbondale: Southern Illinois University Press, 1987. (Original work published in 1934).
Dostoevsky, Fyodor. *The Brothers Karamazov*. Trans. Constance Garnett and Ralph Matlaw. New York: W.W Norton & Co, 1976. (Original work published in 1880).
Doyle, Rob. "The Fall (1956) by Albert Camus, Translated by Robin Buss." *The Irish Times*, December 21, 2019. https://www.irishtimes.com/culture/books/the-fall-1956-by-albert-camus-translated-by-robin-buss-1.4108581.
Drake, Stillman, ed. *Discoveries and Opinions of Galileo*. Garden City: Doubleday, 1957.
Dupuis, Jérôme. "Retour sur le dernier jour d´Albert Camus." *L´Express*, November 2, 2010. https://www.lexpress.fr/culture/livre/retour-sur-le-dernier-jour-d-albert-camus_848459.html.
Ekroth, Gunnel. "Meat in Ancient Greece: Sacrificial or Secular?" *Food and History* 5, no. 1 (2007): 249–72.
Enthoven, Raphaël. "La noblesse d'un but n'excuse jamais l'infamie des moyens." *Europe Matin*, December 13, 2017. https://www.europe1.fr/emissions/le-fin-mot-de-linfo/la-noblesse-dun-but-nexcuse-jamais-linfamie-des-moyens-3519578?fbclid=IwAR3h92umzENUfBh17VSN_P_q7CQsyOkTN9MggNRB5S_P-W5PBJumksnqIgs.
Epictetus. *Discourses of Epictetus*. Trans. George Long. New York: D. Appleton and Company, 1904.
Epicurus. "Letter to Menoeceus." Accessed October 27, 2021. http://classics.mit.edu/Epicurus/menoec.html.
Erickson, John. "Albert Camus and North Africa: A Discourse on Exteriority." In Knapp, 73–88.
Fagles, Robert. Trans. *The Odyssey*. New York: Penguin Books, 1996.
Fauconnier, Bernard, ed. *Albert Camus*. Paris: Magazine Littéraire: Nouveaux Regards, 2013.
Felder, Deborah G. *A Bookshelf of Our Own: Must-reads for Women*. New York: Citadel, 2006.
Festa-McCormick, Diana. "Existential Exile and a Glimpse of the Kingdom." In *Critical Essays on Albert Camus*, edited by Bettina Knapp, 107–15. Boston: G.K. Hall & Co, 1988.
Feuerlicht, Ignace. "Camus's *L'Etranger* Reconsidered." *PMLA* 78, no. 5 (1963): 606–21.
Fiches de lecture: Albert Camus. Accessed February 16, 2020. https://www.fichesdelecture.com/auteurs/albert-camus.
Fielding, Henry. *Tom Jones*. New York: W.W. Norton & Co, 1973. Original work published in 1750).
Finkielkraut, Alain. "Entretient Avec Olivier Todd et Alain Finkielkraut." In Fauconnier.
Foley, John. *Albert Camus: From the Absurd to Revolt*. New York: Routledge, 2014.
Frankl, Viktor. *Man's Search for Meaning*. Trans. Ilse Lasch. Boston: Beacon Press, 1992. (Original work published in 1945).

Freud, Sigmund. *Civilization and Its Discontents*. New York: W.W. Norton & Co, 2010. (Original work published in 1930).
Goethe, Johann Wolfgang von. *Faust, Part I; scenes 1 to 3*. Trans. A. S. Kline. 2013. https://www.poetryintranslation.com/PITBR/German/FaustIScenesItoIII.php (Original work published in 1790).
Gratton, Peter. "Course Materials: 'Care (*Sorge*).'" Accessed March 12, 2020. https://grattoncourses.files.wordpress.com/2014/08/care-sorge.pdf.
Greek Mythology. Accessed April 10, 2020. https://www.greekmythology.com/Myths/Mortals/Sisyphus/sisyphus.html.
Greene, Brian. *Until the End of Time: Mind, Matter, and Our Search for Meaning in an Evolving Universe*. New York: Knopf, 2020.
Guignon, Charles. *On Being Authentic*. London: Routledge, 2004.
Habermas, Jürgen. "Notes on a Post-Secular Society." *Signandsight*, June 18, 2008. http://www.signandsight.com/features/1714.html.
Haidt, Jonathan. *The Righteous Mind: Why Good People are Divided by Politics and Religion*. New York: Pantheon Books, 2012.
Hair, Marilyn and John Sharpe. "Fast Facts About the Human Microbiome." *The Center for Egogenetics and Environmental Health at the University of Washington*. Accessed February 24, 2022. https://depts.washington.edu/ceeh/downloads/FF_Microbiome.pdf.
Hardin, Garrett. *Exploring New Ethics for Survival: The Voyage of the Spaceship Beagle*. New York: Penguin, 1973.
Harlow, Harry. "The Nature of Love." *American Psychologist* 13, no. 12 (1958): 673–85.
Hawes, Elizabeth. *Camus, A Romance*. New York: Grove Press, 2009.
Heidegger, Martin. *Being and Time*. Trans. John Macquarrie and Edward Robinson. London: Blackwell, 1962. (Original work published 1927).
Hobbes, Thomas. *The Leviathan*. 2013. https://www.gutenberg.org/files/3207/3207-h/3207-h.htm#link2HCH0014 (Original work published in 1651).
Hobbes, Thomas. *Man and Citizen (De Homine and De Cive)*. Ed. Bernard Gert. Indianapolis: Hackett Publishing, 1991. (Original work published 1658).
Hogg, James. *The Private Memoirs and Confessions of a Justified Sinner*. Oxford: Oxford University Press, 2010. (Original work published in 1824).
Horowitz, Louise. "Of Women and Arabs: Sexual and Racial Polarization in Camus." *Modern Language Studies* 17, no. 3 (1987): 54–61.
Hume, David. *A Treatise of Human Nature*. Ed. L. A. SelbyBigge. Oxford: Clarendon Press, 1896. (Original work published 1739). Online: https://people.rit.edu/wlrgsh/HumeTreatise.pdf.
Hudon, Louis. "The Stranger and The Critics." *Yale French Studies* 25 (1960): 59–64.
Huxley, Thomas Henry. *Evolution and Ethics and Other Essays*. 1894. http://www.gutenberg.org/files/2940/2940-h/2940-h.htm.
Isaacson, Bertsy. "Silicon Valley is Trying to Make Humans Immortal--and Finding Some Success." *Newsweek*, March 5, 2015. https://www.newsweek.com/2015/03/13/silicon-valley-trying-make-humans-immortal-and-finding-some-success-311402.html.
Jacobs, Alan. "The Liberal Neoplatonist?: A Review of *Existentialists and Mystics: Writings on Philosophy and Literature* by Iris Murdoch." *First Things*, January 1999. https://www.firstthings.com/article/1999/01/006-the-liberal-neoplatonist.
James, William. *The Principles of Psychology, Volumes 1 and 2*. New York: Dover Publications, 1950. (Original work published, 1890).
James, William. *The Will to Believe and Other Essays in Popular Philosophy*. New York: Dover Publications, 1956. (Original work published, 1897).

James, William. *Varieties of Religious Experience: A Study in Human Nature*. New York: Longmans, Green and Co, 1902.
Jörgens, Viktor and Monika Grüsser. "Happy Birthday, Claude Bernard." *Diabetes* 62, no. 7 (July 2013): 2181–2. https://www.ncbi.nlm.nih.gov/pmc/articles/PMC3712027/.
Judt, Tony. *The Burden of Responsibility: Blum, Camus, Aron, and the French Twentieth Century*. Chicago: University of Chicago Press, 1998.
Jurt, Joseph. "Le mythe d'Adam: *Le Premier Homme* d'Albert Camus." In *Mythe des origines: actes du colloque tenu les 8 et 9 mars, 2001, Université Michel de Montaigne-Bordeaux III*, edited by Gérard Peylet, 307–16. Bordeaux: Presses Universitaires de Bordeaux, 2002. https://freidok.uni-freiburg.de/dnb/download/491.
Kierkegaard, Søren. *Philosophical Fragments*. Trans. David Swenson, rev. Howard Hong. Princeton: Princeton University Press, 1936. (Original work published 1844.) http://www.religion-online.org/book/philosophical-fragments/.
Kierkegaard, Søren. *The Sickness unto Death: A Christian Psychological Exposition of Edification & Awakening by Anti-Climacus*. Trans. Alasdair Hannay. New York: Penguin. 1989. (Original work published 1849).
Klein, Daniel. *Every Time I Find the Meaning of Life, They Change It*. New York: Penguin Books, 2015.
Kohak, Errazim. *The Embers and the Stars: A Philosophical Inquiry into the Moral Sense of Nature*. Chicago: University of Chicago Press, 1984.
Konnikova, Maria. "The Power of Touch." *The New Yorker*, March 25, 2015. https://www.newyorker.com/science/maria-konnikova/power-touch.
Koyré, Alexander. *From the Closed World to the Infinite Universe*. Baltimore: Johns Hopkins University Press, 1957.
Kullmann, Wolfgang. "Man as a Political Animal in Aristotle." In *A Companion to Aristotle's "Politics,"* edited by David Keyt and Fred Miller, 94–117. Oxford, Blackwell, 1991.
Langbein, Hermann. *People in Auschwitz*. Trans. Harry Zohn. Chapel Hill: University of North Carolina Press, 2004. (Original published in 1995).
Latour, Bruno. *We Have Never Been Modern*. Trans. Catherine Porter. Cambridge, MA: Harvard University Press, 1993.
Lau, D. C., Trans. *Mencius: A Bi-Lingual Edition*. Hong Kong: The Chinese University Press, 2003.
Lévy-Valensi, ed. *Camus at Combat: Writing 1944–7*. Trans. Arthur Goldhammer. Princeton: Princeton University Press, 2006.
Lewis, C. S. *The Four Loves*. New York: Harcourt Brace, 1960.
Lewis, Charlton and Charles Short. *A Latin Dictionary*. 1879. http://www.perseus.tufts.edu/hopper/text?doc=Perseus:text:1999.04.0059:entry=res.
Lightman, Alan. *Searching for Stars on an Island in Maine*. London: Corsair, 2018.
Lovejoy, A. O. *The Revolt Against Dualism*. La Salle Illinois: Open Court, 1960. (Original work published 1930).
Luther, Martin. "Preface of the Letter of St. Paul to the Romans." Trans. Br. Andrew Thornton OSB. 1983. https://www.ccel.org/l/luther/romans/pref_romans.html. (Original work published 1545).
Macquarrie, John. *In Search of Humanity: A Theological and Philosophical Approach*. New York: Crossroad, 1983.
Marcel, Gabriel. *Homo Viator: Introduction to a Metaphysic of Hope*. Trans. Emma Craufurd and Paul Seaton. New York: Harper & Bros, 1962.

McBride, Joseph. *Albert Camus: Philosopher and Littérateur*. New York: St. Martin's Press, 1992.

McQueen, Paddy. "Social and Political Recognition." *Internet Encyclopedia of Philosophy*. Accessed May 14, 2022. https://www.iep.utm.edu/recog_sp/.

Meagher, Robert Emmett. *Albert Camus and the Human Crisis*. New York: Pegasus Books, 2021.

Meeks, Wayne, Jouette Bassler, Werner Lemke, Susan Niditch and Eileen Schuller, eds. *The HarperCollins Study Bible*. New York: HarperCollins, 1993.

Melville, Herman. *Moby Dick, or, The Whale*. Boston: Houghton Mifflin, 1956. (Original work published 1851).

Melville, Herman. *The Shorter Novels of Herman Melville*. New York: Fawcett Books, 1967.

Merton, Thomas. *The Literary Essays of Thomas Merton*. Ed. Patrick Hart. New York: New Directions, 1981.

Methuselah Foundation. Accessed March 5, 2021. https://www.mfoundation.org/.

Midgley, Mary. *Beast and Man: The Roots of Human Nature*. New York: New American Library, 1978.

Midgley, Mary. *Wisdom, Information, And Wonder: What is Knowledge For?* London: Routledge, 1989.

Midgley, Mary. *Can't We Make Moral Judgments?* New York: St. Martin's Press, 1991.

Midgley, Mary. "Death and the Human Animal." *Philosophy Now* 89 (2012). Accessed February 11, 2021. https://philosophynow.org/issues/89/Death_and_the_Human_Animal.

Monod, Jacques. *Chance Necessity*. Trans. Austryn Wainhouse. London: Fontana, 1974.

Montaigne, Michel de. *Les Essais. Livre I, chapitre, 19*. Trans. Guy de Pernon. 2009. http://www.heracleitos.eu/Textes/Montaigne/Essais_I_19,_trad._G._De_Pernon.pdf. (Original work published 1595).

Moore, Edward. "Gnosticism." *Internet Encyclopedia of Philosophy*, n.d. Accessed March 12, 2021. https://www.iep.utm.edu/gnostic.

Morot-Sir, Édouard. "Actualité de l'Étranger." *La Revue des lettres modernes* 17 (1996): 7–26.

Mounier, Emmanuel. *Le personnalisme. 13e édition*. Paris: Presses Universitaires de France. 1978. (Original work published 1949).

Murdoch, Iris. *Sartre: Romantic Rationalist*. New Haven: Yale University Press, 1953.

Murdoch, Iris. *The Sovereignty of Good*. London: Routledge & Kegan Paul, 1970.

Nabokov, Vladimir. *Speak Memory: An Autobiography Revisited*. New York: Vintage, 1989.

Nietzsche, Friedrich. *The Birth of Tragedy, in The Birth of Tragedy and The Case of Wagner*. Trans. Walter Kaufmann. New York: Vintage Books, 1967. (Original work published 1872).

Nietzsche, Friedrich. *On the Genealogy of Morals*. Trans. Ian Johnston. New York: Penguin Classics, 2014. (Original work published 1877).

Nietzsche, Friedrich. *Thus Spake Zarathustra*. 2008. https://www.gutenberg.org/files/1998/1998-h/1998-h.htm#link2H_4_0081. (Original work published 1885).

Nietzsche, Friedrich. *Beyond Good and Evil*. 2013. https://www.gutenberg.org/files/4363/4363-h/4363-h.htm (Original work published 1886).

Nietzsche, Friedrich. *On the Genealogy of Morality*. Ed. Keith Ansell-Pearson, Trans. Carol Diethe. Cambridge: Cambridge University Press, 1994. (Original work published 1887).

Nietzsche, Friedrich. *The Will to Power*. 2016. https://www.gutenberg.org/files/52914/52914-h/52914-h.htm. (Original work published 1901).

O'Brien, Conor Cruise. "Camus, Algeria, and 'The Fall.'" *NY Review of Books* 13, no. 6 (October 9, 1969). https://www.nybooks.com/articles/1969/10/09/camus-algeria-and-the-fall/.
O'Brien, Conor Cruise. *Albert Camus of Europe and Africa*. New York: Viking, 1970.
O'Donohue, Benedict. "L'Étranger and the Messianic Myth, or Meursault Unmasked." *Journal of Existential and Phenomenological Theory and Culture* 2, no. 1 (2007): 1–18.
Onfray, Michel. *L'Ordre libertaire: La vie philosophique d'Albert Camus*. Paris: Flammarion, 2012.
Ortega y Gasset, José. *The Dehumanization of Art and Other Essays on Art, Culture, and Literature*. Princeton: Princeton University Press, 1968. (Original work published 1925).
Ortega y Gasset, José. *The Revolt of the Masses*. Trans. Anonymous. New York: W.W. Norton & Company, 1932.
Ortega y Gasset, José. *The Modern Theme*. Trans. James Cleugh. New York: Harper Torchbooks, 1961.
Ortega y Gasset, José. *Meditations on Quixote*. Trans. Evelyn Rugg and Diego Marín. New York: W.W. Norton & Company, 1963.
Ortega y Gasset, José. *What is Philosophy?* Trans. Mildred Adams. New York: W.W. Norton & Company, 1964.
Pelluchon, Corine. *Les Nourritures. Philosophie du corps Politique*. Paris: Éditions du Seuil. 2015.
Percy, Walker. *Lost in the Cosmos: The Last Self-Help Book*. New York: Picador, 2000. (Original work published 1983).
Perry, Ralph Barton. *The Thought and Character of William James*. Nashville: Vanderbilt University Press, 1996. (Original work published 1936).
Pingaud, Bernard. *L'Étranger d'Albert Camus*. Paris: Gallimard, 1992.
Plato. *The Collected Dialogues of Plato*, eds. Hamilton, Edith and Huntington Cairns. Bollingen Series LXXI. New York: Pantheon Books, 1963.
Plato. *The Symposium*. Trans. Alexander Nehamas and Paul Woodruff. Indianapolis: Hackett Publishing Co., 1989.
Plotinus. *Plotinus, On the One and Good; being the Treatises of the Sixth Ennead*. Trans. Stephen McKenna. Boston: Charles T. Branford, 1918. https://oll.libertyfund.org/titles/plotinus-on-the-one-and-good-being-the-treatises-of-the-sixth-ennead.
Plotinus. *Enneads V*. Trans. A. H. Armstrong. Loeb Classical Library. Cambridge, MA: Harvard University Press, 1984.
Plutarch. "The Life of Cicero." *The Parallel Lives*. Accessed February 18, 2021. http://penelope.uchicago.edu/Thayer/E/Roman/Texts/Plutarch/Lives/Cicero*.html.
Plutarch. *Plutarch's Lives, Englished by Sir Thomas North*. Vol. 1. London: J.M. Dent, 1898.
Prinz, Jesse. "Morality is a Culturally Conditioned Response." *Philosophy Now* 82, (2011): 6–9. https://philosophynow.org/issues/82/Morality_is_a_Culturally_Conditioned_Response.
Putnam, Robert. "E Pluribus Unum: Diversity and Community in the Twenty-First Century: The Johan Skytte Prize Lecture." *Scandinavian Political Studies* 30, no. 2 (2007): 137–74.
Randall, John Herman and Justus Buchler. *Philosophy: An Introduction*. New York: Barnes & Nobl, 1942.
Rorty, Richard. *Philosophy and the Mirror of Nature*. Princeton: Princeton University Press, 1979.

Rousseau, Jean-Jacques. *Discourse on the Origin of Inequality*. Trans. Donald Cress. Indianapolis: Hackett Publishing Co, 1992. (Original work published 1755).

Rousseau, Jean-Jacques. *The Confessions*. Trans. J. M. Cohen. London: Penguin Classics, 1953. (Original work published 1781).

Rubens, Alain. "Les Femmes d´Albert Camus." *L´Express*, January 15, 2010. https://www.lexpress.fr/culture/livre/les-femmes-d-albert-camus_847025.html.

Russell, Bertrand (1927). "Why I am not a Christian." 1927. https://users.drew.edu/jlenz/whynot.html.

Ryle, Gilbert. *The Concept of Mind*. New York: Routledge, 2009. (Original work published 1949).

Sade, Marquis de. *Philosophy in the Bedroom*. 2018. https://www.globalgreyebooks.com/philosophy-in-the-bedroom-ebook.html. (Original work published 1795).

Said, Edward. *Culture and Imperialism*. New York: Vintage Books, 1994.

Santayana, George. *The Essential Santayana: Selected Writings*. Bloomington: Indiana University Press, 2009.

Sartre, Jean-Paul. "An Explication of *The Stranger*." Trans. Annette Michelson. In Brée. (Original work published 1947).

Sartre, Jean-Paul. "Mon Cher Camus." *Les Temps Modernes* 82 (1952): 334–53.

Sartre, Jean-Paul. *Les Mots*. Paris: Gallimard, 1964.

Sartre, Jean-Paul. *L'existentialisme est un humanisme*. Paris: Les éditions Nagel, 1970.

Sartre, Jean-Paul. *Existentialism is a Humanism*. Trans. Carol Macomber. New Haven: Yale University Press, 1996.

Sartre, Jean-Paul. *Being and Nothingness: An Essay in Phenomenological Ontology*. Special abridged edition. Trans. Hazel Barnes. New York: Citadel Press, 2001.

Schaefer, Jack. *Shane*. New York: Bantam Books, 1983. (Original work published 1949).

Schopenhauer, Arthur. "On the Sufferings of the World." Accessed March 10, 2021. https://ebooks.adelaide.edu.au/s/schopenhauer/arthur/pessimism/chapter1.html. (Original work published 1851).

Serres, Michel. *Les Cinq Sens: Philosophie des Corps Mêlés*. Paris: Bernard Grasset, 1985.

Serres, Michel. *Conversations on Science, Culture and Time with Bruno Latour*. Trans. Roxanne Lapidus. Ann Arbor: University of Michigan Press, 1995a.

Serres, Michel. *Les Messages à Distance*. Montréal: Éditions Fides, 1995b.

Sharpe, Matthew. "Camus on the Virtues (with and beyond Sherman)." *Philosophy Today* 61, no. 3 (2017): 679–708.

Smith, Michael. "Emotivism." *Routledge Encyclopedia of Philosophy*, 1998. https://www.rep.routledge.com/articles/thematic/emotivism/v-1. doi:10.4324/9780415249126-L019-1.

Sontag, Susan. "The Ideal Husband: A Review of *Notebooks, 1935–42* by Albert Camus, Translated from the French by Philip Thody." *The New York Review of Books*, September 26, 1963. https://www.nybooks.com/articles/1963/09/26/the-ideal-husband/?pagination=false.

Sophocle. *Oedipe à Colone*. Trans. Leconte de Lisle. 1877. http://www.theatre-classique.fr/pages/programmes/edition.php?t=../documents/SOPHOCLE_OEDIPEACOLONE.xml.

Spiquel, Agnès. "Le premier homme (1994)." *Société des Études Camusiennes*. http://www.etudes-camusiennes.fr/1994/12/30/le-premier-homme-1994/.

Srigley, Ronald. *Albert Camus' Critique of Modernity*. Columbia: University of Missouri Press, 2011.

Tarrow, Susan. *Exile From the Kingdom: A Political Reading of Albert Camus*. Tuscaloosa: University of Alabama Press, 1985.

Taylor, Charles. *The Ethics of Authenticity*. Cambridge, MA: Harvard University Press, 1991.
Taylor, Charles. "The Politics of Recognition." In *Multiculturalism*, edited by Amy Gutmann. Princeton: Princeton University Press, 1994.
Taylor, Charles. *A Catholic Modernity?: Charles Taylor's Marianist Award Lecture*. New York: Oxford University Press, 1999.
Taylor, Charles. *A Secular Age*. Cambridge, MA: Harvard University Press, 2007.
Tebbani, Ali. "Le Premier Homme de Camus ou l'"amour recouvré." *Synergies Algérie* 9 (2010): 255–60. https://gerflint.fr/Base/Algerie9/Tebbani.pdf.
Tisson-Braun, Micheline. "Silence in the Desert: The Flickering Vision." In Knapp, 42–55.
Todd, Olivier. *Albert Camus: A Life*. Trans. Benjamin Ivry. New York: Alfred A. Knopf, 1997.
Tolstoy, Leo. *The Death of Ivan Ilyich*. Trans. Richard Pevear and Larissa Volokhonsky. New York: Vintage, 2012. (Original work published 1886).
Transhumanism. Accessed January 20, 2022. https://whatistranshumanism.org/.
Trilling, Lionel. *The Liberal Imagination*. New York: Anchor Books, 1950.
Valiant, Leslie. *Probably Approximately Correct: Nature's Algorithms for Learning and Prospering in a Complex World*. New York: Basic Books, 2013.
Vanborre, Emmannuelle Ann, ed. *The Originality and Complexity of Albert Camus's Writings*. New York: Palgrave Macmillan, 2012.
Viggiani, Carl A. "Camus' L'Etranger." *PMLA* 71, no. 5 (1956): 865–87.
Visser, Margaret. *Much Depends on Dinner: The Extraordinary History and Mythology, Allure and Obsessions, Perils and Taboos of an Ordinary Meal*. New York: Collier Books, 1986.
Visser, Margaret. *Beyond Fate*. Toronto: Anansi Press, 2002.
Wahl, Jean. *Vers le Concret. Études d'Histoire de la Philosophie Contemporaine: William james, Whitehead, Gabriel Marcel*. Paris: J. Vrin, 2004. (Original work published 1932).
Ward, Daniel. "Mistaken." 2019. Accessed March 16, 2021. https://aeon.co/essays/i-think-therefore-i-make-mistakes-and-change-my-mind.
Weinberg, Steven. *The First Three Minutes*. New York: Basic Books, 1988. (Original work published 1977).
Wheeler, John Archibald. "Time Today." In *Physical Origins of Time Asymmetry*, edited by J. J. Halliwell, J. Pérez-Mercader and M. H. Zurek, 1–30. Cambridge: Cambridge University Press, 1994.
Wheeler, Michael. "Martin Heidegger." In *The Stanford Encyclopedia of Philosophy*, edited by Edward N. Zalta. Winter 2018 Edition. https://plato.stanford.edu/archives/win2018/entries/heidegger/.
Whitehead, Alfred North. *Science and the Modern World*. New York: Macmillan, 1925.
Williams, Bernard. "The Makropulos Case: Reflections on the Tedium of Immortality." In *Problems of the Self: Philosophical Papers 1956–72*, 82–100. Cambridge: Cambridge University Press, 1976.
Williams, Bernard. "Moral Luck." In *Moral Luck*, edited by Daniel Statman, 35–55. Albany: SUNY Press, 1993.
Wilson, Emily. "What the Ancient Greeks Teach Us: The Value of Athenian Tragedy in an Age of Anxiety." Accessed January 23, 2021. https://www.questia.com/magazine/1G1-587565601/what-the-ancient-greeks-teach-us-the-value-of-athenian.
Wohlleben, Peter. *The Hidden Life of Trees: What They Feel, How They Communicate*. Trans. Jane Billinghurst. Vancouver: Greystone, 2016.

Wolf, Susan. *Meaning in Life and Why it Matters*. Princeton: Princeton University Press, 2012.
Yong, Ed. *I Contain Multitudes: The Microbes Within Us and a Grander View of Life*. New York: Harper Collins, 2016.
Yong, Ed. "Breast-Feeding the Microbiome." *The New Yorker*, July 22, 2016. https://www.newyorker.com/tech/annals-of-technology/breast-feeding-the-microbiome.
Zaretsky, Robert. *A Life Worth Living: Albert Camus and the Quest for Meaning*. Cambridge: Belknap Press, 2016.

Index

absurd, absurdity   3, 4, 14–20, 23–9, 35–42, 48, 50–5, 72–4, 95, 101, 102, 111–19, 126, 135, 143, 149, 155, 158, 171, 174, 190–204, 208 n.5, 211 n.1, 211–12 n.4, 216 n.6, 217 n.8
adaequatio   41, 83
agape   120, 123–5, 143, 144, 152–3
Aristotle   36, 72, 101, 126, 161, 190, 200, 215
Arnold, Matthew   7
Auden, W. H.   116
Augustine, saint   88–90, 107, 211 n.4
Aurelius, Marcus   31–3, 38

Bateson, Gregory   44
Bifurcation, Great   5, 18, 24, 25, 36, 37, 41, 57, 58, 69–74, 77, 102, 106, 110, 114, 162–4, 190, 201
Big Rock Candy Mountain   15, 18
boo-hurrah ethics   5, 69–71, 76–8, 86, 107
Bordo, Susan   161
Buridan, Jean   12–14, 18, 25, 44, 49, 57, 59, 61, 83, 180, 181

choice   2, 3, 13, 18, 20, 32, 33, 45, 49, 51, 55, 59, 63, 71, 77, 83, 95, 98, 106, 162, 169, 175, 178–87
Cicero   33, 45
cogito   42–6, 58, 60, 74, 84, 88, 92, 93, 116, 117, 121, 201, 203, 210 n.5
Condillac, Étienne Bonnot de   38, 39
Cottingham, John   66, 67

death   1, 2, 7, 10, 19, 20, 32, 33, 43–62, 74–6, 90, 113, 117–24, 135, 150–68, 194–6, 210 nn.5, 10, 217 n.10
   of God   7, 12, 56, 57, 61, 75, 76, 124, 145, 161, 165, 168

Descartes   1, 5, 38, 114, 204, 209
Designer, Grand   9–12, 86

ecology   7, 42, 70, 73, 100, 117, 201
embarqué/engagé   108–10
Epicurus   31–3, 38
epistemological subject   36, 37, 40, 45, 95, 98, 100, 109, 117, 183, 184
eris   123–5, 132, 134, 145, 150, 152, 153, 214
eros   119–25, 132, 134, 138, 140–5, 158, 173–88
evil   3, 37, 38, 43, 44, 47, 48, 54, 56, 67–70, 88, 102, 126, 127, 145, 148, 211 n.3, 211–12 n.4
external world   5, 40, 41, 49, 57, 60, 71, 74, 92, 96, 115, 168, 192

fallibilism   83, 97–9, 106, 109, 126, 213 n.1, 214 n.3
Finkielkraut, Alain   157–8
Frankl, Victor   32
freedom   1, 2, 6, 13, 14, 19, 21, 32–3, 51–6, 62, 72, 77–93, 99, 102–8, 130, 135–7, 152, 159–60, 177, 180–7, 200–6, 213 n.3, 215 n.3

Galileo   38, 209 n.2
god, goddess   1, 2, 7–14, 23, 31, 32, 38, 48, 49, 52–7, 61–7, 75–8, 82, 86, 124, 145–55, 161–8, 202, 208 n.5, 212 n.7, 213 n.2, 216 n.6

Habermas, Jürgen   64
Haidt, Jonathan   87, 88
Heidegger, Martin   4, 5, 7, 72–3, 86, 118, 193, 214 n.2, 217 nn.3, 5
Helen's exile   1, 2, 4, 87, 198, 200–3, 214
Hitler   84

Index

home 5, 7, 15–17, 45, 52, 58, 60, 73, 77, 97, 100–10, 117, 122–9, 130–8, 143–50, 154–6, 163, 168, 195–201, 210 n.3, 214 n.4
human nature 4, 7, 71–92, 101, 110, 197, 205, 212 n.1
Huxley, Aldous 2, 69, 70, 201
Huxley, Thomas Henry 7, 192, 193, 197, 204

indifference 13, 16, 44–58, 69, 73–5, 95–106, 109–10, 137, 149, 183–5, 192–7, 210 n.7
infallibilism 98–9, 109, 214
interdependence 5, 26, 39, 104, 118, 168, 194, 203
interrelationship 5, 26, 39, 161
irony 7, 25–30, 91, 125, 183, 189, 199–202, 212 n.9

James, William 4, 5, 91, 195, 196, 199, 201, 209 n.4
job 10

Keaton, Buster 147
Kierkegaard, Søren 13, 24, 178, 179, 210 n.5

liberum arbitrium indifferentiae 88, 98, 99, 102–10, 138, 159, 184, 201, 202
Lightman, Alan 28–9
limit 1, 2, 4, 5, 24, 33, 52, 58, 69, 73–8, 81–92, 98, 102, 130, 135–40, 151, 159, 166, 177, 180, 183, 191, 198, 200–5, 217 n.5
literature 6, 35–7, 114, 117, 189, 191, 205
lived experience 2–7, 18, 23–5, 40, 54, 59, 71, 86, 89, 90, 109–16, 148, 168, 176, 182, 185, 190, 193, 199, 203, 214 n.2
love 7, 9, 14, 26, 28, 33, 39, 43–5, 49, 54, 59, 62, 85, 96, 97, 102–47, 152, 156–9, 173–88, 202, 212 n.9, 215 n.3, 216 n.2, 217 n.10

mattering 36, 42, 43, 55, 56, 60, 71, 73, 77, 96, 109, 110, 182, 205
meaning 2–32, 40, 43, 51, 52, 60, 66–9, 74–8, 90–109, 114–17, 123, 153–9, 168, 174, 175, 190–204, 207 nn.1, 3, 208 n.8, 210–11 n.10, 213 n.1, 214 n.2, 217 n.6
measure 1, 2, 5, 83–8, 138, 166, 169, 202–5, 217
mediation 92, 93
Medusa 143
Melville, Herman 7, 164. *See also Moby Dick*
Mephistopheles 12–19, 136, 138
Merton, Thomas 62, 65
messianism 90, 166
Meursault 35–7, 41–52, 96, 97, 102, 119, 137, 138, 149, 176, 182–4, 191, 209 n.1, 210 nn.4, 7, 210–11 n.10, 211 nn.13, 14, 212 n.1
Midgley, Mary 15–17, 28, 30, 42, 43, 72, 78, 86–8, 185, 196, 206, 213 n.3, 216 n.7
mind 5, 10, 13, 16–18, 21–51, 62, 74, 75, 83–7, 95, 100, 101, 116, 117, 121, 134, 146, 148, 159, 170, 183–6, 190, 201, 209 n.6, 210 n.5, 213 n.1
Moby Dick 164
modernity 3, 38, 41, 44, 82, 167, 168, 191, 193
Montaigne, Michel de 117, 118, 195
Murdoch, Iris 115–17, 130, 208, 217 n.6

Nabokov, Vladimir 162, 163
Nausea (novel) 35, 110, 114
Nemesis 1–5, 52, 55–8, 73, 76, 87, 110, 151–4, 202–5, 217 n.10
Nietzsche, Friedrich 1–13, 25, 56, 61, 74–7, 82, 90, 114, 124, 157, 165–75, 207 n.4, 208 n.5, 209 n.3, 213 n.2, 215–16 n.6, 217 n.10
nihilism 2–20, 51–78, 82–110, 114–43, 149, 165–74, 192, 198–206, 212 n.5, 218 n.11
Nike 124–6, 134, 153

oikos 7, 100
ordinary 6, 7, 23–40, 44, 52–68, 71–8, 90, 91, 110, 115, 117, 120–47, 154–6, 162, 166–78, 180, 186, 194–9, 201–3, 205, 213 n.1

Ortega y Gasset, José   25–32, 40–5, 91, 118, 165, 184, 189, 199, 202, 208 n.2, 209 nn.3, 4
outsider   6, 15–26, 34, 38, 40–8, 53, 60, 98, 100, 109, 116, 125, 150–6, 168, 190, 196, 210 n.3

paradigm   4, 7, 25, 31, 37, 40, 48, 58, 60–7, 81, 89, 108, 110, 114–17, 123, 127, 143, 144, 191–7, 202
paradise   55, 89, 93, 123, 145
philia   120, 123, 125, 132, 137, 138, 141–5, 158
Plato   85–6, 179, 189, 200
Plotinus   90
praxis   53–7, 60–7, 85, 195, 196, 201
Prometheanism   12, 62
Prometheus   1, 3, 11, 19, 54–6, 62, 110, 151

razón vital   7, 25–30, 44, 58, 60, 74, 87, 106, 148, 199, 208 n.2
religion   2, 11–20, 48, 53, 56, 61–7, 75, 77, 89, 123, 124–5, 150, 154, 161, 165, 194, 205, 207 n.1, 212 n.7, 213 n.1, 217 n.7
Renaissance   10, 38, 100, 118, 168, 189, 208–9 n.2
Resistance, French   77
responsibility   1–3, 20, 42, 44, 53–84, 92, 97–9, 102, 104, 126, 129, 136–9, 141, 142, 148–9, 169, 175, 195, 203–5, 213 n.1, 215–16 n.6
revolt   4, 20, 21, 51–8, 61–2, 71, 73–8, 83, 85, 88, 119, 158, 165, 184, 210–11 n.10, 211–12 n.4, 217 n.10
Rieux, Dr.   51–71, 74, 93, 101, 106, 119, 135, 136, 175, 203, 205
risk   54–61, 67, 76, 83, 92, 98, 106, 127, 130, 136–9, 142–5, 152, 166, 170, 180, 184

Rousseau, Jean-Jacques   38, 48, 161, 194, 210 n.4, 211 n.13
Russell, Bertrand   10–13, 19, 25
Ryle, Gilbert   38

Sade, Marquis de   81–8
Sartre, Jean-Paul   2, 3, 35, 37, 41, 46, 58, 71–9, 85, 86, 91, 110, 114, 162, 191, 213 n.1
semiotic   95–6, 100, 109, 136, 167, 170, 193–4
Serres, Michel   96, 130, 21 n.2
Sisyphus   1, 4, 9, 13–35, 51–5, 73, 85, 89, 95, 100–43, 151–63, 174, 176, 183, 184, 186, 190–9, 202–6, 207 n.1, 208 n.1
Sontag, Susan   15, 16, 20, 116
Sophocles   90
spectator   25, 32–49, 53–4, 60, 74, 95, 109, 110, 114–16, 172, 183–5
Srigley, Ron   3, 4, 113, 193, 207 n.2
Stalin   1, 85
Stark, Hans   44
statues   38–50, 117, 210 n.5, 211 n.13
storge   120–3, 132–45, 158, 173, 174, 176, 177, 181–8
surd   18–19, 24, 101, 116

Taylor, Charles   65–7, 204, 212 n.8
Thanatos   119–25
Todd, Olivier   99, 113, 173, 215 n.2

Weinberg, Steven   9
Whitehead, Alfred North   4, 5, 7, 193, 217 n.3
will, faculty of   12–13, 18, 44, 47, 57–63, 77, 83–8, 98, 104, 180–6, 208 n.8, 211 n.4, 215 n.6
Wolf, Susan   52, 208 n.8

www.ingramcontent.com/pod-product-compliance
Lightning Source LLC
Chambersburg PA
CBHW062214300426
44115CB00012BA/2054